Designing Autonomous Agents

Special Issues of Robotics and Autonomous Systems

The titles in this series are paperback, readily accessible editions of the Special Volumes of *Robotics and Autonomous Systems*, produced by special agreement with Elsevier Science Publishers B.V.

Designing Autonomous Agents: Theory and Practice from Biology to Engineering and Back, edited by Pattie Maes, 1991.

Designing Autonomous Agents:
Theory and Practice from Biology to Engineering and Back

edited by Pattie Maes

A Bradford Book

The MIT Press
Cambridge, Massachusetts
London, England

Third printing, 1994

First MIT Press edition, 1990

© 1990 Elsevier Science Publishers B.V., Amsterdam, Netherlands

Printed and bound in the United States of America

Library of Congress Cataloging-in-Publication Data

Designing autonomous agents: theory and practice from biology to engineering and back / edited by Pattie Maes. – 1st MIT Press ed.
     p. cm. – (Special issues of Robotics and autonomous systems)
   "Reprinted from Robotics and autonomous systems, volume 6, numbers 1 & 2 (June 1990)" – T.p. verso.
   "A Bradford Book."
   Includes bibliographical references.
   ISBN 0-262-63135-0 (pbk.)
   1. Self-organizing systems. 2. Artificial Intelligence.
I. Maes, Pattie, 1961-. II. Series.
Q325.D47 1991   90-42396
003'.7–dc20   CIP

Contents

P. Maes
Guest editorial: Designing autonomous agents   1

R.A. Brooks
Elephants don't play chess   3

P.E. Agre and D. Chapman
What are plans for?   17

L.P. Kaelbling and S.J. Rosenschein
Action and planning in embedded agents   35

P. Maes
Situated agents can have goals   49

L. Steels
Exploiting analogical representations   71

D.W. Payton
Internalized plans: A representation for action resources   89

R.C. Arkin
Integrating behavioral, perceptual, and world knowledge in reactive navigation   105

C. Malcolm and T. Smithers
Symbol grounding via a hybrid architecture in an autonomous assembly system   123

T.L. Anderson and M. Donath
Animal behavior as a paradigm for developing robot autonomy   145

R.D. Beer, H.J. Chiel and L.S. Sterling
A biological perspective on autonomous agent design   169

Index   187

Guest Editorial

Designing Autonomous Agents

Theory and Practice from Biology to Engineering and Back

Since 1970 the Deliberative Thinking paradigm has dominated Artificial Intelligence (AI) research. Its main thesis is that intelligent tasks can be implemented by a reasoning process operating on a symbolic internal model. Emphasis is put on explicit knowledge, rational choice and problem solving. This approach has proven successful in knowledge-based task areas such as expert level reasoning. However, only poor results have been obtained in its application to research on autonomous agents. The few systems built show deficiencies such as brittleness, inflexibility, no real time operation, and so on. They also spawned a number of theoretical problems such as the frame problem and the problem of non-monotonic reasoning which remain unsolved (at least within realistic time constraints).

Some researchers view this as evidence that it is unrealistic to hope that more action-oriented tasks could also be successfully implemented by a deliberative machine in real time. For a few years these people have been developing new ideas on how autonomous agents should be organized, which led to radically different architectures. The emphasis in these architectures is on a more direct coupling of perception to action, distributedness and decentralization, dynamic interaction with the

Pattie Maes obtained a PhD in Computer Science from the University of Brussels in 1987, on the basis of a dissertation about Computational Reflection. She holds a position as Research Associate from the Belgian National Science Foundation. She conducts her research activities at the Artificial Intelligence Laboratory of the above-mentioned university, where she leads the research group on Autonomous Agents. She currently maintains a temporary position as a Visiting Faculty Member at the Artificial Intelligence Laboratory of the Massachusetts Institute of Technology. Her interests are in the areas of: Architectures for Autonomous Agents, Theories of Action, Mobile Robots, Learning Robots, and Robotic Collective Intelligence.

North-Holland
Robotics and Autonomous Systems 6 (1990) 1–2

environment and intrinsic mechanisms to cope with resource limitations and incomplete knowledge.

One key idea in these new architectures is that of "emergent functionality". The functionality of an agent is viewed as an emergent property of the intensive interaction of the system with its dynamic environment. The specification of the behavior of the agent alone does not explain the functionality that is displayed when the agent is operating. Instead the functionality to a large degree is founded on the properties of the environment. The environment is not only taken into account dynamically, but its characteristics are exploited to serve the functioning of the system. An important implication of this view is that one cannot simply tell these agents how to achieve a goal. Instead one has to find an interaction loop involving the system and the environment which will converge (in an environment which has the expected properties) towards the desired goal.

A second important idea is that of "task-level decomposition". Distributedness and parallel implementation are viewed as crucial ingredients for fast and robust behavior. An agent is viewed as a collection of modules which each have their own specific competence. These modules operate autonomously and are solely responsible for the sensing, modelling, computation or reasoning, and motor control which is necessary to achieve their specific competence. To avoid unnecessary duplications they may make usage of "virtual sensors" however. Communication among modules is reduced to a minimum and happens on an information-low level. There is no global internal model, nor is there a global planning activity with one hierarchical goal structure. Finally, the global behavior of the agent is not necessarily a linear composition of the behaviors of its modules, but instead more complex behavior may emerge by the interaction of the behaviors generated by the individual modules.

A third idea becoming prevalent in much of this research is the exploitation of reasoning methods which operate on representations which are close to the raw sensor data (e.g. "analogical representations" and also "visual operations"). As such some of the problem solving burden is shifted to processes dealing with perception. Because of this move, the perception task is made less general, and thus more realistic.

Given the short time of their existence, these new architectures have already achieved remarkable successes. They promise to revolutionize the Autonomous Agents area and maybe even AI in general. This book tries to present a first representative sample of this new line of research. It includes articles by the researchers which originated these ideas. It does not make any con-

clusions about the limits of this new approach, as it has only been taken up recently and may as well keep us busy for another 20 years. Some of the papers of this book were discussed at the workshop "Representation and Learning in an Autonomous Agent", held in Lagos, Portugal in November 1988. Some other authors have been invited later to make the selection more complete.

Pattie Maes
Guest Editor

Elephants Don't Play Chess

Rodney A. Brooks

MIT Artificial Intelligence Laboratory, Cambridge, MA 02139, USA

There is an alternative route to Artificial Intelligence that diverges from the directions pursued under that banner for the last thirty some years. The traditional approach has emphasized the abstract manipulation of symbols, whose grounding in physical reality has rarely been achieved. We explore a research methodology which emphasizes ongoing physical interaction with the environment as the primary source of constraint on the design of intelligent systems. We show how this methodology has recently had significant successes on a par with the most successful classical efforts. We outline plausible future work along these lines which can lead to vastly more ambitious systems.

Keywords: Situated activity; Mobile robots; Planning; Subsumption architecture; Artificial Intelligence.

Rodney A. Brooks was born in Adelaide, Australia. He studied Mathematics at the Flinders University of South Australia and received a Ph.D. from Stanford in Computer Science in 1981. Since then he has held research associate positions at Carnegie Mellon University and the Massachusetts Institute of Technology and faculty positions at Stanford and M.I.T. He is currently an Associate Professor of Electrical Engineering and Computer Science at M.I.T. and a member of the Artificial Intelligence Laboratory where he leads the mobile robot group. He has authored two books, numerous scientific papers, and is the editor of the *International Journal of Computer Vision*.

North-Holland
Robotics and Autonomous Systems 6 (1990) 3–15

1. Introduction

Artificial Intelligence research has foundered in a sea of incrementalism. No one is quite sure where to go save improving on earlier demonstrations of techniques in symbolic manipulation of ungrounded representations. At the same time, small AI companies are folding, and attendance is well down at national and international Artificial Intelligence conferences. While it is true that the use of AI is prospering in many large companies, it is primarily through the application to novel domains of long developed techniques that have become passé in the research community.

What has gone wrong? (And how is this book the answer?!!)

In this paper we argue that the *it symbol system hypothesis* upon which *it classical AI* is based is fundamentally flawed, and as such imposes severe limitations on the fitness of its progeny. Further, we argue that the dogma of the symbol system hypothesis implicitly includes a number of largely unfounded great leaps of faith when called upon to provide a plausible path to the digital equivalent of human level intelligence. It is the chasms to be crossed by these leaps which now impede classical AI research.

But there is an alternative view, or dogma, variously called *it nouvelle AI*, *it fundamentalist AI*, or in a weaker form *it situated activity* [1]. It is based on the *it physical grounding hypothesis*. It provides a different methodology for building intelligent systems than that pursued for the last thirty years. The traditional methodology bases its decomposition of intelligence into functional information processing modules whose combinations provide overall system behavior. The new methodology bases its decomposition of intelligence into individual behavior generating mod-

---

[1] Note that what is discussed in this paper is completely unrelated to what is popularly known as *it Neural Networks*. That given, there are nevertheless a number of aspects of nouvelle AI approaches which may be of interest to people working in classical neuroscience.

ules, whose coexistence and co-operation let more complex behaviors emerge.

In classical AI, none of the modules themselves generate the behavior of the total system. Indeed it is necessary to combine together many of the modules to get any behavior at all from the system. Improvement in the competence of the system proceeds by improving the individual functional modules. In nouvelle AI each module itself generates behavior, and improvement in the competence of the system proceeds by adding new modules to the system.

Given that neither classical nor nouvelle AI seem close to revealing the secrets of the holy grail of AI, namely general purpose human level intelligence equivalence, there are a number of critical comparisons that can be made between the two approaches.

● Is either approach epistemologically adequate? (And adequate for what?)
● Are there clear paths for either approach in the direction of vastly more intelligent systems?
● Are nouvellers romantically hoping for magic from nothing while classicists are willing to tell their systems almost anything and everything, in the hope of teasing out the shallowest of inferences?
● Is the claim of emergent properties of nouvelle AI systems any more outrageous than the use of heuristics in classical AI?

In the following sections we address these issues.

2. The Symbol System Hypothesis

The symbol system hypothesis, [30], states that intelligence operates on a system of symbols. The implicit idea is that perception and motor interfaces are sets of symbols on which the central intelligence system operates. Thus, the central system, or reasoning engine, operates in a domain independent way on the symbols. Their meanings are unimportant to the reasoner, but the coherence of the complete process emerges when an observer of the system knows the groundings of the symbols within his or her own experience.

Somewhat more implicitly in the work that the symbol system hypothesis has inspired, the symbols represent entities in the world. They may be individual objects, properties, concepts, desires,

emotions, nations, colors, libraries, or molecules, but they are necessarily named entities. There are a number of effects which result from this commitment.

Recall first, however, that an intelligent system, apart from those which are experiments in the laboratory, will be embedded in the world in some form or another.

2.1. The Interface Between Perception and Symbols

The central intelligence system deals in symbols. It must be fed symbols by the perception system.

But what is the correct symbolic description of the world around the intelligence system? Surely that description must be task dependent.

The default assumption has been that the perception system delivers a description of the world in terms of typed, named individuals and their relationships. For instance in the classic monkeys and bananas problem, the world description is in terms of boxes, bananas, and aboveness.

But for another task (e.g., deciding whether the bananas are rotten) quite a different representation might be important. Psychophysical evidence [32] certainly points to perception being an active and task dependent operation.

The effect of the symbol system hypothesis has been to encourage vision researchers to quest after the goal of a general purpose vision system which delivers complete descriptions of the world in a symbolic form (e.g. [5]). Only recently has there been a movement towards active vision [4] which is much more task dependent, or task driven [1].

2.2. Inadequacy of Simple Symbols

Symbol systems in their purest forms assume a knowable objective truth. It is only with much complexity that modal logics, or non-monotonic logics, can be built which better enable a system to have beliefs gleaned from partial views of a chaotic world.

As these enhancements are made, the realization of computations based on these formal systems becomes more and more biologically implausible. But once the commitment to symbol systems has been made it is imperative to push on through more and more complex and cumbersome systems in pursuit of objectivity.

This same pursuit leads to the well known frame problem (e.g., [27]), where it is impossible to assume anything that is not explicitly stated. Technical deviations around this problem have been suggested but they are by no means without their own problems.

2.3. Symbol Systems Rely on Emergent Properties

In general the reasoning process becomes trivial in an NP-complete space (e.g., [13]). There have been large efforts to overcome these problems by choosing simple arithmetically computed *it evaluation functions* or *it polynomials* to guide the search. Charmingly, it has been hoped that intelligence will somehow emerge from these simple numeric computations carried out in the sea of symbols. [28] was one of the earliest examples of this hope, which later turned out to be only partially correct (his learned polynomials later turned out to be dominated by piece count), but in fact almost all instances of search in classical AI have relied on such judiciously chosen polynomials to keep the search space manageable.

3. The Physical Grounding Hypothesis

Nouvelle AI is based on the physical grounding hypothesis. This hypothesis states that to build a system that is intelligent it is necessary to have its representations grounded in the physical world. Our experience with this approach is that once this commitment is made, the need for traditional symbolic representations soon fades entirely. The key observation is that the world is its own best model. It is always exactly up to date. It always contains every detail there is to be known. The trick is to sense it appropriately and often enough.

To build a system based on the physical grounding hypothesis it is necessary to connect it to the world via a set of sensors and actuators. Typed input and output are no longer of interest. They are not physically grounded.

Accepting the physical grounding hypothesis as a basis for research entails building systems in a bottom up manner. High level abstractions have to be made concrete. The constructed system eventually has to express all its goals and desires as physical action, and must extract all its knowledge from physical sensors. Thus the designer of the system is forced to make everything explicit. Every short-cut taken has a direct impact upon system competence, as there is no slack in the input/output representations. The forms of the low-level interfaces have consequences which ripple through the entire system.

3.1. Evolution

We already have an existence proof of the possibility of intelligent entities – human beings. Additionally many animals are intelligent to some degree. (This is a subject of intense debate, much of which really centers around a definition of intelligence.) They have evolved over the 4.6 billion year history of the earth.

It is instructive to reflect on the way in which earth-based biological evolution spent its time. Single cell entities arose out of the primordial soup roughly 3.5 billion years ago. A billion years passed before photosynthetic plants appeared. After almost another billion and a half years, around 550 million years ago, the first fish and vertebrates arrived, and then insects 450 million years ago. Then things started moving fast. Reptiles arrived 370 million years ago, followed by dinosaurs at 330 and mammals at 250 million years ago. The first primates appeared 120 million years ago and the immediate predecessors to the great apes a mere 18 million years ago. Man arrived in roughly his present form 2.5 million years ago. He invented agriculture a mere 19000 years ago, writing less than 5000 years ago and "expert" knowledge only over the last few hundred years.

This suggests that problem solving behavior, language, expert knowledge and application, and reason, are all rather simple once the essence of being and reacting are available. That essence is the ability to move around in a dynamic environment, sensing the surroundings to a degree sufficient to achieve the necessary maintenance of life and reproduction. This part of intelligence is where evolution has concentrated its time—it is much harder. This is the physically grounded part of animal systems.

An alternative argument to the preceeding is that in fact once evolution had symbols and representations things started moving rather quickly. Thus symbols are the key invention and AI workers can sidestep the early morass and start working directly with symbols. But I think this misses a critical point, as is shown by the relatively weaker performance of symbol based mobile robots as opposed to physically grounded robots. Without a carefully built physical grounding any symbolic representation will be mismatched to its sensors and actuators. These groundings provide the constraints on symbols necessary for them to be truly useful.

[26] has argued rather eloquently that mobility, acute vision and the ability to carry out survival related tasks in a dynamic environment provide a necessary basis for the development of true intelligence.

3.2. The Subsumption Architecture

In order to explore the construction of physically grounded systems we have developed a computational architecture known as the *subsumption architecture*. It enables us to tightly connect perception to action, embedding robots concretely in the world.

A subsumption program is built on a computational substrate that is organized into a series of incremental layers, each, in the general case, connecting perception to action. In our case the substrate is networks of finite state machines augmented with timing elements.

The subsumption architecture was described initially in [6] and later modified in [8] and [16]. The subsumption compiler compiles augmented finite state machine (AFSM) descriptions into a special-purpose scheduler to simulate parallelism and a set of finite state machine simulation routines. This is a dynamically retargetable compiler that has backends for a number of processors, including the Motorola 68000, the Motorola 68HC11, and the Hitachi 6301. The subsumption compiler takes a source file as input and produces an assembly language program as output.

The behavior language was inspired by [23] as a way of grouping AFSMs into more manageable units with the capability for whole units being selectively activated or de-activated. In fact, AFSMs are not specified directly, but rather as rule sets of real-time rules which compile into AFSMs in a one-to-one manner. The behavior compiler is machine-independent and compiles into an intermediate file of subsumption AFSM

specifications. The subsumption compiler can then be used to compile to the various targets. We sometimes call the behavior language the *new subsumption*.

3.2.1. The Old Subsumption Language

Each augmented finite state machine (AFSM) has a set of registers and a set of timers, or alarm clocks, connected to a conventional finite state machine which can control a combinational network fed by the registers. Registers can be written by attaching input wires to them and sending messages from other machines. The messages get written into the registers by replacing any existing contents. The arrival of a message, or the expiration of a timer, can trigger a change of state in the interior finite state machine. Finite state machine states can either wait on some event, conditionally dispatch to one of two other states based on some combinational predicate on the registers, or compute a combinational function of the registers directing the result either back to one of the registers or to an output of the augmented finite state machine. Some AFSMs connect directly to robot hardware. Sensors deposit their values in certain registers, and certain outputs direct commands to actuators.

A series of layers of such machines can be augmented by adding new machines and connecting them into the existing network in a number of ways. New inputs can be connected to existing registers, which might previously have contained a constant. New machines can inhibit existing outputs, or suppress existing inputs, by being attached as side-taps to existing wires. When a message arrives on an inhibitory side-tap no messages can travel along the existing wire for some short time period. To maintain inhibition there must be a continuous flow of messages along the new wire. (In previous versions of the subsumption architecture [6] explicit, long time periods had to be specified for inhibition or suppression with single shot messages. Recent work has suggested this better approach [16].) When a message arrives on a suppressing side-tap, again no messages are allowed to flow from the original source for some small time period, but now the suppressing message is gated through and it masquerades as having come from the original source. A continuous supply of suppressing messages is required to maintain control of a side-tapped wire.

Inhibition and suppression are the mechanisms by which conflict resolution between actuator commands from different layers is achieved. Notice that in this definition of the subsumption architecture, AFSMs cannot share any state, and in particular they each completely encapsulate their own registers and alarm clocks.

All clocks in a subsumption system have approximately the same tick period (0.04 seconds in most of our robots). However, neither the clocks nor the messages are synchronous. The fastest possible rate of sending messages along a wire is one per clock tick. The time periods used for both inhibition and suppression are two clock ticks. Thus, a side-tapping wire with messages being sent at the maximum rate can maintain control of its host wire. We call this rate the *characteristic frequency* of the particular subsumption implementation.

3.2.2. The New Subsumption Language

The behavior language groups multiple processes (each of which usually turns out to be implemented as a single AFSM) into *behaviors*. There can be message passing, suppression, and inhibition between processes within a behavior, and there can be message passing, suppression and inhibition between behaviors. Behaviors act as abstraction barriers; one behavior cannot reach inside another.

Each process within a behavior is much like an AFSM, and indeed our compiler for the behavior language converts them to AFSMs. However, they are generalized so that they can share registers. A new structure, monostables, provides a slightly more general timing mechanism than the original alarm clocks. Monostables are retriggerable, and can be shared between processes within a single behavior.

4. Some Physically Grounded Systems

In this section we briefly review some previous successful robots built with the subsumption architecture and highlight the ways in which they have exploited or epitomize that architecture. The family portrait of all the robots is shown in *Fig. 1*. Most of the robots were programmed with the old subsumption language. Toto and Seymour use the new behavior language.

A key thing to note with these robots is the

Fig. 1. The MIT Mobile Robots include, in the back row, left to right; Allen, Herbert, Seymour and Toto. In front row are Tito, Genghis, Squirt (very small) Tom and Jerry, and Labnav.

ways in which seemingly goal-directed behavior emerges from the interactions of simpler non goal-directed behaviors.

4.1. Allen

Our first robot, Allen, had sonar range sensors and odometry onboard and used an offboard lisp machine to simulate the subsumption architecture. In [6] we described three layers of control implemented in the subsumption architecture.

The first layer let the robot avoid both static and dynamic obstacles; Allen would happily sit in the middle of a room until approached, then scurry away, avoiding collisions as it went. The internal representation used was that every sonar return represented a repulsive force with an inverse square decrease in strength as a function of distance. The vector sum of the repulsive forces, suitably thresholded, told the robot in which direction it should move. An additional reflex halted the robot whenever there was something right in front of the robot and it was moving forward (rather than turning in place).

The second layer made the robot randomly wander about. Every 10 seconds or so, a desire to head in a random direction would be generated. That desire was coupled with the reflex to avoid obstacles by vector addition. The summed vector suppressed the more primitive obstacle avoidance vector, but the obstacle avoidance behavior still operated, having been subsumed by the new layer, in its account of the lower level's repulsive force. Additionally, the halt reflex of the lower level operated autonomously and unchanged.

The third layer made the robot look (with its sonars) for distant places and try to head towards them. This layer monitored progress through odometry, generating a desired heading which suppressed the direction desired by the wander layer. The desired heading was then fed into a vector addition with the instinctive obstacle avoidance layer. The physical robot did not therefore remain true to the desires of the upper layer. The upper layer had to watch what happened in the world, through odometry, in order to understand what was really happening in the lower control layers, and send down correction signals.

In [9] we described an alternate set of layers for the robot Allen.

4.2. Tom and Jerry

Tom and Jerry [14] were two identical robots built to demonstrate just how little raw computation is necessary to support the subsumption architecture. A three layer subsumption program was implemented, yet all data paths were just one bit wide and the whole program fitted on a single 256 gate programmable array logic chip. Physically Tom and Jerry were toy cars with three one-bit infrared proximity sensors mounted on the front and one at the rear. The sensors were individually tuned to a specific distance at which they would fire. The central front sensor fired only on much closer objects than the two side sensors, which pointed slightly outward.

The lowest layer of Tom and Jerry implemented the standard pair of first level behaviors. These used a vector sum of repulsive forces from obstacles to perform an avoidance manuever or to trigger a halt reflex to stop when something was too close ahead, as detected by the central front looking sensor. There were extra complications with Tom and Jerry in that we needed to use the subsumption architecture to implement an active braking scheme because of the high speed of the robots relative to their sensor ranges. Tom and Jerry's second layers were much like Allen's original second layer—an urge to wander about, which was implemented by an attractive force which got added to the repulsive forces from obstacles. The third layer detected moving objects using the front three sensors and created a following behavior. When something was detected, the robot was attracted and moved towards it. The lower level collide behavior stopped the robot from actually hitting the target, however. While the robot was chasing its target, the wander behavior was suppressed.

Tom and Jerry demonstrated the notion of independent behaviors combining without knowing about each other (chasing obstacles but staying back from them a little). Tom and Jerry also demonstrated that the subsumption architecture could be compiled (by hand) down to the gate level, and that it could be run at clock speeds of only a few hundred Hertz.

4.3. Herbert

Herbert [12] was a much more ambitious robot. It has a 24-processor distributed, loosely coupled, onboard computer to run the subsumption architecture. The processors were slow CMOS 8-bit microprocessors (which ran on low electrical power; an important consideration when carrying batteries), which could communicate only by slow serial interfaces (maximum 10 packets each, 24 bits wide per second). Onboard Herbert, the interconnections between AFSMs are physically embodied as actual copper wires.

Herbert had 30 infrared proximity sensors for local obstacle avoidance, an onboard manipulator with a number of simple sensors attached to the hand, and a laser light striping system to collect three dimensional depth data in a 60 degree wide swath in front of the robot with a range of about 12 feet. A 256 pixel-wide by 32 pixel-high depth image was collected every second. Through a special purpose distributed serpentine memory, four of the onboard 8-bit processors were each able to expend about 30 instructions on each data pixel. By linking the processors in a chain we were able to implement quite high performance vision algorithms.

[16] programmed Herbert to wander around office areas, go into people's offices and steal empty soda cans from their desks. He demonstrated obstacle avoidance and wall following, real-time recognition of soda-can-like objects, and a set of 15 behaviors [15] which drove the arm to physically search for a soda can in front of the robot, locate it, and pick it up.

Herbert showed many instances of using the world as its own best model and as a communication medium. The remarkable thing about Herbert is that there was absolutely no internal communication between any of its behavior generating modules. Each one was connected to sensors on the input side, and an arbitration network on the output side. The arbitration network drove the actuators.

The laser-based soda-can object finder drove the robot so that its arm was lined up in front of the soda can. But it did not tell the arm controller that there was now a soda can ready to be picked up. Rather, the arm behaviors monitored the shaft encoders on the wheels, and when they noticed that there was no body motion, initiated motions of the arm, which in turn triggered other behaviors, so that eventually the robot would pick up the soda can.

The advantage of this approach is that there is no need to set up internal expectations for what is going to happen next; this means that the control system can both (1) be naturally opportunistic if fortuitous circumstances present themselves, and (2) it can easily respond to changed circumstances, such as some other object approaching it on a collision course.

As one example of how the arm behaviors cascaded upon one another, consider actually grasping a soda can. The hand had a grasp reflex that operated whenever something broke an infrared beam between the fingers. When the arm located a soda can with its local sensors, it simply drove the hand so that the two fingers lined up on either side of the can. The hand then independently grasped the can. Given this arrangement, it was possible for a human to hand a soda can to the robot. As soon as it was grasped, the arm retracted – it did not matter whether it was a soda can that was intentionally grasped, or one that magically appeared. The same opportunism among behaviors let the arm adapt automatically to a wide variety of cluttered desktops, and still successfully find the soda can.

4.4. Genghis

Genghis [8] is a 1Kg six legged robot which walks under subsumption control and has an extremely distributed control system. The robot successfully walks over rough terrain using 12 motors, 12 force sensors, 6 pyroelectric sensors, one inclinometer and 2 whiskers. It also follows cooperative humans using its pyroelectric sensors.

The subsumption layers successively enable the robot to stand up, walk without any sensing, use force measurements to comply with rough terrain, use force measurements to lift its legs over obstacles, use inclinometer measurements to selectively inhibit rough terrain compliance when appropriate, use whiskers to lift feet over obstacles, use passive infrared sensors to detect people and to walk only when they are present, and to use the directionality of infrared radiation to modulate the backswing of particular leg sets so that the robot follows a moving source of radiation.

In contrast, one could imagine a control system which had a central repository which modeled the robot's configuration in translation and orientation space. One could further imagine high level commands (for instance from a path planner) generating updates for the robot's coordinates. These high level commands would then be hierarchically resolved into instructions for individual legs.

The control system on Genghis has no such repository. Indeed there is not even a central repository for each leg—separate motors on the legs are controlled quite separately in different parts of the network. While there is a some semblance of a central control system for each individual motor, these controllers receive messages from diverse parts of the network and simply pass them on to the motors, without any attempt at integration.

Our control system was also very easy to build. It was built incrementally, with each new capability being a simple addition (no deletion, no change to previous network) of new network structure. The debugged existing network structure was never altered.

The resulting control system is elegant in its simplicity. It does not deal with coordinate transforms or kinematic models. It is not at all hierarchical. It directly implements walking through many very tight couplings of sensors to actuators. It is very distributed in its nature, and we believe its robustness in handling rough terrain comes from this distributed form of control.

We are currently building a new version of Genghis [3] which will be a much stronger climber and able to scramble at around three kilometers per hour. Each leg has three degrees of freedom and three force sensors mounted on load bearing beams. A single-chip microprocessor with onboard RAM and EEPROM is easily able to force servo the complete leg. The total mass of the final robot will be 1.6 Kg. Attila will have batteries which will power it for about 30 minutes while actively walking. Following that, it will have to recharge from solar cells for about 4.5 hours in Earth sunlight.

4.5. Squirt

Squirt is the smallest robot we have built [21]. It weighs about 50 grams and is about 5/4 cubic inches in volume.

Squirt incorporates an 8-bit computer, an onboard power supply, three sensors and a propulsion system. Its normal mode of operation is to act as a "bug", hiding in dark corners and venturing out in the direction of noises, only after the noises are long gone, looking for a new place to hide near where the previous set of noises came from.

The most interesting thing about Squirt is the way in which this high level behavior emerges from a set of simple interactions with the world.

Squirt's lowest level of behavior monitors a light sensor and causes it to move in a spiral pattern searching for darkness. The spiral trajectories are created by a coupling of a forward motion along with a back-and-turn motion, implemented through the use of only one motor and made possible by a unidirectional clutch on the rear axle. Once Squirt finds a dark spot, it stops.

Squirt's second level of behavior is triggered once a dark hiding place has been established. This behavior monitors two microphones and measures the time of arrival of sound at each microphone. By noting the difference, it can localize the direction from which the sound came. Squirt then waits for a pattern of a sharp noise followed by a few minutes of silence. If this pattern is recognized, Squirt ventures out in the direction of the last heard noise, suppressing the desire to stay in the dark. After this ballistic straight-line motion times out, the lower level is no longer suppressed and the light sensor is again recognized. If it is light, the spiraling pattern kicks back in. The end effect is that Squirt gravitates towards the center of action. The entire compiled control system for Squirt fits in 1300 bytes of code on an onboard microprocessor.

4.6. Toto

Toto [24] is our first robot fully programmed with the new behavior language. Toto has 12 radially arranged sonars and a flux-gate compass as its sensors.

At first appearance it may seem that the subsumption architecture does not allow for such conventional items as maps. There are no data structures within the subsumption architecture, and no easy way of having a central repository for more than simple numeric quantities. Our work with Toto demonstrates that these are not critical limitations with regard to map building and use.

Toto has a low level reactive system to keep basic functions running robustly. Its lower level behaviors enable it to wander around avoiding collisions, and successfully follow walls and corridors as if it were explicitly exploring the world. An intermediate level set of behaviors tries to recognize particular types of landmark such as walls, corridors and clutter. Another network is made up of mutually identical behaviors with each layer waiting for new landmarks to be recognized. Each time this happens a behavior allocates itself to be the 'place' of that particular landmark. The behaviors which correspond to physically adjacent landmarks have neighbor relationship links activated between them. A graph structure is thus formed, although the nodes are active computational elements rather than static data structures. (In fact, each node is really a whole collection of computational elements in the form of augmented finite state machines.)

As the robot moves around the environment, the nodes try to keep track of where it is. Nodes become more active if they believe that they correspond to the place at which the robot is currently located. Thus the robot has both a map, and a sense of where it is on the map, but a totally distributed computational model.

When a behavior (such as "go to some place") is activated (via a small panel of push buttons on the robot) a spreading of activation mechanism is used, which spreads from the goal via the neighbor links. This process is continuous and keeps the robot informed as it reaches each place expected from the map.

Mataric's experimental results [25] show how the robot's performance can be incrementally improved by adding new pieces of network. Map building and path planning were initially demonstrated with fewer types of behaviors than finally implemented. Then an idea of expectation, based on temporally generated context was added. This allowed the robot to handle getting lost and to relocate itself in the map later. Then a coarse position estimation scheme was added, based on integrating the compass heading over time. This significantly lowered the level of ambiguity in both map building and map use in more complex environments, and thus increased the robot's overall competence. In all cases we simply added new behaviors to the network to improve the map building and using performance.

The work has also shown that globally consistent maps can be built and emerge in a totally distributed manner. In our experiments they were built by a collection of asynchronous independent agents, without the ability to use arbitrary pointers, or other such traditional data structure techniques. In path planning there is no notion of a global path under this scheme; local pieces of information combine to direct the robot through its dynamics of interaction with the world, to get to the desired place. Overall, these aspects demonstrate that the techniques should scale well.

It has been easy to integrate the maps with the dynamics of navigation, obstacle avoidance and path planning. The representations have a natural ability to integrate temporal aspects of the dynamics since they can use time as its own representation!

The notion of place maps developed for Toto bears striking similarities to what has been observed in the hippocampus of the rat [17].

4.7. Seymour

Seymour is a new robot we are building with all onboard processing to support vision processing of 9 low resolution cameras at approximately 10 frames per second [10]. The cameras feed into different subsumption layers which act upon those aspects of the world they perceive. Seymour is also programmed in the new behavior language.

A number of vision based behaviors developed for Seymour have been prototyped on earlier robots.

[22] describe a subsumption program that controls two simple and unreliable visual processing routines to produce a reliable behavior which follows moving objects using vision. One vision process tracks a single moving blob. It gets bootstrapped by another process which overlays the blob image with an indication of where motion is seen. The robot then tries to servo a selected blob to stay in a fixed location in image coordinates. The blob tracker often loses the blob it is tracking. The motion finder produces a lot of noise especially when the robot is moving, but between the two of them they let the robot reliably follow a moving object (any moving object; we have seen the robot chase a black trash can dragged by a string, a radio controlled blue toy car on a blue floor, a pink plastic flamingo, a grey notebook on a grey carpeted floor, and a drinking mug moved around by hand), by switching back and forth between the visual routines as either one fails. Nowhere internally does the subsumption

program have the notion of an identifiable object, yet to an outside observer it certainly appears to follow a moving object very well.

Using the robot Tito, [29] demonstrated two visually guided behaviors which will be used in support of Seymour. Each behavior used a stereo pair of linear cameras. A vertically mounted pair made use of rotational motions of the base to produce images from which the dimensions of the room could be extracted even though the camera system was uncalibrated. Then employing earlier results from [11], the robot used forward motion to calibrate a horizontally mounted pair of cameras, which were used to find doorways through which the robot drove.

[31] has demonstrated an autonomous eyeball capable of maintaining a steady gaze despite motion of its platform. It recapitulates the primate vestibular-occular system by using vision as a slow calibration system for a gyroscope controlled movable platform which holds the camera.

4.8. Gnat Robots

In all our use and development of the subsumption architecture we have been careful to maintain its simplicity so that programs written in it could be easily and mechanically compiled into silicon. For example, with Toto the map networks were arranged so that the total wire length for connecting the underlying finite state machines need be no more than linear in the number of finite state machines. In general the area of silicon needed for the robots we have built would be quite small. There is a reason for maintaining this restriction.

[18,19] introduced the idea of building complete small robots out of silicon on a VLSI fabrication line. [7] demonstrated how to use the subsumption architecture to control such robots. There is great potential for using such robots in ways previously not considered at all cost effective for robotic applications. Imagine, for instance having a colony of tiny robots living on your TV screen, absorbing energy from the electron beam, whose only purpose in existence is to keep the screen clean. There is potential for a revolution in micro-mechanical systems of the same order and impact as the quiet revolutions brought about in daily life by the advent of the micro-processor.

[20] outlines a series of technological steps necessary to build such robots, including materials, a new type of micro motor based on thin film piezo-electric material, a 3-D fabrication process, and some new types of integrated sensors. Critical to this enterprise is an easy way of controlling the robots, giving them intelligent behavior in unstructured and uncertain environments.

5. Measures of Success

When I give talks about the techniques we have used to build intelligent control systems for our robots, the most common questions I am asked, or assertions I am told, are:
● "If I make *such-and-such* a change to your robot's environment, I bet it would do the wrong thing."
● "Aren't these systems almost impossible to debug?"
● "Surely this can't be scaled up to do *X*", for some value of *X* which has not been part of the talk.

In the next three subsections I argue that these questions are either easy to answer or, in a deep sense, improper to ask.

5.1. Puzzlitis

Since traditional Artificial Intelligence research has concentrated on isolated modules of intelligence that almost never get grounded in the world, it has been important to develop some criteria for successful research. One of the most popular ideas is generality. This quickly leads to a disease I call *puzzlitis*. The way to show generality is to pick the most obscure case within the domain and demonstrate that your system can handle or solve it.

But in physically grounded systems I believe this approach is counterproductive. The puzzles posed are often very unlikely in practice, but to solve them makes the systems much more complex. This reduces the overall robustness of the system! We should be driven by puzzles which can naturally arise in a physically grounded context—this is what gives strength to our physically grounded systems.

One additional argument on this topic is that for most AI programs the creator gets to tell the program the facts in some sort of representation language. It is assumed that the vision guys in the white hats down the corridor will one day deliver world models using these same representations. Many of the puzzlitis failures of physically grounded systems stem from a failure in perception as the stakes have been raised. Standard AI programs have not been forced to face these issues.

5.2. Debugging

In our experience debugging the subsumption programs used to control our physically grounded systems has not been a great source of frustration or difficulty. This is not due to any particularly helpful debugging tools or any natural superiority of the subsumption architecture.

Rather, we believe it is true because the world is its own best model (as usual). When running a physically grounded system in the real world, one can see at a glance how it is interacting. It is right before your eyes. There are no layers of abstraction to obfuscate the dynamics of the interactions between the system and the world. This is an elegant aspect of physically grounded systems.

5.3. But It Can't Do X

Along with the statement "But is can't do *X*" there is an implication, sometimes vocalized, and sometimes not, that therefore there are lots of things that this approach is not good for, and so we should resort to the symbol system hypothesis.

But this is a fallacious argument, even if only implicit. We do not usually complain that a medical expert system, or an analogy program cannot climb real mountains. It is clear that their domain of expertise is somewhat more limited, and that their designers were careful to pick a well circumscribed domain in which to work. Likewise it is unfair to claim that an elephant has no intelligence worth studying just because it does not play chess.

People working on physically grounded systems do, however, seem to be claiming to eventually solve the whole problem. E.g., papers such as this one, argue that this is an interesting approach to pursue for precisely that reason. How can we have it both ways?

Like the advocates of the symbol system hypothesis, we believe that in principle we have uncovered the fundamental foundation of intelligence. But just as the symbol system people are

allowed to work incrementally in their goals, so should the physical grounding people be allowed. Solutions to all problems are not obvious now. We must spend time, analyzing the needs of certain domains *from the perspective of the physical grounding hypothesis* to discern what new structures and abstractions must be built in order to make forward progress.

6. Future Limits

As [30] points out, concerning his symbol system hypothesis:

The hypothesis is clearly an empirical one, to be judged true or false on the basis of evidence.

The same can, of course, be said for the physical grounding hypothesis.

Our current strategy is to test the limitations of the physical grounding hypothesis by building robots which are more independent and can do more in the world. We are tackling aspects of human competence in a different order than that chosen by people working under the symbol system hypothesis, so sometimes it is hard to make comparisons between the relative successes. A further part of our strategy then, is to build systems that can be deployed in the real world. At least if our strategy does not convince the arm chair philosophers, our engineering approach will have radically changed the world we live in.

6.1. Contrasts In Hope

Adherents of both approaches to intelligence are relying on some degree of hope that their approach will eventually succeed. They have both demonstrated certain classes of success, but both can resort only to vague hopes when it comes to generalizability. It turns out that the demonstrations and generalization issues fall along different dimensions for the two approaches.

- Traditional AI has tried to demonstrate sophisticated reasoning in rather impoverished domains. The hope is that the ideas used will generalize to robust behavior in more complex domains.
- Nouvelle AI tries to demonstrate less sophisticated tasks operating robustly in noisy complex domains. The hope is that the ideas used will generalize to more sophisticated tasks.

Thus the two approaches appear somewhat complementary. It is worth addressing the question of whether more power may be gotten by combining the two approaches. However, we will not pursue that question further here.

Both approaches rely on some unanalyzed aspects to gain their successes.

Traditional AI relies on the use of heuristics to control search. While much mathematical analysis has been carried out on this topic, the user of a heuristic still relies on an expected distribution of cases within the search tree to get a "reasonable" amount of pruning in order to make the problem manageable.

Nouvelle AI relies on the emergence of more global behavior from the interaction of smaller behavioral units. As with heuristics there is no a priori guarantee that this will always work. However, careful design of the simple behaviors and their interactions can often produce systems with useful and interesting emergent properties. The user again is relying on expectations without hard proofs.

Can there be a theoretical analysis to decide whether one organization for intelligence is better than another? Perhaps, but I think we are so far away from understanding the correct way of formalizing the dynamics of interaction with the environment, that no such theoretical results will be forthcoming in the near term.

6.2. Specific Problems

Some of the specific problems which must be tackled soon, and solved, by approaches to AI based on the physical grounding hypothesis include

- how to combine many (e.g. more than a dozen) behavior generating modules in a way which lets them be productive and cooperative
- how to handle multiple sources of perceptual information when there really does seem to be a need for fusion
- how to automate the building of interaction interfaces between behavior generating modules, so that larger (and hence more competent) systems can be built
- how to automate the construction of individual behavior generating modules, or even to automate their modification

The first two items have specific impact on whether the approach can scale in principle to larger and more complex tasks. The last two are concerned with the issue of how to build such larger systems even if they are in principle possible.

There is room for plenty of experimentation, and eventually, when we are mature enough, there is also room for much theoretical development of the approaches to Artificial Intelligence based on the physical grounding hypothesis.

Acknowledgements

Pattie Maes encouraged me to write this paper, despite my earlier refusal to do so. She and Maja Mataric made a number of useful criticisms of an earlier draft of this paper.

Funding for this work was provided by a number of government agencies and companies including: the University Research Initiative under Office of Naval Research contract N00014–86–K–0685, the Defense Advanced Research Projects Agency under Office of Naval Research contract N00014–85–K–0124, Hughes Research Laboratories Artificial Intelligence Center in Malibu, Siemens Research Center in Princeton, and Mazda Research Center in Yokohama.

References

[1] Philip Agre and David Chapman, Pengi: An implementation of a theory of activity, *AAAI-86*, Seattle, WA (1987) 268–272.

[2] Colin M. Angle, Genghis, a six legged autonomous walking robot, MIT S.B. Thesis in Electrical Engineering and Computer Science (March 1989).

[3] Colin M. Angle, Attila's cripped brother marvin, MIT Term Paper in Electrical Engineering and Computer Science (May 1989).

[4] Dana H. Ballard, Reference frame for active vision, *IJCAI-89*, Detroit, MI (1989) 1635–1641.

[5] Rodney A. Brooks, Symbolic reasoning among 3-D model and 2-D images, *Artificial Intelligence* 17 (1989) 285–348.

[6] Rodney A. Brooks, A robust layered control system for a mobile robot, *IEEE J. Robotics and Automation*, RA-2, April (1986) 14–23.

[7] Rodney A. Brooks, Micro-brains for micro-brawn; Autonomous microbots, *IEEE Micro Robots and Teleoperators Workshop*, Hyannis, MA (November 1987).

[8] Rodney A. Brooks, A robot that walks: Emergent behavior form a carefully evolved network, *Neural Computation*, 1(2) (Summer 1989) 253–262.

[9] Rodney A. Brooks and Jonathan H. Connell, Asynchronous distributed control system for a mobile robot, *SPIE Vol. 727 Mobile Robots*, Cambridge, MA (November 1986) 77–84.

[10] Rodney A. Brooks and Anita M. Flynn, Robot beings, *IEEE/RSJ International Workshop on Intelligent Robots and Systems '89*, Tsukuba, Japan (1989) 2–10.

[11] Rodney A. Brooks, Anita M. Flynn, and Thomas Marill, Self calibration of motion and stereo for mobile robot navigation, *MIT AI Memo* 984 (August 1987).

[12] Rodney A. Brooks, Jonathan H. Connell, and Peter Ning, Herbert: A second generation mobile robot, *MIT AI Memo* 1016 (January 1988).

[13] David Chapman, Planning for conjunctive goals, *Artificial Intelligence* 32 (1987) 333–377.

[14] Jonathan H. Connell, Creature building with the subsumption architecture, *IJCAI-87*, Milan (August 1987) 1124–1126.

[15] Jonathan H. Connell, A behavior-based arm controller, *MIT AI Memo* 1025 (June 1988).

[16] Jonathan H. Connell, A colony architecture for an artificial creature, MIT Ph.D. Thesis in Electrical Engineering and Computer Science, MIT AI Lab Tech Report 1151 (June 1989).

[17] H. Eichenbaum, S.I. Wiener, M.L. Shapiro, and N.J. Cohen, The organization of spatial coding in the hippocampus: A study of neural ensemble activity. *J. Neuroscience* 9(8) (1989) 2764–2775.

[18] Anita M. Flynn, Gnat robots (and how they will change robotics), *IEEE Micro Robots and Teleoperators Workshop*, Hyannis, MA (November 1987).

[19] Anita M. Flynn, Gnat robots: A low-intelligence, low-cost approach, *IEEE Solid-State Sensor and Actuator Workshop*, Hilton Head, SC (June 1988).

[20] Anita M. Flynn, Rodney A. Brooks and Lee S. Tavrow, Twilight zones and cornerstones: A gnat robot double feature, *MIT AI Memo* 1126 (July 1989).

[21] Anita M. Flynn, Rodney A. Brooks, William M. Wells and David S. Barrett, The world's largest one cubic inch robot, *Proceedings IEEE Micro Electro Mechanical Systems*, Salt Lake City, Utah (February 1989) 98–101.

[22] Ian D. Horswill and Rodney A. Brooks, Situated vision in a dynamic world: Chasing objects, *AAAI-88*, St Paul, MN (August 1988) 796–800.

[23] Pattie Maes, The dynamics of action selection, *IJCAI-89*, Detroit, MI (1989) 991–997.

[24] Maja J. Mataric, Qualitative sonar based environment learning for mobile robots, *SPIE Mobile Robots*, Philadelphia, PA (November 1989).

[25] Maja J. Mataric, A model for distributed mobile robot environment learning and navigation, MIT M.S. Thesis in Electrical Engineering and Computer Science (January 1990).

[26] Hans P. Moravec, Locomotion, vision and intelligence, *Robotics Research* 1, Brady and Paul (eds) (MIT Press 1984) 215–224.

[27] Zenon W. Pylyshyn (ed), The Robot's Dilemma, (Ablex Publishing, Norwood, NJ, 1987).

[28] Arthur L. Samuel, Some studies in machine learning using the game of checkers, *IBM. J. Res. Development* 3(3) (1959).

[29] Karen B. Sarachik, Characterising an indoor environment with a mobile robot and uncalibrated stereo, *Proceedings IEEE Robotics and Automation*, Scottsdale, AZ (May 1989) 984–989.

[30] Herbert A. Simon, The Sciences of the Artificial (MIT Press, Cambridge, MA, 1969).

[31] Paul Viola, Neurally inspired plasticity in oculomotor processes, *1989 IEEE Conference on Neural Information Processing Systems – Natural and Synthetic*, Denver, CO (November 1989).

[32] A.L. Yarbus, Eye Movements and Vision (Plenum Press 1967).

What Are Plans for?

Philip E. Agre and David Chapman *

Computer Science Department, University of Chicago, 1100 East 58th Street, Chicago, IL 60637, USA
* MIT Artificial Intelligence Laboratory, 545 Technology Square, Cambridge, MA 02139, USA

What plans are like depends on how they're used. We contrast two views of plan use. On the plan-as-program view, plan use is the execution of an effective procedure. On the plan-as-communication view, plan use is like following natural language instructions. We have begun work on computational models of plans-as-communications, building on our previous work on improvised activity and on ideas from sociology.

Keywords: Planning; Improvisation; Situated activity.

1. Introduction

What plans are like depends on how they're used. We contrast two views of plan use. On the plan-as-program view, plan use is the execution of an effective procedure. On the plan-as-communication view, plan use is like following natural language instructions. We have begun work on computational models of plans-as-communications, building on our previous work on improvised activity and on ideas from sociology.

The plan-as-program view and the plan-as-communication view offer very different accounts of the role of plans in activity. The plans-as-programs view gives plans a central role. Plan use is only a matter of *execution*, performed by a simple, fixed, domain-independent "interpreter". Plans-as-programs directly determine their user's actions.

The plan-as-communication view gives plans a much smaller role. It requires an account of *improvisation*. Plans, on this account, do not directly determine their user's activity. Indeed, an agent can engage in sensible, organized, goal-directed activity without using plans at all. An agent who does use a plan-as-communication does not mechanically execute it. Instead, the agent uses the plan as one resource among others in continually redeciding what to do. Using a plan requires figuring out how to make it relevant to the situation at hand, a process of interpretation which can be arbitrarily complicated and draw on a wide variety of resources. The plan-as-communication view portrays people and robots as participating in the world, not as controlling it.

Section 2 of this essay describes the plan-as-program view and some of the difficulties with it. The difficulties concern the computational complexity of plan construction, the problem of prediction in a world of uncertainty and change, the necessity of accommodating the simplicity of executives by specifying plans in impractical detail, and the largely unaddressed issue of relating plan texts to concrete situations in the world. This paper is not intended as a thorough survey of the literature on planning; for some useful surveys see [8,18a,50] and [52].

Philip E. Agre is visiting Assistant Professor of Computer Science at the University of Chicago. He received his Ph.D. in Computer Science at M.I.T. in 1988.

David Chapman is a graduate student at the M.I.T. Artificial Intelligence Laboratory.

This report describes research done at the Artificial Intelligence Laboratory of the Massachusetts Institute of Technology. Support for the laboratory's artificial intelligence research is provided in part by the Advanced Research Projects Agency of the Department of Defense under Office of Naval Research contract number N00014-85-K-0124.

North-Holland
Robotics and Autonomous Systems 6 (1990) 17–34

Section 3 outlines our view that everyday activity is improvisatory in nature. Improvisation might involve ideas about the future, but in any event it requires a continual redecision about what to do *now*. Supporting this process of continual redecision is a technical problem that we have addressed in our work. We briefly describe Pengi, a system that employs novel kinds of perception and representation in playing a video game called Pengo.

Section 4 presents the plan-as-communication view and contrasts its views of plan use, representation, and activity with those of the plans-as-programs view. It further illustrates the view with an example of plan use in the real world. Our analysis of this example turns up several ways in which the plan's maker counted on the understandings of everyday reality that he shared with the plan's users.

Section 5 pursues this theme in more detail in relation to an ongoing project. Chapman is constructing a system, Sonja, which uses instructions given in the course of video-game playing. We argue that plan use and instruction use are similar, and sketch some of Sonja's capabilities.

Section 6 summarizes our principal conclusions and proposes that future inquiry conjoin computational analysis and model-building with principled and detailed observation of human plan use in natural settings.

Since we wrote the first version of this paper in 1987, several authors have proposed alternatives to classical planning. An appendix discusses a few of these proposals and compares them to our own.

2. Plans as Programs

The plan-as-program view takes plan use to be like program execution. Almost all implemented executives have been modeled on programming language interpreters. A plan language, on this view, is like a programming language. The plans are built from a set of parameterized primitives (such as PUT–ON(x,y)) using a set of composition operators (to indicate serial execution, for example). Executing a plan means walking over it in a "syntactic," "mechanical" fashion, carrying out its primitive actions and monitoring conditions specified by the planner, and performing little or no new reasoning about the activity in which the agent is engaged. The executive is do-

main-independent: it applies no domain knowledge except that implicit in the plan and the machinery that implements its primitive action types. It makes no interpretations of its sensor inputs except for the monitored conditions and any predicates that might appear in plan conditionals. Nor does it second-guess the planner by performing any interpolations, substitutions, or rearrangements that would count as a departure from the plan. If the executive gets into trouble, it gives up and returns control to the planner.

(The plan-as-program view implies domain-independent *plan execution*, not domain-independent *plan construction*. Plan-as-program construction can be domain-independent or domain-dependent, algorithmic or case-based, formally correct or heuristic.)

This section discusses four reasons to doubt the plan-as-program view. (1) It poses computationally intractable problems. (2) It is inadequate for a world characterized by unpredictable events such as the actions of other agents. (3) It requires that plans be too detailed. (4) Finally, it fails to address the problem of relating the plan text to the concrete situation. These problems with the plan-as-program view do not mean that it is useless. We believe it may lead to practical applications in certain domains. Our arguments only apply to domains, such as the world of everyday life, that are relatively large, uncertain, and changing.

(1) The plan-as-program view makes planning into automatic programming with all its formal undecidabilities. Chapman [8] has proven several negative complexity results, both about the manipulations that need to be performed on partially specified plans and about the spaces through which plan-as-program planners must search. As formalizations of actions and preconditions become more realistic, these results get worse quickly. Complexity theory is, unfortunately, not an ideal tool for proving negative results. The appendix will briefly discuss the possibility that heuristic solutions might work well enough in practice. It is also possible that certain domains have enough useful structure to permit the construction of tractable domain-specific planners. Chapman ([8], page 353) has suggested that plan-construction algorithms at intermediate levels of specialization might capture varieties of formal structure that might be shared by classes of domains.

(2) The original planners made plans to achieve goals in well-behaved simulated worlds. In these imaginary worlds, it was possible to construct a plan which consisted of a representation of a sequence of primitive actions, which, performed in order, would provably achieve the goal. Thus it was possible to formulate the "planning problem" in terms of constructing something that would, when executed, *control* the robot. It has been widely recognized in the last few years that in the real world, execution of a plan brings important risks because unpredictable external processes can change the world and causally affect the robot.

Plans-as-programs are not very flexible. If the robot's interactions with its world fail to work out as the planner expected, the plan itself will fail. If the planner explicitly anticipates a specific, detectable uncertainty, it can either provide the plan with a conditional branch or it can fashion a strategy that works regardless of how the uncertain matter turns out. If the planner fails to anticipate an uncertainty, then a new plan will be required. Reasons to abort or revise a plan can be divided into two classes, contingencies and opportunities. If you're about to walk through the kitchen door to fetch a pen, a closed door is a contingency and a pen on a desk just outside the kitchen is an opportunity. Not all contingencies can be detected through precondition failures: maybe you can put your pants on over your shoes without violating any preconditions, but usually it is not sensible. Opportunities are still harder to test for because they are less obtrusive. An enormous range of circumstances might count as opportunities in one situation or another. In short, a new plan is called for whenever it is no longer sensible to continue following the existing one. This is a grave problem for any executive that does not share the knowledge and reasoning abilities of its planner.

In recent years, more attention has been given to the process of execution. As a result, executives have become increasingly complicated. Much of this complexity has resulted from practical experiences in trying to make plans-as-programs control real robots, experiences that suggest increasing the responsibilities of the executive. In the end, we believe, arbitrary amounts and varieties of domain knowledge can bear on how a plan should be used. This means that an executive must have access to the full cognitive resources of the whole agent. If the full cognitive resources of the agent are devoted to using a plan, there will no longer be a separate executive module whose responsibility that is. The distinction between planner and executive can be eliminated; the whole agent is responsible for both plan making and plan use.

(3) It is generally acknowledged that no system could produce completely detailed plans in domains of realistic complexity. Real activity is too complicated for that. It follows that an executive has to be expected to fill in some details as it goes along. It also follows that a planner needs some idea of what details it can rely on its executive to fill in. A very simple executive will need everything spelled out for it, but if the executive had more knowledge and reasoning abilities then the planner could paint the desired actions with a broader brush. Ideally, a planner would only have to deal with issues that the executive itself cannot. Its plans would not be laden with redundant details. Nor would they prejudge decisions better left to the executive, which after all can base its judgments on the world as it actually turns out, not on models of projected worlds.

The plan-as-program view offers us one account of how a plan can be operational without spelling out every detail. If plans are like programs, then we can make compact plans using a hierarchy of subplans. The planner has a library of subplans, each of which has a contract. These contracts establish a partition between the issues that must concern the planner and the issues that subplans can deal with themselves. They enable the planner to live in a simple, abstract world, reasoning with the preconditions and effects of the top-level subplans.

This subplan-hierarchy view of plans has a number of shortcomings. First, the executive still cannot depart from the plan other than to return control to the planner. Second, it is unclear what sorts of domains permit hierarchical abstraction. The library subplans have to satisfy their contracts regardless of the specific circumstances; this makes them very difficult to construct. In complex real-world domains, where enormous numbers of concrete contingencies can bear on abstract goal ordering issues, truly hierarchical decomposition may not be possible. Lozano-Pérez and Brooks [31] discuss the case of a robot manipulation task: the choice of the initial grasp, the motions of the hand required to position the part, the existence of a path to the destination, and the angles at which compliant forces will be applied are all tightly interconstraining. Moreover, the inevitable sensing and motion errors will propagate from one to another non-locally.

(4) An executive has to establish a causal connection between the text of the plan it is executing and the materials in the concrete situation in front of it. The ontologies of most existing plan languages posit a world made up of individuals, some of which correspond to constant symbols in the agent's axiom set. Thus, for example, the truth of a typical blocks-world proposition like ON(A,B) is determined by a relation corresponding to ON applied to individuals corresponding to A and B. A plan might achieve the goal ON(A,B) by executing an action like PUT–ON(A,B). This requires that the executive be able to determine automatically which individuals in its world correspond to the constant symbols A and B. If every object has a bar-code affixed to it then it's easy enough. But blocks on tables and luggage in airports and cars in parking lots and turns on highways very often take work to distinguish. Arbitrary domain knowledge can, and regularly does, enter into determining which object is the one you want.

The practice of allowing primitive actions to traffic in constant symbols hides not only this problem, but a deeper one as well. Much of the work of using a plan is in determining its *relevance* to the concrete situations that occur during the activity it helps to organize. By hiding this work, an executive that can automatically relate symbols to objects, we feel, falsifies the nature of plan use. Using a plan requires domain-specific skills that a programming language interpreter does not possess and situation-specific improvisations that a programming language interpreter cannot perform.

The difficulties with the plan-as-program view reflect what we feel is a mistaken notion of what plans are for; that is, of what activity is like and of what role plans can play in it. The plan-as-program view understands activity as a matter of problem solving and control. The world presents an agent with a series of formally defined problems that require solutions. A planner produces solutions to these problems. The executive imple-

ments these solutions by trying to make the world conform to them.

The world of everyday life, however, is not a problem or series of problems. Acting in the world is an ongoing process conducted in an evolving web of opportunities to engage in various activities and contingencies that arise in the course of doing so. Most of what you do you already know how to do, and most of the rest you work out as you go along. The futility of trying to control the world is, we think, reflected in the growing complexity of plan executives. Perhaps it is better to view an agent as *participating* in the flow of events. An embodied agent must *lead a life*, not *solve problems*.

We suspect that part of the appeal of the plan-as-program view derives from the word "execution." To execute a command or instruction is to carry it into effect; to execute an action or operation is to perform it. The word is little used except in legal and administrative senses and by football coaches, but even its broader use suggests an activity that takes place in a narrowly specified institutional context, with articulated constraints and strict criteria, and with negligible room and need for variation, interpretation, improvisation, or any other deviation on the part of the person doing the executing. To "execute" a plan isn't just to "follow" it, it's to follow it "to the letter" and "by the book." In short, the word "execution" suggests thinking of a plan as a pretty-well-thorough representation of a sequence of actions, so that execution is a simple process. Perhaps that is why it has seemed so natural to assimilate plan execution to running a program on an programming language interpreter.

3. Participation

What might an alternative to plans-as-programs look like? Let us start by retiring the prejudicial term "execution" and instead speak more neutrally of people (or robots) as "using" plans. This simple terminological change makes some hard questions seem more urgent. First, what can one do with a plan besides executing it? Second, how do plans and plan-making change if plan users can be counted on to use plans sensibly rather than mechanically executing them?

We don't know if these questions must have the same answers for robots as they do for people. But so long as alternatives to the plan-as-program view are in short supply, evidence from human plan use can bring some perspective. Most of what is known has been discovered by social scientists such as Gladwin [21], Hutchins [25], Scher [43], Suchman [48,49], Scribner's group [45,5], and the Soviet activity theorists [54,55]. Our own analysis draws on this material, though a detailed discussion of it would take us too far afield here.

The plan-as-program view gives plans a central role in determining activity. In particular, it claims that an agent acts as it does because it has a certain plan. We do not believe this claim. According to the plan-as-communication view, a plan does not directly determine an agent's actions. Instead, a plan is a resource that an agent can use in deciding what to do. What, then, *does* determine an agent's actions? Answering this question is the job of a *theory of activity*. After briefly summarizing our understanding of activity in this section, we will return to the question of the role of plans in activity.

Our theory of activity has two interconstraining parts: a theory of cognitive machinery and a theory of the *dynamics* or regularly occurring patterns of activity. In studying people we ask (i) how is ordinary human activity organized and (ii) what does this imply for the organization of human cognitive machinery? In studying machines we ask (i) what forms might an agent's activity take and (ii) what sorts of cognitive machinery are compatible with what sorts of activity?

Our answers to these questions are informed by the central theme of participation in ongoing activity whose determination is shared with other processes and agents. Everyday routine activity, we believe, has an orderliness and coherence that is independent of any plan or other representation of it. See [10] for some of this story and [2] for some of the rest. We have found, in the case studies that we have conducted, that participating in the flow of the environment, rather than attempting to control it, can simplify the machinery required to account for the organization of activity.

We built the Pengi system [3] to illustrate some of what we have learned. (For details about Pengi's workings see [2].) Though Pengi engages in complex patterns of activity, its machinery is extremely simple: a visual system based on psychophysically motivated ideas from Ullman's visual routines theory [53], a simple motor system, and a central system made entirely of combinational logic. (For some related projects, see [6,14,28,32,39,41,44].)

Pengi does not follow any plans, but neither is it pushed around by its world. The Pengo games Pengi plays move fast, so Pengi constantly uses the contingencies and opportunities of its environment to help it improvise ways to pursue its projects. Improvisation differs from planning-as-programming in that each moment's action results, effectively, from a fresh reasoning-through of that moment's situation. Yet improvisation, like planning, involves ideas about what might happen in the future.

One of Pengi's contributions is a new participatory theory of representation we call *indexical-functional*, or *deictic* representation [2]. Whereas traditional representations posit a "semantic" correspondence between symbols in an agent's head and objectively individuated objects in the world, our theory describes a causal relationship between the agent and *indexically* and *functionally* individuated *entities* in the world. For example, one of the entities Pengi works with is *the-bee-I-am-chasing*. This entity is individuated indexically in that it is defined in terms of its relationship to the agent ("I"). It is also individuated functionally in that it is defined in terms of one of the agent's ongoing projects (chasing a bee). Whereas in a traditional representation, the symbols BEE-34 and BEE-35 would always refer to the same two bees, different bees might be *the-bee-I-am-chasing* at different times. Pengi uses its visual routines – patterns of directed visual activity – to register *aspects* of various entities, for example *the-bee-I-am-chasing-is-running-away*. The participatory nature of deictic representation means that Pengi deals with its environment through a constant interaction with it rather than through the construction and manipulation of models.

Let us consider a relatively complicated example, starting from the situation illustrated schematically in *Fig. 1*. In this situation, the penguin (played by Pengi) wants to kill the enemy bee by kicking an ice cube at it. Ice cubes, when kicked, slide across the two-dimensional game board in a vertical or horizontal direction. Thus, to kill a bee, an ice cube must be aligned with it in one of the

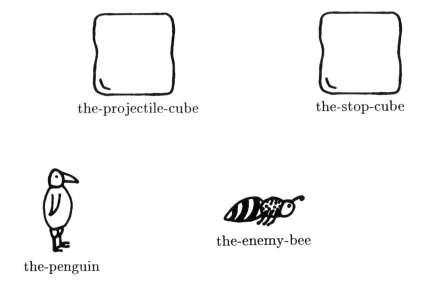

the-projectile-cube   the-stop-cube

the-enemy-bee

the-penguin

Fig. 1. A Pengo situation that requires looking ahead.

two Cartesian dimensions. In this situation, no ice cube is aligned with the bee. However, if the penguin first goes over to the ice cube labeled *the-projectile-cube* and kicks it right, it will collide with the ice cube labeled *the-stop-cube* and come to a halt. (Energy is not conserved in this game.) *The-projectile-cube* will then be aligned with the bee, and can be kicked at it.

A planning system might approach this situation by constructing a four-step plan: go to left side of *the-projectile-cube*; kick *the-projectile-cube*; go to top of *the-projectile-cube*; kick *the-projectile-cube*. The executive that is given this plan must verify the plan's continued applicability by checking a long list of conditions that might have arisen to invalidate it: the bee might wander away, or another bee might draw close and need to be dealt with, or another bee might kick some ice cubes and thereby disturb the configuration in a way that makes carrying out the plan impossible.

Pengi constructs no plans and no models of hypothetical future worlds. It does, however, take probable future circumstances into account; in place of simulation Pengi uses *visualization*. Pengi *looks to see* what might happen next. It engages in visual routines which find particular spatial configurations that predict courses of events and so

suggest actions. For example, when Pengi sees that an ice cube adjacent to the penguin is aligned with a bee, and there are no intervening ice cubes, it kicks it, making it likely to strike and kill the bee. When it sees such an ice cube that is only near, rather than adjacent to, the penguin, it moves the penguin in the direction of the ice cube, because once it gets there the bee might still be aligned. If no ice cubes are aligned but the complex configuration of *Fig. 1* obtains, Pengi sends the penguin over to *the-projectile-cube* in order to kick it at *the-stop-cube*.

Put in the situation of *Fig. 1*, Pengi may well engage in the same course of activity a planning system would, but for quite different reasons. Consider, for example, why each system would take the fourth and final action, kicking *the-projectile-cube* at the bee. The executive would take this action because the value of its program counter is four. Pengi takes the action because, by visualizing, it can see that by doing so it is likely to kill the bee. Once it has gotten to that point, it has no use for the idea that kicking that ice cube is part of a larger pattern of activity.

Even though Pengi's network is only partially implemented, it still plays a pretty decent game of Pengo. We started designing the network by envisioning a series of scenarios, which we call *routines*, of the common patterns of interaction between the player and the game. In practice, Pengi often exhibits these routines. It is relatively unusual, though, for Pengi to carry off one of our envisioned routines without a hitch. Pengi regularly aborts a routine when a contingency arises, tries some action repeatedly until it works or until it notices a more promising option, embarks on a new routine when an opportunity arises, interleaves different routines, and combines its repertoire of activities in useful ways we didn't anticipate. (It also regularly does silly things in situations for which we haven't yet wired it.) Pengi exhibits this flexibility precisely because we did not convert our envisioned scenarios into a repertoire of plans for Pengi to execute. Instead, we analyzed what reasoning should lead Pengi to take what actions in what kinds of situations. When it was possible for these lines of reasoning to conflict, we implemented a simple arbitration scheme that takes various aspects of context into account in deciding which of the various plausible actions to take on each next moment. Pengi thus effectively makes fresh decisions on every cycle of its clock about the nature of its current predicament, what goals it should adopt to deal with that predicament, and what actions it should take to further those goals.

The plan-as-program view may make it a little difficult to grasp the sense in which Pengi creatively improvises. It may seem that, since Pengi will always do just what it's wired up to do, it is completely *un*creative; no more than a wind-up toy. This is, however, equally true of a planner: it too does just what it was programmed to. The apparent difference lies in the fact that a planner explicitly considers and rejects many alternative actions. This seems to give it an infinitely generative combinatorial power that Pengi lacks. Pengi, however, has its own kind of generativity, an infinity of dynamic possibilities rather than an infinity of structural combinations. Like Simon's ant [46], Pengi enters into forms of interaction with its environment which exhibit a great deal of complexity, but for reasons which do not lie in either Pengi or its world alone. Like a planner, Pengi is "given" something and complexity arises from the combinatorial possibilities that arise when that something is put into action. With a planner, these combinatorial possibilities are explored mentally. With Pengi, they are encountered in the course of the activity. We did not design a device that could *simulate* a certain complex way of life; we designed a device that could *live* that life.

It is sometimes said that we should measure a system's achievement by comparing how much it is "given" as compared to how much it "does for itself." By this criterion, though, it is not obvious whether we should prefer Pengi or a conventional planner. Pengi has an invariant part of its architecture (the visual system and the general central system design) and a part varies with the domain (the wiring of the central system). A planner, similarly, has an invariant structure (the plan-space search algorithm) and a part that varies with the domain (at a minimum this includes a set of operators, an axiomatization of the domain, and a set of primitive sensors; to be efficient, it will probably also require a set of domain-specific inference mechanisms and search strategies). It is hard to say which kind of system has the better ratio of "given" to "done-for-itself." Since a real autonomous agent should be able to learn new domains for itself, a real comparison will depend on which is easier to learn; and in the absence of well-worked-out theories of learning for either alternative this is as yet impossible.

The circuitry in Pengi's central system, of course, has a fixed structure. Designing this circuitry is as hard as any other sort of complex programming; we do not believe that such circuitry could arise through general-purpose automatic synthesis. Instead, we believe that this circuitry arises in the course of the agent's interactions with its environment, through a long process of incremental evolution. In earlier work on *running arguments*, Agre [1,2] investigated some of the forms this process might take. He built a fairly general-purpose rule system, a streamlined version of Amord [13], which maintains dependencies on its reasoning. As it runs, it accumulates a large dependency network that can be regarded as a combinational circuit connecting perception and memory elements to primitive actions. Though not entirely realistic, this scheme provides some sense of the form that incremental learning through modification of central-system circuitry might take.

The running argument system's dependency network grows in the course of its interactions with the concrete situations in which it must decide what to do. Faced with any situation at all, the system behaves as though it has forward-chained all of its rules to exhaustion. It does not achieve this behavior, though, by continually undertaking the very expensive process of actually running all those rules. Instead, most of the work is actually done by the previously conducted lines of reasoning stored in the dependency network. The system only runs the new rules that the dependency network does not record, so the amount of actual rule-firing effort that a new situation requires is proportional to how novel it is. Once the running argument system has encountered the normal range of situations that occur in its environment, it needs to run very few rules at all. Since "situations" are counted in terms of their significance for the agent's current understandings and goals and not in terms of an exhaustive enumeration of true propositions, the system's recorded lines of reasoning will apply to a wide variety of future circumstances.

In forms of activity which are generally routine, such a system will be able to engage in rapid, flexible forms of interaction without a prohibitive computational overhead. The principal shortcoming of the particular system described in [1,2] is that it is incompatible with a representation scheme based on constant symbols; this was one of the motivations behind the development of deictic representation. The general strategy of learning through particular occasions of situated reasoning about action is similar in spirit with the notion of case-based planning [23], whose conception of memory structure is much more elaborated.

Pengi illustrates some ideas, but Pengo-playing differs from other human activities in many ways. Most activities are less hectic, have more complex goal structures, require more remembering, involve additional kinds of representation such as visual imagery and internal language, and so forth. Our experience with Pengi has focused the issues for a new round of study of dynamics and machinery.

Pengi, as we have mentioned, neither makes nor uses plans. Pengi engages in a continual, participatory interaction with its environment. Yet its activity is directed toward particular concrete goals: killing certain bees, staying clear of others, becoming adjacent to ice cubes it might usefully kick, and ultimately winning the game. Does this mean that plans are useless? Not at all. Pengi is a study of a certain subset of the dynamics of improvisatory activity. A creature that can participate in this set of dynamics can play Pengo.

Many other activities do require plans. If Pengo got harder, for example, Pengi might sometimes have to refer to a plan. The plan might explain how to deal with some tricky situation, or perhaps what strategic issues bear on the matter of which bees to attack when. But what would be involved in using plans like these? What role can plans play in an improvisatory theory of activity? This is the subject of the remainder of the paper.

4. Plans as Communication

In place of the plan-as-program view, we would like to propose a different account of what plans are for which we will call the plan-as-communication view. The two views differ as to the nature of plan use, the way in which plans are representations, and the nature of activity.

Nature of plan use. For the plan-as-program view, a plan decomposes into primitive actions which can be simply "emitted" by the executive, a simple, fixed, domain-independent device. For the plan-as-communication view, figuring out what activity a plan suggests requires a continual interpretive effort. It can take a lot of work to determine what in the situation the plan is talking about. A plan is operational if a sensible and suitably acculturated agent can use it, somehow, to engage in the activity it describes. A plan is a resource you can draw on in deciding what to do, on an equal basis with other resources such as the arrangement of your equipment, external memory devices like scratch paper, and help from your friends [49]. Unlike executives, people using plans know more or less what they are doing and why. Thus a plan is often well thought of as a mnemonic device. (For another computational interpretation of the idea of plans as resources that, unlike our own notion, maintains a notion of a complete world model, see [40])

Nature of representation. A plan-as-program "represents" a course of action in a very simple sense, insofar as programming languages have roughly compositional semantics. Each primitive of a programming language always occasions the same action, regardless of the context. For the plan-as-communication view, a plan "represents"

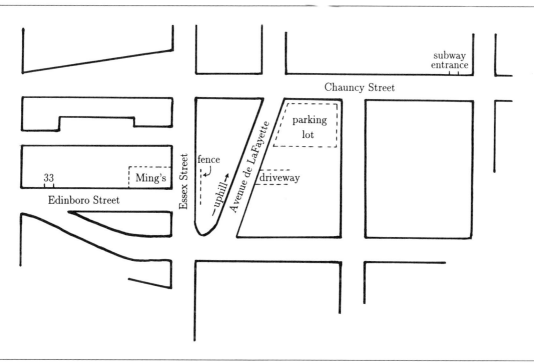

Fig. 2. The route from 33 Edinboro Street to the Washington Street subway station, early 1986. (Not to scale.)

a course of action in a much more complex sense, insofar as a linguistic entity's meaning depends on the context of its use in a hundred different ways. In particular, a program represents its actions "exhaustively" where a linguistic entity cannot and need not.

On the plan-as-program view, plans are abstract mathematical entities. On the plan-as-communication view, plans are social constructions [25,55]. Our ability to make and use plans is built on our ability to use language during activities we share with others. Many plans are physical objects such as wall charts, instruction sheets, blueprints, and bound business plans. Others are spoken utterances, as might be produced in response to the question "So, what's your plan for the afternoon?" The nature and use of these externally represented plans are relatively easy to study. People also make and use plans that are represented only internally. We'll suggest later that these are similar to external ones in important respects. In any case, external plans seem like a good place to start study.

Plans-as-communications, unlike plans-as-programs, do not constitute a unified phenomenon. A lot of disparate sorts of things, used quite differ-

ently, can count as plans-as-communications. Plans-as-communications shade off into a variety of other phenomena, such as mnemonics and conversation and visual imagery and written lists and schedules and workspace arrangement. While you might be able to implement an agent that could use plans-as-communications, the agent's design would not contain a plan-as-communication-using module, since the whole agent must be brought to the task.

Nature of activity. In the plan-as-program view, the only situation given thorough consideration is the "initial situation" passed in to the planner. During the course of execution, the circumstances that arise can only determine conditional branches or cause control to be returned to the planner if something goes obviously wrong.

The plan-as-communication view is part of a theory of "situated activity" [49,30]. Situated activity is not some special variety of activity. The phrase emphasizes that a central feature of *all* activity is that it takes place in some specific, ongoing situation. The plan-as-communication view suggests that the world's independence of your control is not an obstacle to be overcome but a resource to be made use of (*cf.* [48]). If your activity is not rigidly controlled by a plan, contingencies need not be disruptive; instead they can occasion creative improvisation.

In choosing the plan-as-communication view over the plan-as-program view, we implicitly promise to explain the role of plans-as-communications in a broader theory of situated activity. This is a big project. The remainder of this essay sketches some starting points.

Let us consider a typical example of human plan use. The route from my (Agre's) flat in Boston to the subway station, a distance of about three blocks, is hard to describe without drawing maps. (See *Fig. 2*.) Nonetheless, we found that three experimental subjects unfamiliar with the area had no difficulty traversing the route using as a plan only the written instructions "left out the door, down to the end of the street, cross straight over Essex then left up the hill, take the first right and it'll be on your left," which is nothing compared to the actual complexity of the trip.

Consider how much these directions leave out. "The door" is presumably the front door of the building. There's no need to tell you to walk down the street in the direction that "left out the door" will leave you headed; when you're on a path you don't need a plan. No need to label "down to the end" a figure of speech rather than an instruction to descend somewhere. No mention, either, of the fact that Essex Street is not marked as such anywhere near its intersection with Edinboro Street. There's no need to mention it, since it'll be clear which street is meant once you get there. (Our subjects reported being bothered by the lack of a sign but all of them proceeded correctly anyway.) "Left up the hill" will manage to refer to the Avenue de Lafayette rather than to Essex Street because it's the only hill you can see when you're standing at that intersection looking that way. Getting to the Avenue will require a brief rightward detour to get around a fence. No need to mention either this detour or the necessity of crossing the Avenue. When I walk this route myself I typically cut through a parking lot that precedes the "first right." The directions leave out the parking lot altogether; presumably you will have the sense to see the first right coming and cut the corner; and it doesn't matter if you don't. You'll also need the sense not to interpret a drive-

way or the parking lot itself as that first right. Everyone relies heavily on these sorts of things, usually without specifically knowing it, when giving directions. Some people are better at it than others. For example, experienced urban direction-givers know that alleys can confuse people who've been directed to count lefts or rights.

When you're using a plan, your surroundings are available as a resource for interpreting it. A plan that refers to "the hill" counts (roughly speaking) on there only being one hill apparent to someone who has gotten that far in the plan. A plan that instructs you to "take the first right" counts on it being clear which street is indicated. "Counting" and "clarity" are defined reflexively, almost circularly, as that which a given person will be able to figure out in a given situation.

The plan also relies on your experience and skill. The instruction to "walk down to the end of the street" assumes you have the sense to disobey it when the street is full of slush or garbage or dangerous-looking people, as it often is. The plan omits things you already know, like how to cross a street, how to use street signs, how to detect another street coming up, and where it's safe and legal to walk. It also omits things you can be trusted to figure out for yourself, like how to recognize the subway station, how to wind your way past the trash strewn outside Ming's grocery, and how to get some new directions if you get lost.

In short, this plan exploits a long list of ways in which its maker and its user share an understanding of the world. We would like to suggest that this lesson generalizes in several ways: that the list of shared understandings is actually innumerably long; that all plans depend on shared understandings in this way; that action in the real world is sufficiently difficult to specify that plans *must* depend on innumerable shared understandings to be expressible at all; and that all of these points apply regardless of whether the plan's maker and user are the same agent or different agents.

The plan-as-program complexity analysis does not apply to plans-as-communications because they are guides to activity, not solutions to problems. This does not, of course, mean that making plans-as-communications will be easy. One important factor that ought to simplify the process, though, is the knowledge that the plan's user will use it intelligently rather than executing it like a computer program.

Our hypothesis is that the human ability to make plans derives from our formative experiences with using language to communicate about ongoing situated cooperative activity. Our current work explores this view by starting with some simple but, we believe, representative cases.

5. Sonja

Reducing plan use to natural language comprehension might not sound very helpful. We certainly don't want to trivialize the role that natural language plays in situated activity; it's a big topic (see for example [26,47]). We have simplified the problem of plan use by studying *situated instruction use*, the use of instructions given in the course of on-going activity. Situated instruction use is analogous to plan use, with three principal differences: that instructions are given at appropriate times, whereas a plan user must keep track of where it is in the plan; that situated instructions are typically simpler syntactically than full-fledged plans; and that instructions are provided by an external agent, whereas plans may be made by the same agent that uses them. The first two of these differences are straightforward simplifications; the third requires some comment.

External plans you've made for yourself, such as written-down lists of things to do, are perhaps more obviously similar to those made by someone else. The principal difference is that in making a plan for yourself, you can leave out still more detail and be idiosyncratic about abbreviations and conventions. The plan you make for yourself will function more as a mnemonic device than, say, a recipe in a new cookbook. Nonetheless, the same issues of keeping track of the plan's relationship to the concrete circumstances will come up.

We take instructions in internal language (that is, silent speech conducted in ordinary natural languages) as prototypical of internal plans-as-communications. We take literally the phrase "telling yourself what to do." We believe that the ability to instruct yourself in this way is based on your ability to give instructions to others and to follow instructions given to you. This stance has been explored by the psychologist Vygotsky [54]), who explains the similarities between internal and external language and also how internal language becomes abbreviated and idiosyncratic. In [10] we suggested that this internalization process works by part of your brain coming to simulate the external world, thereby "fooling" other parts of your brain into thinking that they are actually engaging in activity when you are actually just thinking; a similar account appears in [42]. In this case, the necessary hardware simulates the process of hearing what you are saying out loud, forming a sort of "null modem" that lets you hear what you are thinking.

Situated instruction use differs from logical advice-taking [35] in that the agent interprets the instructions in relation to its specific ongoing situation. Instructions are understood in terms of the agent's existing ability to understand what is at stake in the situation and to act autonomously to pursue its projects. The instructions thus play only a *management* role.

Chapman (forthcoming) is now constructing a system called Sonja [1] which, like Pengi, can engage in complex activity without use of plans, but which can also use instructions when given them. Sonja is based in part upon an empirical study of video tapes of human video game players who are given advice by a kibitzer, or by another player when two are playing cooperatively. The players in these tapes are already good at video games and at the coordination required for cooperative play; in many cases they are expert at the particular game they are playing. As a result, their activity is largely routine. Moreover, the players see the same screen and have much the same understanding of the game, so they can depend on their shared understanding to achieve most coordination. Thus they need say very little. With rare exceptions, their talk serves only to repair minute differences in understanding. One player might simply say "No!" because there are only two activities the other might plausibly undertake in the current situation. The utterance exploits their commonality of understanding to interpret the listener's moves as constituting a certain activity, judge that activity to be the wrong one, and suggest that he desist from that activity and instead join the speaker in the other one.

To take another example, very often on our tapes one player will say to the other "Turn left!"

---

[1] Sonja is pronounced with an English *j*, "Sahn-djuh," not a Continental one, "Sewn-ya," because it is named after a comicbook character.

Most often, the other player does not immediately turn left. Yet this is not an error, nor is the advice erroneous, nor does the speaker consider that she has been disobeyed. In fact, a viewer will generally agree that the instruction was carried out. Activity other than immediately turning left can count as fulfilling the instruction in many domain-specific ways.

- In some cases, the doorway through which it will be possible to turn has not yet been reached, so that turning left would run you into a wall. In these cases, turning left is deferred.
- When the point at which a turn is possible is reached, there may also be a doorway on the right, and there may be a monster hiding behind the door. If the monster will shoot her in the back when she turns left, the player will turn right and kill the monster before turning back around and proceeding.
- In one case in our collection, the player passes the turn to pick up a valuable energy pod and then returns to comply with the instruction.
- Again, it may be that there is no left turn available, but there is an obviously correct right turn; in this case, the player may well figure that her interlocutor has simply said "left" for "right" in the heat of the moment, and turn right without comment.

The player is only likely to say "huh?" when completely unable to make sense of the instruction.

Not only can instructions be deferred; often they can be enacted with actions that, taken literally, violate them. For example, during a game of Gauntlet one player said "Don't go below that line," pointing at an imaginary line on the screen. Monsters in Gauntlet always head straight for you. Thus it is often important not to pass below the edge of a wall; if you do, monsters will stream around the corner and attack you. However, everyone eventually *did* go below that line without the instruction being explicitly rescinded; they mutually understood that it was now time to go after that particular set of monsters.

Videogame instruction can be so compact because their possible import is heavily constrained by *indexicality, projection,* and *reflexivity.*

Indexicality. We interpret communications with regard to the present circumstances. "No" offers advice about some ongoing activity whose manifestations are visible to both players through the motions of one of the figures on the screen. "Turn left" picks out a certain corridor in the maze, one which is specified in terms of the listener's current location and heading. "Don't go below that line" picks out a certain *imaginary* line that the speaker can point at because both parties know to visualize it. In each case, the players are not making reference to objectively available "features" of the video screen but to shared interpretations of the commonly-visible whirl of colored lights.

Understanding indexical instructions involves complex perceptual processing, which is carried out using Sonja's visual system. (This visual system is similar to, but more sophisticated than, that of Pengi.) This processing often results in a new take on the situation. For example, if Sonja hears "Use the knife!" and it hasn't yet noticed any knives in the scene, it uses a visual routine to find one. Once it can see the knife, it notices properties of it, for example that it is easily accessible, and acts on them.

Projection. Each of us knows what might be expected to happen next. An imperative like "No," "Turn left," or "Don't go below that line" will typically invoke a projection of the specified course of events and another projection of the "or else" that might result if the listener disobeys. Skilled players will generally be able to perform both projections since they are familiar with the ways of the game. Visualization is Sonja's principal means of projection.

Reflexivity. Both the player and the advisor understand that they share an understanding of the situation; since the other person's understanding is part of the situation, this applies recursively. The kibitzer can only expect "No" to communicate if the player understands herself to be engaged in the particular activity "No" recommends against; the player can only make sense of the instruction if she imagines that the kibitzer considers her to be engaged in that activity; the kibitzer must further be able to count on the player imagining this; and so on. Likewise, both players must reflexively understand that "Turn left" picks out a certain corridor and that "Don't go below that line" picks out a certain imaginary line.

In our empirical studies, the players assume to an amazing extent that they both see the evolving game the same way, despite its large number of continually shifting issues. The players *must* make this assumption. If they didn't then they could never finish specifying everything that would be necessary to relate their advice to the evolving game situation. Indeed, we doubt if the players could list their shared understandings if they had to. Communication doesn't pick up a "meaning" from my head and set it down in yours. Instead, communication is part of the work of maintaining a common reality. The players share a common reality because they are competent players and because they use language to keep their shared reality in good repair.

Sonja illustrates certain themes in natural language pragmatics. It makes no attempt to implement a realistic theory of syntax or semantics. However, [9] will sketch a theory of syntax which does not require the creation of parse trees or other datastructures, and which may be implementable in a Pengi-like architecture. This theory, based on *linguistic routines*, might support plan making and might be amenable to internalization. It might, therefore, be the basis of an account of plan-as-communication making and use; but this is all still highly speculative.

6. Conclusion

We have outlined and contrasted two views of the nature of plans and plan use, the plan-as-program view and the plan-as-communication view. We have offered some reasons to doubt the plan-as-program view and speculated briefly about the nature of plans viewed as communications about situated activity. Specifically, we argued that

1. Plan use is not necessary for sensible action. When a plan *is* used, it does not directly determine its user's activity.
2. Plans represent the activity they describe in the way a recipe represents the activity it describes, rather than in the way a program represents the computation it describes.
3. Figuring out how a plan relates to your current situation requires a continual interpretive effort. This interpretation is often difficult and can require arbitrary domain knowledge and reasoning abilities. It can also require concrete actions such as looking around, asking for help, and manipulating the materials at hand to see

how they relate to the ones mentioned by the plan.
4. The ability to make and use plans arises from, and is continuous with, one's experience with cooperative language use in the context of ongoing concrete activity.
5. Plan use relies on an unbounded set of assumptions that the plan's maker and user share concerning activity in the world generally and the evolving concrete situation in particular.
6. Using one's own plans is much like using plans communicated by someone else.

Many of the technical questions raised by the plan-as-communication view are as yet ill-defined, and certainly unanswered. Our initial ideas are only starting points. We do suggest, however, that research into the dynamics of plan making and plan use requires a worked-out view of the nature of everyday activity. Finally, we suggest that a critical and never-ending prerequisite to such an understanding is continual, detailed, sociologically informed observation of the ordinary everyday situated activity of the only truly successful plan makers we know of, namely human beings.

Appendix: Some Other Alternatives

Since we wrote the first version of this paper in 1987, several other papers have appeared reporting projects which address the difficulties that have come up with traditional planning ideas. We cannot conduct a comprehensive review here. Instead we will briefly discuss some of the work that goes by the names of *interleaved planning*, *behavioral modules*, *heuristic planning*, *reactive planning*, and *plans-as-constraints*. These proposals avoid many of the problems we have ascribed to the plan-as-program view, but some of the other problems remain for further research.

Recent interest in mobile robotics has focused attention on embodied activity in various ways. The first and most common response to the difficulties planner-based architectures face in actually acting has been *interleaved* or *incremental* planning [11,20,36,51,56,57,58]. In interleaved planning the planner makes its plan as always. When the executive gets into trouble, it passes control back to the planner, which assesses the situation and makes a new plan.

In order to implement interleaving, an executive needs some notion of when it is in trouble. In a perfect world, the executive would always be able to determine whether continuing with the current plan is the best thing to be doing. In reality, though, an executive has little or no access to the reasoning behind a plan, much less to the courses of action that the planner decided *not* to undertake. Instead, the executive will typically monitor a set of conditions that need to hold at various points during the plan, particularly the preconditions of the various plan steps. Such a system encounters two difficulties. The first is that it does not detect trouble until it has become relatively obvious. It is as if, when driving a car, one did not change direction until one has hit something. The second is that it does not provide a way of registering unexpected opportunities. The triangle table approach of Strips does allow the system to take advantage of opportunities that render planned actions redundant, but it does not help in detecting conditions that would have led the planner to construct a very different plan. This is why we argue that it is best to have as much as possible of the agent's reasoning power on-line, a conclusion that leads us to propose erasing the distinction between plan construction and plan execution and ultimately to a different notion of plans.

Interleaved planning and improvisation differ in their understanding of trouble. In the world of interleaved planning, one assumes that the normal state of affairs is for things to go according to plan. Trouble is, so to speak, a marginal phenomenon. In the world of improvisation, one assumes that things are not likely to go according to plan. Quite the contrary, one expects to have to continually redecide what to do. This is not to say that the resulting activity is chaotic in nature. It is, however, to say that the orderly nature of the activity, on whatever scale, does not arise from its having been mapped out ahead of time through the construction of a plan. Instead, the orderly nature of the activity arises through the interaction of an improvising agent and that agent's familiar world.

We think of this distinction between interleaved planning and improvisation in terms of the theme of control. A system that operates by constructing and executing plans lives, to speak metaphorically, in a sort of fantasy world, the one it

projects when it reasons about its future actions. In this way, the system believes that it has a kind of control over its world that, at least in many domains, is not realistic. When things do not work out as projected, the system is surprised. An improvising agent, by contrast, does not live its life through an alternation between fantasy and surprise. It does not believe that it has complete control over its world. Instead, through a continual give-and-take with its environment, creatively making use of opportunities and contingencies, it participates in the forms of activity that its world affords. On account of this contrast, we feel that the word "reactive" would be much better applied to interleaved planning systems than to improvising systems.

Proposed interleaved planners have all used standard planning techniques. As a result, interleaving the construction and execution of plans does not help with many of the shortcomings of the plan-as-program view. If plan construction is a computationally intractable process at the beginning of a task, it is also going to be an intractable process when trouble arises and a new plan is required.

Some current projects are trying to make plans-as-programs more accommodating of environmental variation using primitive actions, or in Malcolm and Smithers' terms "behavioral modules," that interact in complex but well-understood ways with the physics of the domain to effect specified conditions [33,34]. In both cases the actions slide objects of uncertain locations into specified positions without extensive use of sensors, but the point ought to generalize (see [37]). This idea is closely related to the schemes through which the ethologically inspired robots built by Brooks and his group gain simplicity by relying on regularities in the physics of their interactions with their environment [7,12]. In each case, as in Pengi and Sonja, simplicity of machinery results from close attention to the dynamics of recurrent forms of activity.

Another approach to alleviating the shortcomings of classical planning is heuristic planning. This term actually could mean either of two things: it could refer to heuristics that would help search the space of plans, or it could refer a planner that is only heuristically correct (*i.e.*, sometimes produces incorrect plans).

In order to produce correct plans in a reasonable amount of time, a system must have some way of controlling its search through plan-space. The necessary techniques might be domain-independent or they might be domain-specific. We do not know of any powerful domain-independent heuristics for searching plan spaces. We suspect that none exist, in part because of the results which show domain-independent plan-construction to be as computationally complex as computation in general.

We have more hope for research into plan construction in particular domains or classes of domains. No doubt many domains have structure which the plan construction process can exploit. This might take the form of heuristics that can recognize which plans are most promising before the planner has elaborated them very far [24], or of a plan representation which makes the search space inherently small, perhaps because of locality considerations [29]. Such techniques might work well in certain factory automation tasks, for example, since they take place in a highly structured and constrained environment. Our own concern is with the design of agents that can carry on autonomously in worlds that have the very different kind of structure and constraint that characterizes everyday life. In these worlds, the case for plan-construction search heuristics remains to be made.

Another attractive possibility is a planner that does not always produce correct plans. This approach might circumvent the negative complexity results by posing the planner a less difficult problem. It also addresses the observation that getting along in the world does not require that you do the "right" thing all the time, just that you do well enough. Research on such systems must find a criterion of adequacy other than simple formal correctness. A natural criterion would be probabilistic correctness: the system might be good enough if provably most of its plans were correct. If this fraction is very high, the incorrect plans can be neglected. On the other hand, this seems like a very difficult criterion. People often set out to do something that turns out later not to make sense; at some point they figure out that they are doing the wrong thing and recover. This suggests an alternative criterion of adequacy, that the executive be reliably able to detect incorrect plans in time and to recover, on its own or by getting the

planner to produce a new, provably correct plan. This would demand a lot of the executive. As with interleaved planning, a better approach would be to avoid the modularity of planning and execution, so that as much as possible of the system's reasoning power is available as a plan is used. That way, the agent is much less likely to keep executing a plan that's no longer sensible.

Another recent approach to activity is *reactive planning* [15,16,18,19]. The systems that have gone by this name have consisted of a conventional executive together with an externally generated plan library. Their aim is to act flexibly by having a repertoire of plans available and choosing among them as circumstances evolve. What these systems amount to in practice depends on how big the individual plans are. If the plans are very small, then it is hardly worth calling them plans; the selection mechanism itself is doing all the work that needs to be explained. If the plans are not very small, and especially if they are relatively large, it seems that all of the difficulties with the execution of plans-as-programs will apply to them as well. This ambivalence is already present in the phrase "reactive planning," which seems like a contradiction in terms. A theory of action must explain how action can both have long-term purposes and take account of short-term conditions. Reactive planning systems seem not to resolve this tension: they can only take account of short-term conditions by pursuing the equally short-term goals of their individual plans.

In general, a great deal of dispute has surrounded the term "reactive." Pengi, for example, is often said to be a reactive system. We, however, never use the term ourselves because we feel that it enters into a mistaken opposition. The verb "to plan" takes on two different meanings in AI. The first, more general meaning relates to reasoning about action, and especially about how actions lead to goals, regardless of what form this reasoning takes or how it connects to whatever actions the agent eventually performs. The second, more specific meaning relates to the process of constructing plans in order to execute them. These meanings are distinct because constructing and executing plans might not be the only way of organizing purposive activity. Pengi, for example, reasons about actions but does not construct or execute plans. The word "reactive" usually seems to be opposed to planning in the *first* sense; under this usage, Pengi is not reactive. On the other hand, if "reactive" means neither constructing nor executing plans (the *second* sense), Pengi is in fact reactive. Notice, though, that the second, weaker sense of "reactive" is compatible with all of the phenomena that "planning" is supposed to explain, in particular the pursuit of goals, anticipation of the future, and the complex organization of activity in general. The question is one of what kinds of explanations of these phenomena are possible.

This paper seeks to introduce new terminology to clarify the distinctions that are being created as new ideas are introduced into research on activity. The noun "plan" was once quite well defined in AI; it meant a program, especially one that had been automatically synthesized, that was intended to be executed by a robot. We would like to retain this crisp and useful meaning for discussion, so we refer to it as plan-as-program. We have now proposed another meaning of "plan" to avoid confusion, we refer to it as plan-as-communication.

We can understand the notion of reactivity in terms of loci of control. The plan-as-program view identifies a locus of control for activity in the planner. A chain of command descends from the planner to the executive to the world. We might speculate that "reactivity" means displacing the locus of control from the planner into the executive. Objections to reactivity, though, might rest on the fear that it actually means displacing the locus of control outside of the agent entirely and locating it in the world, leaving the agent to be shoved helplessly around by outside forces. Our solution to this puzzle is to abandon the notion that activity has a particular locus of control at all. Activity arises through interaction, not through control. This transforms our problem from "how do we get this system to control the robot?" to "how do we build this agent to interact with the world in the ways we want?" To answer this question, we need to study the world and we need to find out what sorts of agents can enter into what sorts of interactions with it. In fact, because the agent, the world, and the interactions are interconstraining, we need to design the agent incrementally, tacking back and forth between deepening our understanding of the world, finding new sorts of interactions with it that might occur, and making our agent more sophisticated so that it participate in these sorts of interactions. We

designed Pengi this way. Pengi can't control its world and doesn't try. It is, instead, always ready to participate in various sorts of interactions with bees and ice cubes.

It may be difficult to understand our claim that Pengi uses no plans. In particular, it may seem that Pengi's arbitration network is really a plan; or that the whole central system is; or that whatever state elements Pengi has are plans; or that visualization is really planning. Analogies with some much simpler devices that clearly do not use plans may be helpful.

Some toasters, for example, have photocells that sense when the bread is dark enough. These anticipate the future in the same way Pengi does: they are wired up to act appropriately based on currently perceptible conditions that predict future events. A soda machine, like Pengi, has state elements (forming a coin counter) which are updated based on sensory conditions and their current state, and which determine how the system will behave in the future. An electromechanical elevator controller, like Pengi, engages in complex activity, interacting with other agents whose actions can not be predicted, maintaining state, and using sensors. A well-designed elevator controller, like Pengi, manifests complex, useful dynamics which emerge from its interactions with its environment, rather than being programmed. Yet, we presume, no one would argue that toasters, soda machines, or elevator controllers use plans.

Finally, it is worth mentioning that there is at least one use of the word "plan" current that clearly conforms to neither the plan-as-program view nor the plan-as-communication view. This view, found in some recent work on natural language discourse and on rational action [22,27] might be called "plans-as-constraints." On this view, plans are sets of beliefs and "intentions," which are constraints on possible futures; the view does not specify how these constraints affect action, but rather how they are used to interpret other agents' actions. (Chapman forthcoming) will discuss the relationship between this view and the other two.

Acknowledgments

In working out these ideas about plans and planning, we were greatly aided by conversations with and comments on drafts from John Batali, Rod Brooks, Gary Drescher, Barbara Grosz, Pattie Maes, Drew McDermott, Tomás Lozano-Pérez, Beth Preston, Jeff Shrager, Penni Sibun, Orca Starbuck, Dan Weld, and Ramin Zabih. Lucy Suchman has greatly influenced our thinking by introducing us to ethnomethodology [17,26]. This essay itself descends from position papers we prepared for the DARPA Planning Workshop in Santa Cruz, California in October 1987, and for the COST-13 Workshop On Representation and Learning in an Autonomous Agent in Lagos, Portugal in November 1988. Thanks to Ted Linden and Drew McDermott for organizing the panels where they were presented at Santa Cruz and to Pattie Maes for organizing the Lagos workshop. And finally thanks to Mike Brady, Rod Brooks, and Stan Rosenschein for various sorts of support.

References

[1] Philip E. Agre, Routines, AI Memo 828, MIT Artificial Intelligence Laboratory, 1985.

[2] Philip E. Agre, The dynamic structure of everyday life, Cambridge University Press, forthcoming.

[3] Philip E. Agre and David Chapman, Pengi: An implementation of a theory of activity, Proceedings of AAAI-87.

[4] Philip E. Agre and David Chapman, Indexicality and the binding problem, Proceedings of the AAAI Symposium on Parallel Models, 1988.

[5] King Beach, The role of external mnemonic symbols in acquiring an occupation, in M. M. Gruneberg, P. E. Morris, and R. N. Sykes, eds., *Practical Aspects of Memory: Current Research and Issues*, Volume I, John Wiley and Sons, Chichester, 1988.

[6] Rodney A. Brooks, A robust layered control system for a mobile robot, *IEEE Journal of Robotics and Automation* 2(1), April 1986, pages 14-23.

[7] Rodney A. Brooks, A robot that walks: Emergent behaviors from a carefully evolved network, AI Memo 1091, MIT Artificial Intelligence Laboratory, 1989.

[8] David Chapman, Planning for conjunctive goals, *Artificial Intelligence* 32(3), 1987, pages 333-377.

[9] David Chapman, Instruction use in situated activity, MIT Computer Science Department PhD Thesis, forthcoming.

[10] David Chapman and Philip E. Agre 1986, Abstract reasoning as emergent from concrete activity, in M. P. Georgeff and A. L. Lansky (editors), *Reasoning about Actions and Plans*, Proceedings of the 1986 Workshop at Timberline, Oregon, pages 411–424, Morgan Kaufmann, Los Altos CA (1987).

[11] R. T. Chien and S. Weissman, Planning and execution in incompletely specified environments, *Advance Papers of the Fourth International Joint Conference on Artificial Intelligence*, 1975, pages 169-174.

[12] Jonathan H. Connell, Creature design with the subsumption architecture, *Proceedings of the Tenth International Joint Conference on Artificial Intelligence*, Milan, 1987, pages 1124-1126.

[13] Johan de Kleer, Jon Doyle, Guy L. Steele, Jr., and Gerald Jay Sussman, Explicit control of reasoning, *Proceedings of the ACM Symposium on Artificial Intelligence and Programming Languages*, Rochester, New York, 1977.

[14] Mark Drummond, Situated control rules, *Proceedings from the Rochester Planning Workshop: From Formal Systems to Practical Systems*, University of Rochester, New York, 1989.

[15] R. James Firby, An investigation into reactive planning in complex domains, Proceedings of AAAI-87.

[16] Mark S. Fox and Stephen Smith, The role of intelligent reactive processing in production management, in *13th Meeting and Technical Conference*, CAM-I, November 1984.

[17] Harold Garfinkel, *Studies in Ethnomethodology*, Polity Press, Oxford, 1984. Originally published in 1967.

[18] Michael Georgeff and Amy Lansky, Procedural knowledge, Proceedings of the IEEE, Special Issue on Knowledge Representation, pages 1383-1398, October 1986.

[18a] Michael Georgeff, Planning, in: J. Traub, B. Grosz, B. Lampson and N. Nilsson (eds.), *Annual Review of Computer Science* 2, Annual Reviews, 1987.

[19] Michael Georgeff and Amy Lansky, Reactive reasoning and planning, Proceedings of AAAI-87, pages 677-682.

[20] Georges Giralt, Raja Chatila, and Marc Vaisset, An integrated navigation and motion control system for autonomous multisensory mobile robots, Proceedings of the First Symposium on Robotics Research, MIT Press, 1984, pages 191-214.

[21] Thomas Gladwin, *East is a Big Bird*, Harvard University Press, 1970.

[22] Barbara J. Grosz and Candace L. Sidner, Plans for discourse, in P. Cohen, J. Morgan, and M. Pollack, eds., *Intentions in Communication*, MIT Press, Cambridge Massachussets, 1988.

[23] Kristian J. Hammond, *Case-Based Planning: Viewing Planning as a Memory Task*, Academic Press, 1989.

[24] Caroline Hayes, Using goal interactions to guide planning, Proceedings of AAAI-87, pages 224-228.

[25] Edwin Hutchins, Learning to navigate in context. Manuscript prepared for the Workshop on Context, Cognition, and Activity, Stenengsund, Sweden, August 6–9, 1987. Institute for Cognitive Science, University of California, San Diego, La Jolla, California.

[26] John Heritage, *Garfinkel and Ethnomethodology*, Polity Press, Cambridge, England, 1984.

[27] Kurt Konolige and Martha E. Pollack, Ascribing plans to agents, *Proceedings of the Eleventh International Joint Conference on Artificial Intelligence*, Detroit, 1989, pages 991-997.

[28] Leslie Pack Kaelbling, An architecture for intelligent reactive systems, in Michael P. Georgeff and Amy L. Lansky, eds, *Reasoning about Actions and Plans, Proceed-*

ings of the 1986 Workshop, Timberline, Oregon, 1986, pages 395-410.

[29] Amy L. Lansky and David S. Fogelsong, Localized representation and planning methods for parallel domains, Proceedings of AAAI-87, pages 240–245.

[30] Jean Lave, *Cognition in Practice: Mind, Mathematics, and Culture in Everyday Life*, Cambridge University Press, 1988.

[31] Tomás Lozano-Pérez and Rodney A. Brooks, An approach to automatic robot programming, AI Memo 842, MIT Artificial Intelligence Laboratory, 1985.

[32] Pattie Maes, The dynamics of action selection, *Proceedings of the Eleventh International Joint Conference on Artificial Intelligence*, Detroit, 1989, pages 991-997.

[33] Chris Malcolm and Tim Smithers, Symbol grounding via a hybrid architecture in an autonomous assembly system, in this volume.

[34] Michael A. Erdmann and Matthew T. Mason, An exploration of sensorless manipulation, *IEEE Journal Robotics and Automation* 4(4), pages 369-379, 1988.

[35] John McCarthy, The advice taker, reprinted in Marvin Minsky, ed., *Semantic Information Processing*, MIT Press, 1968. Originally published 1958.

[36] Drew McDermott, Planning and Acting, *Cognitive Science* 2(2), 71–109, 1978.

[37] David P. Miller, Execution monitoring for a mobile robot system, *Proceedings of the SPIE 1989 Conference on Intelligent Control and Adaptive Systems*, Philadelphia, 1989.

[38] George A. Miller, Eugene Galanter, and Karl H. Pribram, *Plans and the Structure of Behavior*, Henry Holt and Company, 1960.

[39] Nils J. Nilsson, Action networks, *Proceedings from the Rochester Planning Workshop: From Formal Systems to Practical Systems*, University of Rochester, New York, 1989.

[40] David W. Payton, Internalized Plans: a representation for action resources, in this volume.

[41] Stanley J. Rosenschein and Leslie Pack Kaelbling, The synthesis of digital machines with provable epistemic properties, in Joseph Halpern, ed, *Proceedings of the Conference on Theoretical Aspects of Reasoning About Knowledge*, Monterey, California, 1986, pages 83-98.

[42] David E. Rumelhart, Paul Smolensky, James L. McClel-land, and Geoffrey E. Hinton, Schemata and sequential thought processes in PDP models, Chapter 14 in James L. McClelland, David E. Rumelhart, and the PDP Research Group, *Parallel Distributed Processing: Explorations in the Microstructure of Cognition*, MIT Press, Cambridge, Massachussets, 1986.

[43] Bob Scher, *The Fear of Cooking*, Houghton-Mifflin, 1984.

[44] Marcel J. Schoppers, Universal plans for reactive robots in unpredictable environments, *Proceedings of the Tenth International Joint Conference on Artificial Intelligence*, Milan, 1987, pages 1039-1046.

[45] Sylvia Scribner, Studying working intelligence, in B. Rogoff and J. Lave, eds, *Everyday Cognition: Its Development in Social Context*, Harvard University Press, 1984.

[46] Herbert A. Simon, *The Sciences of the Artificial*, MIT Press, 1970.

[47] Susan U. Stucky, The situated processing of situated language, CSLI Report 87-80, March 1987.

[48] Lucy Suchman, What is a plan?, ISL Technical Note, Xerox Palo Alto Research Center, 1986.

[49] Lucy Suchman, *Plans and Situated Action*, Cambridge University Press, 1987.

[50] William Swartout, ed, DARPA Santa Cruz Workshop on Planning, *AI Magazine*, Summer 1988, pages 115-131.

[51] Austin Tate, Planning and Condition Monitoring in a FMS, International Conference on Flexible Manufacturing Systems, London, UK, July 1984.

[52] Austin Tate, A review of knowledge-based planning techniques, *The Knowledge Engineering Review* 1(3), June 1985, pages 4-17.

[53] Shimon Ullman, Visual routines, *Cognition* 18, 1984, pages 97-159.

[54] Lev S. Vygotsky, *Thought and Language*, MIT Press, Cambridge Massachussets, 1962.

[55] James W. Wertsch, *Vygotsky and the Social Formation of Mind*, Harvard University Press, Cambridge MA, 1985.

[56] Robert Wilensky, *Planning and Understanding: A Computational Approach to Human Reasoning*, Addison-Wesley, Reading MA, 1983.

[57] David E. Wilkins, Recovering from execution errors in SIPE, SRI Tech Report 346, 1985.

[58] David E. Wilkins, *Practical Planning: Extending the Classical AI Planning Paradigm*, Morgan Kaufmann Publishers, Los Altos CA, 1988.

Action and Planning in Embedded Agents*

Leslie Pack Kaelbling
and Stanley J. Rosenschein

Teleos Research, 576 Middlefield Road, Palo Alto, CA 94301, USA

Embedded agents are computer systems that sense and act on their environments, monitoring complex dynamic conditions and affecting the environment in goal-directed ways. This paper briefly reviews the situated automata approach to agent design and explores issues of planning and action in the situated-automata framework.

Keywords: Intelligent agents; Reactive systems; Planning; Action; Situated-automata theory; Gapps; Embedded agents

Ms Kaelbling received a Philosophy A.B. from Stanford University in 1983 and is currently a Ph.D. candidate with the Department of Computer Science at that University. From 1982 to 1984 Ms Kaelbling acted as a Research and Teaching Assistance at Stanford and in 1984 she joined SRI International's Artificial Intelligence Center as a Computer Scientist, leaving to join Teleos Research as a Computer Scientist in 1988. Ms Kaelbling's research interests include artificial intelligence, machine learning, programming languages and robotics; her Ph.D. dissertation will address learning in embedded systems.

* This work was supported in part by the Air Force Office of Scientific Research under contract F49620-89-C-0055DEF and in part by the National Aeronautics and Space Administration under Cooperative Agreement NCC-2-494 through Stanford University subcontract PR-6359.

North-Holland
Robotics and Autonomous Systems 6 (1990) 35–48

1. The Design of Embedded Agents

Embedded agents are computer systems that sense and act on their environments, monitoring complex dynamic conditions and affecting the environment in goal-directed ways. Systems of this kind are extremely difficult to design and build, and without clear conceptual models and powerful programming tools, the complexities of the real world can quickly become overwhelming. In certain special cases, designs can be based on well-understood mathematical paradigms such as classical control theory. More typically, however, tractable models of this type are not available and alternative approaches must be used. One such alternative is the situated-automata framework, which models the relationship between embedded control systems and the external world in qualititative terms and provides a family of programming abstractions to aid the designer. This paper briefly reviews the situated-automata approach and then explores in greater detail one aspect of the approach, namely the design of the action-generating component of embedded agents.

1.1. The Situated-Automata Model

The theoretical foundations of the situated-automata approach are based on modeling the world

Dr. Rosenschein received his B.A. from Columbia University in 1971 and his Ph.D. in Computer and Information Sciences from the University of Pennsylvania in 1975. After a post-doctorate at the Courant Institute of Mathematics of New York University, a lectureship at the Technion in Haifa, Israel, and a research position at the Rand Corporation, Dr. Rosenschein joined the Artificial Intelligence Center at SRI International in 1980. He became Director of the Center in 1984 and held that post until 1988 at which time he left the Center to found Teleos Research, a research and development company working in artificial intelligence, robotics and advanced computing. Dr. Rosenschein's research has focused on theoretical issues in automated reasoning, knowledge representation, natural language processing, and robotics.

0921-8830/90/$03.50 © 1990 – Elsevier Science Publishers B.V. (North-Holland)

as a pair of interacting automata, one corresponding to the physical environment and the other to the embedded agent. Each has local state that varies as a function of signals projected from the other. The aim of the design process is to synthesize an agent, in the form of an embedded state machine, that causes the desired effects in the environment over time.

In applications of interest, it is often useful to describe the agent in terms of the information available about the environment and the goals the agent is pursuing. It is also desirable that these descriptions be expressed in language that refers to states of the environment rather than to specific internal data structures, at least during the early phases of design. Moreover, the inputs, outputs, and internal states of the state machine will be far too numerous to consider explicitly, which means the machine must be constructed out of a set of separate components acting together to generate complex patterns of behavior. These requirements highlight the need for compositional, high-level languages that compactly describe machine components in semantically meaningful terms.

Situated-automata theory provides a principled way of interpreting data values in the agent as encoding facts about the world expressed in some language whose semantics is clear to the designer. Interpretations of this sort would be of little use were it not also the case that whenever the data structure had a particular value, the condition denoted was guaranteed to hold in the environment. Such considerations motivate defining the semantics of data structures in terms of objective correlations with external reality. In this approach, a machine variable x is said to carry the information that p in world state s, written $s \models K(x, p)$, if for all world states in which x has the same value it does in s, the proposition p is true. The formal properties of this model and its usefulness for programming embedded systems have been described elsewhere [9,11,5,10].

Having established a theoretical basis for viewing a given signal or state in the agent as carrying information content by virtue of its objective correlation with the environment, one can consider languages in which this content might be expressed. In general there will be no single "best" language for expressing this information. For example, one language is the set of signals or states themselves. These can be regarded as a system of

signs whose semantic interpretations are exactly the conditions with which they are correlated. However, the designer will typically wish to employ other, higher-level, languages during the design process. This theme will be expanded upon below in connection with goal-description languages.

1.2. Perception-Action Split

One way of structuring the design process for the cognitive ease of the designer is to separate the problem of acquiring information about the world from the problem of acting appropriately relative to that information. The former we shall label *perception* and the latter, *action*. In terms of the state-machine model, as shown in *Fig. 1*, the perception component corresponds to the update function and the initial state, whereas the action component corresponds to the output mapping.

The perception-action split in itself is entirely conceptual and may or may not be the basis for modularizing the actual system. Horizontal decompositions that cut across perception and action have been advocated by Brooks as a practical way of approaching agent design [2]. The horizontal approach allows the designer to consider simultaneously those limited aspects of perception and action needed to support specific behaviors. In this way, it discourages the pursuit of spurious generality that often inhibits practical progress in robotics.

These attractive features are counterbalanced, however, by the degree to which horizontal decomposition encourages linear thinking. In practice, the methodology of not separating the acquisition of information from its use tends to encourage the development of very specific behaviors rather than the identification of elements that can recombine freely to produce complex *patterns* of behavior. The alternative is a vertical strategy based on having separate system modules that

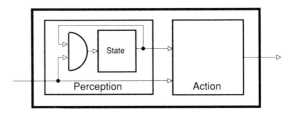

Fig. 1. Division between perception and action components.

recover broadly useful information from multiple sources and others that exploit it for multiple purposes. The inherent combinatorics of information extraction and behavior generation make the vertical approach attractive as a way of making efficient use of a programmer's effort.

The commitment to a decomposition based upon the perception-action split still leaves open the question of development strategy. One approach is to iteratively refine the perception-action pair, more or less in lockstep. The information objectively carried by an input signal or an internal state is relative to constraints on other parts of the system—including constraints on the action component. The more constrained the rest of the system, the more the designer can deduce about the world from a given internal signal or state, hence the more "information" it contains. As the designer refines his design, his model of the information available to the system and what the system will do in response becomes increasingly specific.

An alternative to iterative refinement, suitable in many practical design situations, is the strict divide-and-conquer strategy in which the design of the perception component is carried out in complete isolation from the development of the action component except for the specification of a common interface—the data structures that encode the information shared between the perception and action modules. Although there may be occasions when the designer needs to rely on some fact about what the agent will *do* in order to guarantee that a certain signal or state has the semantic content he intends, if these situations can be minimized or ignored, considerable simplification will result.

1.3. Goals

As we have seen, one way of semantically characterizing an agent's states is in terms of the information they embody. The perception component delivers information, and the action component maps this information to action. In many cases, however, it is more natural to describe actions as functions not only of information but of the goals the agent is pursuing at the moment [12].

Goals can be divided into two broad classes: static and dynamic. A static goal is a statement the agent's behavior is simply designed to make true. In reality, a static goal is nothing more than a specification, and as such the attribution of this "goal" to the agent is somewhat superfluous, although it may be of pragmatic use in helping the designer organize his conception of the agent's action strategy. Dynamic goals are another matter. The ability to attribute to the agent goals that change dynamically at run time opens the possibility of dramatically simplifying the designer's description of the agent's behavior.

Since we are committed to an information-based semantics for reactive systems, we seek an "objective" semantics of goals defined explicitly in informational terms. We can reformulate the notion of having a goal p as having the information that p implies a fixed top-level goal, called N for "Nirvana." Formally, we define a goal operator G as follows:

$$G(x, p) \equiv K(x, p \rightarrow N).$$

In this model, x has the goal p if x carries the information that p implies Nirvana. [1] This definition captures the notion of dynamic goals because p can be an indexical statement, such as "it is raining now," whose truth varies with time. Since this model defines goals explicitly in terms of information, the same formal tools used to study information can be applied to goals as well. In fact, under this definition, goals and information are dual concepts.

To see the duality of goals and information, consider a function f mapping values of one variable, a, to values of another variable, b. Under the information interpretation, such a function takes elements having more specific information into elements having less specific information. This is because functions generally introduce ambiguity by mapping distinct inputs to the same output. For example, if value u_1 at a is correlated with proposition p and value u_2 at a is correlated with q and if f maps both u_1 and u_2 to v at b, the value v is ambiguous as to whether it arose from u_1 or u_2, and hence the information it contains is the disjunctive information $p \vee q$, which is less specific than the information contained in either u_1 or u_2. Thus, functional mappings are a form of forgetting.

---

[1] We observe that under this definition *False* will always be a goal; in practice, however, we are only interested in non-trivial goals.

Under the goal interpretation, this picture is reversed. The analog to "forgetting" is committing to subgoals, which can be thought of as "forgetting" that there are other ways of achieving the condition. For instance, let the objective information at variable a be that the agent is hungry and that there is a sandwich in the right drawer and an apple in the left. If the application of a many-to-one function results in variable b's having a value compatible with the agent's being hungry and there being a sandwich in the right drawer and either an apple in the left drawer or not, we could describe this state of affairs by saying that variable b has lost the information that opening the left drawer would be a way of finding food. Alternatively, we could say that variable b had committed to the subgoal of opening the right drawer. The phenomena of forgetting and commitment are two sides of the same coin.

We can relate this observation to axioms describing information and goals. One of the formal properties satisfied by K is the deductive closure axiom, which can be written as follows:

$$K(x, p \rightarrow q) \rightarrow (K(x, p) \rightarrow K(x, q)).$$

The analogous axiom for goals is

$$K(x, p \rightarrow q) \rightarrow (G(x, q) \rightarrow G(x, p)).$$

This is precisely the subgoaling axiom. If the agent has q as a goal and carries the information that q is implied by some other, more specific, condition, p, the agent is justified in adopting p as a goal. The validity of this axiom can be established directly from the definition of G.

Given these two ways of viewing the semantics of data structures, we can revisit the state-machine model of agents introduced above. Rather than specify the action component of the machine as a function of one argument interepreted in purely "informational" terms, $f(i)$, it may be much more convenient for designers to define it as a function of two arguments, $f'(g, i)$ where the g argument is interpreted as representing the dynamic goals of the agent. Where does the g input come from? Clearly, it must ultimately be computed from the agent's current information state as well as its static goals, g_0. As such, it must be equivalent to some non-goal-dependent specification: $f(i) = f'(extract(i, g_0), i)$. Nevertheless, the decomposition into a goal-extraction module and a goal-directed action module may significantly ease the cognitive burden for the designer while leaving him secure in the knowledge that his design is semantically grounded.

1.4. Software Tools for Agent Design

Although it is conceptually important to have a formal understanding of the semantics of the data structures in an embedded agent, this understanding does not, directly, simplify the programmer's task. For this reason, it is necessary to design and implement software tools that are based on proper foundations and that make it easier to program embedded agents.

Rex [5,7] is a language that allows the programmer to use the full recursive power of Lisp at compile time to specify a synchronous digital circuit. The circuit model of computation facilitates semantic analysis in the situated-automata theory framework. However, Rex only provides, however, a low-level, operational language that is more akin to standard programming languages than to declarative AI languages. For this reason, we have designed and implemented a pair of declarative programming languages on top of the base provided by Rex. Ruler [10] is based on the "informational" semantics and is intended to be used to specify the perception component of an agent. Gapps [6] is based on the "goal" semantics and is intended to be used to specify the action component of an agent. In the rest of this paper, we will describe the Gapps language, its use in programming embedded agents, and a number of extensions that relate it to more traditional work in planning.

2. Gapps

In this section we describe Gapps, a language for specifying behaviors of computer agents that retains the advantage of declarative specification, but generates run-time programs that are reactive, do parallel actions, and carry out strategies made up of very low-level actions.

Gapps is intended to be used to specify the action component of an agent. The Gapps compiler takes as input a declarative specification of the agent's top-level goal and a set of goal-reduction rules, and transforms them into the description of a circuit that has the output of the perception component as its input, and the output of the agent as a whole as its output. The output of the agent may be divided into a number of separately controllable actions, so that we can independently specify procedures that allow an agent to move and talk at the same time. A sample action vector declaration is:

(declare-action-vector

    (left-wheel-velocity int)

    (right-wheel-velocity int)

    (speech string))

This states that the agent has three independently controllable effectors and declares the types of the output values that control them.

In the following sections, we shall present a formal description of Gapps and its goal evaluation algorithm, and explain how Gapps specifications can be instantiated as circuit descriptions.

2.1. Goals and Programs

The Gapps compiler maps a top-level goal and a set of goal-reduction rules into a program. In this section we shall clarify the concepts of goal, goal-reduction rule, and program.

There are three primitive goal types: goals of execution, achievement, and maintenance. Goals of execution are of the form $do(a)$, with a specifying an instantaneous action that can be taken by the agent in the world—the agent's goal is simply to perform that action. If an agent has a goal of maintenance, notated $maint(p)$, then if the proposition p is true, the agent should strive to maintain the truth of p for as long as it can. The goal $ach(p)$ is a goal of achievement, for which the agent should try to bring about the truth of proposition p as soon as possible. The set of goals is made up of the primitive goal types, closed under the Boolean operators. The notions of achievement and maintenance are dual, so we have $\neg ach(p) \equiv maint(\neg p)$ and $\neg maint(p) \equiv ach(\neg p)$.

In order to characterize the correctness of programs with respect to the goals that specify them, we must have a notion of an action *leading to* a goal. Informally, an action a leads to a goal G (notated $a \leadsto G$) if it constitutes a correct step toward the satisfaction of the goal. For a goal of achievement, the action must be consistent with

the goal condition's eventually being true; for a goal of maintenance, if the condition is already true, the action must imply that it will be true at the next instant of time. The *leads to* operator must also have the following formal properties:

$$a \leadsto do(a)$$

$$(a \leadsto G) \wedge (a \leadsto G') \Rightarrow a \leadsto (G \wedge G')$$

$$(a \leadsto G) \vee (a \leadsto G') \Rightarrow a \leadsto (G \vee G')$$

$$cond(p, a \leadsto G, a \leadsto G') \Rightarrow a \leadsto cond(p, G, G')$$

$$(a \leadsto G) \wedge (G \to G') \Rightarrow a \leadsto G'.$$

This definition captures a weak intuition of what it means for an action to lead to a goal. The goal of doing an action is immediately satisfied by doing that action. If an action leads to each of two goals, it leads to their conjunction; similarly for disjunction and conditionals. The definition of *leads to* for goals of achievement may seem too weak—rather than saying that doing the action is consistent with achieving the goal, we would like somehow to say that the action actually constitutes *progress* toward the goal condition. Unfortunately, it is difficult to formalize this notion in a domain-independent way. In fact, any definition of *leads to* that satisfies this definition is compatible with the goal reduction algorithm used by Gapps, so the definition may be strengthened for a particular domain.

Goal reduction rules are of the form (defgoalr G G') and have the semantics that the goal G can be reduced to the goal G'; that is, that G' is a specialization of G, and therefore implies G. By the definition of "leads to", any action that leads to G' will also lead to G.

A program is a finite set of condition-action pairs, in which the condition is a run-time expression (actually a piece of Rex circuitry with a Boolean-valued output) and an action is a vector of run-time expressions, one corresponding to each primitive output field. These actions are run-time mappings from the perceptual inputs into output values, and can be viewed as strategies, in which the particular output to be generated depends on the external state of the world via the internal state of the agent. Allowing the actions to be entire strategies is very flexible, but makes it impossible to enumerate the possible values of an output field. In order to specify a program that controls only the speech field of an action vector, we need to be able to describe a program that requires the speech field to have a certain value, but makes no constraints on the values of the other fields. One way to do this would be to enumerate a set of action vectors with the specified speech value, each of which has different values for the other action vector components. Instead of doing this, we allow elements of an action vector to contain the value $\emptyset$, which stands for all possible instantiations of that field.

A program Π, consisting of the condition-action pairs $\{\langle c_1, a_1 \rangle, \ldots, \langle c_n, a_n \rangle\}$, is said to *weakly satisfy* a goal G if, for every condition c_i, if that condition is true, the corresponding action a_i leads to G. That is,

$$\Pi \text{ weakly satisfies } G \Leftrightarrow \forall i . c_i \rightarrow (a_i \rightsquigarrow G).$$

Note that the conditions in a program need not be exhaustive—satisfaction does not require that there be an action that leads to the goal in every situation, since this is impossible in general. We will refer to the class of situations in which a program does specify an action as the *domain* of the program. We define the domain of Π as

$$\text{dom}(\Pi) = \bigvee_i c_i.$$

A goal G is *strongly satisfied* by program Π if it is weakly satisfied by Π and $\text{dom}(\Pi) = true$; that is, if for every situation, Π supplies an action that leads to G. The conditions in a program need not be mutually exclusive. When more than one condition of a program is true, the action associated with each of them leads to the goal, and an execution of the program may choose among these actions nondeterministically.

Given the non-deterministic execution model, we can give programs a declarative semantics, as well. A program $\Pi = \{\langle c_1, a_1 \rangle, \ldots, \langle c_n, a_n \rangle\}$, can be thought of has having the logical interpretation

$$\left(\bigwedge_i (a_i \rightarrow c_i) \wedge \bigvee_i a_i \right) \vee \neg \bigvee_i c_i.$$

Either the domain of the program is false (the second clause) or there is some action that is executed and the condition associated with that action is true.

2.2. Recursive Goal Evaluation Procedure

Gapps is implemented on top of Rex, and makes use of constructs from the Rex language to provide perceptual tests. There is not room here to describe the details of the Rex language, so we refer the interested reader to other papers [5,7]. Gapps programs are made up of a set of goal reduction rules and a top-level goal-expression. The general form of a goal-reduction rule is

(defgoalr *goal-pat goal-expr*),

where

$$goal\text{-}pat ::= (\text{ach } pat \ rex\text{-}params)$$
$$(\text{maint } pat \ rex\text{-}params)$$
$$goal\text{-}expr ::= (\text{do } index \ rex\text{-}expr)$$
$$(\text{and } goal\text{-}expr \ goal\text{-}expr)$$
$$(\text{or } goal\text{-}expr \ goal\text{-}expr)$$
$$(\text{not } goal\text{-}expr)$$
$$(\text{if } rex\text{-}expr \ goal\text{-}expr \ goal\text{-}expr)$$
$$(\text{ach } pat \ rex\text{-}expr)$$
$$(\text{maint } pat \ rex\text{-}expr)$$

index is a keyword, *pat* is a compile-time pattern with unifiable variables, *rex-expr* is a Rex expression specifying a run-time function of input variables, and *rex-params* is a structure of variables that becomes bound to the result of a *rex-expr*. The details of these constructs will be discussed in the following sections.

The Gapps compiler is an implementation of an evaluation function that maps goal expressions into programs, using a set of goal reduction rules supplied by the programmer. In this section we shall present the evaluation procedure; we have shown that it is correct; that is, that given a goal G and a set of reduction rules Γ, eval(G, Γ) weakly satisfies G.

Given a reduction-rule set Gamma, we define the evaluation procedure as follows:

```
define eval(G)

case first(G)
   do  : make-primitive-program(second(G),
            third(G))
   and : conjoin-programs(eval(second(G)),
            eval(third(G)))
   or  : disjoin-programs(eval(second(G)),
            eval(third(G)))
   not : eval (negate-goal-expr(second(G)))
   if  : disjoin-programs
            (conjoin-cond(second(G),
            eval(third(G))),
```

```
            conjoin-cond(negate-cond(G),
               eval(fourth(G))))
      maint,
      ach : for all R in Gamma such that
            match(G,head (R))
            disjoin-programs(eval(body(R)))
```

We shall now consider each of these cases in turn.

Do

The function make-primitive-program takes an index and a Rex expression and returns a program. The index indicates which of the fields of the action vector is being assigned, and the Rex expression denotes a function from the input to values for that action field. It is formally defined as

make-primitive-program$(i, rex\text{-}expr)$

$$= \{\langle true, \langle \emptyset, \dots, rex\text{-}expr, \dots, \emptyset \rangle \rangle \},$$

with the $rex\text{-}expr$ in the ith component of the action vector. This program allows any action so long as component i of the action is the strategy described by $rex\text{-}expr$.

And

Programs are conjoined by taking the cross-product of their condition-action pairs and merging each of elements of the cross-product together. In conjoining two programs, the merged action vector is associated with the conjunction of the conditions of the original pairs, together with the condition that the two actions are mergeable. The conjunction procedure simply finds the pairs in each program that share an action and conjoins their conditions. We can define the operation formally as

conjoin-programs(Π', Π'')

$$= \{ \langle (c_i' \wedge c_j'' \wedge \text{mergeable}(a_i', a_j'')), $$

$$\text{merge}(a_i', a_j'') \rangle \}$$

for $1 \leq i \leq m$, $1 \leq j \leq n$ where

$$\Pi' = \{\langle c_1', a_1'\rangle, \dots, \langle c_m', a_m'\rangle\}$$

$$\Pi'' = \{\langle c_1'', a_1''\rangle, \dots, \langle c_n'', a_n''\rangle\}.$$

The conjunction operation preserves the declarative semantics of programs; that is, the semantic interpretation of the conjoined program is implied by the conjunction of the semantic interpretations of the individual programs.

Two action vectors are *mergeable* if, for each component, at least one of them is unspecified or they are equal.

mergeable$(\langle a_1, \dots, a_n \rangle, \langle b_1, \dots, b_n \rangle)$

$$\equiv \forall i.(a_i = \emptyset) \vee (b_i = \emptyset) \vee (a_i = b_i).$$

If either component is unspecified, the test can be completed at compile time and no additional circuitry is generated. Otherwise, an equality test is conjoined in with the conditions to be tested at run time.

Action vectors are merged at the component level, taking the defined element if one is available. If the vectors are unequally defined on a component, the result is undefined:

merge$(\langle a_1, \dots, a_n \rangle, \langle b_1, \dots, b_n \rangle)$

$$= \langle c_1, \dots, c_n \rangle, \text{ where}$$

$$c_i = \begin{cases} a_i & \text{if } b_i = \emptyset \text{ or } b_i = a_i \\ b_i & \text{if } a_i = \emptyset \\ \bot & \text{otherwise.} \end{cases}$$

The merger of two action vectors results in an action vector that allows the intersection of the actions allowed by the original ones.

Or

The disjunction of two programs is simply the union of their sets of condition-action pairs. Stated formally,

disjoin-programs$(\Pi', \Pi'') = \Pi' \cup \Pi''$.

Not

In Gapps, negation is driven into an expression as far as possible, using DeMorgan's laws and the duality of ach and maint, until the only expressions containing not are those of the form (ach (not *pat*)), (maint (not *pat*)), and (not (do *index rex-expr*)). In the first two cases, there must be explicit reduction rules for the goal; in the last case we simply return the empty program. The handling of negation could be much stronger if we provided for the enumeration of all possible values of any action vector component and required them to be known constants at compile time. Then (not (do left-velocity 6)) would be the same as $\vee_{i \neq 6}$ make-primitive-program (left-velocity, i); that is, license to go at any velocity but 6. As we noted before, these limitations are too severe for use in controlling a complex agent that has large numbers of possible outputs.

The procedure negate-goal-expression rewrites goal expressions as follows:

$$(\text{not } (\text{and } G_1 \ G_2)) \Rightarrow (\text{or } (\text{not } G_1) \ (\text{not } G_2))$$

$$(\text{not } (\text{or } G_1 \ G_2)) \Rightarrow (\text{and } (\text{not } G_1) \ (\text{not } G_2))$$

$$(\text{not } (\text{not } G)) \Rightarrow G$$

$$(\text{not } (\text{if } c \ G_1 \ G_2)) \Rightarrow (\text{if } c \ (\text{not } G_1) \ (\text{not } G_2))$$

$$(\text{not } (\text{ach } p)) \Rightarrow (\text{maint } (\text{not } p))$$

$$(\text{not } (\text{maint } p)) \Rightarrow (\text{ach } (\text{not } p))$$

If

The evaluation procedure for conditional programs hinges on the definition of the conditional operator $\text{cond}(p, \ q, \ r)$ as $(p \wedge q) \vee (\neg p \wedge r)$. The procedure for conjoining a condition and a program is defined as follows:

$\text{conjoin-cond}(p, \Pi)$

$$= \{\langle p \wedge c_1, \ a_1 \rangle, \dots, \langle p \wedge c_n, \ a_n \rangle\}.$$

Thus,

$\text{disjoin-programs}(\text{conjoin-cond}(p, \Pi'),$

$$\text{conjoin-cond}(\neg p, \Pi''))$$

$$= \{\langle p \wedge c_1', \ a_1' \rangle, \dots, \langle p \wedge c_n', \ a_n' \rangle,$$

$$\langle \neg p \wedge c_1'', \ a_1'' \rangle, \dots, \langle \neg p \wedge c_m'', \ a_m'' \rangle\}.$$

Ach and Maint

Goals of maintenance and achievement are evaluated by disjoining the results of all applicable reduction rules in the rulebase Γ. A reduction rule whose head is the expression (ach pat_1 rex-params) matches the goal expression (ach pat_2 rex-expr) if pat_1 and pat_2 can be unified in the current binding environment. The patterns are s-expressions with compile-time variables that are marked by a leading ?. The Rex expression and parameter arguments may be omitted if they are null. The binding environment consists of other bindings of compile-time variables within the goal expression being evaluated. Thus, when evaluating the (ach (go ?p)) subgoal of the goal (and (ach (drive ?q ?p)) (ach (go ?p))), we may already have a binding for ?p. As in Prolog, evaluation of this goal will

backtrack through all possible bindings of ?p and ?q.

Once a pattern has been matched, Gapps sets up a new compile-time binding environment for evaluating the body of the rule. This is necessary in case variables in the body are bound by the invocation, as in

(defgoalr (ach (at ?p) [dist-err angle-err])

  (if (not-facing ?p angle-err)

    (ach (facing ?p) angle-err)

    (ach (moved-toward ?p) dist-err))).

In the rule above, (at ?p) is a pattern, ?p is a compile-time parameter, dist-err and angle-err are Rex variables, and (not-facing ?p angle-err) will be a Rex expression once a binding is substituted for ?p. A possible invocation of this rule would be:

(ach (at (office-of stan)) [*distance-eps* 10]).

Gapps also creates a new Rex-variable binding environment when the rule is invoked, binding the Rex variables in the head to the evaluated Rex expressions in the invocation. These variables may appear in Rex expressions in the body of the rule. Note that compile-time variables may also be used in Rex expressions, in order to choose at compile time from among a class of available run-time functions.

2.3. Generating a Circuit

Once a goal expression has been evaluated, yielding a program, a circuit similar to the one shown in *Fig. 2*, that instantiates the program is generated. [2] Because any action whose associated condition is true is sufficient for correctness, the conditions are tested in an arbitrary order that is chosen at compile time. The output of the circuit is the action corresponding to the first condition that is true. If no condition is satisfied, an error action is output to signal the programmer that he has made an error. If, at the final stage of circuit generation, there are still $\emptyset$ components in an action vector, they must be instantiated with an arbitrary value. The inputs to the circuit are com-

---

[2] An equivalent, but more confusing, circuit with $\log(n)$ depth can be generated for improved performance on parallel machines.

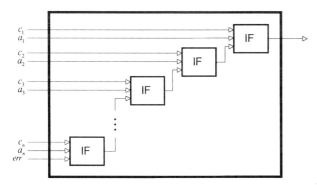

Fig. 2. Circuit generated from Gapps program.

puted by the Rex expressions supplied in the if and do forms. The outputs of the circuit are used to control the agent.

2.4. Reducing Conjunctive Goal Expressions

Conjunctive goal expressions can have two forms: (*ach-or-maint* (and p_1 p_2)) and (and (*ach-or-maint* p_1) (*ach-or-maint* p_2)). Because of the properties of maintainance, the goals (maint (and p_1 p_2)) and (and (maint p_1) (maint p_2)) are semantically equivalent. This is not true, however, for goals of achievement. The goal (ach (and p_1 p_2)) requires that p_1 and p_2 be true simultaneously, whereas the goal (and (ach G_1) (ach G_2)) requires only that they each be true at some time in the future.

Goals of the form (*ach-or-maint* (and p_1 p_2)) can only be reduced using reduction rules whose pattern matches this conjunctive pattern. Goals of the form (and (*ach-or-maint* p_1) (*ach-or-maint* p_2)) can be reduced in two ways: using the standard evaluation procedure for conjunctive goals and using special reduction rules. It is often the case that an effective behavior for achieving G_1 and achieving G_2 cannot be generated simply by conjoining programs that achieve G_1 and G_2 individually. A program for the goal (and (ach have hammer) (ach have saw)) will almost certainly be incomplete when the two tools are in different rooms, because there will be no actions available that are consistent with the standard programs for achieving each of the subgoals. Because of this, we allow reduction rules of the form (defgoalr (and (*ach-or-maint* pat_1 rex-$params_1$) (*ach-or-maint* pat_2 rex-$params_2$)) *goal-expr*) so that special behaviors can be generated in the face of a conjunctive goal.

Following is an example that illustrates both kinds of conjunctive goals. At the top level, the goal is to have the hammer and saw simultaneously, but this reduces to conjunctions of ach and maint goals.

```
(defgoalr (ach (and (have hammer) (have saw))
  (if (have hammer)
      (and (maint have hammer)
           (ach have saw))
      (if (have saw)
          (and (maint have saw)
               (ach have hammer))
          (if (closer-than hammer saw)
              (ach have hammer)
              (ach have saw)))))
```

The agent will pursue the closer object until he has it, then pursue the second while maintaining posession of the first. We might need a similar rule for reducing the conjunctions of goals of achievement and maintenance. Instead of the specific rule above, we could write a more generic sequencing rule, like the following:

```
(defgoalr (ach (and ?g1 ?g2)
          [g1-params g2-params])
  (if (holds ?g1 g1-params)
      (and (maint ?g1 g1-params)
           (ach ?g2 g2-params))
      (if (holds ?g2 g2-params)
          (and (maint ?g2 g2-params)
               (ach ?g1 g1-params))
          (if (better-to-pursue ?g1 g1-params
                                ?g2 g2-params)
              (ach ?g1 g1-params)
              (ach ?g2 g2-params))))).
```

The generic form of the rule assumes that there is a Rex function, holds, that takes a compile-time parameter and generates a circuit that tests to see whether the predicate encoded by the compile-time parameter and the run-time variables is true in the world.

2.5. Prioritized Goal Lists

It is often convenient to be able to specify a prioritized list of goals. In Gapps, we can do this with a goal expression of the form (prio *goal-expr₁ ... goal-exprₙ*). The semantics of this is

$$\text{cond}(\text{dom}(\Pi_1), \Pi_1,$$
$$\quad \text{cond}(\text{dom}(\Pi_2), \Pi_2, \ldots,$$
$$\quad\quad \text{cond}(\text{dom}(\Pi_{n-1}), \Pi_{n-1}, \Pi_n) \ldots)),$$

where $\Pi_i = \text{eval}(goal\text{-}expr_i)$. The domain of a program (true in a situation if the program has an applicable action in that situation) is the disjunction of the conditions in the program. A program for a prio goal executes the first program, unless it has no applicable action, in which case it executes the second program, and so on. At circuit-generation time, this construct can be implemented simply by concatenating the programs in priority order, and executing the first action whose corresponding condition is satisfied.

An example of the use of the prio construct comes about when there is more than one way of achieving a particular goal and one is preferable to the other for some reason, but is not always applicable. We might have the rule

(defgoalr (ach in-room r)

    (prio (ach follow-planned-route-to r)

      (ach use-local-navigation-to r))).

This rule states that the agent should travel to rooms by following planned paths, but if for some reason it is impossible to do that, it should do so through local navigation. The same effect could be achieved with an if expression, but this rule does not require the higher-level construct to know the exact conditions under which the higher-priority goal will fail.

2.6. Prioritized Conjunctions

An interesting special case of a prioritized set of goals is a prioritized conjunction of goals, in which the most preferred goal is the entire conjunction, and the less preferred goals are the conjunctions of shorter and shorter prefixes of the goal sequence. We define (prio-and $G_1 G_2 \ldots G_n$) to be

(prio (and $G_1 G_2 \ldots G_n$)

    (and $G_1 G_2 \ldots G_{n-1}$) ...

    (and $G_1 G_2$)

    G_1).

Isaac Asimov's three laws of robotics [1] are a well-known example of this type of goal structure. As another example, consider a robot that can talk and push blocks. It has as its top-level goal

(prio-and (maint not-crashed)

    (ach (in block1 room3))

    (maint humans-not-bothered)).

It also has rules that say that any action with the null string in the talking field will maintain humans-not-bothered; that (in ?x ?y) can be achieved by pushing ?x or by asking a human to pick it up and move it; and that any action that keeps the robot from coming into contact with a wall will maintain not-crashed. As long as the robot can push the block, it can satisfy all three conditions. If, however, the block is in a corner, getting in a position to push it would require sharing space with a wall, thus violating the first subgoal. The most preferred goal cannot be achieved, so we consider the next-most-preferred goal, obtained by dropping the last condition from the conjunction. Since it is now allowed to bother humans, the robot can satisfy its goal by asking someone to move the block for it. As soon as the human complies, moving the block out of the corner, the robot will automatically revert to its former pushing behavior. This is a convenient high-level construct for programming flexible reactive behavior without the need for the programmer to explicitly envision every combination of conditions in the world. It is important to remember that all of the symbolic manipulation of the goals happens at compile time; at run time, the agent simply executes the action associated with the first condition that evaluates to true.

3. Extending Gapps

Gapps is an appropriate language for specifying action maps that can be hard-wired at the compile time of the agent. In this section, we will consider ways of extending and augmenting Gapps to do exhaustive planning at compile time, to do run-time planning, and to do run-time goal reduction.

3.1. Universal Planning with Goal-Reduction Schema

Schoppers [13] has introduced the notion of a *universal plan*. A universal plan is a function that, for a given goal, maps every possible input situation of the agent into an action that leads to (in an informal sense) that goal. The program resulting from the Gapps-evaluation of a goal can be thought of as a universal plan, mapping situations to actions in service of the top-level goal.

Schoppers' approach differs from Gapps in that the user specifies the capabilities of the agent in an operator-description language. This language allows the user to specify a set of atomic capabilities of the agent, called operators, and the expected effect that executing each of the operators will have on the world, depending possibly on the state of the world in which the operator was executed.

Another way to characterize operators is through the use of a *regression function* [8]. The relation $q = regress(\alpha, p)$ holds if, whenever q holds in the world, the agent's performing action α will cause p to hold in the world as a result. In general, the regression function will return the weakest such q. Regression is usually used to look backwards from a goal-situation p; the proposition q describes a set of situations that are only one "step" or operator application away from the set of situations satsifying p. We know that if the agent can get to a situation satisfying q, it can easily get to a situation satisfying p.

The following schematic Gapps rule allows it to do the exhaustive backward-chaining search that is typically done by a planner, in order to construct a universal plan. The Gapps compiler must be augmented slightly by giving it a depth-bound for its backward chaining, because this rule would, by default, cause infinite backward chaining.

```
(defgoalr (ach (before ?p ?q))
  (if (holds ?q)
    fail
    (if (holds ?p)
      (do anything)
      (if (holds (regress ?a ?p))
        (do ?a)
        (ach (before (regress ?a ?p)
                     (regress ?a ?q)))))))
```

The reduction rule is for goals of the form (ach (before ?p ?q)); that is, the goal is to achieve some condition ?p before some other condition ?q obtains. This form of achievement goal is, we think, typical—it is rare that an agent has a goal of achieving something no matter how long it takes. The rule works as follows: if ?q is true in the world, the agent fails; if ?p holds in the world, then the agent can do anything because it has achieved its goal; otherwise, if, for any action ?a, (regress ?a ?p) holds (that is, performing action ?a will cause ?p to hold next time) then this goal reduces to the goal (do ?a); finally, this goal can be reduced to achieving, for any action ?a, (before (regress ?a ?p) (regress ?a ?q). The final reduction says that it is good for the agent to get into a state from which action ?a achieves the goal ?p before the agent gets into a state from which action ?a achieves the releasing condition ?q, because once that has been done, all the agent must do is do action ?a.

Consider the application of this process to the standard 3-block blocks-world problem. The actions are named atoms, like *pab*, which signifies "put a on b." The world is described by predicates like *ca*, which signifies "clear a" and *obt*, which signifies "on b table." An additional predicate, *time*(i), is true if the time on some global clock, which starts at 0, is i. We will use the abbreviation t_i to stand for *time*(i). Given the goal (ach (before (and oab obc) (time 2))), the evaluation procedure returns a program that is described propositionally as follows:

$$\{ \langle (\neg t_2 \wedge obc \wedge ca \wedge cb), pab \rangle,$$

$$\langle (\neg t_2 \wedge \neg t_1 \wedge obc \wedge ca \wedge cb), pat \rangle,$$

$$\langle (\neg t_2 \wedge \neg t_1 \wedge obc \wedge oab \wedge ca), pat \rangle,$$

$$\langle (\neg t_2 \wedge \neg t_1 \wedge ca \wedge cb \wedge cc), pbc \rangle,$$

$$\langle (\neg t_2 \wedge \neg t_1 \wedge oba \wedge cb \wedge cc), pbc \rangle \}.$$

According to this program, if b is on c, a and b are clear, and it is not time 2, then the agent can put a on b; otherwise, if it is neither time 1 nor time 2, the agent can do a variety of other things. For instance, if b is on c and a and b are clear, the agent can put a on the table. This illustrates the generality of the program. Because it is not yet time 1, it is acceptable to undo progress (we might have some other reason for wanting to do this), because there is time to put a back on b before time 2. Notice that this program is not complete. There are situations for which it has no action, because there are block configurations that cannot be made to satisfy the goal in two actions. Notice also that, because this is a program of the standard form used by Gapps, it can be conjoined in with programs arising from other goals, such as global maintenance goals. Its generality, in allowing any sequence of actions that achieves the first condition before the second, makes it more likely that conjoining it in with a program expressing some other constraint will result in a non-null program.

3.2. Working in Parallel with an Anytime Planner

When the size of the state space is so large that doing exhaustive planning at compile time is impractical, it is possible to solve problems described as planning problems by integrating a run-time planning system with the Gapps framework.

We can express the planning process as an incremental computation, one step of which is done on each tick. On each tick the process generates an output, but it may be one that means "I don't have an answer yet." After some number of ticks, depending on the size of the planning problem, the planner will generate a real result. This result could be cached and executed as in a traditional system, or the agent could just take the first action and wait for the planner to generate a new plan.

Because time may have passed since the planner began its task, we must take care that the plan it generates is appropriate for the situation the agent finds itself in when the planner is finished. This can be guaranteed if the planner monitors the conditions in the world upon which the correctness of its plan depends. If any of these conditions becomes false, the planner can begin again. This behavior will be correct, though not always optimal. In the worst case, the planner will continuously emit the "I don't know" output and the agent will react reflexively to its environment without the benefit of a plan.

The kind of planner discussed above is a degenerate form of an anytime algorithm [3]. An anytime algorithm always has an answer, but the answer improves over time. In the example given above, the answer is useless for a while, then improves dramatically in one step. It might be

useful to have planning algorithms that improve more gradually. Such algorithms exist for certain kinds of path planning, for instance, in which some path is returned at the beginning, but the algorithm works to make the path shorter or more efficient. There is still a difficult decision to be made, however, about whether to take the first step of a plan that is known to be non-optimal or to spend more time planning. For many everyday activities, optimality is not crucial, and it will be sufficient to act on the basis of a simple plan, if a plan is required at all.

From the perspective of Gapps, the anytime planner is just a perceptual process that has state. It is "perceiving" conditions of the form: "the world is in a state such that if I do action α followed by action β, followed by action γ, my goal will be achieved." The following Gapps program makes use of such a planner, but also has the potential for reacting to emergency situations:

```
(defgoalr (ach (in room) [r t])
  (if (know-plan-for-getting-to-room r t)
    (ach execute-first-step
        (plan-for-getting-to-room r t))
    (if (time-is-critical-for-getting-to-room r t)
        (ach drive-in-the-direction-of-room r)
        (maint sit-still))))).
```

If the agent has the goal of being in room r at time t, and he knows a plan for getting there, then he should execute the first step of that plan; otherwise, if it looks like time is running out, the agent should do the best action he can think of at the moment; if there is no problem with time, his best course of action is to sit still and wait until the perception component has produced a plan. These issues of combining planning and reactive action are explored more fully by Kaelbling [4].

3.3. Run-Time Goals

So far, we have only addressed the case in which the agent's top-level goal is specified at compile time. It will often be the case that it is useful to think of the agent as acquiring goals at run time.

3.3.1. Dispatching

The simplest case of responding to run-time goals is to consider them to be another type of perceived information and write goal-reduction rules that are conditional on the given goal. As an example of this, an agent could be given the static compile-time goal of following orders and reduction rules of the following form:

```
(defgoalr (maint follow-orders)
   (if (current-request-pending)
      (ach goal-encoded-by
         (perceived-command))
      (do twiddle-thumbs)))
(defgoalr (ach goal-encoded-by params)
   (if (move-command params)
      (ach do-move-command
         (get-destination params))
      (if (stop-command params)
         (ach stopped)
         ...))).
```

The agent will carry out requests as it perceives them by dispatching to the right goal-reductions based on the nature of the request. This method is sufficient for many cases, but requires the run-time goals to be of a few limited types, because the different types must be tested for and dispatched to directly.

3.3.2. Run Time Goal Reduction

An alternative to explicit dispatching on the types of goals is to interpret Gapps-style goal-reduction rules at run time. An interpreter for Gapps is very similar to the evaluation procedure, except that the result at each step is a set of possible actions, rather than a set of condition-action pairs. This is because the interpretation is taking place at run time, which allows all of the conditions to be evaluated during the interpretation process, rather than combined into a program that is to be evaluated later. Any action can be chosen from the set resulting from interpreting the top-level goal in the current situation.

Given a reduction-rule set Gamma, we define the interpretation procedure as follows:

```
define interp(G)

case first(G)
   do  : make-action-set(second(G),
           rex-eval(third(G)))
   and : conjoin-action-sets(interp(second(G)),
           interp(third(G)))
```

```
   or  : disjoin-action-sets(interp(second(G)),
           interp(third(G)))
   not : interp(negate-goal-expr(second(G)))
   if  : if rex-eval(second(G)) then
           interp(third(G)) else
           interp(fourth(G))
   maint,
   ach : for all R in Gamma such that
           match(G,head(R))
           disjoin-action-sets(interp(body(R)))
```

The function make-action-vector takes an index and a value and returns the singleton set containing the action vector with the field specified by the index set to the indicated value. That is,

$$\text{make-action-vector}(i, v) = \{\langle \emptyset, \ldots, v, \ldots, \emptyset \rangle\}.$$

The value is calculated by evaluating, in the current state of the world, the Rex expression specifying the primitive action. Using the functions mergeable and merge described in Section 2.2, the conjunction of action sets can be defined as

$$\text{conjoin-action-sets}(A', A'')$$
$$= \{\text{merge}(a'_i, a''_j) \mid \text{mergeable}(a'_i, a''_j)\}$$

for $1 \leq i \leq m$, $1 \leq j \leq n$ where

$$A' = \{a'_1, \ldots, a'_m\}$$
$$A'' = \{a''_1, \ldots, a''_n\}.$$

The disjunction of two action sets is simply the union of the sets:

$$\text{disjoin-action-sets}(A', A'') = A' \cup A''.$$

The crucial difference between the interpretation procedure and the evaluation procedure is in the if case. When the interpreter encounters an if goal, it can simply test the condition in the current state of the world and go on to interpret the subgoal corresponding to the result of the test. This obviates the need for manipulating formal descriptions of conditions during the goal-interpretation process.

If the rule set is fixed at compile time and is not recursive, interpretation can be done by a fixed circuit (written, perhaps, in Rex) whose depth is equal to the length of the maximum-length chain of rules in the rule set. If the rule set is recursive, a depth bound will have to be imposed in order to guarantee real-time response. Another possiblity would be to make this into an anytime algorithm by using iterative-deepening search over the course of a number of ticks, and being careful that conditions that have already been evaluated do not change their values during the search process.

If the agent acquires goal reduction rules at run time, perhaps through learning, then the interpretation process can by carried out by general-purpose goal-reduction machinery. It can either be done in real time by a fixed circuit or over time by an anytime search procedure. If interpretation is to happen in real time, there must be a limit on the number of reduction rules that can be applied, in order to make the circuitry be of fixed size.

4. Conclusions

The Gapps goal-reduction formalism provides a flexible, declarative method for describing the action component of agents that must operate in real-time in dynamic worlds. It has a formal semantic grounding and has been implemented and used in a variety of robotic applications. In addition, it can be extended in a number of ways for use in domains with different types of complexity.

References

[1] Isaac Asimov, *I, Robot* (Fawcett Crest, New York, 1950).

[2] Rodney A. Brooks, A robust layered control system for a mobile robot, Technical Report AIM-864, MIT Artificial Intelligence Laboratory, Cambridge, Massachusetts (1985).

[3] Thomas Dean and Mark Boddy, An analysis of time-dependent planning, in *Proceedings of the Seventh National Conference on Artificial Intelligence*, Minneapolis-St. Paul, Minnesota (1988).

[4] Leslie Pack Kaelbling, An architecture for intelligent reactive systems, In Michael P. Georgeff and Amy L. Lansky (eds), *Reasoning About Actions and Plans*, (Morgan Kaufmann, 1987) 395–410.

[5] Leslie Pack Kaelbling, Rex: A symbolic language for the design and parallel implementation of embedded systems, in *Proceedings of the AIAA Conference on Computers in Aerospace*, Wakefield, Massachusetts (1987).

[6] Leslie Pack Kaelbling, Goals as parallel program specifications, in *Proceedings of the Seventh National Conference on Artificial Intelligence*, Minneapolis-St. Paul, Minnesota (1988).

[7] Leslie Pack Kaelbling and Nathan J. Wilson, Rex programmer's manual, Technical Report 381R, Artificial Intelligence Center, SRI International, Menlo Park, California (1988).

[8] Stanley J. Rosenschein, Plan synthesis: A logical perspective, in *Proceedings of the Seventh International Joint Conference on Artificial Intelligence*, Vancouver, British Columbia (1981).

[9] Stanley J. Rosenschein, Formal theories of knowledge in AI and robotics, *New Generation Computing*, 3(4) (1985) 345–357.

[10] Stanley J. Rosenschein, Synthesizing information-tracking automata from environment descriptions, in *Proceedings of Conference on Principles of Knowledge Representation and Reasoning*, Toronto, Canada (1989).

[11] Stanley J. Rosenschein and Leslie Pack Kaelbling, The synthesis of digital machines with provable epistemic properties, in Joseph Halpern (ed.) *Proceedings of the Conference on Theoretical Aspects of Reasoning About Knowledge* (Morgan Kaufmann, 1986) 83–98. An updated version appears as Technical Note 412, Artificial Intelligence Center, SRI International, Menlo Park, California.

[12] Stanley J. Rosenschein and Leslie Pack Kaelbling, Integrating planning and reactive control, in *Proceedings of NASA/JPL Conference on Space Telerobotics*, Pasadena, California (1989).

[13] Marcel J. Schoppers, Universal plans for reactive robots in unpredictable environments, in *Proceedings of the Tenth International Joint Conference on Artificial Intelligence*, vol. 2, Milan (Morgan Kaufmann, 1987) 1039–1046.

Situated Agents Can Have Goals

Pattie Maes

AI-Laboratory, Vrije Universiteit Brussel, Pleinlaan 2, B-1050 Brussels, Belgium, pattie@arti.vub.ac.be, and
AI-Laboratory, Massachusetts Institute of Technology, 545 Technology Square, Cambridge, MA 02139, USA, pattie@ai.mit.edu

This paper discusses the problem of action selection for an autonomous agent. We argue that the so-called "situated agents", which have been built in response to the limitations observed with classical planners, do not provide a satisfactory solution to this problem because of their lack of goals and run-time arbitration. We present a novel action selection theory which allows arbitration among goals and actions while producing fast and robust activity in a tight interaction loop with the environment. The theory models action selection as an emergent property of an activation/inhibition dynamics among the actions the agent can select and between the actions and the environment. A handful of global parameters make it possible to smoothly mediate between several action selection criteria. For example, one can balance goal-orientedness against situation-orientedness, bias towards ongoing plans (inertia) against adaptivity, thoughtfulness against speed, and adjust sensitivity to goal conflicts.

Keywords: Action selection; Theories of action; Architectures for autonomous agents; Situated activity; Planning; Goal-directed behavior.

Pattie Maes obtained a PhD in Computer Science from the University of Brussels in 1987, on the basis of a dissertation about Computational Reflection. She holds a position as Research Associate from the Belgian National Science Foundation. She conducts her research activities at the Artificial Intelligence Laboratory of the above-mentioned university, where she leads the research group on Autonomous Agents. She currently maintains a temporary position as a Visiting Faculty Member at the Artificial Intelligence Laboratory of the Massachusetts Institute of Technology. Her interests are in the areas of: Architectures for Autonomous Agents, Theories of Action, Mobile Robots, Learning Robots, and Robotic Collective Intelligence.

North-Holland
Robotics and Autonomous Systems 6 (1990) 49–70

1. Introduction

One of the main concerns of Artificial Intelligence research is the development of mechanisms for action selection which an autonomous agent can use to determine what to do next. The problem has been approached in two very different ways. Since 1970 the "deliberative thinking" paradigm has dominated AI in general, and thus also theories of action selection. Its main thesis is that intelligent tasks can be implemented by a reasoning process operating on a symbolic internal model. More specifically for action selection, this implies that an agent has an internal representation of actions, goals and events, and that this representation is used by a reasoning process, called "planning", to determine what sequence of actions will achieve the goals [5]. This "plan" is then handed to an execution process, which more or less blindly performs the specified actions.

Although the deliberative thinking approach has proven successful for certain other tasks, only poor results have been obtained with planning, in particular, when applied in real autonomous agents operating in complex, dynamic environments. The few systems built show major deficiencies such as brittleness, inflexibility and slow response times. They also spawned a number of theoretical problems such as the frame problem and the problem of non-monotonic reasoning which so far remain unsolved in satisfactory ways [22]. More recently, some researchers have been viewing this as evidence that it is unrealistic to hope that action-oriented tasks can be successfully implemented by a deliberative machine in real time. This led to the development of radically different architectures, such as, reactive systems [8,17], situated automata [15], situated agents, interactional systems, routines [1], subsumption architectures [3], behavior-based architectures [4], universal plans [18], action networks [14], etc.

The emphasis in these architectures is put on direct coupling of perception to action, distributedness and decentralization, dynamic interaction with the environment and intrinsic mechanisms to cope with resource limitations and incomplete knowledge. One interesting idea shared by these architectures is that of "emergent functionality". The functionality of an agent is viewed as an emergent property of the intensive interaction of the system with its dynamic environment. The specification of the behavior of the agent alone does not explain the functionality that is displayed when the agent is operating. Instead, the functionality to a large degree depends on the static and dynamic properties of the environment. The environment is not only taken into account dynamically, but its characteristics are exploited to serve the functioning of the system. An important implication of this view is that one cannot simply tell these agents how to achieve a goal. Instead, one has to find a "dynamics", or interaction loop or servo control loop, involving the system and the environment which will converge towards the desired goal. The interaction process only comes to a rest (or a fixed pattern) when the goals are achieved.

These new theories of action selection, which we will refer to as "situated agents" in the remaining part of the paper, have already demonstrated remarkably reliable and successful performance in real autonomous agents. In this paper, we argue that the currently existing situated activity systems do, however, have some important limitations because of their lack of explicit goals and goal-handling capabilities, and relatedly, because they require the designer of the systems to wire-up or precompile the action selection. We further present a novel approach in which action selection is modeled as an emergent property of an activation/inhibition dynamics among actions. The mechanism proposed combines characteristics of both traditional planners and situated agents: it produces fast and robust activity in a tight interaction loop with the environment, while at the same time allowing for some prediction and planning to take place.

The main difference between our approach and current situated activity systems is that we neither hard-wire nor precompile the action selection. Arbitration among actions is a run-time process which differs according to the goals of the system and the situation it finds itself in. It, therefore, constitutes a simpler, more flexible and more general solution to the problem. It differs from classical planners in the way this run-time arbitration is organized. Instead of programming in advance the

central control structure that regulates the arbitration, this new approach control structure emerges in a distributed fashion by parallel local interactions among actions and between actions and the environment. So, in conformity with the underlying philosophy of situated agents, an interaction loop or servo control loop involving the system and the environment is set up which converges towards the desired functionality. Its dynamics makes a selection of action(s) emerge in response to environmental conditions and internal goals of the agent.

The paper starts with a discussion of the problem of action selection and the limitations of the planning approach and the situated agents approach. It then goes on to present a concrete action selection algorithm which combines the best of both worlds. In addition, the algorithm provides global parameters, which one can use to tune the action selection behavior to the characteristics of the task environment. In this way, one can smoothly balance several action selection criteria, such as goal-orientedness against situation-orientedness, bias towards ongoing plans (inertia) against adaptivity, thoughtfulness against speed, and adjust its sensitivity to goal conflicts. The results obtained with this algorithm are reported upon in detail. The paper concludes with a critical discussion of those results.

2. The Problem of Action Selection

2.1. The Need for Run-Time Arbitration

The main purpose of this section is to demonstrate that the new architectures for action selection which have been proposed lately as an alternative for classical planning [8,9,15,18,1,17,3,14] have important limits as theories of activity for an autonomous agent. The way these systems organize activity is by hard-wiring the action selection at compile time. The agent is equipped with some circuitry which implements a set of situation-action rules. Care is taken either that the situation descriptions are exclusive, so that there is no problem of arbitration among different rules (e.g. [8]) or that the arbitration among rules is hand-coded [3]. The rules themselves are either hand-coded again [3,1] or compiled on the basis of a declarative description of the desired behavior of the agent [9].

In the case of hand-coding, the result typically demonstrates very good performance, but at the price of requiring a great effort for a very specific solution. For example, the Pengi system [2,1] consists of a set of very specific "tricks" (or routines, or rules) for playing the Pengo game. These tricks have been devised by the programmers of the Pengi system, after a deep analysis of the strategies that are useful in playing the game. To the contrary, planning leaves more of the burden of figuring out what to do with the agent instead of the programmer. A planner has explicit knowledge about action selection in general, i.e. it knows that one has to take action X before action Y if Y undoes a precondition of X, etc. If classical planning is trying to solve the automatic programming/planning problem, then instead, the current situated agents approach relies on the designer of the system to do all the hard work.

Also, the second approach, which precompiles the action selection on the basis of a compile-time description of the goals, has limitations. Both approaches require that one can anticipate what the best action is to take in all of the occurring situations. We believe that there are limits to how far one can precompile an optimal solution. For more complex tasks, too few constraints may be known at compile time to be able to make the problem analyzable. The reason is that action selection happens on the basis of information. Some of this information is available at compile time, some of it at run-time. For complex agents in complex environments, the latter will dominate. This would imply that a precompiled solution might involve an explosive (or even infinite) number of situations.

A second limitation is that in neither of the two approaches do the resulting agents have explicit goals. Explicit goals (and, therefore, also run-time arbitration among them) is crucial for an autonomous intelligent agent for a number of reasons:

- It is important that new or changed goals can be communicated to an agent without having to reprogram the agent. If only because we want to be able to affect its behavior at run-time, for example, to help it when it gets stuck, or to give it some advice and by that bias its selection of action. Notice that we do not demand that the agent can just be given any arbitrary goal.

- Even if one does not care about being able to communicate goals to the agent, "internal" goals still are important. Any complex (intelligent) agent has different modes or drives. Its behavior and action selection varies according to these internal goals and how important they are. E.g., when you are really thirsty, you reach for a cup. You do not reach for a cup when you are not thirsty. But you can, if you want to[1].

- Having a particular goal makes selection of action easier because it helps in biasing/restricting the possible choices. One of the functions goals can fulfill is as memory of the global picture one is working on (or committed to), in case one might forget it while working out local details of a task. When an agent does not have explicit goals (or some sort of state to memorize the global picture), every situation has to carry complete information for deciding what the best next action is. For many tasks this is an unrealistic requirement: often the agent has to go through situations which seem worse from a local perspective to obtain the globally desired results.

- A complex agent has complex goals. First of all, it has many goals, second the goals it has vary over time, third they have different priorities, and fourth their priorities vary according to the situation and according to their interrelationships. So it is definitely important that an autonomous agent can mediate among goals and handle their conflicts or even try to exploit their interrelationships to optimize their achievement over time.

- Finally, goals are a crucial ingredient for self-consciousness. They are in particular important for an agent to be able to learn or improve its performance. An agent needs an explicit notion of what its goals are in order for it to (i) know when it is doing better at something[2] and (ii) in order for it to bias its learning efforts. An additional advantage of having explicit goals is that an action learned in the context of one goal, can once learned, be applied in the context of a different goal.

---

[1] This particular example stems from a personal communication with Marvin Minsky.

[2] This doesn't hold for reinforcement learning, which only requires that one can sense success. For complex agents that have to perform many tasks in their environment, this might prove not to be enough to allow fast learning.

So an intelligent autonomous agent does need full-fledged goals and goal-handling capabilities (run-time decision making). A solution which has been proposed by some of the researchers in situated agents is to have goals as an extra condition in the description of a situation. However, this solution is not satisfactory because (i) it would imply that for every situation description of a rule one writes a large disjunction of all the goals (and subgoals) the action possibly contributes to, and (ii) this still does not allow arbitration among actions on the basis of the number of goals they contribute to and their relative importances. Another suggestion which has been made [16] is to integrate a traditional planner into a reactive system. The idea is to have a planning component which continuously tries to produce a plan. If it succeeds before changes in the environment make the plan invalid, it is taken into account by the reactive, situated system. It is not yet clear how satisfactory this solution is, but some of the disadvantages we expect are (i) that the resulting behavior might appear very discontinuous or irregular, and (ii) that the amount of time available for planning or the required quality of the plan are not tunable. Ideally, one would like to be able to trade off quality of the plan for time spent in producing it.

2.2. Trading Off Different Criteria

Imagine an autonomous agent which has to achieve a number of global goals in a complex dynamic environment. An example could be a rover that has to explore Mars and collect samples of soil. What actually is "the most appropriate" or "the most relevant" next action that agent should take at a particular moment? It is very difficult to come up with a exact definition of the best choice of action. Nevertheless, some of the characteristics the action selection mechanism should demonstrate are evident:

- it favors actions that are goal-oriented, in particular, actions that contribute to several goals at once,
- it favors actions that are relevant to the current situation, in particular it exploits opportunities and is adaptive to unpredictable and changing situations,
- it favors actions that contribute to the ongoing goal/plan (unless another action rates a lot better), i.e., it 'sticks' onto a particular goal (because it has already invested time and energy in that goal), unless there is a good reason to start working on something different.
- it looks ahead (or 'plans'), in particular to avoid hazardous situations and handle interacting and conflicting goals,
- it is robust (exhibits a graceful degradation when any of its components fail),
- and it is reactive and fast.

Important constraints for the action selection mechanism are that it has to operate with incomplete or even incorrect knowledge about the world and limited computational resources and time resources. This implies that the action selection cannot be completely "rational" or optimal. Furthermore, the desired characteristics listed above are contradictory. For example, an agent cannot be at the same time completely adaptive to changes in the environment as well as biased to ongoing plans. The right "mixture" of the above characteristics depends on characteristics of the environment and the task, such as how critical the environment is, what the pace of changes is, or the time available for decisions, how predictable the environment is, or what precision is required for the task, etc. Ideally, we would like an action selection mechanism that can smoothly mediate along different dimensions to adapt to the characteristics of the environment and task.

3. Dynamic Action Selection

3.1. Hypotheses

The remaining sections of this paper describe an action selection mechanism for a situated agent which allows for some "planning" (looking ahead, looking backwards from the goals, arbitrating among goals) to take place while avoiding the pitfalls of classical AI planners. It combines the "aesthetics" of the new architectures, such as decomposition along tasks instead of along functions, distributedness, de-emphasized role of internal models and emergent functionality, with the goal-handling capabilities of traditional planners, in an elegant way. It makes it possible to vary the action selection behavior along certain dimensions so as to match the characteristics of the environment.

The hypothesis we are testing is whether action selection can be modeled as an emergent property of an activation/inhibition dynamics among the different actions the agent can take. We try to avoid having "bureaucratic" modules at all (i.e. modules whose only competence is determining which other modules should be activated or inhibited) nor do we have global forms of control. The idea is to get a similar functionality as that provided by the deliberative control taking place in classical planners in a different way. The "deliberation" of our action selection mechanism is implicit: it is an emergent property of a dynamic process. Rational control schemes emerge in a distributed fashion by parallel local interactions between a set of simple modules.

We are studying the adequacy of these hypotheses and attempting to determine which activation/inhibition dynamics is appropriate. To this end, we are developing a series of algorithms and testing them in computer simulations. One such algorithm was discussed in [11]. This paper describes a variation on the algorithm (see also [12] for a longer account) which is simpler and produces more interesting results [3]. Experiments have been performed for several applications. The resulting systems do exhibit the desired properties of goal-orientedness, situation-orientedness, adaptivity, robustness, looking ahead, etc. Furthermore, a handful of global parameters make it possible to smoothly mediate between these action selection criteria. As such one can balance goal-orientedness against data-orientedness, adaptivity against inertia, thoughtfulness against speed, and adjust sensitivity to goal conflicts.

3.2. Algorithm

This section of the paper describes the algorithm and illustrates it with a very simple example. [12] discusses a mathematical model and includes more complicated examples.

The algorithm views an autonomous agent as a set of modules each having its own specific com-

---

³ In particular, this algorithm also makes use of 'inhibition' among modules, which makes it possible to deal with interacting goals. Further, there are new results on how the global parameters can be used to tune the action selection behavior along different dimensions.

```
PICK-UP-SANDER
  :action ...
  :condition-list '(hand-empty, sander-on-
    table)
  :add-list '(sander-in-hand)
  :delete-list '(hand-empty, sander-on-table)
  :activation-level 18.678
```

Fig. 1. An example competence module. The way the competence is achieved (i.e. the exact actions taken by the module) is not made explicit.

petence [13,3]. These competence modules resemble the operators of a classical planning system. A *competence module i* can be described by a tuple $(c_i, a_i, d_i, \alpha_i)$. c_i is a list of preconditions which have to be fulfilled before the competence module can become active. a_i and d_i represent the expected effects of the competence module's action in terms of an add list and a delete list. In addition, each competence module has a level of activation α_i. A competence module is *executable* at time t when all of its preconditions are observed to be true at time t. An executable competence module whose activation level reaches a certain threshold, may be selected, which means that it performs some real world actions. The operation of a competence module (what computation it performs, what actions it takes and how) is not made explicit, i.e., competence modules could be hard-wired inside, they could perform logical inference, or whatever. *Fig. 1* shows an example of a competence module.

Competence modules are linked in a network through three types of links: successor links, predecessor links, and conflicter links. The description of the competence modules of an autonomous agent in terms of a precondition list, add list and delete list completely defines this network (this is the only purpose of these lists):

- There is a *successor link* from competence module x to competence module y ('x has y as successor') for every proposition p that is member of the add list of x and also member of the precondition list of y (so more than one successor link between two competence modules may exist). Formally, given competence module $x = (c_x, a_x, d_x, \alpha_x)$ and competence module $y = (c_y, a_y, d_y, \alpha_y)$, there is a successor link from x to y, for every proposition $p \in a_x \cap c_y$.
- A *predecessor link* from module x to module y ('x has y as predecessor') exists for every suc-

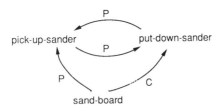

Fig. 2. A small example network. Pick-up-sander and put-down-sander are mutual predecessors and therefore also mutual successors. Pick-up-sander is a predecessor of sand-board, because it makes the latter's precondition 'sander-in-hand' true. Further, put-down-sander is a conflictor of sand-board, because it makes the condition 'sander-in-hand' of the latter undone.

cessor link from y to x. Formally, given competence module $x = (c_x, a_x, d_x, \alpha_x)$ and competence module $y = (c_y, a_y, d_y, \alpha_y)$, there is a predecessor link from x to y, for every proposition $p \in c_x \cap a_y$.

- There is a *conflicter link* from module x to module y ('y conflicts with x') for every proposition p that is a member of the delete list of y and a member of the precondition list of x. Formally, given competence module $x = (c_x, a_x, d_x, \alpha_x)$ and competence module $y = (c_y, a_y, d_y, \alpha_y)$, there is a conflicter link from x to y, for every proposition $p \in c_x \cap d_y$.

Fig. 2 shows an example network.

The intuitive idea is that modules use these links to activate and inhibit each other, so that after some time the activation energy accumulates in the modules that represent the "best" actions to take given the current situation and goals. Once the activation level of such a module reaches a certain threshold, and provided the module is executable, it becomes active and takes some real actions. The pattern of spreading activation among modules, as well as the input of new activation energy into the network is determined by the current situation and the current global goals of the agent:

- *Activation by the Current Situation*
  There is input of activation energy coming from the currently observed situation towards modules that partially match this situation. A competence module is said to partially match the current situation if at least one of its preconditions is observed to be true in the current situation. Notice that we do not make the assumption that there is a global continuously updated world model. Instead, in a real robot,

each proposition would be delivered by a virtual sensor, which is a module that decides upon the basis of real sensor data whether a certain proposition should be considered true. The "currently observed situation" consists of the union of all the propositions that are currently observed by their associated virtual sensor.

- *Activation by the Goals*
  A second source of activation energy are the global goals of the agent. They increase the activation level of modules that achieve one of the global goals. A module is said to achieve one of the global goals if one of the goals is a member of the add list of the competence module. Notice that we distinguish two types of goals: *once-only* goals have to be achieved only once, *permanent* goals have to be achieved continuously. An example of the first is the goal 'spray-paint-car', an example of the second would be 'battery-half-loaded'.

- *Inhibition by the Protected Goals*
  Further, there is an external inhibition (or removal of activation) by the global goals of the agent that have already been achieved and should be protected. These 'protected goals' remove some of the activation from the modules that would undo them. A module is said to undo one of the protected goals when one of the protected goals is a member of the delete list of the module.

These processes are continuous: there is a continual flow of activation energy towards the modules that partially match the current situation and towards the modules that realize one of the global goals. There is a continual decrease of the activation level of the modules that undo the protected goals. This means that the environment and the global goals may change unpredictably at any moment in time. If this happens, the external input of activation automatically flows to other competence modules.

Besides the impact on activation levels from the current situation and goals, competence modules also activate and inhibit each other. Modules spread activation along their links as follows:

- *Activation of Successors*
  An executable competence module x spreads activation forward. It increases (by a fraction of its own activation level) the activation level of those successors y for which the shared pro-

position $p \in a_x \cap c_y$ is not true. Intuitively, we want these successor modules to become more activated because they are "almost executable", since more of their preconditions will be fulfilled after the competence module has become active. Formally, given that competence module $x = (c_x, a_x, d_x, \alpha_x)$ is executable, it spreads forward through those successor links for which the proposition that defines them $p \in a_x$ is false.

– *Activation of Predecessors*

A competence module x that is not executable spreads activation backward. It increases (by a fraction of its own activation level) the activation level of those predecessors y for which the shared proposition $p \in c_x \cap a_y$ is not true. Intuitively, a non-executable competence module spreads to the modules that 'promise' to fulfill its preconditions that are not yet true, so that the competence module may become executable afterwards. Formally, given that competence module $x = (c_x, a_x, d_x, \alpha_x)$ is not executable, it spreads backward through those predecessor links for which the proposition that defined them $p \in c_x$ is false.

– *Inhibition of Conflicters*

Every competence module x (executable or not) decreases (by a fraction of its own activation level) the activation level of those conflicters y for which the shared proposition $p \in c_x \cap d_y$ is true. Intuitively, any module will try to prevent a module that undoes one of its true preconditions from becoming active. Notice that we do not allow a module to inhibit itself (while it may activate itself). In case of mutual conflict of modules, only the one with the higher activation level inhibits the other. This prevents the phenomenon that the most relevant modules eliminate each other. Formally, competence module $x = (c_x, a_x, d_x, \alpha_x)$ takes away activation energy through all of its conflicter links for which the proposition that defines them $p \in c_x$ is true, except those links for which there exists an inverse conflicter link that is stronger.

As an example, consider the network in *Fig. 3*. Suppose the state of the environment is $S(0) =$ {sprayer-in-hand, sander-on-table}. The goals are $G(0) = $ {board-sanded}. The external spreading of activation would be as follows: the current situation gives put-down-sprayer a lot of new activation energy because both of its conditions are

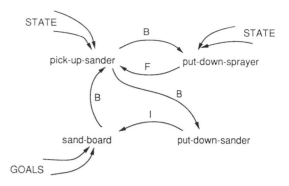

Fig. 3. A toy example. The initial situation is $S(0) = $ {sprayer-in-hand, sander-on-table}, the initial goal is $G(0) = $ {board-sanded}. This situation implies the flow of activation energy indicated by the arrows. "B" stands for backward spreading of activation (towards a predecessor), "F" for forward spreading (towards a successor), and "I" for inhibition (taking away activation energy of a conflictor).

fulfilled. Further, it also gives some activation energy to pick-up-sander because one of its conditions is fulfilled (namely that the sander is on the table). The goals of the agent increase the activation level of sand-board, because it promises to achieve the goal when activated. The internal spreading of activation goes as follows. Put-down-sprayer is executable (all its conditions are fulfilled), so it spreads activation energy forward to its successor pick-up-sander. Sand-board, pick-up-sander and put-down-sander are not executable, so they spread activation energy backwards to their predecessors. In particular, sand-board will increase the activation level of pick-up-sander with a fraction of its own activation level, pick-up-sander will increase the activation level of put-down-sprayer, and put-down-sander will increase the activation level of pick-up-sander (although since its own activation level is very low or zero, this won't have much effect). The same spreading of activation pattern will go on (as long as the situation or goals don't change) and make activation energy accumulate in put-down-sprayer. When this one has reached a certain threshold, it will become active and execute its actions, i.e. the sprayer will be put down.

Consequently, the state of the environment will change and thus also the external and internal patterns of activation [4]. In particular, pick-up-

---

[4] We assume in this example, that all of the modules successfully complete their actions. Later in the paper, we show how the system handles situations in which the environment changes in an unexpected way.

sander will after a while accumulate enough activation energy and become active. After that, sand-board and put-down-sander will be executable. Sand-board will, however, accumulate enough activation energy faster than put-down-sander, first of all because it receives activation energy from the goals and second because it takes away activation energy from put-down-sander, since put-down-sander is a conflictor of sand-board for the proposition 'sander-in-hand'. After sand-board has been active, the goal will be achieved.

The global algorithm performs a loop, in which at every timestep the following computation takes place over all of the competence modules:

1. The impact of the current situation, goals and protected goals on the activation level of a module is computed.
2. The way the competence module activates and inhibits related modules through its successor links, predecessor links and conflicter links is computed.
3. A decay function ensures that the overall activation level remains constant.
4. The competence module that fulfills the following three conditions becomes active: (i) it has to be executable, (ii) its level of activation has to surpass a certain threshold and (iii) it must have a higher activation level than all other competence modules that fulfill conditions (i) and (ii). When two competence modules fulfill these conditions (i.e. they are equally strong), one of them is chosen randomly. The activation level of the module that has become active is reinitialized to 0 [5]. If none of the modules fulfills conditions (i) and (ii), the threshold is lowered by some percentage (e.g. 10%).

These four steps are repeated infinitely. Interesting global observable properties are: the sequence of competence modules that have become active, the optimality of this sequence (which is computed by a domain-dependent function), and the speed with which it was obtained (the number of timesteps a competence module has become active relative to the total number of timesteps the system has been running).

Four *global parameters* can be used to 'tune'

the spreading activation dynamics, and thereby the action selection behavior of the agent:

1. θ, the threshold for becoming active, and related to it, π the mean level of activation. θ is lowered with 10% each time none of the modules could be selected. It is reset to its initial value when a module could be selected.
2. ϕ, the amount of activation energy a proposition that is observed to be true injects into the network.
3. γ, the amount of activation energy a goal injects into the network.
4. δ, the amount of activation energy a protected goal takes away from the network.

Example values for these parameters could be $\theta = 45$, $\pi = 20$, $\phi = 20$, $\gamma = 50$, and $\delta = 40$. These parameters also determine the amount of activation that modules spread forward, backward or take away. More precisely, for each false proposition in its precondition list, a non-executable module spreads α to its predecessors. For each false proposition in its add list, an executable module spreads $\alpha(\phi/\gamma)$ to its successors. For each true proposition in its precondition list a module takes away $\alpha(\delta/\gamma)$ from its conflictors. These factors were chosen this way because the internal spreading of activation should have the same semantics/effects as the input/output by the current situation and the goals. The ratios of input from the situation versus input from the goals versus output by the protected goals are the same as the ratios of input from predecessors versus input from successors versus output by modules with which a module conflicts. Intuitively, we want to view preconditions that are not yet true as subgoals, effects that are about to be true as 'predictions', and preconditions that are true as protected subgoals.

The algorithm as it is described until now, has a drawback that has to be dealt with. The length of a precondition list, add list or delete list affects the input and output of activation to a module. In particular, a module which has a lot of propositions in its add list and precondition list has more sources of activation energy than a module that only has a few. Therefore, all input of activation to a module or removal of activation from a module is weighted by $1/n$, where n is (i) the number of propositions in the precondition list (in the case of input coming from the current situation and from the predecessors), (ii) the number of

[5] If this were not be the case, modules could become active a couple of times in a row without this really being desirable.

propositions in the add list (in the case of input from the goals or from successors), or (iii) the number of propositions in the delete list (in the case of removal of activation by the protected goals or by modules with whom the module conflicts).

Finally, we want modules that achieve the same goal or modules that use the same precondition to compete with one another to become active (we view them as representing a disjunction or choice point). Therefore, the amount of activation that is spread or taken away for a particular proposition is split among the affected modules. For example, for a particular proposition p that is observed to be true the situation divides ϕ among all of the modules that have that precondition in their precondition list. The same not only holds for the effect of the goals and the protected goals, but also for the internal spreading of activation. For example when a large number of modules achieve a precondition of module m, the activation α_m that m spreads backward for that proposition is equally divided among all of these modules. When on the other hand there is only one other module that can make this precondition true, module m increases the activation level of that module by its own activation level α_m. One implicit assumption on which this is based is that the preconditions are in conjunctive normal form. A disjunction of two preconditions would be represented by a single proposition, for which two competence modules exist that can make it true.

4. Results

The algorithm presented in this paper can be modeled by a system of differential equations. This system is, however, too complicated to solve, so that exact predictions about the resulting action selection behavior are not available. Nevertheless, important qualitative results can be obtained, for example, on possible phase transitions with the growth of parameters, such as the size of the network, the mean fanout of a node, etc. [7]. We have evaluated the algorithm empirically by performing a wide series of experiments using several example applications. *Fig. 4* shows a bitmap of the simulation environment. The networks had such diverse properties as being very 'wide', very

'long', containing cycles, local high concentrations of links, unlinked subnetworks, destructive modules, conflicting and mutually conflicting modules, etc. All of the problems presented were solved for large ranges of parameters. The initial results are very promising, and will, therefore, be followed by more systematic studies. The following subsections discuss the results observed in detail.

4.1. Planning Capabilities

The actions selected by the simulated networks cannot be said to show a 'jump-first think-never' behavior. The networks do exhibit planning capabilities. They 'consider' to some extent the effects of a sequence of actions before actually embarking on its execution. If a sequence of competence modules exists that transforms the current situation into the goal situation, then this sequence becomes highly activated through the cumulative effect of the forward spreading (starting from the current situation) and the backward spreading (starting from the goals). If this sequence potentially implies negative effects, it is weakened by the inhibition rules.

More specifically, goal-relevance of the selected action is obtained through the input from the goals and the backward spreading of activation. Situation relevance and opportunistic behavior are obtained through the input of the current situation and the spreading of activation forward. Conflicting and interacting goals are taken into account through inhibition by the protected goals and inhibition among conflicting modules. Further, local maxima in the action selection are avoided, provided that the spreading of activation can go on long enough (the threshold is high enough), so that the network can evolve towards a better activity pattern. And finally, the algorithm automatically biases towards ongoing plans, because these tend to have a shorter distance between current situation and goals and are favored by the remains of the past spreading activation patterns. Moreover, the global parameters serve as controls by which one can mediate smoothly among these different action selection characteristics. All of these results are reported upon in more detail later in subsequent sections.

The notion of a plan here is very different from the classical one existing in AI. A network does

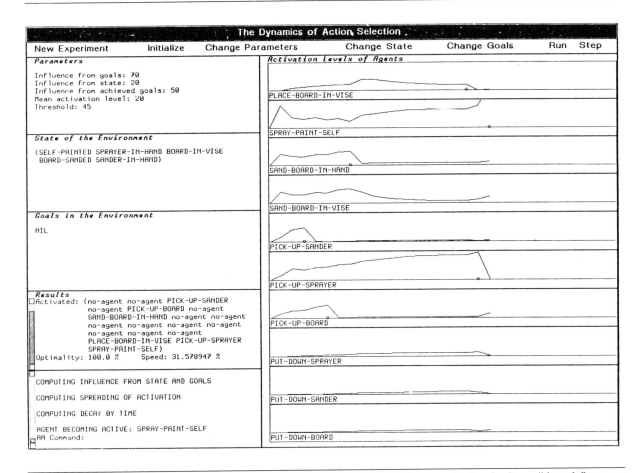

Fig. 4. The user interface of the simulation environment. The upper pane is a menu of commands. It makes it possible to define a new network, to initialize the current network, to change the global parameters, to change the state of the environment, to change the goals of the network and to run or step through the behavior of a network. The left-hand panes display the parameters, the current state of the environment, the current goals of the network and the results of the simulation (among which is the list of activated modules). The right-hand panes display the activation levels of competence modules over time (the X-axis represents time, while the Y-axis displays the activation level). The little circles tell when a competence module has become active.

not construct an explicit representation of a single plan, but instead expresses its "intention" or "urge" to take certain actions by high activation levels of the corresponding modules. Another important difference is that there is no centralized preprogrammed search process. Instead, the operators (competence modules) themselves select the sequence of operators that are activated, and this in a non-hierarchical, highly distributed way. There is no search tree constructed, i.e. there is no explicit representation built of state changes after taking certain actions.

Consequently, the system does not suffer from the disadvantages of search trees such as: that information is duplicated in several parts of a tree; trees grow exponentially with the size of the problem; trees only make a strict representation of a plan possible (it is impossible to work with uncertainties); etc. In addition, the spreading activation process is a much cheaper operation. Of course, these advantages are not cost-free. The action selection produced is less 'rational' than that of the sophisticated deliberative planners built in AI. On the other hand, the latter systems, when applied in autonomous agents, suffer from brittleness and slowness. What is particularly interesting about the algorithm presented here is that it provides parameters to mediate between adaptivity, speed and reactivity on the one hand and thought-fulness and rationality on the other hand.

4.2. Goal-Orientedness

The algorithm selects actions that contribute to the global goals of the agent. Given that g is a global goal of the network, then γ of new activation energy is put into the modules that achieve this goal. These modules will in turn per subgoal (false precondition) increase the activation level of the modules that make this subgoal true, and so on. This backward spreading of activation takes care that modules that contribute to goal g are more activated than modules that do not. Furthermore, modules that contribute to different goals (or subgoals) receive activation for each of these goals and will, therefore, be favored over modules that only contribute to one.

If the agent has more than one goal, modules that contribute to the goal that is 'closest' are favored. 'Closest' here means that the path from the goal-achieving modules to the situation-matching modules is the shortest. The algorithm also favors modules that have little competition. For example, if the agent has two goals $g1$ and $g2$, and if there is one module that achieves $g1$ and there are two modules that achieve $g2$, then the algorithm favors the module that achieves $g1$, and, therefore, the probability of $g1$ being realized first is higher (because the 2 modules that achieve $g2$ have to share the amount γ of activation energy put into the network by goal $g2$). All of these comments hold for subgoals as well as for goals, since subgoals (false preconditions of modules) are treated the same way as goals.

The behavior can be made more or less *goal-oriented* in its selection by varying the ratio of γ to ϕ (the amount of activation energy injected by the current situation per true proposition). For example, if $\phi = 0$, traditional backward chaining is performed (i.e., the selection is completely goal-oriented). On the other hand, the system now takes less advantage of opportunities, it is less reactive, and less biased by what is currently observed and what is predicted to become true in the near future. Furthermore, it is also slowed down because the current state of the environment does not bias the action selection. Ideally, we want a system that is mainly goal-oriented, but does take advantage of interesting opportunities. This can be obtained by choosing $\gamma > \phi$. The optimal ratio

is of course problem dependent (more on choosing the parameter values in section 6.4).

4.3. Situation Relevance

The algorithm activates the modules that are relevant to the current situation more than the ones that are not. The processes responsible for this are the input of activation energy coming from the state of the environment and the spreading of activation energy by executable modules towards their successors (which implements some sort of prediction/projection of what will be true next). As already mentioned in the previous section, the advantages are that (1) the system biases its search and thereby speeds up the action selection and (2) the system is able to exploit opportunities (let its action selection be driven more by what is happening in the environment). The importance of (2) for an autonomous agent has recently been recognized by the AI community as is witnessed by the growth of interest in so-called reactive systems. The characteristic of situation-orientedness can be exploited to a higher or lesser degree by varying the parameter ϕ. *Fig. 5* shows the results of experiments with different ratios for the parameters γ and ϕ.

The forward spreading rules take care that a module receives activation from the current situation in proportion to how 'close' it is to being executable given the current state of the environment. A module is closest to being executable if it really is executable (i.e., if all its preconditions are fulfilled). For non-executable modules, 'closeness' is inversely proportional to the weighted sum of the lengths of a path from executable modules to the module itself for each of the preconditions of the module. This implies, for example, that a module that has two preconditions $p1$ and $p2$ of which one, for example $p1$, cannot be made true given the current state, receives relatively less activation from the situation and, therefore, has less probability of being part of a "plan" [6].

4.4. Adaptivity

The action selection process is completely "open". The environment as well as the goals may

---

[6] It may, however, receive a lot of activation from the goals and use that activation to urge its predecessors to make its preconditions true.

```
┌─────────────────────────────────────────┐   ┌─────────────────────────────────────────┐
│                                   The │   │                              ` The C │
├─────────────────────────────────────────┤   ├─────────────────────────────────────────┤
│ New Experiment      Initialize   Change Par│  │ New Experiment      Initialize   Change Par│
├─────────────────────────────────────────┤   ├─────────────────────────────────────────┤
│ Parameters                              │   │ Parameters                              │
│                                         │   │                                         │
│ Influence from goals: 50                │   │ Influence from goals: 50                │
│ Influence from state: 0                 │   │ Influence from state: 10                │
│ Influence from achieved goals: 50       │   │ Influence from achieved goals: 50       │
│ Mean activation level: 20               │   │ Mean activation level: 20               │
│ Threshold: 40                           │   │ Threshold: 40                           │
│                                         │   │                                         │
├─────────────────────────────────────────┤   ├─────────────────────────────────────────┤
│ State of the Environment                │   │ State of the Environment                │
│                                         │   │                                         │
│ (HAND-IS-EMPTY A-TOWER-IS-BEING-BUILT   │   │ (HAND-IS-EMPTY A-TOWER-IS-BEING-BUILT   │
│ A-TOWER-IS-BEING-BUILT A-TOWER-IS-BEING-BUILT│ │ A-TOWER-IS-BEING-BUILT A-TOWER-IS-BEING-BUILT│
│ A-FIRST-BLOCK-IS-LAYED FREE-SPACE)      │   │ A-FIRST-BLOCK-IS-LAYED FREE-SPACE)      │
│                                         │   │                                         │
├─────────────────────────────────────────┤   ├─────────────────────────────────────────┤
│ Goals in the Environment                │   │ Goals in the Environment                │
│                                         │   │                                         │
│ (A-TOWER-IS-BEING-BUILT)                │   │ (A-TOWER-IS-BEING-BUILT)                │
│                                         │   │                                         │
├─────────────────────────────────────────┤   ├─────────────────────────────────────────┤
│ Results                                 │   │ Results                                 │
│                                         │   │                                         │
│ Activated: (no-agent no-agent no-agent no-agent│ │ Activated: (no-agent no-agent no-agent SEE GRASP│
│            SEE GRASP no-agent FIND-PLACE BEGIN│ │            FIND-PLACE BEGIN no-agent no-agent SEE│
│            no-agent no-agent SEE GRASP MOVE│ │            GRASP MOVE no-agent no-agent SEE│
│            no-agent no-agent no-agent SEE GRASP│ │            MOVE FIND-PLACE no-agent SEE GRASP│
│            MOVE no-agent no-agent no-agent SEE│ │            MOVE)                         │
│            GRASP MOVE)                   │   │ Optimality: 85.71429 %    Speed: 63.636364 %│
│ Optimality: 100.0 %    Speed: 50.0 %    │   │                                         │
└─────────────────────────────────────────┘   └─────────────────────────────────────────┘
```

Fig. 5. These results show that one can mediate between goal-orientedness of the action selection and data-orientedness by varying the ratio of γ to φ. In the first experiment, the network performs traditional backward chaining (φ = 0). In the second experiment there is some forward spreading going on, but φ is still smaller than γ. The input from the current situation and forward spreading bias the search so that the action selection is now much faster. The resulting action selection is however less optimal (the action selection is more data-driven, which makes that actions that are not relevant to the goal may get selected. In this example, the module 'find-place' is activated a second time, without this contributing anything to the goal of building a tower).

change at run time. As a result, the external input/output as well as the internal activation/inhibition patterns will change reflecting the modified situation. Even more, the external influence during "planning" or spreading activation is so important that plans are only formed as long as the influence or input/output (or 'disturbance') from the environment and goals is present.

Because of this continuous 're-evaluation', the action selection behavior adapts easily to unforeseen or changing situations. For example, if after the activation of module 'pick-up-board', the board is not in the robot's hand (e.g. because it slipped away), the same competence module becomes active once more, because it still receives a lot of activation from the competence modules

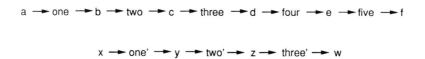

Fig. 6. A toy network to test adaptivity versus bias (inertia). $y \rightarrow three$ stands for proposition y is a precondition of module *three*, while *three* $\rightarrow y$ stands for proposition y is in the add list of module *three*.

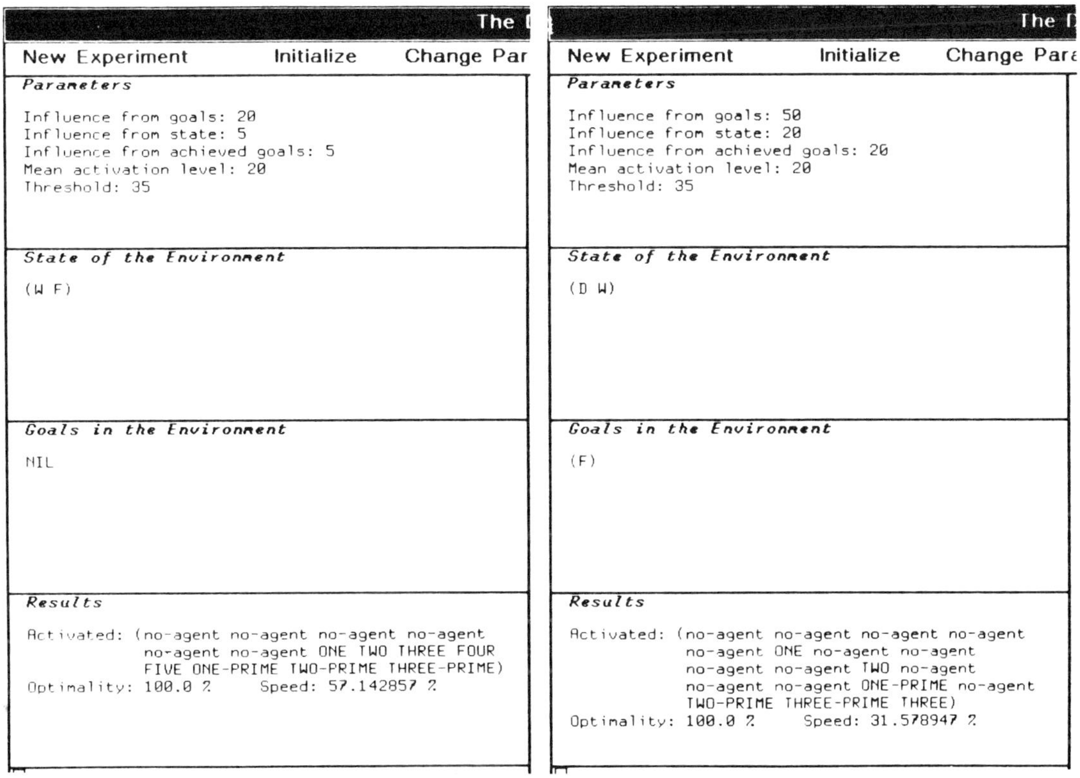

Fig. 7. The action selection behavior can be made less adaptive and more biased towards ongoing plans by choosing γ and φ relatively small in comparison with π as in the first experiment. After module *one* had been active, we added the goal *w*. Although there are less modules required to achieve this goal, the system continues working on goal *f*. In the second experiment, the system is less biased towards ongoing goals, because γ and φ are relatively high in comparison with π.

that want the board to be in the robot's hand. Or if there would be a second module which can make that condition become true, than that one will be selected (because 'pick-up-board's activation level will have been reset to 0). Serendipity is another example of this ability to adapt. If a goal or subgoal would suddenly appear to be fulfilled, the modules that contributed to this goal will no longer be activated. All of these experiments have been simulated with success. Notice that such unforeseen events do not mean that the system has to 'drop' the ongoing plan and 'build' a new one. Actually the system continuously compares the different alternatives. When some condition changes, this may have the effect that an alternative (sub-)plan becomes more attractive (more activated) than the current one.

Notice also that it is not the case that the system replans at every timestep. The 'history' of the spreading activation also plays a role in the action selection behavior since the activation levels are not reinitialized at every timestep [7]. So just as there is a tradeoff between goal-orientedness and situation-orientedness, we here have a tradeoff between adaptivity and bias towards the ongoing plan (see also next section). One can smoothly mediate among the two extremes by selecting a

---

[7] The remainings of the past spreading activation implement some sort of "state" functionality. The problem of incorrect or outdated information is solved by decaying the activation levels (diminishing the impact of past information and data on the selection of action).

particular ratio of the parameters γ and ϕ versus π (the mean level of activation).

Consider as an example the modules of *Fig. 6.* The initial observed situation is (a, x), the goal is f. After module 'one' had been active, we added w to the global goals. When γ and ϕ are relatively small in comparison with π, the internal spreading activation has more impact than the influence from the state of the environment and the global goals. The resulting action selection behavior is, therefore, less adaptive. Specifically, it means that, although for goal w the path from situation to goals is shorter, the system continues working on goal f, and only after f is achieved, starts working on goal w (cf. *Fig. 7*). Again the appropriate solution lies somewhere in the middle. The parameters should be chosen such that the system does not jump between different goals all the time, but that it does exploit opportunities and adapts to changing situations.

Notice finally that the algorithm also exhibits another type of adaptivity, namely *fault tolerance*. This is a consequence of the distributed nature of the algorithm. Since no one of the modules is more important than the others, the networks are still able to perform under degraded preconditions. It is possible to delete competence modules and the network still does whatever is within its remaining capabilities.

4.5. Bias to Ongoing Plans

The algorithm demonstrates an implicit bias mechanism. It favors modules that contribute to the ongoing goal and subgoals except when there is enough urge to start working on something different. The main reason bias is exhibited is that the activation levels are not reinitialized every time a module is activated. As a consequence, the history of past activation spreading plays a role in the selection of action, in particular when the effect of the situation and goals is relatively small in comparison with the mean activation level. But

even if that is not the case, the algorithm exhibits bias towards ongoing plans. More specifically, it demonstrates two types of bias: horizontal and vertical.

1. *Horizontal Bias*
    A first type of bias demonstrated by the action selection algorithm is the favoring of actions that contribute to the current goal (the goal on which it was working before). Consider the set of modules in *Fig. 8* and an initial situation $S(0) = (a, x)$, and global goals $G(0) = (f, r)$. One to five are the competence modules necessary to achieve goal f, while one' to five' are the modules that contribute to goal r.
    When simulated this network does not jump back and forth between modules that contribute to f and modules that contribute to r. Instead, it starts working on one goal, completes it and then works on the other goal (cf. *Fig. 9*). This is the case, because when either module one or one' is chosen, the distance of that path to the goals is shorter than that of the other path. Therefore, the spreading of activation backwards has a larger effect and makes sure that the started path is finished first. As the paths from current situation to goals grow longer, the threshold has to be increased to obtain this effect (more on the effect of the threshold in the next section).

2. *Vertical Bias*
    A second type of bias is the favoring of actions that contribute to a 'brother' goal (a subgoal of the same overall goal). Consider the modules in *Fig. 10*. The initial state of the environment is $S(0) = (a1, c1, e1, g1, a2, c2, e2, g2)$, the goals are $G(0) = (k1, k2)$.
    Again, if the threshold is high enough, this network first executes all the actions that contribute to one of the two global goals and then starts working on the second one (cf. *Fig. 11*). The reason is that once a predecessor of a module has been active, the node itself receives more activation energy from the state of the

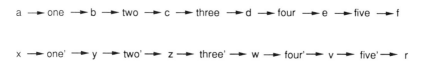

Fig. 8. A toy network to test horizontal bias.

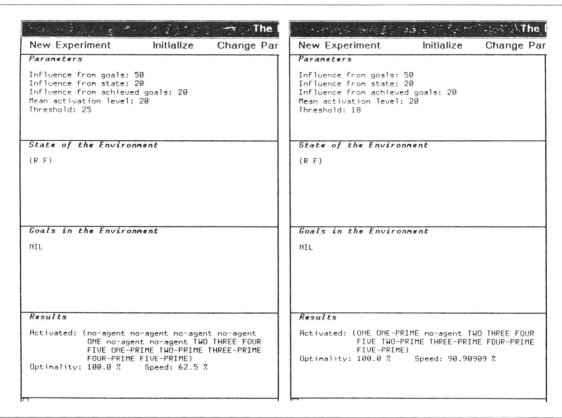

Fig. 9. When the threshold is high enough, the action selection behavior exhibits a horizontal bias (left-hand experiment). When the threshold is not high enough, the system jumps between modules contributing to one goal and modules contributing to the second goal (right hand experiment).

environment. Therefore, it has more activation to spread to its remaining predecessors.

As already stated in the previous section, the

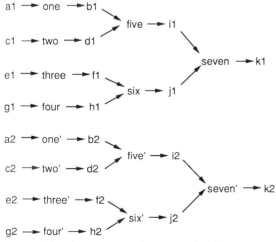

Fig. 10. A toy network to test vertical bias.

system can be given a higher or lesser degree of 'inertia' with respect to the changing environment and goals by selecting the ratio of the global parameters appropriately. Especially in very dynamic environments, it might be necessary to make the system adapt slower, otherwise, it might never get anything done.

4.6. Avoiding Goal Conflicts

A bad ordering of actions can dramatically increase the number of actions necessary to achieve a goal, or even prevent a solution from ever being found. Any action selection algorithm should, therefore, to some degree be able to arbitrate among conflicting actions. Our algorithm is able to do so because of inhibition rules. The modules in a network that undo a protected goal are weakened by a factor of δ. If δ is large enough (in

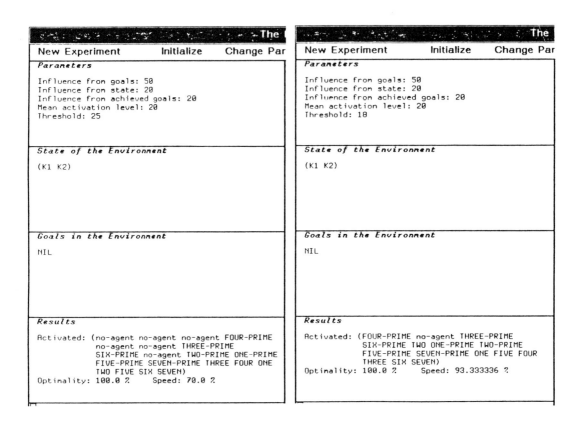

Fig. 11. When the threshold is high enough, the action selection behavior exhibits vertical bias (left-hand experiment). When the threshold is not high enough, the system jumps between modules contributing to the first goal and modules contributing to the second goal (right hand experiment).

particular in relation to γ and ϕ), this results in an action selection that protects global goals.

The same is true for subgoals (or preconditions of modules). Every module decreases the activation level of modules that undo its true conditions. Again, this results in an action selection behavior

Fig. 12. A classical conflicting goals example. The initial observed situation is $S(0) = (clear\text{-}a, clear\text{-}b, a\text{-}on\text{-}c)$, the goals are $G(0) = (a\text{-}on\text{-}b, b\text{-}on\text{-}c)$. The system should first achieve the goal b-on-c and then the goal a-on-b. It is tempted however to immediately stack a onto b, which may bring it in a deadlock situation (not wanting to undo the already achieved goal).

in which 'subgoals' are protected and, thereby, goal conflicts are avoided. To illustrate how this happens, we reimplemented a classical anomalous situation example from the blocks world [21]. *Fig. 12* illustrates the problem. *Fig. 13* shows some of the competence modules involved in this example.

```
(defmodule stack-a-on-b
  :condition-list '(clear-a clear-b)
  :add-list '(a-on-b clear-c)
  :delete-list '(clear-b a-on-c))
(defmodule stack-b-on-c
  :condition-list '(clear-c clear-b)
  :add-list '(b-on-c clear-a)
  :delete-list '(clear-c b-on-a))
(defmodule take-a-from-c
  :condition-list '(clear-a a-on-c)
  :add-list '(clear-c)
  :delete-list '(a-on-c))
```

Fig. 13. Some of the modules involved in the blocks world domain.

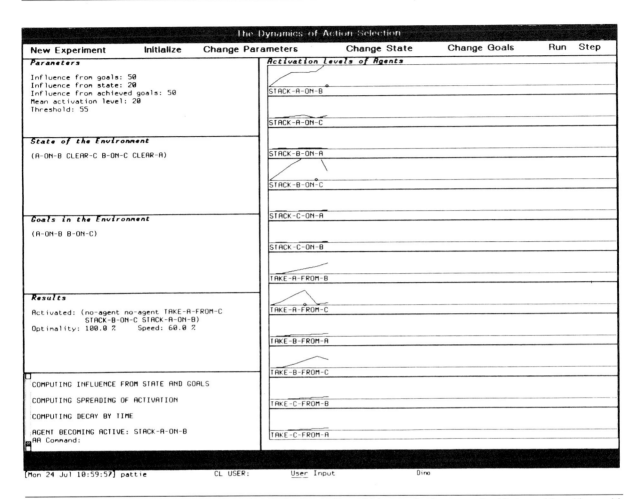

Fig. 14. When the influence from protected goals and the threshold are high enough, the system is able to avoid problems with conflicting goals.

Fig. 14 and *15* show the results obtained. In the first experiment δ has the same value as γ which is far greater than ϕ. The result is that the inhibition of 'stack-a-on-b' by 'stack-b-on-c' for condition 'clear-b' is far more important than its activation by the current situation. Because of this, the module 'take-a-from-b' dominates over 'stack-a-on-b', despite the fact that the latter one achieves a goal. If δ is not high enough (as in the second experiment), the urge to fulfill the goal 'a-on-b' dominates over the urge to avoid 'clear-b', so that the system does start by stacking a on b. It is however still able to restore the situation and obtain the two goals, since the influence from the protected goals is not high enough to keep the

system from undoing the achieved goal 'a-on-b'. Again, a balance has to be found between not caring about goal conflicts at all and being so rigid as to never undo an achieved (sub-) goal, thereby risking deadlocks.

4.7. Thoughtfulness

A network only looks ahead in a local neighborhood (in time) which is determined by the threshold θ. The behavior can be made more or less *thoughtful* by increasing the threshold θ. This makes the spreading activation process go on for a longer time before a specific action is selected. As such, it allows the network to look ahead further,

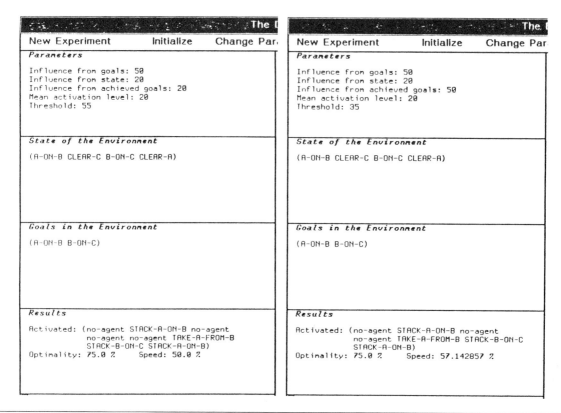

Fig. 15. In both these experiments the system reacts opportunistically, not taking into account conflicting goals. In the first experiment, the parameter γ is low, so that the system is not very sensitive to goal-conflicts. In the second experiment, the threshold is not high enough, so that the system chooses a local maximum.

thereby avoiding local maxima (in time) of activation levels. For example, in the blocks-world example above, the module 'stack-a-on-b' initially has the highest activation level (since it receives direct input from both the current situation and the goals). The threshold has to be put high enough to avoid that this module is chosen right away, so that the network can go on taking into account the conflicts among modules.

Ideally, we would like to set the threshold to a very high value (for example, equal to the total activation of the whole network). This would guarantee that the spreading activation process goes on long enough so that the 'optimal' action can be selected. The problems with putting the threshold high are first, that the action selection process would require too much time (especially for an agent operating in a rapidly changing environment) and second, that the result would be

that the agent would get bogged down trying to take into account the effects of actions it might take in the far future. This is most probably a wasted effort in an unpredictable environment. Therefore, we do want the agent only to look ahead to the near future. The desired amount of looking ahead for a particular application can be obtained by choosing a proper value for the threshold.

4.8. Speed

The counterpart of thoughtfulness is speed. The action selection behavior can be made *faster* by varying the threshold θ as explained above. The resulting action selection is however less 'thoughtful', which means that it is less goal-oriented, less situation-oriented, that it takes conflicting goals less into account and that it is less biased towards ongoing plans. Nevertheless, it may sometimes be important to react fast or it may be a wasted effort to be very thoughtful (i.e. make a lot of plans and predictions). Fortunately, the algorithm is not complex, so that it allows speed to be obtained without sacrificing too much thoughtfulness.

5. Discussion

5.1. Complexity of the Algorithm

The algorithm performs some sort of computation bearing similarities with search processes, so one could wonder whether it suffers from the same problems as traditional AI search. More specifically, that the efficiency necessarily goes down as the number of modules involved in a plan grows (the so-called 'combinatorial explosion' problem). The following arguments make us believe that we will not run into this problem:

- The computation the algorithm performs is much less costly. Actually, it resembles marker passing algorithms more than the AI notion of search. The maximum number of steps the system takes to select one action is bounded by the "width" of the network (distance from executable modules to goal-achieving modules) multiplied by some linear function of the threshold. The system does not construct a search tree, nor does it maintain a current hypothetical state and partial plan. In addition, it evaluates different paths in parallel, so that it does not have to start from scratch when one path does not produce a solution, but smoothly moves from one plan to another.
- The system does not 'replan' completely at every timestep. The algorithm does not reinitialize the activation-levels to zero whenever an action has been taken. This implies that it may take some time to select the first action to execute, but from then on, the network is biased towards that particular situation and set of goals. This means that it will take much less time for the following actions to be selected, in particular when little has changed in the meantime with respect to the goals or current situation.
- We believe that for real autonomous agents (e.g. mobile robots) the networks will grow "de-

eper" instead of "wider", because typically, the agent will have more tasks/goals instead of having tasks/goals that require more actions to be taken (and therefore more 'planning'). Also, large subparts may exist in the network that appear to be unconnected. As a result, the efficiency of the system will not be affected so much. Even if some paths from situation matchers to goal achievers would be very long, the system would still come up with an action because it does not await a convergence in the activation levels and decreases the threshold with time. The selected action might, however, be non-optimal.
- The same simple spreading activation rules are applied to each of the modules. In addition, there are only local, fixed links among modules. This opens interesting opportunities for a parallel implementation, which would imply a considerable speed up.

5.2. The Issue of Variables

The algorithm does not incorporate classical variables and variable-passing. As a matter of fact, a lot of its advantages would disappear if they would be introduced. For example, one reason a lot of search is eliminated is exactly because there are no variables in the algorithm. A first implication of the absence of variables is that one cannot specify goals using variables (e.g. goto-location(x, y)). A second implication is that all modules/operators of the domain have to be instantiated beforehand.

We try to avoid the need for variables altogether by using *deictic representation*, i.e. using only *indexical-functional aspects* to describe relevant properties of the immediate environment [2,1]: objects in the environment are internally represented relative to the purposes and circumstances of the agent. The module 'spray-paint-self' for example only has to be instantiated with one parameter, namely 'the-sprayer-I-am-holding-in-my-hand'. Because of this, it is not necessary to create new operators/modules for every new object that is introduced in the world. There is no exhaustive combination of operators and objects.

The idea of indexical-functional aspects is particularly interesting for autonomous agents because it makes more realistic assumptions about what perception can deliver. In particular, it does not demand that the perceptual system produces the identity and exact location of objects. The absence of variables does constrain the language one can use to communicate with the system, but not in a too strong way. All it requires is a new way of thinking about how to tell an agent what to do. More specifically, one does not use unique names of objects when specifying goals. Instead, goals are specified in terms of indexical or functional constraints on the objects involved. For example, one would not tell the agent to go to location (x, y), but one would tell the agent that the goal is to be in a location that is a doorway (a small area where it is able to 'go through' a wall).

Nevertheless, it is not necessarily impossible to incorporate variables into the current algorithm. For example, a copy of a competence module could be created every time we have to instantiate that module with a different set of variable values. This would, however, require more machinery than there is now. The approach we take is to see how far we can get using only indexical-functional representations. The algorithm will only be extended to full-fledged variables when we feel the need for them.

5.3. Emergent Control Flow

The main difference between the algorithm discussed in this paper and classical planning lies in the way they each organize the task of producing an action sequence. A classical planner uses a preprogrammed, sequential, centralized search process. A sequence of actions is searched for, which according to the internal model, when executed will bring the system into a goal state. Instead, in this algorithm the control structure regulating when a particular action is activated is emergent: the dynamics of interaction between the actions (modules) themselves establishes the sequence of selected actions in a completely distributed way in response to environmental conditions and to the global goals.

The same "philosophy" of emergent functionality underlying the development of individual competence modules in situated agents is applied here to the problem of dynamic control structure. The two are instances of a more general view on how to go about designing systems that have to function in a complex environment, sometimes referred to as as "bottom-up" construction [10,6,13]. The key idea is that functionality is made to emerge as a global side-effect of some intensive, local interactions among components that make up the system [8]. There are no rules or programs that specify how the functionality of the global system should be obtained. Instead, a dynamics takes place which forms structure in response to environmental conditions. Advantages of the bottom-up approach to designing complex systems are:

- The result is more natural and fluid. The reason is that in bottom-up systems a dynamics takes place that makes functionality emerge in response to environmental conditions which demand some response. Another reason is that bottom-up systems show a more continuous and dense behavior. They do not categorize the environment into discrete types of situations for which (radically) different actions are required.
- The result is more flexible. Hierarchically organized functionality is typically very inflexible. One reason is that whenever the situation or operation conditions change, this change has to be propagated from the top node through all of the abstraction layers, down to the bottom of the hierarchy, where these changes should imply a real difference. Another reason is that all of the possible situations have to be foreseen in advance, so that it can be programmed what actions the system should take in each of them. In a system relying on emergent functionality the interactions with the environment happen directly in parallel through all of the bottom level components.
- The result is more robust. Systems with emergent functionality tend to be more fault-tolerant. They are less brittle when the environments in which they operate change or when components in the system itself fail. One reason is that there is no central, critical component which makes the whole system break down when it doesn't function properly. Another reason is that if one or more of the components break down, the system shows a smooth performance degradation. And finally, these systems often have redundant components and, therefore, more

---

[8] Notice that aspects of the environment are also viewed as components of this dynamical system.

robust results. In the algorithm described above one can, for example, add new competence modules or modify existing ones or even delete existing ones. The dynamics will automatically adapt to the new situation and still do whatever is in its possibilities. In contrast, classical planners to a large degree depend on the fact that every component works perfectly.

Disadvantages of systems with emergent functionality are that the resulting behavior is less predictable, and related to this, that it is less understood how to obtain the desired global functionality.

5.4. Limits and Extensions

There are a number of limits to the algorithm as it is now. One is that loops in the action selection may emerge. They only occur very rarely and spring from the fact that the system does not maintain a history of what it did in the past. As such it might make the same "mistake" in its selection of action over and over again. It is questionable whether a solution to such impasses should be built in. The hypothesis could be adopted that in a real environment the situation and goals will change anyway after some time Δt that is very small. This changes the spreading activation patterns and, therefore, gets the network out of its impasse. If we insist on avoiding (even temporal) impasses, this cannot be guaranteed by a careful selection of the parameters. One very simple solution, however, could be to introduce some randomness in the system. Another solution might be to use a second network to monitor possible loops in the first network and take actions whenever this happens. Finally, we could implement some *habituation* mechanism for some or all of the modules. This mechanism would take care that every time a module is activated, it is less likely to become active in the future (i.e. have local thresholds that vary over time).

Another problem is that it is not clear how, given a specific application, one can select values for the global parameters that produce the desired action selection behavior. The parameters to a large degree determine the effectiveness and characteristics of the action selection behavior. They are problem dependent, not only because every problem area requires different degrees of goal-orientedness, situation-orientedness, speed, adap-

tivity, etc. But also because the size and structure of the network also determines these characteristics. For example, in an application with a very big network, the threshold has to be put higher to obtain the same results. At the moment we hand-tune the parameters during a series of experiments. We plan to automate this task by building a second network of competence modules that would look at the results of the first one and tune its parameters so as to obtain the action selection characteristics specified by the user.

Finally, other extensions to the current theory seem useful and are a topic of current research. One is the introduction of parallelism in the action selection, another is the introduction of action selection on different abstraction levels. Yet another deals with more realistic, possibly noisy, sensor data. The solutions being developed resonate with the current philosophy and the merits it has.

6. Conclusions

We argued that neither classical planning, nor the currently popular situated activity systems provide a satisfying solution to the problem of action selection for an autonomous agent. We presented a new approach to the problem which combines the "aesthetics" of the latter, such as distributedness, physical grounding, and interaction, with the former's general capability of handling goals.

Acknowledgements

Paul Viola, Ian Horswill, Rod Brooks and Jeff Inman proofread an earlier version of this paper and provided valuable comments. Supported by Siemens with additional support from the University Research Initiative under Office of Naval Research contract N00014-86-K-0685, and the Defense Advanced Research Projects Agency under Office of Naval Research contract N00014-85-K-0124. The author is a research associate of the Belgian National Science Foundation. She currently holds a position as visiting professor at the M.I.T. Artificial Intelligence Laboratory.

References

[1] P. Agre, and D. Chapman, Pengi: An implementation of a theory of activity, *Proceedings of the Sixth National Conference on Artificial Intelligence, AAAI-87* (Morgan Kaufmann, Los Altos, California, 1987).

[2] P. Agre, The dynamic structure of everyday life, MIT Artificial Intelligence Laboratory, Technical Report 1085 (1989).

[3] R. Brooks, A robust layered control system for a mobile robot, IEEE J. Robotics and Automation, RA-2 (1) (1986).

[4] R. Brooks, Elephants don't play chess, this volume.

[5] M. Georgeff, Planning, *Annual Review Computer Sci.*, 2 (1987) 359-400 (Annual Reviews Inc, Palo Alto, California).

[6] D. Hillis, Intelligence as emergent behavior; or, The songs of Eden, in: *The Artificial Intelligence Debate; False Starts, Real Foundations* (MIT Press, 1988).

[7] B. Huberman, and T. Hogg, Phase transitions in artificial intelligence systems, *AI-Journal* 23 (2) (1987).

[8] L. Kaelbling, An architecture for intelligent reactive systems, *Reasoning about Actions and Plans: Proceedings of the 1986 Workshop* (Morgan Kaufmann, Los Altos, California, 1987).

[9] L. Kaelbling, Goals as parallel program specifications, *Proceedings of the Seventh National Conference on Artificial Intelligence*, Minneapolis-St. Paul, Minnesota (1988).

[10] C. Langton, Artificial Life (Addison Wesley, 1989).

[11] P. Maes, The dynamics of action selection, *Proceedings of the IJCAI-89 Conference*, Detroit (1989).

[12] P. Maes, How to do the right thing, *Connection Science J.*, special issue on Hybrid Systems, 1(3) (February 1990). Also MIT AILAB Memo 1180.

[13] M. Minsky, *The Society of the Mind* (Simon and Schuster, New York, 1986).

[14] N. Nilsson, Action Networks, *Proceedings of the Rochester Planning Workshop: From Formal Systems to Practical Systems*, J. Tenenberg, et al. (eds.), University of Rochester, New York (1989).

[15] S. Rosenschein, and L. Kaelbling, The synthesis of digital machines with provable epistemic properties, in J.F. Halpern (ed.), *Proceedings of the 1986 Conference on Theoretical Aspects of Reasoning about Knowledge* (Morgan-Kaufmann, Los Altos, California, 1987).

[16] S. Rosenschein, and L. Kaelbling, Acting and planning in autonomous agents, this volume.

[17] J. Sanborn, and J. Hendler, A model of reaction for planning in dynamic environments, *Internat. J. AI in Engineering* (1988). Special Issue on Planning.

[18] M. Schoppers, Universal plans for reactive robots in unpredictable environments, *Proceedings of IJCAI-87*, Milan, Italy (1987).

[19] L. Steels, Connectionist problem solving, an AI perspective, in: *Connectionism in Perspective*, R. Pfeiffer, Z. Schreter, F. Fogelman and L. Steels (Elsevier Science Publishers, Amsterdam, 1989).

[20] L. Steels, Cooperation between distributed agents through self-organization, *Proceedings of the workshop on Multi-Agent Cooperation*, Cambridge, U (August 1989) (Elsevier Science Publ., Amsterdam) in press.

[21] G. Sussman, *A Computer Model of Skill Acquisition* (Elsevier Science Publ., New York, 1975).

[22] Z.W. Pylyshyn (ed.), *The Robot's Dilemma. The Frame Problem in Artificial Intelligence* (Ablex Publishing Corp. Norwood, New Jersey, 1987).

Exploiting Analogical Representations

Luc Steels

VUB AI Lab, Pleinlaan 2, 1050 Brussels, Belgium

The paper discusses the use of internal models for autonomous agents. It proposes to use analogical instead of symbolic representations and to annotate these representations dynamically with markers and structures that emerge by the parallel local activity of simple computational agents. Two experiments illustrate the ideas of the paper: one in hand-eye coordination and one in the acquisition of a world map by a wandering mobile robot.

Keywords: Analogical representations; Emergent functionality.

Luc Steels studied at the University of Antwerp and the Massachusetts Institute of Technology. He was formerly associated with the Schlumberger-Doll Research Laboratory where his prime interest was in geological expert systems. At present Steels is professor of computer science and artificial intelligence at the Free University of Brussels and director of the AI laboratory. His publications include several books and numerous articles.

North-Holland
Robotics and Autonomous Systems 6 (1990) 71–88

1. Introduction

There is a trend in research on sensorimotor systems to downplay the role of internal representations, even going so far as to eliminate them altogether [1]. This has lead to purely reactive systems which work immediately on the output of sensors and have a direct mapping between sensors and effectors. Such reactive systems constitute a healthy change from earlier AI research that was heavily based on highly complex symbolic models, such as geometrical models of the objects in the work space [8], mechanics models of effectors [9], or logical models of actions to allow planning [4]. The change is healthy for the following reasons:

● It was often not clear how enough information could be extracted in real time from sensors to build up or maintain the assumed symbolic models. Despite enormous efforts to extract general purpose symbolic descriptions from visual data (see e.g. [11]), no such "vision module" is expected to arrive soon, and some leading vision researchers have expressed doubts whether this will ever be possible ([20]).

● A model is always approximate to reality. This means that there will always be aspects that are not fully covered by the model. For example, even in simple mechanical manipulations, there are unpredictabilities due to friction, irregularities of the objects, small deviations in the execution of an action by an effector, etc. This makes systems relying on these models occasionally unrealistic and always brittle (see the discussion in [10]).

● It is assumed that the human designer constructs the models. Although this is often done with great ingenuity, such a design is necessarily based on what the designer believes the task will be and what the environment is going to look like. This makes model-based systems inflexible and brittle. As soon as there are situations that were not foreseen by the designer they will break down.

On the other hand the 'reactive systems movement' in its extreme form may have gone too far as well. Autonomous agents without internal models will always be severely limited. For example, if

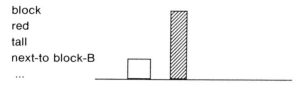

block
red
tall
next-to block-B
...

Fig. 1. (a) categorial representation. (b) analogical representa-tion.

a goal can only be represented by fixating on an object in the external world, then the goal will be lost as soon as this object is not directly perceivable, as would be the case if there is temporarily an obstacle that obscures the view. It is also obvious that agents may occasionally want to check out the consequences of an action in an internal model before actually doing the action. After all this is the essence of planning. An autonomous agent without internal representations can therefore not plan, it can at best select from its existing repertoire of actions the one that is most appropriate in a particular circumstance.

In this paper we propose a number of ideas that try to save the advantages of reactive systems while reintroducing the power of internal representations. The first idea is to have internal representations that are similar and close to sensor outputs, i.e. analogical representations [17,14]. Next we will propose to have non-symbolic operators directly over these representations. These operators are themselves built up from more primitive reaction-diffusion operations. They create dynamic structures over analogical representations such as gradient fields, or waves. These structures then yield additional information which can be used by the agent to decide what an appropriate action will be. The decision is implemented by an internal sensor linked to an effector, just like reactive systems link directly external sensors to effectors. Steels [18] is a preliminary report on the present research. It contains also other examples of the approach.

The structure of this paper is as follows. The first sections develop the ideas further. We explain the difference between analogical and categorial representations (2), describe the operations over analogical representations (3), and introduce a general computational architecture to implement systems this way (4). Then we describe two experi-

ments that were implemented to illustrate and explore the ideas. The first experiment (5) concerns an autonomous agent that learns about the location of food sources in its environment. The second experiment (6) is from the domain of hand-eye coordination. Some conclusions (7) end the paper.

2. Analogical vs. Categorial Representations

Symbolic or categorial representations are based on a categorisation of reality. A category is an invariant property of a set of objects. It can be given a name and represented internally by a pointer. Given a repertoire of categories we can then describe a particular situation and deduce more information from it using logical inference or some other deductive mechanism [1]. For example, a block A on a table could be described using a set of categories like block, tall, next-to block-B (*Fig. 1*).

In contrast, an analogical representation represents a situation without prior categorisation. The extreme form of an analogical representation is reality itself or a picture of it. Mostly the representation is however a transformation of the original. A typical example is a spatial map in which the positions of objects are represented by locations on a map rather than coordinate descriptions or descriptions relative to the position of other objects as in "next to". Another example is a tactile or somatosensory map in which the location of a tactile stimulus is represented as a spot on a map. *Fig. 2* (from [3]) displays the areas on the hand of a monkey and the corresponding tactile map. This example illustrates that maps are also used in biological sensori-motor systems.

Analogical representations can be built for any kind of sensory information: a frequency map, a sonar map, a "smell" map, a colour map. They can also be a filtered version of that information

---

[1] Most neural networks, particularly perceptron-like networks [16] also work with categorial representations, even if they are not coded in terms of explicit symbols but in terms of patterns of activation over a collection of units. The major difference between connectionist representations and symbolic ones is that categories cannot be accessed from a distance through pointers or names.

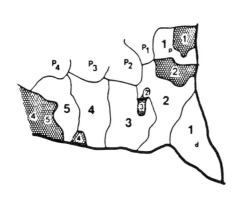 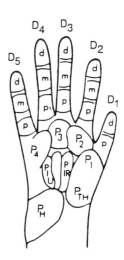

Fig. 2. Sensory map of hand in monkey.

while still preserving the implicit relationship to the underlying reality, as in a contour map (*Fig. 3*) which only represents contours of the objects, or a map of free space which can be computed by taking the inverse of an obstacle map. Analogical representations can also take the form of annotations of maps. For example, we could put a token in a particular position on a spatial map to indicate a goal location. This is already a mixture of purely analogical representations (like pictures) and categorial representations because it involves a category namely "this is a goal location". The representations that we will use are mostly of this mixed type.

We will implement analogical representations by markers put on a grid. The markers form a set M of numerical quantities. The grid $G = I \times J$

CONTOUR VALUE

Fig. 3. Contour map.

consists of a set of regularly connected cells C. Each cell $c \in C$ has a position $pos(c) = \langle i, j \rangle \in I \times J$ and an associated set of markers $markers(c) \subset M$. For example, to represent a contour map we use contour-markers. The cells which are located on the contour have a positive value for this marker. Those which do not have a zero value. Most markers are a continuously varying quantity. For example a gradient field is represented by a marker in each cell which has a varying degree of strength.

Analogical representations have a number of advantages compared to categorial representations:

- They do not assume a complex interpretation process to transform sensory data into a symbolic representation. Often analogical representations can be derived in quasi real-time from sensors.
- They contain more precision than categorial representations. For example, if we say that a block is tall we do not know how tall it really is, whereas if we represent length in an analogical way, a precise but relative indication of the length is retained in the representation.
- An analogical representation can easily be mapped onto an "active" memory, i.e. the processing array of a data-level parallel computer. Operations over analogical representations can therefore be executed in parallel

Fig. 4. Experimental setup containing camera mounted on arm and lightsource.

which may sometimes radically change their computational complexity.

- The most important advantage however is that this kind of representations makes it possible to use quite different operations during problem solving. This topic is discussed in more detail in the next section.

3. Operations

In a purely symbolic approach, sensory interpretation, planning, action selection, and motor control take place by performing manipulations of symbolic structures. Analogical representations require a different approach. What we propose is to create various spatio-temporal structures which can then be used by other processes to make decisions. We could for example create a gradient field and let decisions on where to go next be guided by this field (see also [15]). These decisions are based on the output of internal sensors over the analogical representations just as in reactive systems decisions are based on the output of external sensors.

The following simple experiment illustrates the idea. [2] The experiment is an instance of the tracking problem, i.e. the problem of executing a body-action to align yourself to a sensory stimulus or follow it. It is operationalized in an experimental setup where a camera is mounted on a robot-arm (*Fig. 4*). A sensory stimulus in the form of a lightsource is presented within the field of view of the camera. The camera's focal point is equal to the center position of this field. The camera should turn so that the center of the lightsource is equal to this focal point. To simplify the exposition we assume that the camera has 2 degrees of freedom: left-right and up-down.

Here is a solution to this problem along the lines advocated in this paper. We use an analogical representation of the lightsource in the form of a filled circle of lightsource-markers (*Fig. 5b*) Our experiments have shown that this representation can be derived virtually in real time from the camera by introducing a simple intensity filter

---

[2] All the experiments discussed in this paper have been implemented.

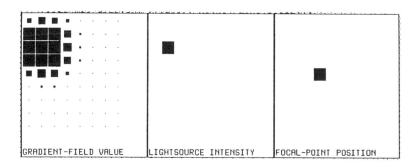

Fig. 5. (a) Gradient from diffusion. (b) Lightsource. (c) Focal point.

which translates points of high intensity to lightsource markers. Next we project onto that an analogical representation of the focal point of the camera. This representation is a focal point marker in the cell on the grid where the focal point is located. The point is fixed. It is located in the middle of the grid (*Fig 5c*).

The tracking problem is then solved by establishing a gradient field emanating from the lightsource (*Fig. 5a*). This gradient field is represented by markers which have a strength equal to the strength of the field at the point where the marker is located. Hence the marker diminishes in strength as the distance to the lightsource increases. An internal sensor attached to the cell containing the focal point marker measures what the direction of highest gradient is in the neighbourhood of this cell. This measurement is directly connected to the instructions controlling the arm. For example, if the highest gradient is north of the cell containing the focal point, then the arm will move up. The speed of arm movement can be linked to the quantity of gradient-marker so that the arm moves quickly when far from the lightsource and slows down when it is close to it.

We have implemented in our laboratory the tracking problem this way. The resulting system performs in quasi real-time with considerable robustness and flexibility. The lightsource can be moved when the arm is already under way. The size or shape of the lightsource does not really matter. There is no training or adaptation involved as would be the case if a categorization would have to be learned first (as in the neural net approach of the same problem discussed in [7]). Moreover everything is very dynamic. The relationship between the focal point and the lightsource changes dynamically as the camera moves. This dynamical relation is handled smoothly without having to pauze for recategorization.

But so far this looks very much like a reactive system without internal representations. Indeed decisions take place over representations which are very close and continuously linked to sensory data. Consider therefore the problem of tracking a lightsource that blinks once and then disappears. In this case, there is no longer immediate feedback from sensors possible so that a system without internal representations would stop moving as soon as the stimulus disappears and the gradient field has died out. But given that we have an internal representation we can do things differently. We can change the relationship between the sensors and the analogical representation such that the internal representation of the lightsource does not disappear when the sensory data is no longer present. Instead it disappears, and is replaced by, a new representation when a new light source is presented to the camera.

Our approach has some similarities with the visual routines advocated by [20] or potential field approaches [6]. The major difference is that these approaches assume markers and structures that are deposited once by an algorithm that operates globally using computational geometry. Moreover they are consulted by special purpose routines which again are global. We will use instead dynamic spatio-temporal structures that emerge due to the primitive operations of diffusion of markers or reaction between markers which take place in parallel over the grid. For example, the gradient field will renew continuously by the spreading of markers out of the marker representing the lightsource. When the spot moves, the field moves along. When it dies out, the diffusion stops and the field gradually disappears. This makes our approach more adaptive. Also no central supervisor to construct or maintain the internal representations is needed and parallelism can be maximally exploited.

4. Computational Architecture

It is possible to think up many operations over analogical representations and code them in an ad hoc way. But there are clear advantages in trying to formulate a general computational architecture for implementing analogical systems. If we can find a common kernel, this can be implemented efficiently to act as the foundation of a programming language with which systems can be built in a more modular fashion. Based on the development of a wide variety of applications we have arrived at two generalizations:

- At the lowest level we use an architecture based on the idea of agents.
- At the second level we use a set of primitive operations that are inspired by the biochemical metaphor of reaction-diffusion.

Both levels are now briefly discussed.

4.1. Multi-agent Automata

Various frameworks have been developed in the past for modeling concurrent distributed systems. One example is the actor model of computation [5]. It assumes that concurrent computation can be modeled in terms of the passing of messages between computational objects called actors. Each actor has a script that specifies how it should respond to a message and a set of acquaintances which are other agents to which messages can be sent. Some of these acquaintances hold the state of the agent.

In the original actor model there is no notion of spatial distance between actors. Two actors may communicate with each other even if they are far apart, as long as they are acquaintances. Also

there is no notion of (global) time. Each actor executes its script as soon as it has all the information and it has been given the resources to do so. The model that we have adopted is similar to the actor model in many respects, except that we make actors localized both in time and in space. We call these localized actors *agents* and the resulting model a *multi-agent automaton*. Multi-agent automata can be viewed as generalizations of cellular automata [19]. They add the idea of objects with internal state and local rules.

A multi-agent automaton operates on a grid of cells $G = I \times J$. Agents are located in specific cells on this grid. An agent α is a computational entity with two components $\alpha = \langle s, b \rangle$:

- $s = \langle s_0, \ldots, s_n \rangle$ is a sequence of numerical quantities which represents the *state* of the agent.
- b is a procedure, i.e. a finite state automaton with registers. It represents the *behavior* of the agent.

The behavior defines the actions that the agent will execute. Possible actions are: to change state, to change the state of other agents, to move, or to instantiate new agents. All these actions are restricted to the immediate neighborhood of the agent which consists of the cell itself or the cells bordering immediately on the cell in which the agent is located. Thus agents can move to neighboring cells but are not allowed to jump to an arbitrary location somewhere else on the grid. They can change the state of other agents but only when those agents are located in the same cell or in a neighboring cell. In deciding which action to take, an agent may only consult its own variables or the variables of the agents in its immediate neighborhood.

The behavior of agents is not only localized in space but also in time. There is a global clock that has two phases. At the first phase the agents are executing the procedure defining their behavior. This generates a set of proposed changes. The changes are however not executed immediately. This happens at the second phase.

Given its local nature, multi-agent automata are well adapted to data-level parallelism. We have implemented a multi-agent system (MAS) to make experimentation possible. The language for defining agents is LISP-based but uses the DAP, a data-level 1000 processor machine, as target of the compiler. The language also contains abstraction

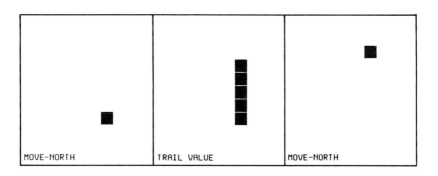

Fig. 6. Move-north agent leaving behind a trail.

facilities to make it possible to define agent types and subtypes in the style of object-oriented programming. The run-time environment includes tools for inspecting and displaying graphically the behavior of agent systems. It is used in all the experiments reported on in this paper. [3]

For example, an agent that moves north on the grid and leaves behind another agent called the trail-agent which contains a positive value for trail is defined as follows.

(def-agent move-north ()

:behavior 'move-north-behavior)

where *move-north-behavior* is defined thus:

(defun move-north-behavior (self self-x self-y)

(put-agent (trail-agent 10) self-x self-y)

(move-agent self self-x self-y

self-x (- self-y 1)))

Self, self-x, and self-y are variables referring to the agent itself, and its x and y coordinates on the grid.

(put-agent $\alpha \times y$) puts an agent α in the position x, y on the grid.

(Move-agent α old-x old-y new-x new-y) moves an agent α from a given position ⟨old-x,old-y⟩ to a new position ⟨new-x,new-y⟩.

(trail-agent 10) creates a new instance of the trail-

agent with initial trail value 10. The trail-agent is defined as follows:

(def-agent trail-agent (value)

:vars ((trail-value value)))

This agent has no behavior. It contains only a local variable called trail-value which is initiated to be value when the instance is created.

Fig. 6 contains a few snapshots of these agents in action. In *Fig 6a* a move-north agent was instantiated in a random location. *Fig. 6b-c* show how the the move-north agent has moved up the grid and how at the same time instances of the trail-agent with a particular value for trail-value have been created.

4.2. Reaction-diffusion

It is not difficult to see how agents can be used to implement analogical representations and operations over them. For example, to represent the lightsource we would have a lightsource agent that is instantiated with positive values wherever there is a high intensity of the lightsource. Internal sensors, like one detecting the highest value of a particular quantity in a nearby cell, are also implemented as agents whose behavior does the required internal sensing. What is particularly interesting is that most operations taking place over analogical representations can be classified as being of two types:

● Diffusion operations: They diffuse information over the grid. An example from the experiment described earlier is the establish-

[3] Work on the agent model was financed by ESPRIT project P440.

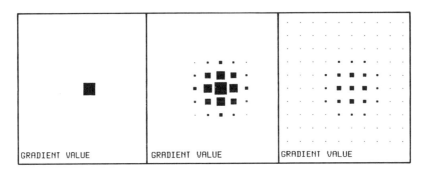

Fig. 7. Different snapshots of progressing diffusion.

ment of a gradient field out of a particular location. Another example discussed later in the paper is a wave that starts from a particular location and expands progressively over the rest of the grid.

● Reaction operations: They combine information to generate new information. An example is the creation of markers that are the source of the gradient field whenever there is a marker for the lightsource. Another example discussed later are markers representing obstacles inhibiting the diffusion of other markers that are in the process of establishing a gradient field.

This commonality makes it worthwhile to introduce a second layer of abstraction that consists of typical reaction-diffusion operations. The parallel with reaction-diffusion systems which underly most biological and chemical systems is striking and mechanisms generating spatio-temporal structures in biology form an important source of inspiration for building analogical systems. Indeed most forms of regulation and self-organization in biological systems are based on reaction-diffusion mechanisms.

Thinking in terms of reaction and diffusion makes it also possible to describe the operations over analogical representations in terms of equations, such as the following difference equation which describes simple diffusion of m with a mass transfer coefficient $k \leq 1/9$ [2].

$$m(t, \langle x, y \rangle) = \sum_{i \in N} km(t - 1, i) + m(t - 1, \langle x, y \rangle)$$
$$- 8km(t - 1, \langle x, y \rangle)$$

N is the set of pairs $\langle i, j \rangle$ which are immediate neighbors of a cell c with position $pos(c) = \langle x, y \rangle$. Such general equations can be readily translated into the behavior of agents. For example, we could construct a gradient field by having gradient-field agents instantiated in every cell which have a value indicating the strength of the field in that cell. This strength is stored in a value variable initialized to be 0:

```
(def-agent gradient-field ()
    :vars ((value 0))
    :behavior 'diffusion)
```

The behavior of this agent is defined by the following function:

```
(defun diffusion (self self-x self-y)
 (let
   ((influx
     (apply '+
       (mapcar
          #'(lambda (neighbor)
              (* *diffusion-constant*
                (find-one-var 'gradient-value
                  'value
                  (+ (car neighbor) self-x)
                  (+ (cadr neighbor) self-y)))))
       *neighbors*)))
    (remainder
      (- (my 'value)
        (* 8 *diffusion-constant* (my 'value)))))
   (add-var self 'value
      (- (+ influx remainder)
        (my 'value)))))
```

This code illustrates typical actions of an agent: (my x) fetches the value of the variable x in the agent bound to self, (add-var v q) proposes the addition of a certain quantity q to the variable v of the self agent,

(find-one-var α v x y) retrieves the value of a particular variable v in a neighboring agent of type α located in the cell x, y.

When this gradient field is instantiated in all cells of the grid and one of them is given a positive quantity for the variable value then there will be a positive quantity for the marker spreading out like a drop of ink on the grid. This is illustrated in *Fig. 7.*

Operations like diffusion, inhibition, decay, or wave formation, have been brought together in a reaction-diffusion library called RDL which runs on top of MAS. Experiments can now be implemented more easily by instantiating elements from this library. *Fig. 8* illustrates for example the formation of a wave by wave agents instantiated in every cell of the grid.

5. Acquiring a Map

We now discuss two experiments to illustrate the ideas put forward in this paper. The first experiment involves a simple mobile robot wandering around in an environment in which there are a set of objects. Some of the objects contain food of a particular type. The robot does not know the environment when it starts out. After exploring the environment it should recall where food sources are and go towards them. The objects as well as the associated types of food may change their location dynamically. We assume a simple autonomous robot that has a set of behaviors possibly coupled in a subsumption architecture [1,12] describes a physical robot for a similar experiment.

This is clearly an experiment where an internal model of the world is necessary. The representation that will be used is in the form of an analogical map. On this map obstacles as well as food sources are indicated using markers. Various reaction-diffusion operations will be executed over this map in order to find out how to get to the food. For the sake of the experiment it is assumed that the robot knows where it is, i.e. that it can relate its current position to a point on its internal map.

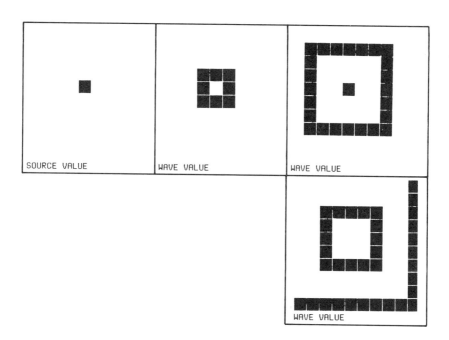

Fig. 8. Waves emerging when wave agent is given positive value.

We have done the experiment through a software simulation. This meant that both the internals of the robot and the world had to be simulated. The world is simulated with agents representing the objects. They are called world-object agents. These world-object agents have an associated food type and may suddenly change position in a random fashion with a probability of 1/100.

```
(def-agent world-object (food-type)
  :vars ((food food-type))
  :behavior
  #'(lambda (self self-x self-y)
      (if (one-out-of 100)
          (move-agent self
            self-x self-y
            (+ self-x (random-between -1 1))
            (+ self-y (random-between -1 1)))))))
```

The external aspects of the robot (such as its position in the world) are modeled by a robot agent that moves around on the grid in a random fashion:

```
(def-agent robot ()
  :vars ((goal 0))
  :behavior
  'robot-behavior)
```

The internal map of the robot is implemented as an analogical representation isomorphic to the external world. It consists of map-object agents which also have an associated food type:

```
(def-agent map-object (food-type)
  :vars ((food food-type)))
```

Let us first investigate how this internal map is built up and then turn to how the map is used.

Wandering Behavior

The first behavior of the robot is to wander around in a random fashion. To make the robot more efficient a trail is left behind in the internal map. The trail is in the form of a location agent which has a variable called explored. The robot avoids locations that it thinks were already visited, although this is not always possible, for example, if it has worked itself into a corner. The trail progressively decays so that spots that were visited

a while ago may be revisited again. This ensures that exploration continues so that changes in the world are detected. The definition of the location agent implementing the trail is as follows:

```
(def-agent location ()
  :vars ((explored 10))
  :behavior
  #'(lambda (self self-x self-y)
      (decay self 'explored)))
```

The behavior of the robot so far is defined as follows:

```
(defun robot-behavior (self self-x self-y)
  ; remembering where you have been
  (let
    ((location (find-one-agent 'location self-x self-y)))
    (if
      location
      (add-var location 'explored 10)
      (put-agent (location) self-x self-y)))
  ; deciding where to go next
  (let
    ((neighbors
        (collect-unexplored-neighbors
          *neighbors* self-x self-y)))
    (if
      (null neighbors)
      ; all of them explored so move to random
location
      (move-agent self self-x self-y
              (random-point self-x)
              (random-point self-y))
      ; otherwise select randomly out of non-explored
      (let
        ((new-location
            (nth (random (length neighbors))
              neighbors)))
        (move-agent self self-x self-y
                (+ (delta-x new-location) self-x)
                (+ (delta-y new-location) self-y))))))
```

Map Building Behavior

There are two possibilities: either the robot stands above an object or it stands above empty space.

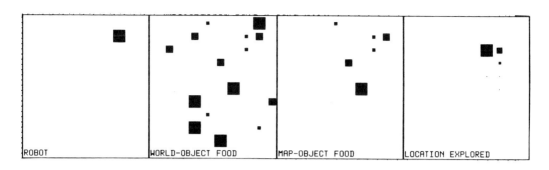

Fig. 9. Gradually acquiring a world map.

1. When the robot stands above an object, i.e. when there is a real world object at the location where the robot finds itself, the following actions take place:

● If no object was expected, the robot updates its internal world map by instantiating a new object at this location. If the world object contains a certain type of food, this instance is given the same food type.

● If an object was expected the robot checks whether the object is still there and has the same food type. If this is not the case the internal world model is updated.

2. When the robot does not stand above an object the following actions take place:

● If no object was expected, no change to the internal map is needed.

● If an object was expected, this object is removed from the internal world map.

Executing this behavior gradually leads to the construction and possibly updating of an internal world map. *Fig. 9* shows a state where six objects

have already been incorporated in the internal world map. The trail is given in the window location explored.

We now add an additional behavior to the robot to create an internal desire for a particular type of food. This desire is stored as an additional variable in the state of the robot. Once the robot has a desire it wants to go as quickly as possible to a particular location where it suspects food of a certain type to be available. Our strategy will be to create spatio-temporal structures on the analogical representation that can be used to derive the required information. Two structures are needed: one to find out where food of a certain type is located on the map, and one to help go towards the location of the food.

Waves

Waves with a fixed wave-length will be used to solve the first problem because waves are a way to communicate specific information from a given location to all other agents on the grid. It is like a

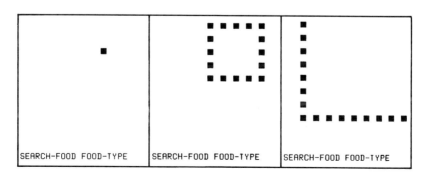

Fig. 10. Propagation of wave over the grid.

general broadcast but given the local nature of the agents it takes time. When the robot wants a particular type of food, a wave is created emanating from the current position of the robot. The wave has a particular wave length which is equal to the type of food that is wanted. The wave emerges in search-food agents which are instances of the generic RDL wave agent. The wave-length is called food-type. This is illustrated in *Fig. 10*. The robot has generated a desire for a particular food type in *Fig. 10a*. This is propagated as a wave over the grid (*Fig. 10b-c*).

The Gradient Field

The second problem can be solved using a gradient field. This gradient field starts from the position of an object with the desired food type and propagates over the grid. An internal sensor is incorporated in the robot that allows it to detect the direction of highest gradient and this sensor is coupled to the decision where to go next. We call this gradient field the pull-field because it metaphorically pulls the robot to the food source. Pull-field creation starts when a map-object senses that a wave is passing through which has a wave length equal to the food type that it stores.

```
(def-agent map-object (food-type)
  :vars ((food food-type))
  :behavior 'map-object-behavior)

(defun map-object-behavior (self self-x self-y)
  (let
    ((food-wanted
       (read-var-agent
         'search-food 'food-type self-x self-y)))
    (if
      (and food-wanted
           (= food-wanted (my 'food)))
```

```
(add-var (find-one-agent 'pull-field self-x
    self-y)
    'value
    1000))))
```

The gradient field itself is created with the diffusion mechanisms discussed earlier on. All this is illustrated in *Fig. 11*. A gradient field emanates from the location where the robot thinks the food it wants was located. This field attracts the robot to the food source.

The different behaviors (map-guided behavior, wandering behavior, and map-building behavior) are coupled as follows:

1. As long as there is no gradient field wandering continues. This is necessary because no food location may be known yet or the food may no longer be at the desired location in which case exploration must continue until food of the assumed type is found.

2. Map-guided behavior overrides the wandering behavior if there is a gradient field.

3. Map building behavior continues all the time because the robot might encounter objects on the way that it did not yet know about and it therefore may have to update its map.

This experiment illustrates several of the principles of this paper:

1. Global functionality emerges by the parallel interaction of local behaviors. This is true for the world itself of course, but also for the robot behaviors and for the formation of the internal representations and their usage.

2. Analogical representations play a key role. Although there are some symbolic elements (such as the type of food), the location of the objects is encoded in an analogical way and this representation is exploited for solving problems like finding

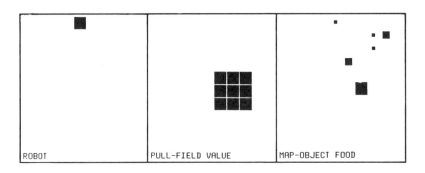

Fig. 11. Gradient field pulling robot to desired food location.

the shortest distance to a nearby foodsource. This is an alternative to problem solving based on the development of a search space.

3. The system has many of the features that we want of AI systems such as ability to handle dynamical situations, and flexibility (if the robot is suddenly moved to another spot solutions will still be found).

6. Hand Eye Coordination

The second experiment is from the domain of hand-eye coordination. There is a camera looking at a set of bottles (the camera is located under a glass table). There is an arm that can grasp the bottles and move them around. The objective of the experiment is to move a bottle (called m) to a particular target position (called g). The bottle is to be moved in small steps so that we can see what

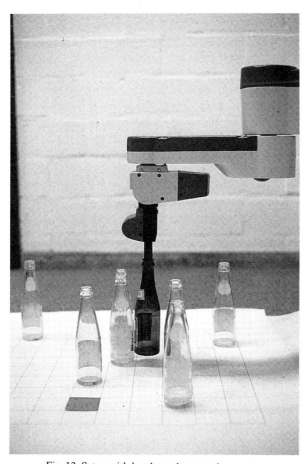

Fig. 12. Setup with bottles to be moved around.

is going on. An example setup of the bottles is given in *Fig. 12*. The dark bottle is the one that needs to be moved. We will first do a simple version of the experiment, namely one where the bottles can be moved around or in between the obstacles. Then we do a more difficult experiment in which a bottle can only be lifted to a certain height so that bottles need to be moved out of the way when m is moved along the shortest distance to g.

Moving around obstacles

As expected we will use an analogical representation of the situation in terms of a grid with markers for the obstacles, i.e. the bottles, the goal g, and the object to be moved m. Each of these markers is associated with different agents: a goal agent, an obstacle agent, and a moving-object agent.

To find out how the bottle needs to be moved we create a gradient field emanating from g which we call again the pull-field. The agent responsible for creating the pull-field is called the pull-field agent. It is an instance of the gradient-field agent discussed earlier. Pull-field agents have been instantiated in all cells of the grid so that they only need to be given a positive value, for example 100, to start their work. This value is supplied by the goal-agent:

```
(def-agent goal-agent ()
    :vars ((g 0))
    :behavior
    #'(lambda (self self-x self-y)
        (if ( > (my 'g) 0)
            (add-var 'pull-field
                'value
                self-x self-y
                100)))))
```

To take care of the obstacles, the obstacle agent inhibits the gradient, so that there are no positive markers representing the gradient wherever there are obstacles. Inhibition is implemented by proposing a high negative value less than −10.000 for the gradient.

```
(def-agent obstacle-agent ()
    :vars ((obstacle 10))
    :behavior
```

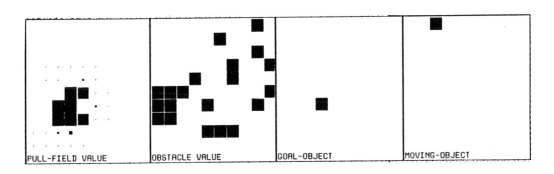

Fig. 13. Diffusion process around the obstacles.

```
#'(lambda (self self-x self-y)
    (if (and (> (my obstacle) 0)
             (> (find-one-var 'pull-field
                              'value self-x self-y)
                - 10000))
        (add-var 'pull-field 'value
                 self-x self-y
                 - 10000))))
```

Note that the inhibition only takes place as long as there is a positive value for the obstacle marker. The operation of these agents is illustrated in *Fig. 13*. *Fig. 13b* displays the obstacle markers. *Fig 13c* displays the goal location. *Fig 13a* displays diffusion out of this location and around the obstacles.

The only thing left to do is put an internal sensor in the cell where m is located that translates the direction of highest gradient into an instruction to the arm. Sensors are also implemented by agents located on the grid.

```
(def-agent arm-movement-sensor ()
    :behavior
    #'(lambda (self self-x self-y)
        (let
            ((direction
              (find-direction-highest-value
               'pull-field 'value
               self-x self-y)))
          (if direction
              (pick-and-move self-x self-y
                             (direction-x direction self-x)
                             (direction-y direction self-y))))))
```

Find-direction-highest-value returns the direction (zero, up, down, left, right, etc.), expressed as $\langle \Delta x,$

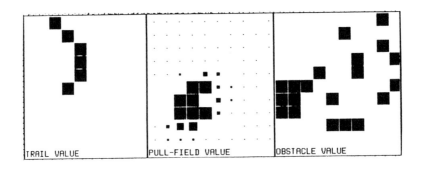

Fig. 14. Movement of object m to reach g.

$\Delta y\rangle$, in which the highest value of a particular variable (here value) in an agent (here pull-field) is found. This is directly translated to an action of the robot-arm to pick up the object at $\langle$self-x,self-y$\rangle$ and move it to the new position. *Fig. 14* shows the behavior of these agents starting from the initial situation given in the previous figure. The object m is moved to g by successive steps. A trace is left behind so that the sequence can be followed. This trace is constructed by the arm-movement-sensor agent similar to the way the move-north agent put down a trail as it moved over the grid.

It is not difficult to see that this mechanism will solve the problem. The gradient field effectively computes the distance from any given point to the goal g. The sensor reads off this information and makes the decision. There are no local minima, as in similar solutions using potential fields, because integration of the different elements in the decision (shortest distance, presence of obstacles) is done in the representation by the reaction between markers. Our experiments (both in software and with a real arm) show that the solution also works out in practice.

We can also begin to see the advantages of the approach:

1. The shape of the obstacles does not really matter because inhibition takes place from each obstacle agent. The solution is therefore flexible in the sense that it does not make detailed assumptions about what obstacles will occur.

2. The shape of the obstacles does not have to be categorized as being square or round or any other shape category. The solution therefore avoids costly interpretation processes.

3. Although there is an implicit search space in the problem because the object may have to be moved first away from the goal position to avoid obstacles, there is no search space in the traditional sense of exploring different world states using operators that transform one world state into another. Instead the search is taken care of by the diffusion process and exploits the analogical representation.

4. Everything is dynamic. Obstacles may move dynamically. If they do, they start inhibiting from their new locations. The goal g may be moved in which case the source of diffusion changes to the new position. Also m may be moved to a new location or it may end up in a new location due to

execution failure. In each case there is automatic replanning because the spatio-temporal structures that are used to guide behavior are dynamic.

Moving Obstacles out of the Way

Now we tackle the task of moving the object m to its goal location g along the shortest route, moving the other bottles out of the way. The problem is non-trivial because removal of a bottle to make room might involve removing first other bottles that stand in the way. So we need an internal model to think first which bottle needs to be moved. In a traditional symbolic planner, this can be done relatively easily. There is a set of primitive operations, like move north, move south, remove bottle, etc. With these operators a search space can be constructed. The planner then develops enough of the search space to find the best solution. There is in principle no fundamental difficulty with the search approach, except that it ignores the problem how the agent makes contact with the world: How will the agent be capable to interpret the situation in terms of the symbolic representations needed to build up the search space and how will the agent be able to replan when an action failed or after the world changed dynamically.

Here is how this problem can be solved without the traditional search space built up by a classical planner:

1. We first have to find out to which location m should move. We call this location the target location. This can be done by diffusing from g a gradient field as before, but now ignoring the obstacles, i.e. inhibition no longer takes place. An internal sensor in the cell in which m is located can detect the cell with highest gradient and thus the target location.

2. Next we have to find out whether there is free space at the target location. Free space is represented analogically by having markers in those cells where there are no objects. This can easily be computed in parallel directly from the sensory map by an intensity filter.

3. If there is free space at the target location, then instructions are given to the arm to move the object to that cell.

4. If there is no free space at this place, then we need to remove the obstacle first. But of course it may be surrounded by obstacles as well. So what we do is diffuse a new gradient field, called the

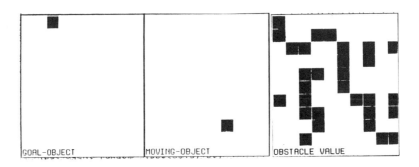

Fig. 15. Begin situation for problem with obstacle removal.

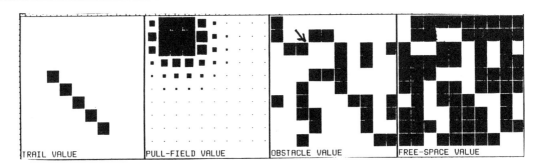

Fig. 16. Movement when there is free space.

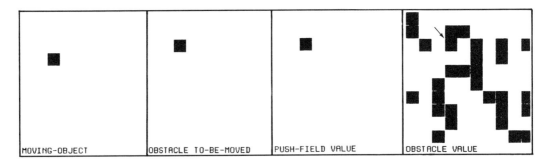

Fig. 17. Putting an obstacle out of the way.

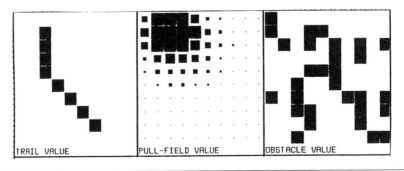

Fig. 18. Complete path with removal of obstacles.

push-field, starting from the target location. If a push-field marker arrives at a cell where there is also a free-space marker, an obstacle can be moved there and instructions are given to the arm to do so. This goes on until the obstacle that occupies the target location is moved out of the way and then g itself can move.

The following figures illustrate the behavior of these mechanisms. *Fig. 15* gives the begin situation. In *Fig. 16* m has made a few moves towards the goal based on the gradient in the pull-field (*Fig. 16b*) but now it stands in front of an obstacle (indicated with the arrow). *Fig. 16a* shows the trail.

A marker for 'obstacle to be moved' is created and the push-field starts (*Fig. 17b + c*). As there is already free space next to the obstacle, it can move there and consequently m itself can also move to the position it wants to go. *Fig. 17d* (arrow) shows that the obstacle has moved to the right. *Fig. 18* shows the complete trail and all obstacles removed.

7. Conclusions

There are three contributions of the present work to autonomous agents research. The first one is the emphasis on internal models in the form of analogical representations which is an alternative both to systems with elaborate symbolic world models and to systems which do not have internal models but react directly to their sensory inputs. An analogical representation is close to sensory output. It is therefore easier to derive from sensors or to use as a way to specify actions of effectors as symbolic representations. But it re-introduces the capability to look ahead or to remember where you have been which purely reactive agents without internal models do not have.

The second contribution concerns the way in which new information may be derived in analogical representations. Although other researchers such as Ullmann [20] have also used markers and structures over analogical representations, we have introduced the idea that these structures could be dynamic and emergent: dynamic in the sense that they adapt continuously to changing circumstances, emergent because the structures are generated by the parallel local activity of smaller units instead of a global algorithm.

We have provided evidence in the form of a series of implemented experiments that these two ideas lead to working solutions. The solutions have a number of interesting properties, such as robustness, ability to cope with dynamical worlds, flexibility, ease of coupling to sensors and effectors, and efficient use of data-level parallelism.

The third contribution of our research has been the development of a particular style for developing analogical sensori-motor systems and an associated software environment MAS to practice this style. MAS consists of tools for defining and simulating agents. An agent is a computational entity with internal state and behavior. It is located in a particular cell on a grid but it can move to its local neighbors. At every time step all agents execute their complete behavior. On top of MAS we have RDL, a library of generic agents that implement various reaction-diffusion mechanisms such as diffusion, wave formation, activation, inhibition, decay, etc. The code given throughout the paper illustrates that a particular application can be constructed by modularly putting together a set of behaviors whose interaction has the desired global effect.

Acknowledgement

Several members of the VUB AI Lab (particularly Peter Strickx and Sven van Caekenberg) have helped with the implementation of some of the experiments. Interesting feedback has come from Jo Decuyper, Didier Keymeulen, Bernard Manderick and other members of the lab's complex dynamics group. Pattie Maes has stimulated the writing of this paper.

References

[1] R. Brooks, Intelligence without representations, to appear in *Artificial Intelligence.*

[2] E.L. Cussler, *Diffusion, Mass Transfer in Fluid Systems* (Cambridge University Press, Cambridge 1987).

[3] Y. Demazeau, O. Bourdon, and M. Lebrasseur Contours et illusions de contours: un Gabarit Elastique pour l'extraction de formes. Dans les *Actes du 1er Workshop Regional de Sciences Cognitives, LASCO3*, Grenoble (March 89).

[4] M. Genesereth, and N. Nilsson, *Logical Foundations of Artificial Intelligence* Morgan Kaufmann, Los Angeles 1987).

[5] C. Hewitt, (1977) Viewing control structures as patterns of passing messages, *Artifical Intelligence* 8: (August, 1977) 323–364.

[6] O. Khatib, Real-time obstacle avoidance for manipulators and mobile robots, *Internat J. Robotics Res.* 5(1) (1986).

[7] M. Kuperstein and J. Rubinstein, Implementation of an adaptive neural controller for sensory-motor coordination, in. Pfeifer et al. (ed.) *Connectionism in Perspective* (Elsevier Science Publ. Amsterdam, 1989) 49–61.

[8] T. Lozano-Perez, (1981) Automatic planning of manipulator transfer movements, *IEEE Trans. Sys. Man, Cyber SMC*-11(10) (1981) 681–689.

[9] M. Mason, Mechanics and planning of manipulator pushing operations, *Intern. J. of Robotics Res.* 5 (3) (Fall 1986).

[10] C. Malcolm, this volume.

[11] D. Marr, (1984) *Vision* (Freeman, San Francisco 1984).

[12] M. Mataric, Environment learning using a distributed representation, *IEEE J. Robotics and Automation* (1990).

[13] Merzenich et al., Somatosensory cortical map changes following digit amputation in adult monkeys, *J. Comp. Neurol.* 224 (1984) 591–605.

[14] M. Mohnhaupt, and B. Neumann, Understanding object motion: recognition, learning and spatiotemporal reasoning, to appear in *Internat. J. Robotics*.

[15] D. Payton, this volume.

[16] D.E. Rumelhart and J. McClelland, *Parallel Distributed Processing-Explorations in the Microstructure of Cognition* (MIT Press, Cambridge, Ma, 1986).

[17] A. Sloman, Afterthoughts on analogical representations, in: *Proc. TINLAP* (Cambridge Ma. 1975). Reprinted in R. Brachman and H. Levesque (ed.) *Readings in Knowledge Representation* (Morgan Kaufmann. Pub. Inc., Los Angeles).

[18] L. Steels, Steps towards common sense, *Proceedings ECAI-88 Munchen* (Pitman Pub, London 1988) 49–54.

[19] T. Toffoli and N. Margolis *Cellular Automata Machines* (MIT Press, Cambridge, Ma. 1987).

[20] S. Ullmann Visual routines. *Cognition* 18 (1984).

Internalized Plans:
A Representation for Action Resources

David W. Payton

Artificial Intelligence Center, Hughes Research Laboratories,
3011 Malibu Canyon Road, Malibu, CA 90265, USA

In the ongoing pursuit to produce intelligent autonomous agents that can operate in real world environments, emerging concepts about the relationships between planning and action are inspiring new alternatives in plan representation. The simple yet elusive concept that plans must serve as resources for action rather than as programs for action has significant ramifications. In this paper we examine methods for compiling world knowledge into forms which serve only to enhance performance, rather than to dictate a specific course of action. We present the notion of *internalized plans*, which can be thought of as representations that allow the raw results of search in any abstract state space to be made available for direct use within continuous real-time decision-making processes. In the case of map-based plans, we find that by abandoning the notion that a specific path must be defined by a route plan we are free to make direct use of the map data and search results that are normally used to generate route plans. As a result of this simple change in outlook, we can more easily solve problems requiring opportunistic reaction to unexpected changes in the environment.

Keywords: Autonomous vehicles; Mobile robots; Reactive planning; Route planning; Subsumption architectures; Plans as resources

David W. Payton received the B.S.E.E. degree from the University of California at Los Angeles in 1979, and the S.M. degree in Electrical Engineering and Computer Science from the Massachusetts Insitute of Technology in 1981.

From 1981–1982, he was a software developer at Lisp Machine Inc., Boston, Mass. Since December, 1982, he has been with the Hughes Research Laboratories, Malibu, CA, working with the Artificial Intelligence Department. Since 1985, he has been head of the Autonomous Systems Section. His research interests have included the development of knowledge representation and control strategies for context-based object recognition. His most recent work has been in the development of software architectures for autonomous vehicle control.

Mr. Payton is a member of Phi Beta Kappa.

North-Holland
Robotics and Autonomous Systems 6 (1990) 89–103

1. Introduction

In the endeavor to develop intelligent autonomous agents capable of interacting with a dynamic environment, there has been a growing awareness that traditional planning methods may not be compatible with the demands for real-time performance. Recent efforts to re-evaluate the relationship between plans and action have cast a shadow on traditional notions of plans as programs, shedding new light on a promising view of plans as *resources* for action [1]. The quest for suitable action resources yields provocative insights into how plans might be best represented to serve in this manner.

In this paper we examine methods for compiling world knowledge into forms having maximal utility for guiding the action of a mobile robot. While we refer to this compilation of knowledge as "planning," it is distinguished from conventional planning by the fact that the resultant plans are used optionally and serve only to enhance performance, rather than to dictate a specific course of action. From this new perspective, we find that representing plans through conventional methods of abstraction tends to prevent the information generated during the planning process from being exploited to its fullest potential. Instead, we present the notion of *internalized plans*, which can be thought of as representations that allow the raw results of search in any abstract state space to be made available for direct use within continuous real-time decision-making processes. In the case of map-based plans, we find that by abandoning the notion that a specific path must be defined by a route plan we are free to make direct use of the map data and search results that are normally used to generate route plans. As a result of this simple change in outlook, we can more easily solve problems requiring opportunistic reaction to unexpected changes in the environment. Alternatives are inherent in the representation, so replanning is rarely needed.

0921-8830/90/$03.50 © 1990 – Elsevier Science Publishers B.V. (North-Holland)

Some researchers who are specifically addressing the problems of operating in a dynamic real-
world environment have purposely de-emphasized
the need for plans; instead, they are focusing on
the issues of being able to produce appropriate
action in any given situation. Work by Brooks, for
example, is aimed at avoiding the use of plans
altogether [6]. In this approach, intelligent action
is a manifestation of many simple processes operating concurrently and coordinated through the
context of a complex environment. While there is
no tangible representation for plans in such a
system, plans are implicitly designed into the system through the pre-established interactions between behaviors. Similarly, Agre and Chapman
have shown how a system that determines its
actions through the constant evaluation of its current situation can perform complex tasks that
might otherwise have been thought to require
planning [2]. Despite their emphasis on the theme
that action is obtained by always knowing what to
do at any instant, Brooks, Agre, and Chapman do
not discard the notion that look-ahead and anticipation of future events are desirable activities.
While these activities are normally associated with
planning, there is a difference in how the resultant
"plans" are represented and used in their systems.

Agre and Chapman, for example, draw a sharp
distinction between the concept of plans as communication and the more traditional view of plans
as programs [1]. The key difference is the idea that
plans must be constructed as a resource to the
plan user, not as an explicit set of instructions to
be followed [25]. As a resource, plans must serve
as sources of information and advice to plan users
that are already fairly competent at dealing with
the immediate concerns of their environment. In
contrast, the traditional view of plans puts them in
the role of specifying a distinct course of action to
systems which are often incapable of doing anything without them.

2. Representation of Plans

Employing plans as resources for action places
a substantial responsibility on the plan user for
their proper interpretation. This brings forth the
important issue of how plans might be best represented to allow a plan interpreter to take greatest
advantage of them. The significance of ap-

propriate plan representation is evidenced by performance failures resulting from inadequate representations. For illustration, we can analyze one of
several experimental cross-country runs of the
DARPA Autonomous Land Vehicle (ALV), performed by members of the Hughes Artificial Intelligence Center in August and December, 1987
[10,13].

2.1. The Example: The ALV Experiment

In the cross-country experiment, a very simple
abstraction of a map-based plan was used to assist
a set of sensor-based reflexive behaviors [13] that
were independently competent at avoiding obstacles. As shown in *Fig. 1*, the basic mission
objective was for the vehicle to get from one
location to another, bypassing a gully and
maneuvering around a large rock outcrop in the
process. Throughout this traversal, it was important that the vehicle maintain line-of-sight contact with a remote radio tower so that it could
receive control commands from an off-board computer. Compensating for the potential loss of radio contact behind the rock outcrop, a map-based
planner [19] generated a route plan and abstracted
a sequence of intermediate sub-goals to represent
the critical points along this path. A portion of
this sequence is illustrated in *Fig. 1* as Goals 1, 2,
and 3. To accomplish the mission, the sensor-based
behaviors were designed to bias their selection of
heading toward the current sub-goal whenever
possible. As soon as the vehicle got within a
specified radius of its current sub-goal, that goal
would be discarded and the next sub-goal would
be selected. On paper and in simulation, it seemed
that this approach would be effective.

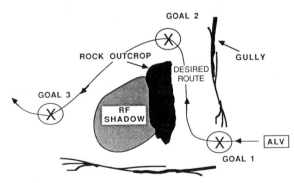

Fig. 1. An ALV route plan expressed as a sequence of intermediate goal points.

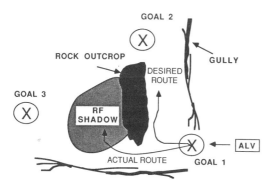

Fig. 2. Errant vehicle action while executing its route plan.

When the vehicle attempted to perform the mission, the deficiencies of this method became strikingly clear. *Fig. 2* shows what happened. After achieving Goal 1, the vehicle attempted to reach Goal 2. Because of the rock outcrop straight ahead and extending to the vehicle's right, the perception system indicated that the local terrain to the left of the vehicle was far more traversable than to the right. The bias in favor of going left was so strong that the vehicle did not turn right, thus failing to follow the desired route. Of course, this action was known to be undesirable from the map, yet the advice contained in the abstract route description gave no indication of a problem with going behind the rock. As it happened, contrary to expectations, radio contact was not lost behind the rock. The vehicle could have proceeded to Goal 3 and completed its mission, but it unnecessarily persisted in its attempt to reach Goal 2. This highlights the system's inability to take opportunistic advantage of unexpected situations when such situations are not properly accounted for in the abstract plan. We know from our understanding of the mission constraints that Goal 2 was merely an intermediate waypoint intended to keep the vehicle away from the RF shadow. Looking at the abstract plan in isolation, however, there is no way of knowing why a particular sub-goal has been selected. The Goal 2 location could just as easily have been a critical choke point along the only path to Goal 3. It is only through our understanding of the underlying mission constraints that we can analyze the vehicle's failure to turn right and see the opportunity that arose as a result.

2.2. The Problem: Information Loss From Abstraction

The apparent shortcoming of the plan is that it lacks environmental and mission constraints that are quite evident in the map. A more suitable plan might have detailed the concern about staying out of the RF shadow. We therefore might wish to add more of this type of information to the plan. Once we start augmenting the plan, however, we have to ask how we might ever know when a sufficient amount of information has been added to prevent other types of mistakes. Consider, for example, the system's failure to realize that the intermediate sub-goal could be skipped when the opportunity arose. Although the plan user may appear to be at fault, the real flaw is in the plan, inasmuch as it fails to indicate the true purpose of the sub-goal. However, if the plan could include all the reasons for when and why the particular sub-goal was significant, then the location itself would become inconsequential. Clearly, the simple sequence of sub-goals is both an overspecification and an underspecification. It's like someone telling you which lane to be in while you're driving down the highway, when what you really need to know is where to turn off. The problem is inherent in the fact that we are attempting to build an abstraction of the map data. Inevitably, some information will be lost.

3. Communicated Plans

One alternative form of plan representation, as advocated by Agre and Chapman, is to express plans in linguistic forms similar to those that people use to communicate plans [1]. It is suggested that viewing plans as communication is distinct from viewing plans as programs, because linguistic plans are not exhaustive descriptions of action, and the meaning of their primitives depends heavily on the context of the situation in which they are interpreted. Accordingly, the plan user is viewed as a dynamic and creative decision-making entity, continuously selecting actions based on whatever information is relevant at the time. For such a plan user, the ideal plan is a source of information, and not a specific set of instructions to be followed blindly. In this sense, a linguistic plan is truly a resource for action.

A possible linguistic plan for the cross-country example above might be something like "cross the gully near the lower end, then take a hard right and go around the high end of the big rock so you can maintain radio contact." In looking at this plan, we can almost build our own map of the terrain. We know that there is a gully, and that on the other side of the gully is a big rock. We also know that we have to do something special around the big rock in order to ensure reliable radio contact. Knowing that rocks might interfere with radio reception, we can then infer which side of the big rock should be avoided and also conclude that maintaining radio contact is an important concern for this mission.

The sequence of actions specified by the linguistic plan is much less significant than the understanding about the environment conveyed through the plan's description. Even if the specific actions are ignored, there is still a great deal of valuable information gleaned from knowing what the vehicle was supposed to have done. Suppose, for example, that the vehicle could not make a right turn after passing the gully. Inferences from the linguistic plan could indicate that going the other way around the rock might cause radio interference problems, so the vehicle would have to think of something else to do. Using a plan as a resource, then, may require that the plan user do some planning of its own.

Once we start requiring that a plan user be capable of doing some of its own planning, we open the possibility that there may be much more to plans than what is communicated. This raises the question of whether there should be a distinction between internal representations of plan knowledge and representations of communicated plans. This is a prominent implementation concern for mobile robots. As Brooks argues, for example, plans can create unnecessary abstraction barriers that get in the way of making a robot "do the right thing" [7]. Thus, while there may still be value in performing search and look-ahead activities, it may be best to avoid molding the results of these activities into an abstract plan representation. Intuitively, we see that because communicated linguistic plans are constrained by the natural bandwidth limitations and sequentiality of human speech, they inherently create abstraction barriers. While this does not obstruct their use as a resource to the human plan user, linguistic plans

are neither simple to generate nor simple to interpret within a machine.

4. Internalized Plans

It seems that if all relevant knowledge can be organized with respect to a given problem and thereafter can be provided in full without abstraction to the plan user, then that knowledge can become an ideal resource for action. Such a structured compilation of knowledge might be called an "internalized plan." In many ways, a thorough understanding of a problem domain is the best possible resource for action. When humans produce plans, it is often helpful for the intended plan user to be involved directly in the planning process. Through the activity of exploring alternatives and deriving the constraints of a problem, those who participate in planning can create new chunks of knowledge about their problem domain. Accordingly, a plan user who is involved in the planning process will be more capable of dealing with unexpected situations than one who is merely given a set of instructions. This puts a different light on the role of communicated plans. It seems likely that when a person generates a plan for his own use, and records it in some way such as through writing, the plan then serves primarily as a reminder of the issues addressed during plan generation. (Maybe this is why you can't give someone else your grocery list and expect the "plan user" to come back with what you really wanted.)

The ideal internalized plan for a mobile robot would allow all pertinent mission constraints to be utilized directly by the robot's real-time decision-making processes. As obstacle avoidance behaviors negotiated through the sensed environment, their decisions could be biased in favor of alternatives which might best satisfy mission criteria. The proper representation of an internalized plan would not only enable the vehicle to do a better job of avoiding costly errors, but it would also allow unexpected opportunities to be recognized whenever they might arise. In creating such a plan, we must view mission and map planning processes as the means for exploration and organization of a problem space, explicating constraints of the problem for immediate use during action.

The idea of compiling knowledge into a form that provides for immediate action brings to mind aspects of situated-automata theory [23], yet there are some marked differences between internalized plans and situated-automata. Situated-automata theory offers a formal mechanism for synthesizing machines through the compilation of world knowledge. This mechanism facilitates the construction of intelligent mobile robots which have their static world knowledge built-in to their real-time decision-making circuitry. All world knowledge, however, is expressed in terms of discrete states. Machines are modeled by discrete input and output processes which, in turn, are described in terms of discrete sets of locations, states, and instants in time. When world knowledge is compiled to form a machine, the final system is limited to dealing with the environment exclusively in terms of those states that were used to express the original knowledge base. Hence there is a strong dependence on the accuracy and availability of the necessary state information. In contrast, even though internalized plans themselves are expressed in terms of discrete states, they are designed for interpretation by continuous non-state-oriented processes. By serving as a resource, they can be ignored by these processes whenever the knowledge of state required for their interpretation is unavailable or inaccurate. Furthermore, there is no limit to the number of separate internalized plans that might be simultaneously employed, so there is no bound on the realm of states that might influence action.

4.1. Internalized Route Plans

To illustrate the unique qualities of internalized plans, it is helpful to review the earlier example in which a sequence of sub-goals was used to guide the vehicle around a rock outcrop to reach its final goal. In the example, we found that the simple sub-goal description of the plan was too weak to properly convey the underlying objective of maintaining radio contact. The plan had no provision for integrating the knowledge about the RF shadow into the real-time decision-making processes of the reflexive behaviors.

4.1.1. A Gradient Representation

Consider, instead, a gradient description of a plan to achieve the same objectives, as illustrated in *Fig. 3*. There is no explicit plan shown, yet the plan user can always find the best way to reach the goal simply by following the arrows. Such a representation would not ordinarily be thought to be a plan because it provides no specific course of action. As a resource for guiding action, however, the gradient type of representation is extremely useful. No matter where the vehicle is located, and no matter how it strays from what might have been the ideal path, a reflexive behavior can always bias turn decisions in favor of following the arrows.

Upon closer examination of *Fig. 3*, we can see not only how the mistake of entering the RF shadow could be avoided, but we see also how the system could be opportunistic should the vehicle

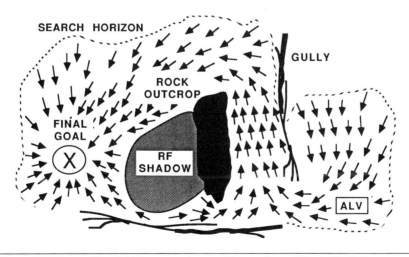

Fig. 3. A gradient field representation provides one form of internalized plan.

happen to enter the shadow and be able to continue onward. First, when the vehicle had to make a choice between going left or right near the bottom of the rock outcrop, the gradient field would strongly bias its decision in favor of going right. If the vehicle got too close to the shadow on the left, the gradient field would actually be telling it to turn around. Further, should the vehicle happen to be forced to go below the rock outcrop and enter the RF shadow, then it would continue to be directed toward the final goal despite the radical deviation from its expected path. This type of behavior is opportunistic in that the vehicle is not constrained to reach any arbitrary pre-established sub-goals, and, therefore, all action can be directed exclusively toward achieving the mission objectives.

With all its potential advantages, one of the most exciting aspects of this approach is that gradient field information is available as a by-product of existing route planning algorithms [18]. These algorithms begin by assigning a cost to each grid cell of a digital terrain map. By associating high costs with locations that are undesirable according to mission criteria, a combination of mission constraints can be represented. Whether an A* [21], or Dijkstra [11] search algorithm is employed in the cost grid, the net result of the search is a score for each grid cell, indicating the minimum cost remaining to get from that cell to the goal. From any given grid cell, the best incremental step to get to the goal is the neighboring grid cell which has the lowest score. Ordinarily, when we use these scores to compute a standard route plan, we simply begin at the starting point and locally choose the lowest-score adjacent cell until we finally reach the goal. The record of our steps along the way gives us the minimum cost path to the goal. If we look at these scores in a slightly different way, we see that they establish a scalar function for which a gradient can be computed. The direction of the steepest descent indicated by the gradient values gives the best heading from any grid cell to the goal.

Essentially, gradient field information has been available to us all along, yet it has been overlooked because we are so accustomed to representing plans in ways designed for human interpretation. One basic tenet of the dynamic programming field has been the idea of representing the set of optimal incremental decisions to be made from any state of a system [4]. More recent efforts in path planning have resulted in general methods for computing shortest path maps [16,20] which yield a combinatorial description of all shortest paths to a goal. In earlier work, graph search algorithms such as A* and Dijkstra have frequently been used to compute shortest path trees which, when represented in a grid, form a discrete approximation to a continuous gradient surface. It is interesting to note, however, that even when this information has been exploited [17,9], it has been applied exclusively in the context of providing an abstract route plan. In such

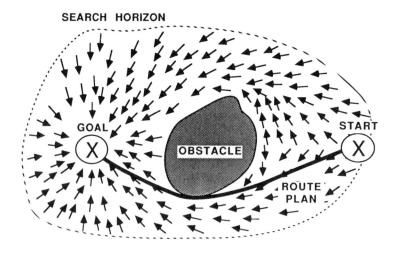

Fig. 4. Alternative paths are inherent in the gradient field representation.

instances, the utility of the shortest path tree concept has been limited to allowing the fast generation of a new plan should the constraints of the original plan be violated. Unfortunately, this type of over commitment inhibits opportunistic behavior. Whenever a route plan is abstracted from the shortest path map, any opportunities that are not deliberately represented in the abstract plan will be lost. Only by viewing shortest path maps as a direct resource for action can we get full benefit of all the information they provide.

4.1.2. Alternative Paths

To clarify the distinction between using an abstract route plan and using a gradient field, see *Fig. 4*. In the figure, the goal can be reached by going around either side of the obstacle, so there are two nearly equivalent cost paths between the start and the goal. To create an abstract route plan for this situation, we would generally use the gradient field data to select a single route, producing a description for the shortest of the two possibilities. In contrast, to use the gradient field directly, all we need to do is bias local turn decisions in favor of the gradient arrows shown in the

figure, making no a priori selection of a preferred route. When the vehicle sets out for the goal, we can expect these two approaches to produce markedly different vehicle behavior in the event that unexpected obstacles must be avoided. In the first case, using the abstract plan, the vehicle may stray from the planned path, but it will continue to attempt to go around the specified side of the obstacle until it gets so far off course that a failure is detected and a new plan must be generated. In the second case, the gradient field plan will keep the vehicle moving toward the goal regardless of how it might stray while avoiding obstacles. This latter plan allows the vehicle to go around either side of the obstacle without the need to replan. The gradient field data allows the vehicle to opportunistically select the most appropriate route at any instant in time, while the route plan limits the vehicle's options to what was thought to be best at the time the plan was generated.

4.1.3. Multiple Goals

A second illustration of the differences between using a route plan and the gradient field representation can be seen with problems involving multi-

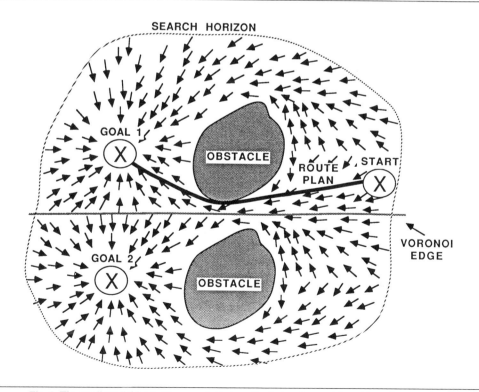

Fig. 5. The gradient field provides a useful internalized plan for reaching either of two goals.

ple disjunctive goals. This type of problem is often referred to as the "Post Office Problem" [12] because it can be likened to the task of finding a route to the nearest of several post offices in a neighborhood. The first step to solving this type of problem generally involves computing a Voronoi diagram which divides the map up into distinct regions associated one for one with each post office. Since the boundaries between regions indicate points which are equidistant between post offices, one can determine the closest post office merely by determining which region encompasses his location. This same technique holds with or without obstacles present so long as obstacles are included in the distance metric [20].

Suppose a mission requires that a mobile robot reach either of two distinct goal locations. As shown in *Fig. 5*, the gradient field computed for multiple goals is fairly similar to that of the single goal case. Instead of initiating the search from a single goal point, however, the search is propagated simultaneously from the two goals. In the single goal case, the search propagates like a wave from the goal, splitting when it encounters an obstacle, but then converging on the other side to form a divergent gradient at the seam. Similarly, we see that the search wavefronts from two goals meet to form a divergent gradient at their seam as well. This seam is, in fact, a Voronoi edge. Note that the search is equivalent to a wildfire algorithm, except that because it terminates when it reaches the starting point, we can benefit by using A* techniques. Note also that gradient fields can be computed independently for each goal, and then, during execution, the fields can be compared to determine which one to follow. This is more costly than computing just a single field, but it provides a better resource for action by allowing for a goal to be abandoned simply by ignoring the gradient for that goal.

If we were to extract a route plan from the gradient field result, we would invariably have to select a route to the closest goal, as shown in *Fig. 5*. The route plan suffers from its inability to capture the relationship between the two goals and the fact that the second goal is nearly as close as the first. In contrast, by using the gradient field directly, a commitment toward either goal is never

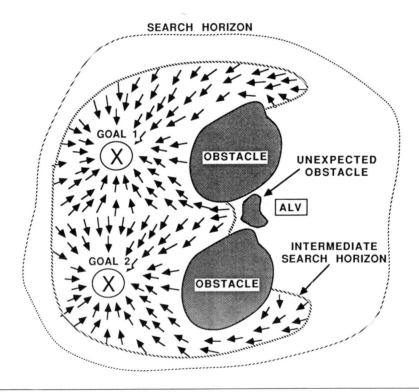

Fig. 6. To replan, the map is updated to account for the unexpected obstacle, and we revert to an intermediate stage of the original search.

made, because the vehicle approaches whichever goal is most accessible at the moment.

4.1.4. Dynamic Replanning

Although the gradient field representation generally elides the need for replanning, there are still certain situations where replanning is necessary. The simplest case is when the vehicle somehow strays outside of the initial search horizon while avoiding local obstacles. When this happens, the vehicle need not stop. A simple heuristic can be applied to guide the vehicle back into the search region, and, meanwhile, if appropriate information is saved, the search can be continued from its previous state until the search horizon reaches the vehicle's current position.

A more complex case for replanning occurs when an unexpected obstacle is found to block a passageway. When this happens, the map must be updated and the gradient field must be partially re-computed. Imagine, for example, that an unexpected obstacle is detected during the execution of the earlier multiple goal problem as shown in *Fig. 6*. Here, a critical choke point has been blocked,

so replanning is necessary. To perform replanning, first the new obstacle is inserted into the map data. The exact extent of the obstacle is not known, but it is inserted to block the choke point appropriately. Next, because information is recorded at various stages during the original search, the planner can revert back to an intermediate stage of the search that is not affected by the change to the map. Because the search is analogous to a propagating wavefront, it is easy to identify stages of the search where the wavefront had not yet reached the obstacle location. Resuming the search as if the vehicle had strayed outside the intermediate search horizon, a new gradient field is computed as shown in *Fig. 7*. The newly detected obstacle will always be near the vehicle's current location, so this replanning process has the benefit of searching only an incremental amount relative to the entire path length.

4.1.5. Relation to Potential Fields

Since other researchers have used *artificial potential field* methods to perform local obstacle avoidance [15,14], it is important to observe the

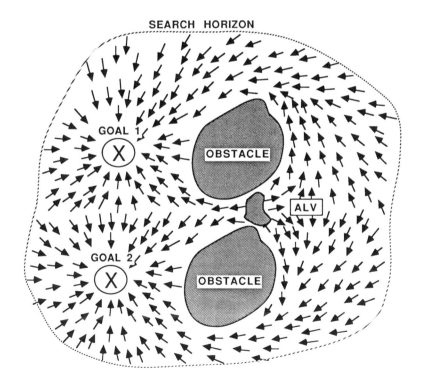

Fig. 7. Resuming the search yields a new gradient field.

distinction between our gradient field method and
potential field methods. Although the two appear
similar in nature, they are not created in the same
way and they have very different properties.
Artificial potential fields are computed through a
process analogous to assigning electrostatic charges
to obstacles and goals and then combining the
fields of these charges through superposition. In
contrast, the gradient field is created through a
graph search process which propagates like a wave
from the goal, moving fastest through low cost
regions and slowest through high cost regions.
Superposition allows the potential field vector at
any point to be computed quickly by adding up
the contributions from each charge. On the other
hand, the search required to compute a gradient
field can be time consuming, especially for points
far from the goal. A gradient field, however, yields
a set of optimal paths to the goal, while a potential field provides only a heuristic guide for avoiding obstacles enroute to the goal. Often, potential
fields contain local minima and traps requiring
additional heuristics to enable the vehicle to proceed to its goal. Such a problem never arises in a
gradient field, because the underlying scalar function decreases monotonically toward the goal. In
light of all these factors, the gradient field really
has little in common with a potential field.

Although potential fields do not yield optimal
paths, they do offer a useful mechanism for fusing
action commands from multiple concurrent behaviors, and they may therefore serve as a means for
incorporating gradient field information in action
decisions. In Arkin's schema-based approach, for
example, potential fields provide a means for fusing commands from independent motor schema
[3]. By independently assigning repulsive fields
around observed obstacles and varying the field
strengths appropriately, Arkin shows that strategies for road following and obstacle avoidance can
be implemented. Unfortunately, in using piecewise
linear segments to describe the desired route, this
approach does not extend the application of
potential fields beyond the problem of short-term
sensor-based control. If, instead, we were to use
superposition to combine the gradient field produced from the map with potential fields created
from sensed data, we would have a straightforward mechanism for using the map data as an
immediate resource for action. Extending this idea
beyond gradient fields, it is possible to envision

using potential fields to combine information from
a large number of distinct internalized plans. This
opens the door to a wide range of useful resources
for action.

4.2. Other Internalized Plans

As we examine map data and mission knowledge for other useful resources for action, it becomes clear that the gradient field described earlier
is just the tip of the iceberg. By compiling a priori
knowledge into specialized representations, the
system can use such information directly in the
computation of immediate actions.

4.2.1. Resource Usage Constraints

For example, a mobile robot mission might
impose resource constraints such as a limit on
total fuel consumption and a time deadline for
reaching the specified goal. Concomitant with the
gradient field computation, one could also compute an estimate of the total fuel and the total
time required to get from any point to the goal.
While this information would not directly indicate
a course of action, it would allow available fuel
and time resources to be monitored constantly
and compared with expected needs. If there were
barely enough fuel to succeed but plenty of time
available, the vehicle might be able to switch to a
simple fuel conserving strategy such as reducing
its speed. If time and fuel were both in short
supply, then replanning would be required. Although no new obstacle features could be added
to the map, various constraints such as safety
could be relaxed, thereby altering the cost of
traversal over different types of terrain. The gradient field would then be recomputed to see if time
and fuel constraints could be met.

4.2.2. Raw Map Data

Another way to exploit the map as a resource
for action is to probe it directly during execution.
As the vehicle is traveling, the system might examine the portion of the map corresponding to the
area just in front of the vehicle to determine what
types of features should be detected. This understanding of the local environment can have a
direct bearing on how sensor data is interpreted
for action. Remember, for example, the problem
illustrated earlier in *Fig. 2*. Here, one of the main
reasons the vehicle failed to avoid the RF shadow

was that its sensors indicated a clear path in this area. This error could be overcome by differentiating between obstacles that are observable and those that are not, and then appropriately discounting sensor readings that are known to be inapplicable. Thus, by treating the map as if it too were sensor data, the value of real sensor data can be greatly enhanced.

4.2.3. Landmarks

Map data also can be processed to help find prominent landmarks. For landmark knowledge to be a true resource for action, it must be independent of any specific route. All prominent landmarks should be identified a priori, and visibility regions for these landmarks should be computed. In this way, several queries could be answered at any point during mission execution: "What landmarks should be visible from the current position?," "Are we in a good viewing region?," "Where is the nearest viewing region?," and "What heading is best for viewing landmarks?"

4.2.4. Circulation

One critical stumbling block for many of the above techniques is that they rely heavily on a fairly accurate estimate of vehicle position relative to the map. There are many locations in the map, such as near the gully in *Fig. 3*, where a slight error in position could yield a gradient vector that is completely opposite to the desired direction. The mathematical concept of *circulation* can help to better characterize the nature of this problem. Circulation is defined as the line integral around a closed contour as described by the expression

$$\oint \boldsymbol{v} \cdot \mathrm{d}\boldsymbol{s}$$

where $\boldsymbol{v}$ is a vector field, and $\mathrm{d}\boldsymbol{s}$ is a vector directed along the tangent of the curve at every point. Those areas where gradient vectors tend to point along a curve would be areas of nonzero circulation, and areas where all gradient vectors point in the same direction would have zero circulation. Regions where gradient vectors are opposite but emanating from the same point, such as along a Voronoi edge, would also have zero circulation. Regions where the gradient vectors are antiparallel, such as along a gully, would have extremely high circulation. From this we can see that in most areas a position error will not impair

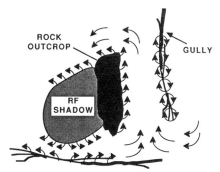

Fig. 8. The circulation of a gradient field plan provides an indication of salient mission-related map features.

the usefulness of the gradient field, but in areas with an extremely high circulation, accurate knowledge of the vehicle's position is essential. *Fig. 8* shows an approximation of the circulation that might be obtained from the gradient field in *Fig. 3*.

A circulation map may be obtained for a gradient field grid $\boldsymbol{G}$ by convolving $\boldsymbol{G}$ with a 2×2 mask $\boldsymbol{M}$ whose vector elements are defined by $\vec{\boldsymbol{m}}_{i,j} = \langle -2i + 3, \ -2j + 3 \rangle$ where $i, j \in \{1, 2\}$. This definition of $\boldsymbol{M}$ creates a matrix of four vectors which can be thought of as being tangent to a circle at the center of the matrix. This can be shown graphically as:

$$\boldsymbol{M} = \begin{bmatrix} \nearrow & \searrow \\ \nwarrow & \swarrow \end{bmatrix}$$

The convolution of $\boldsymbol{M}$ with $\boldsymbol{G}$ is the same as a convolution between two scalar matrices except that dot products are computed between vectors where multiplication of scalars would ordinarily be performed. This provides a discrete approximation to the continuous line integral formula for circulation.

While, in one sense, the presence of circulation in a gradient field plan diminishes the utility of the gradient field for guidance, in another, it provides the means for improving navigational accuracy. Regions of high circulation correspond directly to critical features in the environment that can seriously impede the vehicle's progress toward it's specified goal. The highest circulation in *Fig. 8*, indicated by the tight circular loops, occurs along the gully. This tells us that the gully is a highly salient obstacle with respect to the given mission. Assuming that appropriate perception resources are devoted to this task, this also means that the vehicle should have a good chance of determining which side of the gully it is on when it gets near the gully. This information is all that is needed to preserve the utility of the gradient field. High circulation regions can thus serve both as an aid to understanding sensor requirements and as an aid to navigation.

High circulation occurs only around objects that can seriously impede progress to the goal. Not all obstacles will hinder progress to the goal. Gullies that are parallel to the gradient field, or small obstacles that require only a minor detour will have very little circulation around them. The presence of circulation can thus serve as an indicator of features that should be closely monitored by the available sensors. In *Fig. 8*, for example, high circulation is found at the upper right gully. Medium circulation is found below the gully and above the rock outcrop. Because they are in areas that require special vehicle attention or action, features identified by high and medium circulation may be closely related to the cues used in a linguistic route plan.

4.2.5. Symbolic Data

Although the discussion in this paper has focused primarily on internalized plans based on map data, it is also possible to consider internalized plans based on symbolic data such as that found in more general problem-solving domains. There are some significant differences, however, between symbolic data and maps. In maps, state can be defined by position and orientation, and proximity between states is easily estimated by a Euclidian metric. In more complex domains, state may be difficult to define and even more difficult to sense. Proximity of states may be determined only through knowledge of what state transitions are achieved by various operations. However, when a domain can be divided into a set of recognizable states, and these states can be linked according to their accessibility to one another, then internalized plans can be produced. Just as with map data, search through an abstract state space can indicate the progression of states required to reach a desired goal. If this knowledge can be used as advice within a system that can move between states on its own accord, then we have an internalized plan.

In his concept of "universal plans," Schoppers has shown that by breaking away from linear plan descriptions, one can obtain plans which allow opportunistic reaction to a dynamic world [24]. Universal plans are similar to a gradient field in that they indicate the precise action to perform from any given state. In this way, they constitute a significant departure from traditional plan representations by eliminating all abstraction barriers. However, universal plans are still designed to serve as a program for action, requiring that all action be determined from knowledge of discrete states and explicitly labeled objects. Consequently, universal plans cannot truly be viewed as a resource for action, as they do not allow symbolic world knowledge to be used as advice. There could be value to finding universal plan representations that provide a gradient field for arbitrary state spaces. Tremendous benefits might be realized if concepts such as circulation can be applied to these state spaces.

5. A System Perspective

All of the above approaches to using plans as resources for action are meaningful only if they can be applied in the context of a working mobile robot system. In developing autonomous systems, it is best to eschew traditional hierarchical control schemes and resist system architectures which are oriented toward plan-directed control. Plans used as resources serve only to aid a system already capable of independently solving the more immediate problems in its world. Consequently, various plan-driven hierarchical control schemes may be incapable of using plans as resources, since all detailed actions are produced from the transformation of high-level plans through successive refinements at different abstraction levels.

Hierarchical planning approaches may suffer also from the abstraction barriers created at each planning level. Whenever plans are transformed from one representation to another within a hierarchical planner, information is distorted or lost, and abstraction barriers are inevitably created. By the time a suitably refined set of subgoals and constraints is made available for generating action, the underlying basis for those goals and constraints may be lost. From the viewpoint of using plans as resources, however, it is the underlying basis for goals and constraints that is needed most. The arbitrary subgoals and constraints generated from this basis become super-fluous.

The abstraction barrier problem was present in our own hierarchical architecture even though our reflexive behaviors could produce reasonable actions without the aid of any plans at all [22]. The original intent of our architecture was to allow abstract symbolic plans to modify the performance characteristics of low-level behaviors in accord with changes in goals and environmental context. In a typical plan-driven manner, high-level plans were to be passed down and refined through successive stages of the hierarchy until appropriate effects on behavior were produced. To make things work, however, we found ourselves bypassing intermediate stages in the hierarchy and providing plan data directly to the behaviors. Effectively, we were treating the data as sensory input. While we once saw this as the exception, we now see it as the rule.

When plans are used properly as resources for action, they do not control a robot's behavior any more than does the robot's sensory input. Instead, all control of the system is effected by behaviors that interpret and respond to external and internal information sources. In a way, internalized map and mission plans can be treated as if they were supplementary sensory inputs. The gradient field, for example, can be thought of as a phantom compass that always gives a general idea of the right way to go. Additionally, just because we do not think of the robot as being directed by its plans, it does not follow that the robot can ignore important mission requirements. A mission constraint can no more be overlooked than an obstacle in the robot's path.

One architecture which seems highly amenable to the incorporation of internalized plans is the layered architecture advocated by Brooks [5]. The layered approach differs from a hierarchical approach in that there is no abstraction of data between layers. Each layer uses its own internalized sources of information either to influence vehicle behavior directly or to influence the activity in other layers. Because of this, we can imagine various layers making direct use of different internalized plan representations such as illustrated in *Fig. 9*. Each layer can make use of whatever plan information applies to the decisions being made at that level. Since the layered architecture provides the fundamental levels of competence needed by

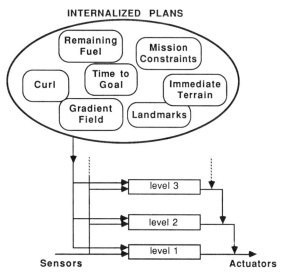

Fig. 9. Internalized plans are easily integrated into a layered system architecture.

the robot to survive, the addition of internalized plans merely adds another information reservoir to enhance the robot's overall competence. The concept of expressing behaviors as simple difference engines, as suggested by Cudhea [8], should make the incorporation of internalized plans straightforward because, as in the gradient field example, it is often fairly easy to estimate the difference between the current vehicle state and the desired state as specified by the plan.

6. Conclusion

In the ongoing pursuit to produce intelligent autonomous agents that can operate in real world environments, emerging concepts about the relationships between planning and action are inspiring new alternatives in plan representation. The simple yet elusive concept that plans must serve as resources for action rather than as programs for action has significant ramifications. The feasibility of constructing purposeful and competent autonomous systems which are not dependent on plans affords us the opportunity to focus on the information content of plans rather than their ability to direct a specific course of action. In doing so, we find that many forms of compiled data which would not ordinarily be regarded as plans can provide better action resources than can be obtained through conventional plan representations.

We have shown that a thorough understanding of the constraints of a problem may provide an extremely useful resource. In an autonomous system, this understanding comes about through the organization and analysis of available information with respect to the problem at hand. Ideally, all contributing information is furnished whole to the plan user, allowing the context of the plan user's surroundings to determine how the data will be used. To designate that aggregate of relevant knowledge specifically organized relative to a given problem, we have used the term "internalized plans." Internalized plans are predicated on the notion that there is more to a plan than what is seen in externally expressed representations.

If we accept the notion that a plan is a device containing advice for action, then our approach indeed internalizes real plans, albeit very expansive ones. To give the system the greatest ability to comprehend and to negotiate within its environment, we have supplied a ubiquitous type of plan that suggests a desirable course of action in every situation. This contrasts with the traditional type of plan, a single, linear, highly abstracted procedure that requires adherence to a predetermined course of action. While the compact expression of knowledge, such as in a linguistic route plan, has a prominent role in communication and may also be a valuable resource, this abstraction may not be necessary if all knowledge can remain internal to the system. In many existing planning algorithms, abstraction is an unnecessary final step that only serves to obscure far more valuable information.

Although we treat the plan user as an independently competent agent, capable of performing most fundamental tasks in its environment, internalized plans do not require a great deal of intelligence or reasoning power to be interpreted. A properly represented internalized plan gives straightforward advice for a specific set of situations. The breadth of the representation provides an efficiency of interpretation as opposed to an efficiency of space. At the current state of autonomous system technology, this trade-off is necessary to produce efficacious real-time action.

What is especially fortuitous about the internalized plan concept is its eloquent simplicity and the fact that all needed elements are already available. The implementation of internalized plans as a resource for action should be straightforward, and the search for new forms of internalized plan representations is conducive, we believe, to a wealth of further innovation.

Acknowledgments

Many of the concepts presented in this paper were fostered through frequent discussions with David M. Keirsey, J. Kenneth Rosenblatt, and Charles Dolan. I am extremely grateful for their contributions and insights. The advice of Joseph Mitchell and Rodney Brooks was also very helpful in bringing to light many important areas of related work. Many thanks also to Jimmy Krozel, and, of course, my wife, Karen, who helped make sure I said what I really meant.

References

[1] P. Agre and D. Chapman, What are plans for? AI Memo 1050, MIT Artificial Intelligence Laboratory (1987) (see also this issue).

[2] P. Agre and D. Chapman, Pengi: An implementation of a theory of activity, *Proc. Sixth Nat. Conf. Artificial Intelligence*, Seattle, Washington (July 1987) 268–272.

[3] R. Arkin, Motor schema based mavigation for a mobile robot: An approach to programming by behavior, *IEEE Conf. Robotics and Automation* (March 1987) 264–271.

[4] R. Bellman, *Dynamic Programming* (Princeton University Press, Princeton, New Jersey, 1957).

[5] R.A. Brooks, A robust layered control system for a mobile robot, *IEEE J. Robotics Automat.*, RA-2(1) (April 1986).

[6] R.A. Brooks, Intelligence without representation, *Preprints Workshop Foundations of Artificial Intelligence* (Endicott House, Dedham, MA, June 1987).

[7] R.A. Brooks, Planning is just a way of avoiding figuring out what to do next., presented at the DARPA Planning Workshop, Santa Cruz (October, 1987).

[8] P.W. Cudhea and R.A. Brooks, Coordinating multiple goals for a mobile robot, *Preprints of Intelligent Autonomous Systems* (North-Holland, Amsterdam, December 1986) 168–174.

[9] Y.K. Chan and M. Foddy, Real time optimal flight path generation by storage of massive data bases, *IEEE National Aerospace and Electronics Conf. (NAECON)*, Dayton, OH (May 1985).

[10] M. Daily, J. Harris, D. Keirsey, K. Olin, D. Payton, K.Reiser, J. Rosenblatt, D. Tseng, and V. Wong, Autonomous cross-country navigation with the ALV, *Proc. DARPA Knowledge-Based Planning Workshop*, Austin, Texas (December 1987) (also appearing in *Proc. IEEE Conf. on Robotics and Automation*, Philadelphia, PA, April 1988).

[11] E.W. Dijkstra, A note on two problems in connection with graph theory, *Num. Math.* 1 (1959) 269–271.

[12] H. Edelsbrunner, *Algorithms in Combinatorial Geometry* (Springer-Verlag, Berlin, 1987) 298–299.

[13] D.M. Keirsey, D.W. Payton, and J.K. Rosenblatt, Autonomous navigation in cross country terrain, *Proc. Image Understanding Workshop*, Boston, MA (April 1988).

[14] O. Khatib, Real time obstacle avoidance for manipulators and mobile robots, *IEEE Conf. Robotics and Automation* (March 1985) 500–505.

[15] B.H. Krogh, A generalized potential field approach to obstacle avoidance control, *Int. Robotics Res. Conf.*, Bethlehem, PA (August 1984).

[16] D.T. Lee, F.P. Preparata, Euclidian shortest paths in the presence of rectilinear boundaries, *Networks* 14 (1984) 393–410.

[17] T.A. Linden, J.P. Marsh and D.L. Dove, Architecture and early experience with planning for the ALV, *IEEE Int. Conf. Robotics and Automation* (April 1986) 2035–2042.

[18] J.S.B. Mitchell and D.M. Keirsey, Planning strategic paths through variable terrain data, *SPIE Conf. on Applications of Artificial Intelligence*, Arlington, VA (May 1984) 172–179.

[19] J.S.B. Mitchell, D.W. Payton, and D.M. Keirsey, Planning and reasoning for autonomous vehicle control, *Int. J. Intelligent Systems* 2 (1987).

[20] J.S.B. Mitchell, Planning shortest paths, Research Report 561, Artificial Intelligence Series No. 1, Hughes Research Laboratories, Malibu, CA (Also as PhD Thesis, Stanford University, Department of Operations Research, and to appear, *J. ACM*).

[21] N.J. Nilsson, *Problem Solving Methods in Artificial Intelligence* (McGraw-Hill 1971).

[22] D.W. Payton, An architecture for reflexive autonomous vehicle control, *IEEE Robotics Automation Conf.*, San Fransisco (April, 1986) 1838–1845.

[23] S.J. Rosenschein and L.P. Kaelbling, The synthesis of digital machines with provable epistemic properties, *Theoretical Aspects of Reasoning about Knowledge, Proceedings 1986 Conf.* J.Y. Halpern (ed.) (Morgan Kauffman Publ.) 83–98.

[24] M.J. Schoppers, Universal plans for reactive robots in unpredictable environments, *Proc. Tenth Int. Joint Conf. Artificial Intelligence*, Milan, Italy (August, 1987) 1039–1046.

[25] L. Suchman, *Plans and Situated Actions: The Problem of Human – Machine Communication* (Cambridge University Press, 1987).

Integrating Behavioral, Perceptual, and World Knowledge in Reactive Navigation

Ronald C. Arkin

School of Information and Computer Science, Georgia Institute of Technology, Atlanta, GA 30332-0280, USA

Reactive navigation based on task decomposition is an effective means for producing robust navigation in complex domains. By incorporating various forms of knowledge, this technique can be made considerably more flexible. Behavioral and perceptual strategies which are represented in a modular form and configured to meet the robot's mission and environment add considerable versatility. *A priori* world knowledge, when available, can be used to configure these strategies in an efficient form. Dynamically acquired world models can be used to circumvent certain pitfalls that representationless methods are subject to.

The Autonomous Robot Architecture (AuRA) is the framework within which experiments in the application of knowledge to reactive control are conducted. Actual robot experiments and simulation studies demonstrate the flexibility and feasibility of this approach over a wide range of navigational domains.

Keywords: Mobile robots; Reactive control; Knowledge-based systems; Artificial intelligence; Schemas.

Ronald C. Arkin was born in New York, N.Y., in 1949. He received the B.S. Degree from the University of Michigan in 1971, the M.S. degree from Stevens Institute of technology in 1977 and a Ph.D. in Computer Science from the University of Massachusetts, Amherst in 1987. From 1977 until 1985 he was a member of the faculty of Hawthorne College in Antrim, N.H., serving as the Computer Science Department Chair for the last three years. After receiving his Ph.D. in 1987, he assumed the position of Assistant Professor of Information and Computer Science at the Georgia Institute of Technology.

His research interests include reactive control and action-oriented perception for the navigation of mobile robots, dynamic replanning in hazardous environments, fault tolerant survivable control systems, navigation in three dimensional environments, and cognitive models of perception. He is included in several *Who's Who* publications including *Who's who in the World*.

1. Introduction

Considerable success has been achieved of late in the design and implementation of working robotic systems that can cope with a dynamically changing world. Several of the companion papers in this volume describe such systems. They are characterized by robust navigational capabilities and rapid, real-time response to the environment.

It is equally important to design for flexibility and adaptability in mobile robot navigational systems. Our approach, embodied in the Autonomous Robot Architecture (AuRA), allows for such freedom. It affords the decided advantages of reactive navigation: modular and incremental design; the ability to cope with a changing world; and the production of intelligent emergent behavior. In AuRA, however, both the motor behaviors and perceptual strategies can be readily reconfigured based on current environmental conditions, available *a priori* knowledge, and the robot's intentions based on the current mission's needs.

This paper describes how knowledge can be used to allow a robot to exhibit different navigational abilities under different circumstances. The methodology of reactive navigation is described in Section 2. Section 3 outlines the forms of knowledge that are especially pertinent to this form of mobile robot control.

The Autonomous Robot Architecture is presented in Section 4. AuRA is designed as much as possible to be a generic architecture, suitable for use over a multiplicity of domains. These include navigation in buildings, in outdoor campus settings, in aerospace or undersea applications, over contoured landscapes, in manufacturing environments and other settings. Representative examples, both with actual robot experiments and simulation studies are presented in Section 5. A summary and conclusions regarding the role of knowledge in reactive control complete the paper.

North-Holland
Robotics and Autonomous Systems 6 (1990) 105–122

2. Reactive Navigation

Reactive navigation is a form of robot control that is characterized by a stimulus-response type of relationship with the world, not unlike the viewpoint held by the behaviorist psychologists, epitomized by Skinner [30]. Mentalistic (representational) structures are eschewed and the organism (in our case, robot) reacts to the immediacy of sensory information in what we would term a very low-level non-cognitive manner.

Complex behaviors emerge as a combination of simple low-level responses to the rich variety of stimuli the world affords. Typically this involves decomposition of tasks into a collection of distributed parallel sub-tasks. Further, sensor data is normally channeled directly to the individual sub-tasks, reducing significantly the computational demand typically found in navigational regimes requiring world model building.

There are many representative examples of this form of navigation, a few of which will be described here. Brooks' subsumption architecture [15] has demonstrated robust navigation for mobile vehicles in dynamically changing domains. It is a layered architecture, well-adapted for hardware implementation [18]. It has been used in a wide range of robots, including legged ones [17]. Much of Brooks' work has been motivated by the desire to produce artificial insects. There is a deliberate avoidance of world modeling which is captured by the statement that *the world is it's own best model* [16].

Payton has described a collection of motor responses that are termed "reflexive behaviors" [27]. These behaviors react directly to sensory information yielding intelligent emergent behavior. Payton, Brooks, and several other proponents of reactive control incorporate the concept of *arbitration*. Multiple behaviors compete for control of the vehicle with a winner-take-all mechanism deciding the result. Only one behavior dominates the vehicle at any time, although the dominant behavior can change frequently in rapid response to environmental sensing. Earlier work by Kadonoff [22] also employs an arbitration scheme.

Kaelbling has developed a reactive architecture [23] that is an extension of Brooks' work. The emphasis is on embedded systems for real-time control. A hierarchical competency level for behaviors is established which is mediated by a high-level controller. The switching mechanism results in a decision as to which behavior is in control of the robot at any given time.

Firby has developed a different form of reactive control by utilizing modules called RAPs (Reactive action packages) which encapsulate tasks for a robot [19]. Situation-driven execution via goal satisfaction is the predominant mode of operation. Unsatisfied tasks are selected along with methods for their achievement that are consistent with the current world state. RAPs provide a hierarchical building block mechanism consistent with the task decomposition methodologies ubiquitous in reactive navigation.

Agre and Chapman in their PENGI system [1] have used reactive control in the domain of game playing. Several behaviors are active at any time, controlling the strategies used by a video game penguin and its relationship with other objects and entities in the world. An arbitration strategy is in evidence here as well.

Reactive navigation in AuRA [9] addresses reactive control in a manner that is significantly different than the approaches described above. Arbitration is not used for coordinating the multiple active agents; potential field formulations are employed to describe the reactions of the robot to the world; and explicit representational knowledge is used to select and configure both the motor and perceptual strategies used for reactive control.

Just as many psychologists moved away from behaviorism as an acceptable description of human information processing to cognitive psychology, our research has expanded to include many of the concepts forwarded by this relatively new discipline. Within AuRA, we do not abandon the unquestioned advantages of reactive control in the behaviorist sense as described above. It is our premise, however, that by encapsulating these stimulus-response behaviors in a form that is more flexible, adaptable, and controllable at a cognitive level above the reactive regime, robots can be created that are intrinsically more useful for a variety of missions over a wide range of task domains. The following section describes the structures that are used to represent these behavioral and perceptual techniques for navigation within AuRA and their motivation by modern psychology and neuroscience.

3. Applicable Knowledge

Despite the assumptions of early work in reactive control, representational knowledge *is important* for robot navigation. The fundamental problem lies in representing what is appropriate for the task. Amarel's classic paper [2] shows the importance of appropriate knowledge representation for problem solving using artificial intelligence.

The question is first what needs to be represented for successful general-purpose mobile robot navigation and then second how it is to be represented. Our answer to the first question is threefold: motor behaviors that are used to describe the set of interactions the robot can have with the world; perceptual strategies that provide the required sensory information to the motor behaviors; and world knowledge (both *a priori* and acquired) that is used to select (and reconfigure when necessary) the motor behaviors and perceptual strategies that are needed to accomplish the robot's goals. The remainder of this section answers the question as to how to represent this knowledge.

3.1. Schemas

Although it is not our goal to create robots that function internally in an identical or even similar manner as humans or animals do, it is our belief that tremendous insights can be drawn from these biological systems which already successfully achieve the tasks we would like our robots to perform. By studying psychological, ethological (behavioral), and neuroscientific theories, some of the models developed to explain these behavioral systems can serve well to motivate our approaches to robot navigation.

3.1.1. Motivation

Schema theory has been developed within cognitive psychology as a means for the codification and coordination of motor action and perceptual activity [14,21,28]. In particular, Neisser [25] describes the role of schemas within the context of the action-perception cycle. Perceptions are derived from the environment which in turn modify a cognitive map of the world resulting in motor actions which alter both the state of the world and the perceptions which arise from it. Norman and Shallice [26] have also used schema theory as a means for differentiating between willed and automatic behavior. Their studies provide motivation for the co-existence of both hierarchical and reactive control systems as is found in AuRA.

Psychologists have defined schema in a variety of ways. For our purposes, they are the primitives that serve as the basic building blocks of perceptual and motor activity. Arbib [3] was the first to apply schema theory to the robotics domain. This involved studies in the application of schema theory to dextrous hand control [4]. Other related research delves into neuroscientific models for schema operation within the brain itself.

The approach used in AuRA for developing navigational techniques in a new problem domain is as follows. First, the motor behaviors (motor schemas) required for the particular robotic application and domain are determined and then tested in simulation. Next, the perceptual strategies required to provide the information necessary for those motor schemas are designed and then implemented on the actual robotic vehicle. The techniques involving motor and perceptual schema design are discussed next.

3.1.2. Motor Schemas

Motor schemas, as used within AuRA, comprise a collection of individual motor behaviors each of which reacts to sensory information gleaned from the environment. The output of each individual motor schema is a velocity vector representing the direction and speed at which the robot is to move given current environmental conditions. A partial listing of some of the available motor schemas for our robot include (see also *Fig. 1*):

- **Move-ahead** – Move in a general compass direction.
- **Move-to-goal** – Move towards a discernable goal.
- **Avoid-static-obstacle** – Move away from a detected barrier.
- **Stay-on-path** – Move towards the center of a path.

– **Dock** – Combine aspects of ballistic and controlled motion to achieve a safe trajectory for mating with a docking workstation.
– **Noise** – A random process used for handling problems with local minima.
– **Move-up** – Move uphill on undulating terrain.
– **Move-down** – Move downhill on undulating terrain.
– **Maintain-altitude** – Follow isocontours on undulating terrain.

The first six schemas listed above have also been formulated for three-dimensional navigation as might be found in aerospace or undersea robotic applications (Sec. 5.2).

Each of these schemas is instantiated as separate asynchronous computing agents with parameters reflecting current world knowledge. The computations for each schema are very simple, usually involving a couple of additions or subtractions and at most one or two multiplications or divisions (with the exception of docking which includes a transcendental function). It should be noted that the entire potential field is never computed by the robot (although it is depicted in the figures to aid the reader's comprehension). Only the point where the robot is currently located needs to be computed. So each process is performing relatively simple mathematical operations, outputting a single vector expressing the robot's desired motion for that behavior.

The output of each primitive motor schema is combined using vector summation and normalization (keeping the resultant vector within the constraints of the actual robot's capabilities). This simple process can result in quite complex trajectories and behaviors as illustrated in the simulations shown in *Fig. 2*.

3.1.3. Perceptual Schemas

Action-oriented perception is the founding tenet for perceptual schema construction and usage. Each individual perceptual strategy is created to produce *only* the information that is necessary for the particular task at hand. Perceptual schemas are embedded within motor schemas providing the information that is required for them to compute their reaction to the world. In contrast to other non-reactive navigational approaches, no abstract model of the world is built using sensory data which is then reasoned over by perceptual processes during plan execution.

With this technique it becomes possible to exploit expectation-based mechanisms by using *a priori* knowledge of objects, constraints on positional uncertainty obtainable from a spatial uncertainty map [7], and adaptive models based on processing performed by previous sensing. By matching perceptual techniques to motor requirements, computational demand is greatly reduced.

Current sensors for our mobile vehicle include 24 ultrasonic sensors, a monocular CCD video camera, and shaft encoders. Simulation studies have used inclinometer data [12]. The example below using vision for docking operations describes the coordination between multiple perceptual strategies.

Docking with a manufacturing workstation is a complex operation. It requires a wide range of perceptual skills and knowledge (See [11] for a more detailed description of the perceptual processing). When the robot is located at a large distance from the workstation, it is impossible to discern the dock's structure. A salient feature however is the presence of motion (activity) due to the workstation's normal operation. A temporal activity detection algorithm has been designed to provide information regarding the location of the workstation relative to the robot given constraints on the location of the robot relative to a world map. As the robot gets closer to the workstation, it becomes necessary to positively identify it. A more computationally expensive algorithm, exploiting a spatially constrained version of the Hough transform is used to get a positive location. For final positioning, adaptive tracking is performed which abandons the *a priori* model of the workstation after it has been located and uses feedback from previous images to finally position the robot relative to the dock. An adaptive version of a fast region segmentation routine followed by texture-based positioning completes the sequence of perceptual techniques for docking in a complex manufacturing setting.

The above sequence can be likened to the strategies used by someone who is given instructions to turn right at the second flashing traffic light. At first the person walks along looking for some long-distance perceptual event. After detection of a candidate event (something flashing), models of what traffic lights look like (as opposed to car's turn signals) are brought to bear for a positive identification of the flashing object as a

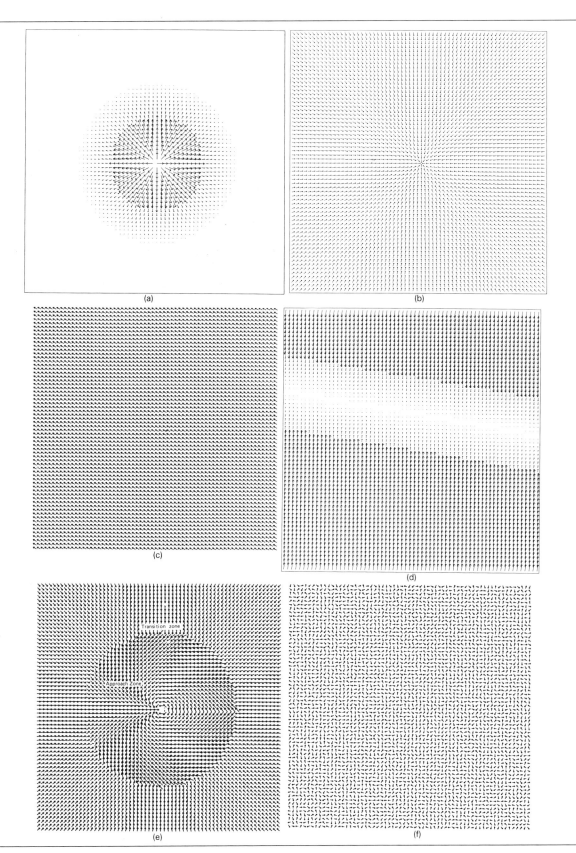

Fig. 1. Motor Schemas. a) **Avoid-static-obstacle**; b) **Move-to-goal**; c) **Move-ahead**; d) **Stay-on-path**; e) **Dock**; f) **Noise**.

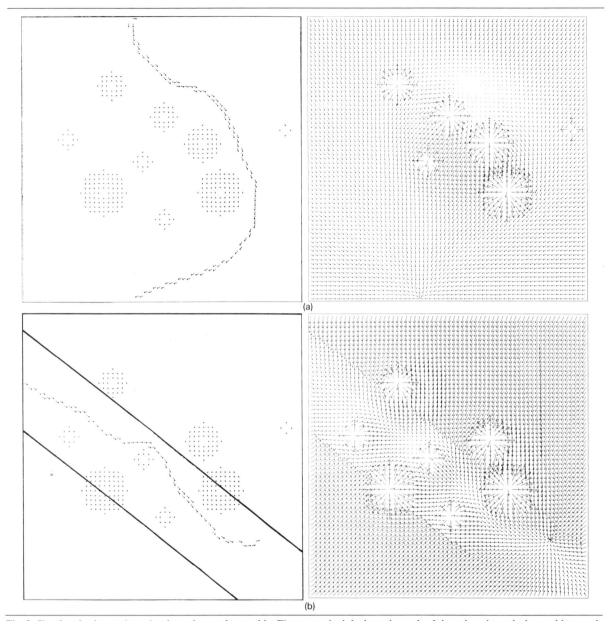

Fig. 2. Simulated robot trajectories through complex worlds. Figures to the left show the path of the robot through the world towards the goal. Figures to the right indicate a typical field present at some point during the robot's travel. a) **Move-to-goal** and 9 obstacles. Only 6 **avoid-static-obstacle** schemas are active in the field to the right as the other obstacles are out of range. b) **Move-to-goal**, 8 obstacles, and **stay-on-path** schemas. Only 7 **avoid-static-obstacle** schemas are active in the right-hand figure.

traffic light. Once this is identified, the preconceived notion of an *a priori* model of a traffic light is abandoned, allowing the user to continuously monitor the perceived object in an adaptive manner, updating their understanding (acquired model) of what that object is only in terms of

what is necessary to perform the motor action of turning at the correct point.

This strategy is loosely consistent with the concept of affordances as espoused by Gibson [20]. Only the information that is required to perform a motor action is extracted from the environment and little or nothing more. This computational economy underscores the principle that perception is meaningless without the context of motor action.

Some of the perceptual schemas that we have developed in addition to the four described above include: ultrasonic sensing used for obstacle avoidance; fast region segmentation using computer vision for road/path following; fast line finding for landmark identification and road following; depth-from-motion algorithm for obstacle avoidance; inclinometers for moving on non-planar outdoor terrain; and the use of shaft encoders for direction and approximate goal location.

3.2. World Knowledge

Most reactive systems are unconcerned with the use of world knowledge. It is our contention that world knowledge plays a vital role in a robot's interaction with the world. It is not a prerequisite for navigation, but it is a prerequisite for *efficient, flexible, and generalizable* intelligent navigational techniques.

Two types of world knowledge can be utilized. *A priori* information about the robot's environment that can be considered relatively static for the duration of the mission is termed *persistent* knowledge. This data typically arises from object models of things the robot might expect to see within it's world, models of the free space within which it navigates, and an ego-model of the robot itself. The knowledge base within which this information resides is termed long-term memory (LTM), indicative of the persistence of this data.

Transitory knowledge is dynamically acquired by the robot as it moves through the world. It is remembered within the context of short term memory (STM). World models constructed from sensory data fall into this category. Although this data is not used for reactive navigational control, it is brought to bear when difficulties are encountered with the reflexive/reactive techniques used in the absence of this form of knowledge. Much work has been undertaken in dynamic world model acquisition in mobile robotics (e.g., [13,24]). It should be noted that dynamically acquired world models should only be used when needed, as indicated by the failure of reactive control to cope with difficult situations. Even then, that data should only be used to reconfigure the reactive

control regime and not to supplant it. Transitory knowledge is forgotten (fades) as the robot moves away from the locale within which that information was gathered. Learning mechanisms could be constructed to migrate knowledge from STM to LTM (assuming that semantics could be developed to distinguish persistent environmental objects from transitory ones) but this currently is not one of our research thrusts.

For both persistent and transitory knowledge, the choice of representational structure and format is less important than merely the availability of the knowledge itself for use within a navigational system using reactive control for plan execution. Persistent knowledge allows for the use of pre-conceived ideas of the relationship of the robot to the world, enabling more efficient use of its resources than would be accomplished otherwise. Transitory knowledge on the other hand, if misused, could interfere, with the simplicity and efficiency of reactive control. Nonetheless, when difficulties with a reflexive control regime arise, it is important to have a bigger picture available to help resolve them. This can result in solutions to problems such as the *fly-at-the-window* situation in reactive control when an insect, striving to go towards the light of the sun entering from the outside of a window, but rebuffed by the glassy barrier, expends all of its energy trying to solve the problem with its fixed set of behaviors and dies. If transitory models of the environment are constructed under these conditions, a robot could use this information to circumnavigate the barrier.

4. The Autonomous Robot Architecture

The Autonomous Robot Architecture (AuRA) was designed to provide general purpose navigational capabilities over a wide-range of problem domains. It has been used as the framework to conduct navigational experiments in the interior of buildings [9], outdoor campus settings [5], and manufacturing environments [6]. Simulation studies in three dimensional domains [8,29] and rough outdoor terrain [12], have also been performed.

AuRA (*Fig. 3*) is comprised of 5 basic subsystems:

1. *Perception:* The gateway for all sensory data into the system. Sensory information is shunted in two primary directions: to the motor schema

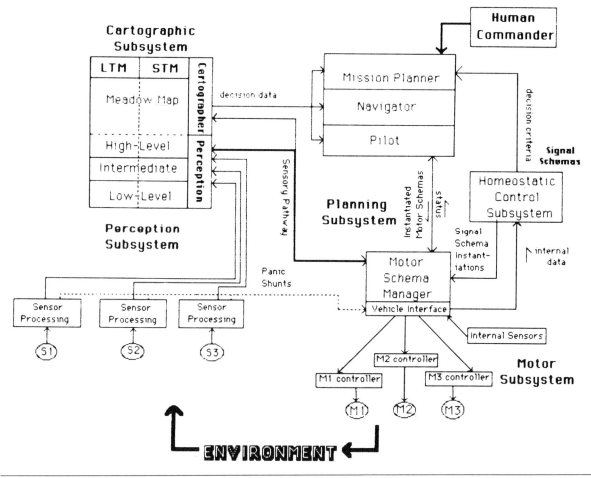

Fig. 3. The Autonomous Robot Architecture.

manager for processing by the perceptual schemas providing data for the reactive motor behaviors; and to the cartographer for construction of dynamically acquired world models within short-term memory. Specific sensor preprocessing and information flow control occurs within the perception subsystem.

2. *Cartographic:* World knowledge, both *a priori* knowledge stored in long-term memory and perceived world models stored in short-term memory, is constructed and maintained within this subsystem. It is available for use by the planning subsystem. Spatial uncertainty management is also maintained within the cartographic subsystem, providing data for the generation and control of expectations used for perceptual processing.

3. *Planning:* The planning subsystem consists of both a hierarchical planner and a distributed reactive plan execution subsystem. The hierarchical planner determines, via a series of actions involving changes in planning scope, first a global path through the modeled world (*Fig. 4a*) that consists of a series of piecewise linear path segments (*Fig. 4b*) that fit the constraints of the overall mission. Each segment is translated sequentially into a collection of motor and perceptual schemas that will accomplish the subtask (*Fig. 4c*). These schemas are then instantiated concurrently for plan execution, driving the robot to successful completion of each leg (*Fig. 4d*).

4. *Motor:* The motor subsystem is the interface to the actual robot. It is intended to be the only

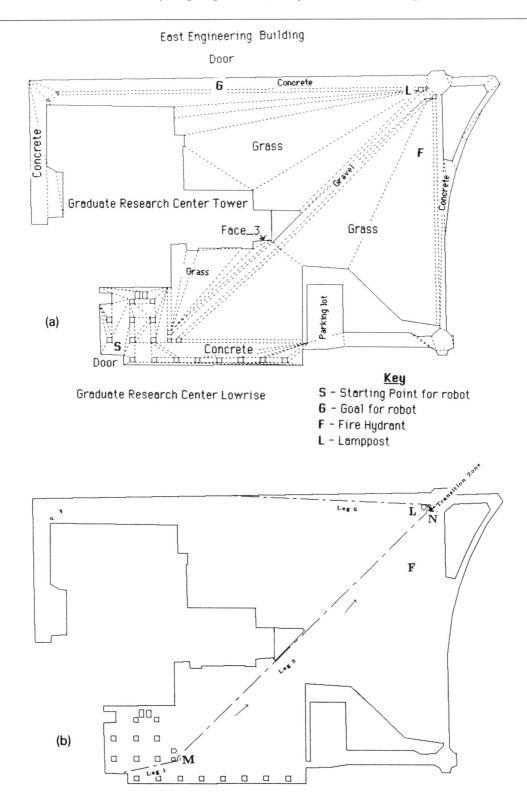

Fig. 4. Planning in AuRA. (a) (*top*) World model of a campus setting. (b) (*bottom*) Navigational path computed through world model.

A. **Stay-on-path(find-path**(gravel))
B. **Move-ahead** (NNE — 30 degrees)
C. **Move-to-goal**(right(**find-landmark**(LAMPPOST-107),3))
D. **Move-to-goal(find-transition-zone**(gravel,concrete))   **(c)**
E. **Find-landmark**(HYDRANT-2)
F. **Find-landmark**(GRC-TOWER(face-3))
G. **Avoid-obstacles**

(d)

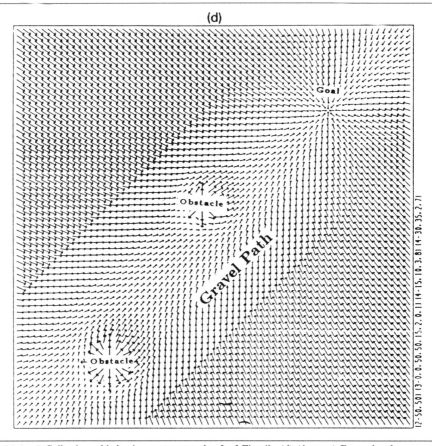

Fig. 4 (continued). (c) (*top*) Collection of behaviors to traverse leg 3 of Fig. 4b. (d) (*bottom*) Example of a potential field generated during path traversal where the robot is approaching the goal in the presence of unmodeled obstacles.

vehicle dependent component of the architecture. The velocity signal provided by the planning subsystem is translated into a correct set of steering and drive commands for the particular robot, in our case, George – a Denning mobile robot (*Fig. 5*).

5. *Homeostatic Control:* This subsystem monitors internal conditions of the robot (e.g., available fuel, internal temperature) and feeds the data to both the higher level planning mechanisms and the motor schemas themselves. Knowledge of the robot's current condition can thus affect

high-level planning and also modify reactive behavior in a manner that can minimize the internal stress on the system. Schema-based techniques are employed that exploit an analog of the mammalian control system to allow for dynamic replanning in hazardous environments. See [10] for additional information.

AuRA in its current state is only partially completed. Most of the modules exist in operational form, but are yet to be fully integrated. Section 5 presents examples of the navigational successes already achieved within the existing framework.

Fig. 5. George – a Denning mobile robot.

5. Reactive Navigational Examples

Section 3.1 has already presented simulation results for two-dimensional terrestrial schema-based navigation. In this section, results using our actual mobile robot are presented in addition to simulation studies in more complex worlds.

5.1. Mobile Robot Experiments

The concepts in this paper have been developed and tested on our mobile robot. The first sequence (*Fig. 6*) illustrates door entry behavior (using an earlier Denning robot – HARV) by a combination of **move-ahead** and **avoid-static-obstacle** schemas. 24 Ultrasonic sensors provide the perceptual data for the robot. The **move-ahead** schema is pointing obliquely into the wall, while the **avoid-static-obstacle** is concurrently repulsing the robot from the

wall. The net emergent effect has been termed the *drunken sailor behavior*, where the robot follows the contour of the wall (as someone drunken might lean against the wall while progressing forward) and when the robot (or the sailor) encounters a sufficiently large opening, falls through. World knowledge is exploited to indicate when a door might be present without relying on the shaft encoders or other correlation mechanisms to find its position accurately. The result is successful passage through a doorway.

Docking in a complex, cluttered environment is shown in *Fig 7*. Here the robot is under the influence of **docking**, **avoid-static-obstacle**, and **noise** schemas. The robot never computes a global path, but continuously reformulates its reactions to the world (using ultrasonic and shaft encoder data), to maneuver around obstacles and satisfy its final positioning requirements. We have also demonstrated the robot's ability to cope with moving obstacles using the same schema configuration for this domain.

5.2. Three-dimensional Simulation

Schema-based navigation has been extended to three-dimensional domains [8] that afford six degrees of freedom for the robot (3 translational, 3 rotational). The schemas used for 2D navigation have been reformulated in a straightforward manner to produce three dimensional vectors instead of two. As the simulation studies show, the navigational technique generalizes very well.

The first example (*Fig. 8a*) shows the robot's path while maintaining its position in a channel, moving towards a goal and avoiding obstacles along the way. The second example (*Fig. 8b*) illustrates docking in the presence of obstacles. Remember that a global path is never computed and the robot reacts from its current position to its perceived world using combinations of schemas that have been selected by higher level planning mechanisms. The simulation studies incorporate uncertainty in perception to reflect more realistically actual conditions.

5.3. Reactive Navigation over Contoured Terrain

Rough terrain can also provide an interesting test domain for schema-based navigation. Using inclinometer data that provides pitch and roll information for a mobile robot, the vehicle can react directly to the topography of the land. This can result in literal artificial intelligence "hill-climbing" behavior. A discussion of the issues of sensor design and the role of noise in dealing with local maxima and minima appears in [12]. The simulation studies presented here are based on actual Defense Mapping Agency data obtained from the North Georgia region.

Fig. 9a shows the results for a robot striving to move up in the world and using noise to rock it off of local maxima. The figure to the right of the schema path shows the robot's altitude as it move through the world. *Fig. 9b* shows a combination

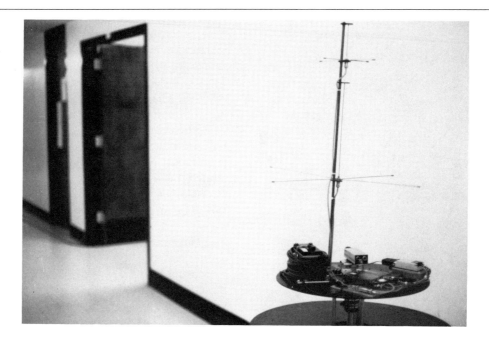

Fig. 6. Door entry via a combination of **avoid-static obstacle schema** and **move-ahead** schemas.

of **move-down** and **move-to-goal** schemas successfully completing the robot's mission. Space prevents illustration of other interesting combinations of inclinometer behaviors (including **maintain-altitude** with other schemas such as **avoid-static-obstacle**, **move-ahead**, and **stay-on-path** (see [12]).

6. Conclusions

Reactive navigation is an important general purpose navigational technique that can be applied to a wide variety of problem domains. It is characterized by its independence of world models

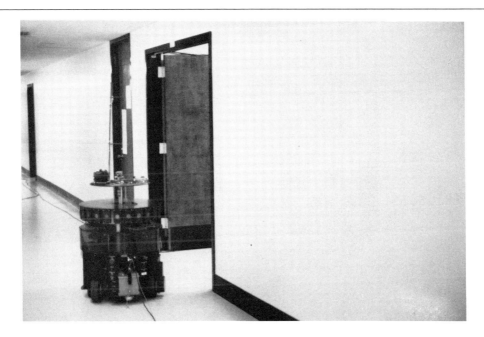

Fig. 6 (continued).

during plan execution. Knowledge of various forms, however, plays a crucial role for flexible and generalizable reactive navigation. Flexibility can be readily incorporated by modularizing behavioral patterns and perceptual strategies (schemas within AuRA). In this manner, behaviors drawn from a library of motor skills and sensory algorithms can be configured to meet the needs of a particular high level mission and any known environmental constraints.

World models play an important role in configuring these behaviors. We have seen that world models are unnecessary for low-level actions, but in order to efficiently explore the environment, *a*

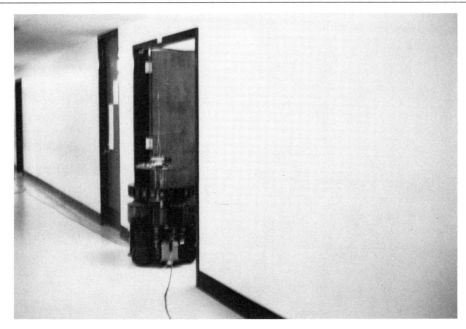

Fig. 6 (continued).

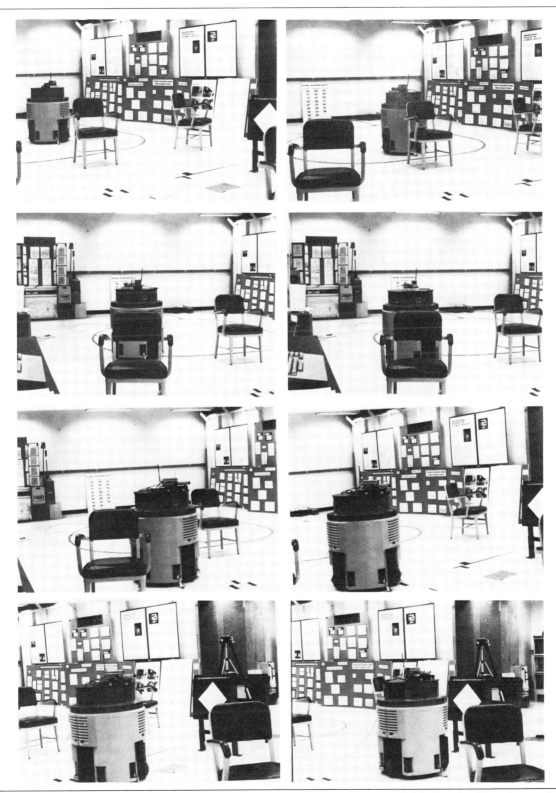

Fig. 7. Docking in a complex environment. The robot winds its way through a world cluttered with obstacles ultimately assuming the correct position and orientation relative to the docking workstation.

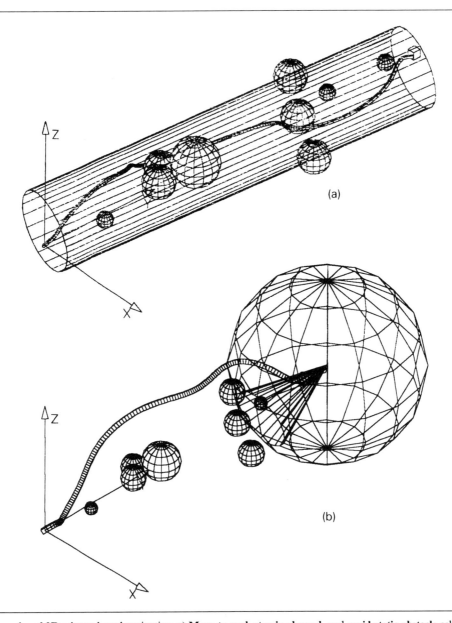

Fig. 8. Two examples of 3D schema-based navigation. a) **Move-to-goal**, **stay-in-channel**, and **avoid-static-obstacle** schemas produce the robot's path through the cluttered channel to the goal on the right. b) **Docking** and **avoid-static-obstacle** schemas produce a safe traversal through the cluttered environment to the dock in the center of the controlled motion zone. The outer sphere of the **docking** demarcates the transition from ballistic to controlled motion, while the inner cone distinguishes the approach zone from the coercive region.

priori knowledge of both objects to be perceived and the navigational free-space of the robot should be exploited when available. Dynamically acquired world models also play a role, but only when problems are encountered using reactive tech-

niques. Routine navigation can be conducted in the absence of such short-term memory data.

The Autonomous Robot Architecture is one framework in which world knowledge is used to facilitate reactive navigation. Potential field meth-

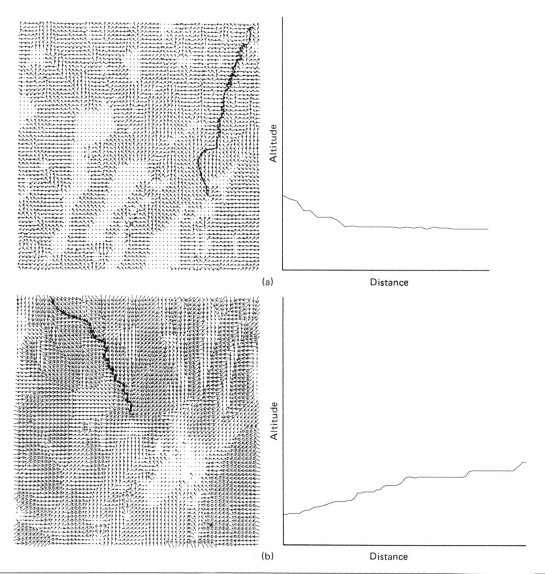

Fig. 9. Inclinometer schema-based navigation. a) **Move-up** and **noise** schemas produce the steady climb over rough terrain. b) **Move-down** and **move-to-goal** schemas produce the path shown. The robot overcomes local minima due to the pressure exerted on it by the goal.

ods afford an effective means for combining multiple active motor behaviors concurrently, without arbitrating between them. The simulations and experiments in this paper have demonstrated the viability of this methodology.

Acknowledgments

The author would like to thank Robin Murphy and Warren Gardner for their assistance with the experiments and simulations. This research is supported in part by the Georgia Tech Computer Integrated Manufacturing Systems Program and the Materials Handling Research Center.

References

[1] P. Agre and D. Chapman, Pengi: An implementation of a theory of activity, Proc. AAAI-87, 268-272.

[2] S. Amarel, On representations of problems of reasoning about actions, *Mach. Intelligence* 3 (1968) reprinted in *Readings in Artificial Intelligence*, Eds. Webber and Nilsson (Tioga, 1981) 2-22.

[3] M. Arbib, Perceptual structures and distributed motor control, *Handbook of Physiology – The Nervous System II*, Ed. Brooks (1981) 1449-1465.

[4] M. Arbib, T. Iberall and D. Lyons, Coordinated control programs for movements of the hand, COINS Technical Report 83-25 Dept. of Comp. and Info. Science, University of Massachusetts, Amherst, Ma., 1983 (also *Exp. Brain Res. Suppl.*, 10, (1985) 111-129).

[5] R.C. Arkin, E. Riseman and A. Hanson, AuRA: An architecture for vision-based robot navigation, *Proc. 1987 DARPA Image Understanding Workshop* (Los Angeles, CA, 1987) 417-431.

[6] R.C. Arkin, Intelligent mobile robots in the workplace: Leaving the guide behind, *Proc. First International Conference on Industrial and Engineering Applications of Artificial Intelligence and Expert Systems* (1988) 553-561.

[7] R.C. Arkin, Spatial uncertainty management for a mobile robot and its role in expectation-based perception, *Robot Control 1988 (Syroco '88)* (Pergamon Press, Karlsruhe, W. Germany, Oct. 1988) 279-284.

[8] R.C. Arkin, Three dimensional motor schema based navigation, *Proc. NASA Conference on Space Telerobotics*, Pasadena, CA (Jan. 1989).

[9] R.C. Arkin, Motor schema-based mobile robot navigation, *Int. J. Robotics Res.* 8 (4) (August 1989) 92-112.

[10] R.C. Arkin, Dynamic replanning for a mobile robot based on internal sensing, Proc. 1989 IEEE International Conference on Robotics and Automation, Scottsdale, Arizona, (May 1989) 1416-1421.

[11] R.C. Arkin, R. Murphy, M. Pearson and D. Vaughn, Mobile robot docking operations in a manufacturing environment: Progress in visual perceptual strategies, *Proc. IEEE International Workshop on Intelligent Robots and Systems 89*, Tsukuba, Japan, 147-154.

[12] R.C. Arkin and W.F. Gardner, Reactive inclinometer-based mobile robot navigation, submitted to 1990 IEEE Conf. on Robotics and Automation, May 1990.

[13] N. Ayache and O. Faugeras, Building, registration, and fusing noisy visual maps, *Proc. Int. Conf. on Computer Vision* (1987).

[14] F.C. Bartlett, *Remembering: A Study in Experimental and Social Psychology* (London, Cambridge Univ. Press, 1932).

[15] R. Brooks, A robust layered control system for a mobile robot, *IEEE J. Robotics Automation* RA-2 (1) (1986) 14-23.

[16] R. Brooks, Intelligence without representation, Research paper, AI lab, Mass. Institute of Tech. (1988).

[17] R. Brooks, A robot that walks; Emergent behaviors from a carefully evolved network, *Proc. 1989 IEEE Conf. on Robotics and Automation*, Scottsdale, AZ. (May 1989) 692-694.

[18] R. Brooks and J. Connell, Asynchronous distributed control system for a mobile robot *Mobile Robots*. Eds. W. Wolfe and N. Marquina, *Proc. SPIE* Vol. 727 (Bellingham, Wash. SPIE) 77-84.

[19] R.J. Firby, Adaptive execution in complex dynamic worlds, *Ph.D. Dissertation*, YALEU/CSD/RR #672, Yale University, Jan. 1989.

[20] J.J. Gibson, The theory of affordances, *Perceiving, Acting, and Knowing*, Ed. R. Shaw and J. Bransford (Erlbaum, 1977).

[21] H. Head and G. Holmes, Sensory disturbances from cerebral lesions, *Brain* 34 (1911) 102-254.

[22] M. Kadonoff, F. Benayad-Cherif, A. Franklin, J. Maddox, L. Muller and H. Moravec, Arbitration of multiple control strategies for mobile robots, Mobile Robots - *SPIE Proc.* 727 (1986).

[23] L. Kaelbling, An architecture for intelligent reactive systems, *SRI Technical Note 400*, SRI International (Oct. 1986).

[24] H. Moravec, Sensor fusion in certainty grids for mobile robots, *AI Magazine* 9 (2) (1988).

[25] U. Neisser, *Cognition and Reality: Principles and Implications of Cognitive Psychology* (Freeman, 1976).

[26] D. Norman and T. Shallice, Attention to action: Willed and automatic control of behavior, from *Consciousness and Self-regulation: Advances in Research and Theory*, Eds. Davidson et al., 4 (Plenum, 1986) 1-18.

[27] D. Payton, An architecture for reflective Autonomous vehicle control, *IEEE Conf. Robotics and Automation* (1986) 1838-1845.

[28] J. Piaget, *Biology and Knowledge* (Univ. of Chicago Press, 1971).

[29] T.M. Rao and R.C. Arkin, 3D path planning for flying/crawling robots, to appear in *Proc SPIE Conference on Mobile Robots IV*, Advances in Intelligent Robotics Systems, Philadelphia, PA, November 1989.

[30] B.F. Skinner, *About Behaviorism* (Knopf (Random House), 1974).

Symbol Grounding via a Hybrid Architecture in an Autonomous Assembly System

Chris Malcolm and Tim Smithers

Department of Artificial Intelligence,
University of Edinburgh,
5 Forrest Hill,
Edinburgh EH1 2QL, Scotland

We describe the architectural principles of our SOMASS robotic assembly system. It requires little more information than the shape of the desired assembly and the shape of the parts from which to construct an assembly plan, which is executed reliably by a robot system. It is a *hybrid* system, comprising a careful marriage of a PROLOG assembly planning system with a plan execution agent designed to control uncertainty (including the use of sensors) by means of *behavioural modules* which accomplish useful motions of the parts. The key notions are the simplification of the planner resulting from increasing the competence of the plan execution agent, and grounding the planner through a *single* hierarchy of behavioural modules instead of a *twin* hierarchy of sensing and action. We develop new terms for this discussion, since the old ones – such as "subsymbolic" – beg the questions we wish to address.

Keywords: Assembly robots; Assembly planning; Behaviour-based; Cognitive; Hybrid; SOMA; Subsumption; Symbolic; Symbol grounding; Uncertainty.

Presented at the Workshop on Knowledge Representation and Learning in an Autonomous Agent, November 16–18, 1988, Lagos, Portugal.

DAI Research Paper No 448, 1989

After twenty years in the computer industry as a systems programmer, latterly specialising in communications operating systems, **Chris Malcolm** joined the Dept. of Artificial Intelligence in 1981 as an RA on a robot dynamics project. In 1987 he received an MSc in IT/AI at Edinburgh. The topic of the MSc dissertation, for which he shared the Xerox prize, was the SOMASS system described in this paper. In 1987 he became a lecturer in Intelligent Robotics in the Dept., and is now in charge of a SERC (UK Science and Engineering Research Council) grant-funded project (ACME GR/E/68075) based on this system, which began in Jan 1989. With his colleagues John Hallam and Tim Smithers he leads the Behaviour-based Systems Research Group (BSRG) at Edinburgh, which coordinates within a long-term research agenda a number of research projects in robotics.

North-Holland
Robotics and Autonomous Systems 6 (1990) 123–144

1. Introduction

We consider the representational and architectural lessons we have learned from our implementation of an automated robotic assembly system which makes and executes assembly plans. It is necessary to develop some new terms for this discussion, since the conventional ones – such as *symbolic* and *subsymbolic* – beg some of the questions we wish to address. Thus we begin with a general introduction, in which we explain the classical Explicit-World-Model paradigm of (artificial) creature construction, and how our approach, which we call the Behaviour-based paradigm, differs from this.

1.1. The Knowledge Representation Hypothesis

One of the long term aims of Artificial Intelligence is the emulation of intelligent human behaviour. This is too difficult to attempt directly, so must be approached by degrees. One way is to divide human mentality into separate packages which can be studied in relative independence; which presumes that mentality is (at least to some extent) functionally modular [1]. Another way is to follow the same kind of developmental path as

Tim Smithers has a BSc in Aeronautical Engineering from Kingston Polytechnic, London, obtained in 1977. After which he joined the Engineering Department at Cambridge University, from which he received his PhD in 1981 for work on numerical methods for structural design. He then spent a year as a Research Assistant in the Radio Astronomy Group at the Cavendish Laboratory, Cambridge, working on the Structural design of the James-Clerk Maxwell millimeter wave telescope, now operating on Mona Kea, Hawaii. This was followed by a period with FEGS Ltd., a small engineering software company in Cambridge, during which he worked on parallel algorithms and hardware architectures for finite element analysis and results visualization techniques. In 1984 he joined the Department of Artificial Intelligence in Edinburgh as a Research Fellow working on a project to investigate intelligent design support systems for mechanical design. In 1986 he became a lecturer in Intelligent Robotics in the Department, and now leads the AI in Design research programme and robotics research in Behaviour-based mobile robots and low-level Behaviour-based control techniques.

Fig. 1. The computational metaphor.

evolution: to start with simple but complete creatures, and proceed by incremental development [1]. Most AI research has assumed functional modularity of a particular kind, concentrating on experimental implementations of such human competences as planning, reasoning, game playing, diagnosis, and language understanding. Typically the input to these implementations arrives already coded, in the form of input either directly typed on a keyboard, or ultimately derived from such input; and their output is similarly some symbolic encoding intended for human interpretation. One might say that the input and output consist of "paperwork", or symbols. Thus this kind of artificially intelligent system is a *program* which performs an (intelligent) *transformation* between its (symbolic) *input* and its (symbolic) *output*. Thus it is analogous to the standard model of information processing, i.e., a program performing some transformation between between its input and its output data [2]. This kind of intelligent transformation is sometimes referred to as *symbolic* computation to distinguish it from the data processing kind.

Not all computer systems fit easily within this program model of computation. Three obvious examples are operating systems, word processors, and blackboard systems, where the variety and discontinuity of input forces some kind of parallelism on the functional decomposition of the system, in the sense that at any particular time there may be many different partly completed tasks in process, some of which depend on or affect others.

In such cases the attempt is often made to characterise these more complex systems as collections of programs with suitable communication interfaces. Hoare has challenged the utility of this view of such systems in general [3], and Lyons suggests quite explicitly that it is inappropriate for complex robots, i.e., robots with sensors:

> As robotics has progressed it has become clear that sensory input and motor output are *not* simply analogues of the peripheral read and write commands in computer programming languages. We argue here that they are the *primal* structuring concepts for describing robot behaviour in computational terms. Just as Hoare revolutionised interprocess communication by stating that data input and output operations are not extensions to a programming model but *the* fundamental structures in it, we shall also argue that sensory input and motor output are *not* examples of peripheral read and write commands but the fundamental operations of the robot domain.
>
> [4, p. 48].

The poverty of support in programming languages for the non-hierarchical program structuring methods based around co-routines [2] reflects the difficulty we have in understanding this kind of non-hierarchical complexity. So, since not even all information processing systems fall naturally within the hierarchical model of computation, it would not be surprising if the same proved true of artificially intelligent systems.

This suggestion that input and output (sensing and action) are the fundamental operations of the robot domain is not new, e.g. [5], but it is only recently that it has received suggestive confirmation from the experimental success of those who are implementing the coupling of sensing and action at low levels (rather than via a world model). The best known examples are Brooks's family of subsumption-based mobile robots at MIT [6–8],

---

[1] Incremental development also requires a certain kind of modularity (i.e. the increments), but this is not *functional* modularity, and is moreover one which we have existence proof is workable – the incremental development by which we evolved from lesser creatures.

[2] This model model derives naturally from the terms of the Church-Turing thesis, and is made explicit in the *transform-centered morphology* of Yourdon and Constantine [2], where analytic program decomposition continues in the same terms, with the central transformation module receiving its input from a hierarchy of efferent modules, and supplying its output via a hierarchy of afferent modules.

and the work at Rochester on dynamic vision [3], which shows how the use of simple vision-servoed motions of the kinds employed by primate vision can considerably simplify the processing required to decode the symbolic information in the image plane, e.g. [10,11 (contained in ref. 12)].

Returning to our story-line, in the early days of AI it was supposed that intelligence would consist essentially of some powerful reasoning machine, ingeniously deriving the conclusion from the the premises, much after the fashion exhibited by mathematicians' rational reconstructions of theorem proving [13]. It proved difficult to make these highly general systems effective in specific domains, and in reaction to this systems were tried in which specific skills were implemented procedurally. The disadvantage these procedural systems manifested in their turn was the difficulty of achieving general and modular behaviour in their specific domains. Computer science by then had recognised the advantages of generality and modularity resulting from declarative rather than procedural encoding of data in computer programs, and this led in AI to the *Knowledge-Based* paradigm which currently dominates AI research. The essential feature of this is the declarative expression of knowledge in propositional form, either explicitly recognisable as this knowledge, or implicit (derived by the operations of the accompanying reasoning processes from the explicit knowledge) [4]. The basic hypothesis underlying this Knowledge-Based paradigm (that artificial intelligence is (will be) essentially based on propositionally encoded knowledge) has been nicely characterised by Brian Smith.

The Knowledge Representation Hypothesis: Any mechanically embodied intelligent process will be be comprised of structural ingredients that a) we as external observers naturally take to represent a propositional account of the knowledge that the overall process exhibits, and b) independent of such external semantical attribution, play a formal but causal and essential role in engendering the behaviour that manifests that knowledge.

[16, p. 2].

As Smith points out, it is an open question whether this is the only way of contriving intelligent processes, merely the most convenient, or even true at all; but it is interesting because it underlies a great deal of AI research (and robotics), even to the extent that it is often presumed by the terms we use to describe intelligent systems.

1.2. Symbolic and Subsymbolic Systems

Systems whose behaviour depends upon propositionally encoded knowledge, and reasoning mechanisms operating on this knowledge base, are sometimes called *symbolic systems*. Expert systems are a well known example of the type. We will explain the assumptions underlying this use of "symbolic", and some criticisms of these.

There are many varieties of computational system which do not depend on this kind of knowledge base. There are systems whose extensive knowledge is procedurally encoded, such as the system of co-ordinated joint servos which drive the end of the jointed arm of an industrial assembly robot in a straight line. There are systems whose knowledge is wired into the hardware substrate, such as floating point arithmetic processors or analogue computers. And there are systems which do use a large representational knowledge base, but one which is analogically rather than propositionally encoded.

These different kinds of system are often referred to not just as *non*symbolic systems, but as *sub*symbolic systems, because it is presumed that a symbolic system will naturally form the controlling pinnacle of the architecture of any artificial creature, and that all these other nonsymbolic kinds of system are naturally fitted to the more menial tasks of supporting the input/output of the symbolic system. The input system processes the raw sensory input signals, and turns them into the symbols necessary for input to the symbolic system; the output system turns the symbols output by the symbolic system into actuator control signals. This is sometimes referred to as the symbol/signal transformation [17]. Just as computer

---

[3] We prefer to use *dynamic* vision to refer to vision which employs relative motion between observer and observed, in line with Beni and Hackwood's term *dynamic sensing* [9]; reserving *active* vision for vision which emits the illuminating radiation.

[4] In using the the terms *explicit, implicit*, and *tacit* to categorise types of knowledge representation we follow Dennett's usage [14] except that we restrict *implicit* to implications within the scope of the inference engine, i.e.: *explicit* is explicitly encoded; *implicit* can be inferred (made explicit) by the system in question; the other sense of Dennett's *implicit* (embedded in some way which cannot be made explicit) we call *tacit*, following [15].

science has extended the program-based model of computation into the notion of a program with standard input and output streams, which are supported by the operating system, with its file managers, device drivers, etc., so this is a similar extension of the Knowledge-Based paradigm of AI into the realm of artificial creatures. We will call this extension the Explicit-World-Model paradigm, since in the case of an artificial creature the knowledge naturally comprises the creature's model of its world. This Explicit-World-Model paradigm presumes the world model to be implemented (at least in part) as a classical Knowledge-Based system, and so it shares the features of that kind of system.

This approach is not without its critics. Harnad refers to this as the symbolic functionalist approach, and criticises its presumption that the symbolic processing component of an artificial creature can be devised in hygienic and comfortable isolation from the problems of handling sensors and effectors, and that these subsymbolic components can be bolted on afterwards at the symbolic interface. He suggests that it is likely to be so difficult to handle sensors and effectors in ways useful to the hosting of intelligence that the ways this can be done will dominate and interpenetrate the design of the symbolic system [18–20]. Dennett has pointed out that the usefully predictive *description* of a system as a knowledge-based system is quite a distinct matter from the *implementation* containing knowledge as a recognisable ingredient, i.e., in the way described by Brian Smith's Knowledge Representation Hypothesis above [21,22] [5] Brooks argues against the need for any kind of world model or cognitive level at all, on the grounds that these things exist purely in the mind of the observer, i.e., we have made the mistake of reifying the intentional description [6] [6]. Rosenschein and Kaelbling have shown how a knowledge-based (or symbolic) description may be compiled into a nonsymbolic implementation (at least in simple cases) [24]. Steels has shown that some problems usually regarded as exemplary

demonstrations of the utility of the symbolic approach can equally well be solved by complex dynamics acting on an analogical (nonsymbolic) representation [25].

Brooks goes further, pointing out that in a real artificial creature, embedded in its world, some of the information processing which the creature has to perform in going about its business need not necessarily be performed by a computer at all – it can be performed by taking advantage of the physical properties of certain sensor and effector implementations, e.g., a cylindrical lens can be used to emphasise vertical edges in a camera image [8]. In assembly robotics the mechanical remote centre compliance [7] in effect uses linkages and springs to perform computations. Maturana points out that in any biological creature going about its business in its environment of evolutionary adaptation, these kinds of effects extend beyond taking advantage of properties of sensors and effectors, to what he calls *structural coupling* between the whole creature and its environment, so that some features of what we as observers may construe to be components of the mentality of the creature may be inextricably dependent on the complex embeddedness of the creature in its environment, and not discernible within the bounds of the creature itself at all [27]. Bateson long ago argued this as a general property of cybernetic systems, e.g. [28].

Most of the chapters in this book in one way or another dispute the presumptions which underlie the classical Explicit-World-Model paradigm of an artificial creature, including this hierarchical symbolic/subsymbolic division of the architecture. Consequently we will use the term *nonsymbolic* rather than *subsymbolic* in order to avoid the presumption that nonsymbolic processing must necessarily subserve symbolic processing; and we introduce the terms *cognitive* and *subcognitive* to describe the hierarchy in functional terms without presuming the symbolic (subsymbolic, nonsymbolic) status of the elements as they may be implemented. It is an open question whether a cognitive/subcognitive division within the implementa-

---

[5] Using an analytic description of a behaviour as an ingredient of an implementation of that behaviour is often a computationally expensive implementation.

[6] This is by no means a novel *philosophical* point of view e.g., [23], but it *is* novel as the underpinning of a robot architecture.

[7] There is a problem in trying to insert a slightly misaligned peg into a chamfered hole, which is that the resulting forces tend to cause jamming. The remote centre compliance is a device which translates these forces into a movement of the peg tending to correct the misalignment [26].

tion of the mentality of an artificial creature is necessary or convenient. In our SOMASS system described here we do find it (at least) convenient.

1.3. Cognitive and Subcognitive Systems

The term *cognitive* refers etymologically to and implies a knower. When discussing component parts of systems which *know*, whether human, animal, or artificial, it is necessary to be clear what *knower* is presumed. For example, *we* may see knowledge embedded in the design of a creature, or even explicitly represented, without this particular knowledge being known or knowable by the creature in question. On the other hand, a certain creature may know something which people are in principle incapable of knowing. Furthermore, one of the points of Dennett's intentional level of description of a creature is that one may use terms like *knowledge* in describing the behaviour of a creature without presuming that this knowledge is in some way a distinguishable ingredient of the creature; cognitive *behaviour* does not necessarily imply cognitive *components* of mind. Finally, it may be the case that a closed modular component of a creature may be cognitive, while the entire creature does not itself have a topmost controlling cognitive level, e.g., a creature which consists of a society of component creatures. In other words, a cognitive *part* does not necessarily imply a cognitive *whole* (and vice versa). Thus, when talking about *knowledge*, we must always remember that knowledge is relative to the viewpoint of the supposed *knower*. This knower may be an autonomous system, or even just a component part of one.

The hybrid architecture exemplified by our SOMASS system comprises a cognitive component, which performs the higher mental functions (in this case planning), and a subcognitive component, which controls the actuators and sensors of the robot. The subcognitive component hosts the cognitive component in the sort of way the operating system of a computer, with its device drivers etc., hosts the programs, but is more complex than this, since it is required to provide the basic instinctive competences whose existence is taken for granted by the cognitive level. Indeed, there is no reason why the subcognitive component should not be more complex and computationally demanding than the cognitive component. It so

happens that the cognitive component of our SOMASS system *is* a symbolic system, and a simple monolithic one, but we do not presume that this is necessarily a feature of cognitive systems in general. In other words, this kind of hybrid architecture is only one of the possible architectures of a creature exhibiting cognitive behaviour. If, as in the case of the SOMASS system, the cognitive component is also a symbolic system, then the subcognitive assembly component will perform the interfacing signal/symbol transformations which are a necessary part of the support or grounding of a symbolic system.

Our SOMASS system has a hierarchical assembly planner with dependency-directed backtracking [29], written in PROLOG. We call this a cognitive system because of the kind of function it performs – planning. It so happens that its behaviour is determined by means of explicit propositional representations of knowledge and computations performed using them, in the manner indicated in Brian Smith's Knowledge Representation Hypothesis above, and consequently it is also a symbolic (i.e. Knowledge Based) system. We see no reason, however, why the kind of assembly plans our system requires could not in principle be generated by a *non*symbolic system, such as a complex dynamical system operating on an analogical representation – but it would still be performing the same task and producing the same results. So the fact that it would no longer be a symbolic system is a design decision, and we would still call it a cognitive system because it would still perform the job of planning.

The SOMASS system also executes these plans. The planner and the plan execution agent are two complementary parts of the complete SOMASS system. The kinds of things this plan execution agent can do determine the terms in which the plans must be expressed, and these competences (or Behaviours) give semantic significance to the planner. Without the assembly agent, the planning system would be simply a formal syntactic process, lent second-hand semantic significance only by the minds of its human observers. So because the assembly agent provides this semantically grounding substrate to the (cognitive) planner, we call it a subcognitive system. It so happens that it is also a nonsymbolic system. This is unlikely to remain the case in the next version of the SOMASS system.

1.4. Inherent and Borrowed Semantics

Where there exists a clearly defined symbolic interface between the cognitive and subcognitive components of a system (as there does in the SOMASS system) then it might so happen that the implementation of the cognitive component was finished first. In this case it would be pedantry to refuse to suppose it cognitive until the subcognitive component had also been finished, on the grounds that until then it was an ungrounded (purely formal) system without inherent semantics.

No, we would naturally deem it cognitive in the reasonable expectation that the necessary subcognitive support would later arrive. One month later? Two years later? Maybe in a few decades? At what stage does this expectation cease to be reasonable (and consequently the cognitive system fail to be grounded)? We might, for example, decide to specialise in research into cognitive systems only, building them to symbolic interfaces which we reasonably expected were in principle supportable, but without intending ever to bother devising this subcognitive support. In this case these systems can be called cognitive as a *semantic loan* which we consider in principle redeemable. Some of the criticisms of the Knowledge-Based paradigm of AI come down to assertions – for various reasons – that the implied semantic loan is *not* redeemable, i.e., that it could never be cashed because the appropriate kind of subcognitive component is *not* implementable.

2. The Architecture of Artificial Creatures

A critical problem in the construction of both mobile robots and assembly robots proves to be the handling of the uncertainties of the real world. So many systems which worked wonderfully in an ideal simulated world have foundered upon this rocky problem. When complete autonomous systems are divided into modular components to be distributed between the implementation team, or when research institutions decide to specialise in one particular aspect of artificial intelligence, the problem of handling uncertainty is frequently defined to be the problem of someone else, and so disappears conveniently in the cracks between the module interfaces until the embarrassing time of system integration. In our opinion the problem of

uncertainty provides a serious constraint upon the architecture of artificial creatures, and consequently should be addressed from the outset rather than being postponed.

2.1. The Problem of Uncertainty in Assembly Robots

If one is dealing with a sensorless robot (which can therefore only perform fixed sequences of motion) the problem of uncertainty [8] can be dealt with by carefully engineering the robot and its environment so that everything will work. Consequently the planner (whether human, artificial, or some combination) can think in terms of the ideal mathematical models with the reasonable expectation that the plans will work in practice. Unfortunately the cost of ensuring this reliable performance (by engineered control of uncertainty) seriously restricts the industrial applicability of sensorless assembly robots, and removes the whole point of using them: to substitute software (programming) for hardware (engineering).

Now in general to bring the management of uncertainty within the domain of software requires the introduction of sensors. This raises the problem of how to program sensor use.

It was considered obvious [9] that the robot was like an output peripheral and the sensors were like input peripherals. Connecting the two was the robot control program, whose job was to perform the appropriate transformations upon the input data (sense data) in order to arrive at the output data (robot motions). Since to duplicate the richness of the human vision system – which spreads an apparent model of the 3D world before our mind's eye in real time – is currently beyond the scope of both our technology and our understanding, it was obviously necessary to build systems which already knew a lot about their world (possessed a well-developed world model) and were thereby able to make use of the clues provided by

---

[8] The inevitable variations of the form and location of the parts, the inevitable inaccuracies in the robot's motions, the vagaries of friction and stiction, and all other kinds of deviation of the real world from the ideal mathematical models, are known generically in assembly robotics as *uncertainty*. It is often characterised by bounds such as tolerances, e.g., [30], although Durrant-Whyte argues persuasively for proper statistical modelling, e.g., [31].

[9] It followed naturally from the program model of computation and the Knowledge Representation Hypothesis.

simpler sensors (such as proximity sensors, visual image edge detectors) to keep this model of the world up to date. This is the Explicit-World-Model paradigm of robot construction we have already mentioned. The world model is updated by the sensor processing hierarchy, corresponding to the input streams of a program. Consideration of the state of this world model by the cognitive system produces a decision about what action to take. This action is then effected through the effector control hierarchy, corresponding to the output streams of a program. Since the control of uncertainty involves the combined use of sensors and effectors, the two processing hierarchies of which are combined only at the level of the world model, then it follows that the control of uncertainty must involve cognitive activity based on the world model [10]. An underlying presumption is that the three activities of sensing, thinking, and action, can be decoupled in this way.

As far as assembly robots are concerned, a further assumption of the Explicit-World-Model paradigm has been that the position controlled robot, such as those controlled by VAL2 (Unimate, Adept) or AML (IBM), is a usefully general enough interface to the assembly process, and that all higher levels – such as planning – should be compiled down into this level. Indeed, the German IRDATA DIN interface standard is an attempt to define a general assembly robot programming interface at just this level. There is no doubt that it is *possible* to use this level of interface in the sense that it is theoretically possible to program any algorithm in machine code; the important question is whether or not it is in practice so tedious or intractable as not to be worth the bother of trying.

2.2. The Virtual Robot and the Subsumption Architecture

It is instructive to see how a lower level uncertainty problem – the problem of controlling the motion of the assembly robot – has already been solved. The typical industrial assembly robot has a number of revolute joints powered by electric mo-

tors, with some kind of rotation sensor, so that the angle of rotation of the joint can be inferred. Each motor and sensor pair is wrapped up in a servo control loop, which tries to keep the joint at the particular commanded angle. When perturbed by being pushed, the motor resists, and when the servo loop is given a new commanded angle, it drives the joint rapidly and without overshoot to the new angle. If all the joint servos are set to new angles, as would be required to move the whole arm to some new attitude, then the servos fight it out between themselves (since the acceleration of each one perturbs its neighbours) until one by one they stop (i.e., settle down into holding the achieved position), and the arm finally reaches its new position.

The trajectory by which it reaches the new position will be both irreversible and hard to predict unless some further control is added, so the next level of control is to determine the length of time the slowest motor will take to reach its destination, and then to control all the others in speed so that they all stop at the same time. In practice this means that each joint servomechanism must be both sufficiently powerful and conservatively controlled so that it can handle the worst loads that the other motors can impose on it without losing control of its own trajectory (i.e., deviating by more than the permitted error). Thus the whole arm executes a smooth and reversible trajectory in Cartesian space (in fact a straight line in joint space) in what is known as joint-interpolated motion [11].

Economical algorithms for solving the inverse kinematics of the robot arm [12] for certain geometries of arm have been found – but unfortunately not economical enough to be solved within the tens of milliseconds loop time of the joint control servos. Fortunately small joint-interpolated motions approximate to straight lines. So straight line motion in Cartesian space of the end of the robot arm is implemented by dividing the straight line into small straight-enough segments of joint-interpolated motion. In this way is implemented the

---

[10] Whether the world model need exist only in the programming (or off-line) part of the system, and can be compiled away in the consequent execution (or on-line) system is an interesting question we do not pursue here.

[11] It is possible to construct robot geometries in which this is not true; robot geometries in practice are constrained to those for which it is true, at least within the main part of the working volume.

[12] What set(s) of joint angles correspond to the end of the robot being at a certain position in Cartesian space.

standard industrial assembly robot, the end of which can be commanded to move in a straight line from its current position to a new position, regardless of the contortions of the joints required to achieve this [32].

What the observer sees is a robot which is told to go to a new position, and moves there in a straight line, and stops. At the bottom level this is implemented as a bunch of servos which are permanently active in parallel. They never stop, and all they do is monitor the difference between the commanded joint angle and the actual joint angle, controlling the motor current to keep it that way. Their interaction with one another (accelerating any one joint will always impose a reactive load on the others) is controlled purely by the fact that each is trying to do its own job – a society of joint controllers. What it does is determined by the error signal derived from the difference between its own sense input and its goal. Thus at the lowest level this is like a layer or two of a subsumption architecture [7], but instead of hosting further layers, it hosts a virtual machine interface – the virtual robot described by the robot programming language, the motion commands of which are implemented by this hierarchical servo system [13].

This illustrates the point that not only is it possible for a subsumption-type architecture to host a virtual machine interface, but that it might actually be the simplest and most elegant way of doing it in this kind of environment – handling many interacting sensors and effectors. Indeed, this is the point made by Lyons in his proposal for a schema-based architecture for the control of the Utah hand [4]. We have pointed out the analogy between Behaviour-based robot control systems, implementing virtual robots, and the current VLSI design and construction techniques which are used to implement the machine code interface (the virtual computer) of our current computers [33]. It happens that Brooks, the primary protagonist of the subsumption architecture, goes to considerable lengths to avoid the slightest taint of symbolic computation in his implementations. This may well be the only way of convincing those whose

imaginations have suffered from overexposure to LISP of the important point that there are truly no symbolic ghosts in his machines, but it should not divert our attention from the special virtues of this kind of architecture for providing a virtual machine interface to a cognitive system – which may in implementational fact happen to be a symbolic system. As will soon become apparent, however, the kind of relationship in the Behaviour-based approach between the subcognitive component and the cognitive component is radically different from that envisaged (or at least presumed by default) by the Explicit-World-Model approach.

2.3. The Grounding of Symbolic Systems

The problem of attaching meaning (with respect to the creature) to the symbols it employs is often called the problem of *symbol grounding*. Established usage calls this *symbol* grounding even though it is the entire system of knowledge and the inference and access machinery which acts upon it which must be grounded, rather than the symbols being grounded individually, as the phrase suggests. The symbolic representations in the computer can be connected to the world by engineering suitable input/output devices and drivers, such as the sensors and actuators of a robot. In an uncertain world there are difficult problems of maintaining a proper correspondence between the system's explicit world model and reality – grounding the symbols. We showed in Section 2.1 that in the Explicit-World-Model paradigm this problem has to be dealt with at the cognitive level.

Consequently the very difficult topics of representing and reasoning about uncertainty, and default and non-monotonic reasoning, are being actively researched by those following this paradigm.

2.3.1. Grounding in Expert Systems

Some of these problems can be avoided in symbolic systems which depend upon human mediation between the system and the real world. For example, a medical diagnosis expert system asks questions of people, and may request actions, such as testing blood samples. Human mediation allows these systems to use highly idealised and simplified views of the world. Without the highly competent actions and interpretations of people these systems would not work at all. In effect, expert systems are grounded by human mediation.

---

[13] With respect to the demands of the assembly task on robot control this is both an *incomplete* and an *ambiguous* virtual machine, but that is an implementation detail that does not concern us in this paper..

In other words, the subcognitive substrate supporting expert systems, into which dependency they are carefully dovetailed (as any cognitive system must dovetail into the subcognitive substrate which gives it inherent semantics and causal powers) is borrowed from the mentally most sophisticated creatures we know of – ourselves. Consequently, while not denigrating the utility of these artificial extensions of our own cognitive faculties (expert systems), they may well bear no useful resemblance to the cognitive level appropriate to the very much simpler creatures whose implementation we can currently hope for as research goals [14].

2.3.2. Grounding in Assembly Robots

In the case of an artificial creature rather than an expert system the situation is very different. Autonomous systems must handle for themselves the problems of maintaining a reliable and appropriate representation of the uncertain and changing world. Trying to solve this problem at the symbolic level gives rise to characteristically intractable problems. In the case of assembly robotics the critical problem is making the transition from the *motions of the parts* which would suffice to perform the assembly in an ideal world to those *motions of the robot* (partially instantiated from sensor readings) which are necessary to accomplish (the purpose of) these part motions reliably in an uncertain world. It is here that the representations and inferences concerning the effects of the various forms of uncertainty tend to develop an exponential greed for computation. In effect the cognitive component is trying to perform the virtually impossible task of compensating for the extreme incompetence of the subcognitive component, for it is generally the case that the less competent the plan (or program) execution agent, the more complex the plan (or program) must be.

In the case of assembly robots the classical presumption is that the executing agent is a robot which should be instructed in some suitably decorated variation of a standard computer programming language, where the decorations consist of support for the kind of position-controlled virtual assembly robot already described. In terms of general competence in the real world this is probably the ultimate degree of incompetence and stupidity short of complete inability that can be devised. Witness to this, despite decades of research into the automation of assembly, is the tediousness and complexity of getting modern assembly robots to perform even the simplest assembly tasks with adequate reliability, even without sensors. Where sensors are necessary, they are employed in an ad hoc fashion to repair the practical deficiencies of an underlying sensorless program, not because we are careless, but because it is the best we can currently do (within the Explicit-World-Model paradigm). The programming and engineering skills routinely deployed in even this primitive level of assembly automation, not to mention the human common sense on which much of these skills depend, make it clear that automation of the programming of sensor-based assembly robots (by this method) is still very far away.

2.3.3. The Movable Cognitive / Subcognitive Interface

What has been overlooked is the radically different nature of the cognitive and the subcognitive components of the complete system and the fact that the interface between them is movable. The interface is determined by the competent behaviours of which the subcognitive system is capable, which in effect defines a virtual machine. Like the familiar virtual machines of computer science, this is a movable interface: the more competent the plan execution agent, the less complex need be the plan. Moving this interface is in effect shifting the solution of certain problems between the planner and the assembly agent – the cognitive and the subcognitive systems. And since these systems necessarily employ very different styles of representation and architecture (reflecting their different tasks and resources) it is likely that some problems will be significantly easier to solve in one part of the system than the other.

Our contention is that the attempt to bolt classical cognitive systems directly onto the kind of assembly robot systems manufacturers are making today is based upon a mistaken decision about where in the system to solve the problem of uncertainty. This has led to the need for implementations of such complexity and computational power that they are quite beyond the scope of today's

---

[14] It is of course an open question just how complex a creature must be to require a cognitive level – if indeed a cognitive *level* is ever required at all.

technology. We assert that this complexity is not inherent in the problem, but is an artefact of this particular method of solution. In general we agree with Harnad that symbol grounding is a very difficult problem, perhaps solvable in only very few ways, and that the subcognitive component of the intelligence of a robot system which does the symbol grounding will so determine and permeate the design of the cognitive component that it would be folly to construct the cognitive component without first very carefully considering the subcognitive substrate which will host it [18].

The argument may be even stronger than this. It is commonly the case that lower level programming languages (such as assembler) can be directly compiled from higher level ones (such as Pascal), but there are some cases (such as LISP and PROLOG) where this is not possible, and an intermediate interpreted virtual machine interface is required [15]. It would be very nice if the part motions required to accomplish the assembly could be compiled down into robot motions and sensor readings plus appropriate computational glue. For example, this was the implicit presumption behind the development of Edinburgh's high-level RAPT assembly programming language [34]. Unfortunately, while this is possible in many simple cases, there are no *a priori* reasons for supposing that this is even possible, let alone feasible, in sensor-based assembly in general. In other words, it may not just be *easier* to do it the Behaviour-based way – it may be the *only* way to do it.

In fact, although we have spoken so far as though the important decision was in which part of the computational system to solve certain problems (the cognitive or subcognitive parts), we have already mentioned that in the case of real robots computations are not necessarily restricted to being performed by computers, and may in the extreme case be performed not even by the robot's hardware, but by some aspect of its embeddedness in its world. In this paper, however, we illustrate this general theme with the particular example of the benefits to be gained by solving the problems of uncertainty in assembly robotics, not in the assembly planner, but in the assembly agent, and consequently will emphasise the division of labour

between these two components of the *computational* part of the robot's mentality.

2.3.4. Grounding Cognitive Systems via Behavioural Modules

All this, however, (*pace* Brooks) does not damn cognitive systems in themselves, but only this classical Explicit-World-Model approach to connecting them to the real world. Their natural place in the architecture of an artificial creature is as a highly abstracted reasoning system, operating in an idealised world from which all the complex details irrelevant to that *problem* have been removed. Note the emphasis on *problem*: we agree with Winograd and Flores [35] that it is a mistake to try to construct comprehensive world models suitable for the solution of *all* the kinds of problem with which the autonomous system may be faced. To do so is to invite explosive complexity and consequent intractability. Rather we suppose that problems should be solved – in autonomous systems as in animals and people – in terms specifically and narrowly contrived for their solution, and which can be easily related to economically available subcognitive abilities. As Chapman and Agre point out, this is a point of view which is gaining acceptance among cognitive scientists outside as well as inside AI [36].

In a simple cognitive system, not able to carry out problem abstraction for itself, the abstractions required for those problems it has been designed to solve are accomplished by the implanted practical competences of the subcognitive system. We call the modular units from which this subcognitive system is built *Behavioural modules*, because they encapsulate useful elements of practical behaviour. Note that although these Behavioural modules are inspired by the same attitudes which underlie Brooks's development of the subsumption architecture, this *encapsulation* of useful behaviours is an important way in which these Behavioural modules differ from the state machines of the subsumption architecture. There is no need for Brooks's state machines to *encapsulate* behaviours – it suffices if the required behaviours emerge as the creature goes about its business. Since our Behavioural modules must not only implement the required behaviours, but also define the virtual machine which comprises the interface to the planner, then it is necessary that they do encapsulate those aspects of the robot's

---

[15] Of course LISP and PROLOG compilers exist, but they do require at run time an intermediate interpreted level, at least for the use of the special cases which demand it.

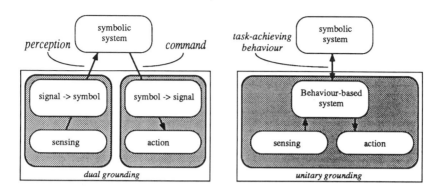

Fig. 2. Two kinds of symbol grounding.

behaviour in terms of which the planner will construct its plans [16]. This difference arises because we are concerned to construct systems which have an explicit cognitive level, whereas Brooks eschews explicitly cognitive ingredients as an illusion of the (human) mind's eye.

Thus these Behavioural modules serve not only as modular units of functional capability, they also act as the abstraction devices which enable the existence of an idealised and tractable representation of the problem. It is by means of the effective and reliable capabilities of these Behavioural modules that the cognitive reasoning of the system (the planning) is securely grounded in the real world. These two aspects of symbol grounding, the *abstraction*, and the *effective capability*, are performed by *one* unit, the Behavioural module. This is an important difference from the Explicit-World-Model paradigm, which grounds these two aspects by *two* distinct components, performing the abstraction by the sensor processing hierarchy, and the effective action by the motor control hierarchy (*Fig. 2*). The Explicit-World-Model paradigm simplifies the subcognitive system into these two parallel hierarchies (of sensor interpretation and motor control) at the expense of sweeping so many prob-

lems into the world model as to make it intractable for all but the simplest of autonomous systems.

2.4. The Hybrid Architecture

We refer to autonomous systems built from a careful marriage of cognitive and subcognitive systems as *hybrid* systems, to distinguish them from purely cognitive systems on the one hand [17], and on the other hand, from systems without any explicitly cognitive ingredients, such as Brooks is currently investigating. Thus the term *hybrid* is used to indicate an autonomous system built from these two kinds of component: a cognitive component, such as the Knowledge-Based systems of classical AI; and the Behaviour-based kind of subcognitive system as advocated by Brooks and others for mobile systems, and – with the differences we have already mentioned – by us for the subcognitive component of robotic assembly systems [33,37]. The cognitive component is char-

---

[16] There is no need to encapsulate those aspects of the robot's behaviour, however important to the task in question, which are *not* terms in which the planner will construct its plans. In the construction of these kinds of system, deciding what are the terms which need to be made explicit is a black art; and the grounds on which to base these decisions is an interesting and fundamental research question.

[17] As we have explained, systems cannot be *purely* cognitive if they are connected to the real world via sensors and effectors as opposed to being connected via human mediation, but the negligence with which the subcognitive component is often treated in the Explicit-World-Model paradigm suggests the presumption that the problems of the cognitive and subcognitive components are decoupled without further ado. Such a careless liaison can hardly be dignified as a *marriage*, and consequently we do not refer to these as *hybrid* systems in the sense defined above. We suggest that it may indeed be possible to decouple the cognitive and subcognitive components by means of a virtual machine interface – but that contriving this requires care.

acterised by a functional description in terms of knowledge representations and reasoning mechanisms which are cognitively penetrable, i.e., could be affected by the changing goals and states of the creature. We do not, however, as we have already explained, agree with Pylyshyn's assertion that cognitive penetrability necessarily entails implementation of the cognitive system as a symbolic system [17] – though this may happen to be the case.

The subcognitive component is characterised by cognitive impenetrability [18] and modularity of competence [19], but once again, while using Pylyshyn's useful terminology, we do not agree, as we have explained, that cognitive impenetrability necessarily entails a nonsymbolic implementation.

We like to suppose (*pace* Harnad and Brooks) that the interface between the cognitive and subcognitive components of the system should constitute a virtual machine, but whether this elegance can be maintained as such hybrid systems become more complex than the currently very simple SOMASS system remains to be seen. Note that this virtual machine need not necessarily reflect the structure of the subcognitive system as implemented – it could be a rational reconstruction.

3. The SOMASS Soma Assembly System

3.1. The Experimental Approach

Very little is as yet known about the business of designing and building artificial creatures; we merely have suspicions, hunches, and some plausible arguments to support them. In many cases our suspicions are supported more by what we know *hasn't* worked than what we know *has*. In brutal terms, our current ideas are quite possibly wrong. Under these circumstances we think it would be unwise to devise large long-term implementation experiments where we would have to wait many years before the crucial questions were answered. What we require are the simplest possible experi-

mental domains which focus us on the important problems, and which test our assumptions as soon as possible.

Since these assumptions may well be wrong, we cannot afford the luxury of presuming a problem decomposition and experimenting with simulations of the parts; our simple domains and robot systems must be complete and real. In other words, the only kind of simplifying abstraction available to us under these circumstances is the choice of suitably simplified tasks in the real world. Brooks has devised such a domain for his autonomous mobile system research [8].

Assembly is the fitting together of parts of various shapes to make a whole. It is characteristic of assembly that these parts only fit together in certain ways dependent on their shapes, and that they can only be moved into these fitting positions in ways dependent on their shape. This *shape-dependent part-fitting* is the essential feature of the assembly problem which the experimental domain must capture.

The SOMASS soma assembly system is a fully automated hybrid assembly planning and execution system. It needs to be told the shape of the final assembly it is to construct, the shape of the parts it is to use, and their approximate positions and orientations on the worktable [20]. *Fig. 3* shows the seven soma4 parts. *Fig. 4* shows some of the different assemblies which can be made from these parts. *Fig. 5* shows the various sizes of the parts with which we exercise the system. The size of of the cubies from which they are constructed varies from 1 centimetre to 3.5 centimetres a side. They are not too carefully made: there are errors of form of up to about 0.05 of the size of the basic cubie.

This experimental world was chosen for three main reasons.

1. It is as simple as possible, while capturing the essential characteristic of the assembly problem: the parts fit together, and must be moved into their fitted positions, in ways dependent upon their shape. The blocks world, for exam-

---

[18] i.e., impenetrable to the cognitive component, not the system designer.

[19] It is this modularity which permits the construction of a virtual machine interface between the cognitive and subcognitive components.

[20] Of course, working out how the parts should be disposed within the assembly is not usually considered to be part of the industrial assembly problem, but this is a useful facility in an experimental research system. One of the benefits is that it is a tireless inventor of new system tests, in the form of new assemblies to plan and make.

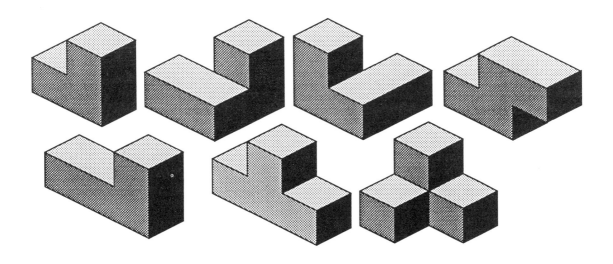

Fig. 3. The soma4 set.

ple, is too simple – blocks don't *fit* together, they can only be assembled by simple abutment relationships which are not strongly constrained by their shapes.

2. It is extendable. As the number of parts, and the number of cubies comprising the parts, are increased, the assembly problem becomes more complicated. For example, if more than one example of each soma4 part is permitted, then cyclic part adjacencies create the need for new part fitting strategies and for subassemblies [38]; in the soma5 world there is a tongue-in-slot assembly problem; in the soma7 world there is a square-peg-in-hole assembly problem.

3. It is combinatorially rich. Excluding rotations and reflections there are 240 different ways of

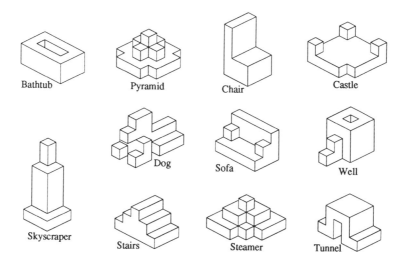

Fig. 4. Some soma4 assemblies.

Fig. 5. Various sizes of soma parts.

disposing the 7 soma4 parts within a 3 × 3 cube [39], each one of which constitutes a different assembly problem [21].

3.2. Reliability and Robustness

The planner produces an assembly plan which is then executed reliably by a robot system – our robot system has executed one of these plans 100 times, at twice the design speed, without failure. This was part of a reliability trial involving about 4,000 lines of automatically generated robot code, comprising about 50 different assembly plans, run for a total of about 45 hours, and involving part sets of two different sizes [22]. Less than three per cent of these plans failed in execution. These failures were almost entirely simple and easily fixed bugs (the majority in the planner) due to the fact that almost all of these assemblies were being planned and performed for the first time by the system [37].

It is a key feature of the approach that reliability of execution is achieved without the need for human intervention at any stage. For the system to lack that basic kind of autonomy would beg too many difficult questions about the role of the human intervention in the system, diluting the essential symbol grounding function which we wish the subcognitive plan execution system to perform for the cognitive planning system.

3.3. Interpretation versus Compilation

The SOMASS soma assembly system was designed as a complete unit. A Behavioural interpreter was implemented on top of the conventional programmable Cartesian position controller of the robot (VAL2). This interpreter consists of a set of Behavioural modules which achieve the motions of parts. We claim that it is a fundamental mistake, which has mired classical assembly robotics research in endless complexity, to try to decompose (i.e. compile) an assembly plan into motions of the *robot*. If the plan is instead decomposed into terms of ideal motions of the *parts* with the run-time Behavioural interpreter hiding both uncertainty and the use of robot motions and sensings to manage it, this turns out to be a computationally much less complex way of handling uncertainty, and permits the planner to be very much simpler. It is computationally less complex, because systems which control perturbations by servo-like task-achieving operations, using specific error perception and minimisation actions, are inherently less complex and more capable than systems which attempt to analyse the possibilities of perturbation in advance, and to devise comprehensive control-

---

[21] In fact, as far as the robot is concerned, which of the six ways up (i.e. which face is on the table) each of these assemblies may be done constitutes a different problem, because of gravity. Thus there are 1440 different *assembly* problems in the cube shape alone. Limitations of the current system (e.g. the robot has only 5 axes) mean that only about half of these possible assemblies can in fact be assembled.

[22] The plans are size independent; size is instantiated at run time.

ling strategies in terms of robot motions, reasoning from much more detailed world models. The planner can then be much simpler because it can plan in the simple general terms of an ideal world. From the point of view of the planner, the Behavioural modules are abstraction devices which both provide its ideal problem representation and ground it in effective real-world behaviour.

3.4. Representation

The issue of representation in computational systems and artificial creatures is as yet only poorly understood. There is a lot of dispute about the membership, propriety, and defining characteristics of such categories as *declarative* and *procedural*, and *analogical* and *symbolic*. Therefore the account we give here of the representation within the SOMASS system is not systematic, but we have tried to make it a complete list of the salient representational features which a systematic account should cover.

The division of labour between the subcognitive Behaviour-based assembly agent and the cognitive planning system is the first and most important representational consideration. As explained earlier, we require that the Behaviours which constitute the operators used by the planner are individually encapsulated as Behavioural modules, rather than emerging as the collaboration of a number of modules. Finally, since we make use of standard industrial assembly robots and their controllers, and in this initial implementation do not use sensors [23], the code component of our Behavioural modules [24] looks like ordinary subroutines or programs, with communication effected largely through conventional software methods such as parameter or message passing. These differences of architecture partly reflect the difference in the nature of the mobile and assembly problems, and partly reflect our use of a standard commercial robot (the ADEPT). It does not reflect a fundamental difference of approach. We share with Brooks the same concerns about

the close marriage of sensors and effectors, the local control of uncertainty, the use of the world where possible instead of representations, the importance of computational economy, and what kind of principles should motivate the modularisation of the system – an approach we sometimes call the *insect metaphor*. And although we do specifically make use of a standard symbolic system embodying explicit symbolic representations (the assembly planner), we have been very careful to make this cognitive component as *ignorant* as possible. This is achieved partly by improving the competence of the robot system which performs the plans, and partly by making the representations and reasoning as problem oriented as possible. Some suggest that this approach is less amenable to generalisation than a more widely knowledgeable system (e.g., which "knows" about Newton's equations of motion); we suggest that while such systems may indeed be more easily generalisable, they are fundamentally not implementable.

Thus the planning agent of the soma assembly system is unlike conventional AI planners. Where they tend to be designed to make as much as much of the knowledge involved explicit, the soma planner is designed to be as *ignorant* as possible – by making as much use of *tacit* knowledge as possible. Because the nature of the task is already well-defined (to construct an assembly from the given parts) the planning does not so much consist of the selection of appropriate operators, as the sequencing of the assembly, and the parameterisation of standard part-fitting schemas. There are two part fitting schemas: *pick up part, put part in assembly*; and, where this is not possible (the pick-up and put-down grasps cannot be equated), *pick up part, regrasp, put part in assembly*. The problems which forbid certain sequences and parameterisations (such as the obstruction of a particular grasp by some other component) can't be discovered by consulting lists of pre-conditions, but have to be established by computation, in a kind of envisioning. These kinds of things are what makes assembly planning different from resource and project planning.

3.4.1. The Structure of the Assembly Planner

The planner is hierarchical, in the sense that it forms a complete plan at a certain stage of abstraction, before going into further details and

---

[23] The architecture is designed to incorporate sensing, which is now (1989) being introduced.

[24] There is more to a Behavioural module than its code – indeed, in the extreme case, it has no more code than is necessary to constitute a software interface to the noncomputational implementation.

forming a complete plan at a lower level of detail. The stages of the hierarchy are as follows [38]:

1. Find a disposition of the parts within the assembly (usually many solutions). This level corresponds to a "materialisation" operator, i.e., this would constitute an assembly plan if it were possible to "materialise" each part directly into its final position (and the parts were perfect in form). This will backtrack through all possible dispositions.

2. Find a gravitationally stable ordering of the above in which each part can move into its final position along an unobstructed vertically downwards trajectory (always many solutions). This level corresponds to a telekinetic operator, i.e., this would constitute an assembly plan were it possible to command the parts to fly through space (and the parts were perfect in form). This backtracks through all possible stable orderings.

3. Find a way of gripping each part as it is put into the assembly (mostly fails). This level corresponds to an operator which causes the part to materialise in the required attitude in the robot's gripper. It so happens that the parts cannot *all* be placed in some assemblies using only vertical trajectories. In some cases the finger holding the last part cannot avoid being inside the assembly, consequently requiring a sideways displacement of that part. In these cases the part in question must also (as well as a vertical fitting trajectory) be capable of moving into position along a horizontal trajectory.

   The part must be gravitationally stable in this offset position. Because a failure here is always due to some other previously placed part getting in the way, this part of the search is pruned by identifying the obstructive part and using dependency-directed backtracking to leap directly to the next stable ordering in which that part has been re-ordered in the assembly sequence.

4. Find either a get-grasp which matches a put-grasp, or else a regrasping strategy (sometimes fails). This corresponds to the final assembly plan in the sense that all of the operators used here (pick up, regrasp, etc.) correspond to Behavioural modules in the assembly system. Planning proper is now finished, in the sense that neither of the two subsequent stages can fail, i.e., the searching which is characteristic of

(this implementation of) planning has concluded. Execution of this plan would always fail, since it is still based on the assumption that the parts are perfect in form and can be fitted into the assembly using ideal fitting trajectories with zero clearance between the parts.

5. Calculate the offsets necessary between the parts to allow spaces between all the horizontally adjacent faces (this always succeeds). This is known as *spacing out*, and is an important part of a tacit strategy [25] for handling uncertainty. These spaces accommodate the errors of form of the parts, plus the cumulative errors of location, which together comprise the presentation uncertainty at this point of fitting the part into the assembly. The errors are "trapped" (hygienically isolated) in these spaces during the assembly process. The robot concludes the assembly process by nudging the assembly together so as to close up the spaces. Note that while this spacing-out calculation always succeeds, it involves a search process which just happens to be both independent of the other constraints and guaranteed to succeed. This is an accident of the single soma4 world, and does not hold in either the multiple soma4 world or the higher orders (soma5, soma6, etc.) [38]. Thus in the soma5 world, this stage will still be part of the search in plan-space.

6. Translate this plan into VAL2 code for the robot system (this always succeeds). This is a simple context-free syntactic transformation. The code consists largely of parameterised subroutine calls to Behavioural modules [26].

3.4.2. Explicit Representations

The planner is told the shape and orientation of the parts as supplied, and the shape and orientation of the required assembly. It is not told the locations or sizes – these are communicated to the assembly system only at plan execution time (this is part of the strategy of maximising its ignorance). Since the parts (and assembly) are constructed

---

[25] i.e., "unknown" to the planner because built into the design of the entire system.

[26] This strictly serial delegation of control is only possible in the sensorless SOMASS 1 system. The SOMASS 2 system will involve parallel distributed behaviours, with control mediation via the environment.

according to a cubical grid these shapes are represented very simply as a list of those cubical cells (cubicles) which are occupied. A cubicle is represented as a triple of three (usually small) integers: (x,y,z). The planner also needs to know what rotations the five-axis robot can accomplish, which is held as a list of all possible rotations. This is all the explicitly represented knowledge.

3.4.3. Implicit Representations

The transformations of a shape list under rotation and translation are procedurally encoded, and the new shape list can be deduced after any movement of the shape. Thus knowledge of all possible shape movements is implicit, in the sense that the given operations on the given knowledge can make it explicit.

During the process of planning the assembly the system maintains two lists representing the partially complete assembly: a list of already occupied cubicles; and a list of still empty cubicles. Thus the basic question of whether a given part can be fitted into the assembly is answered by searching the possible rotations and translations of the shape list of the part for one which is a subset of the list of empty cubicles.

The system also has a set of basic procedures for such operations as discovering which part owns a given cubicle, the projection of shape lists into planes, the intersection of shape lists with planes, and so on.

The notion of gravitational stability is procedurally encoded, and consists of a simplified subset of full Newtonian stability such that everything considered stable by the system will really be stable. The cubical modularity makes the computations involved very simple matters of integer arithmetic. This procedurally encoded knowledge is regarded as implicit since it results in explicit knowledge, i.e., knowing whether or not a certain configuration is stable.

The planner is also concerned with temporary occupations of cubicles by its fingers and hand, since these sometimes get in the way, and is equipped with simplified procedurally encoded heuristics for computing these.

Since the planner is written in PROLOG one could pedantically argue that there is no such thing as procedurally encoded knowledge beyond the PROLOG interpreter itself. We adopt here the convention that explicitly represented knowledge

is that which one naturally takes to be a direct representation of given facts, whereas procedurally encoded knowledge is that which one naturally takes to be encoded in the form of the algorithm by means of which it can be derived. There are trivially disputable cases of no significant consequence. Sloman has well explicated these subtleties [40].

3.4.4. Tacit Representations

Tacit representations are those which the system cannot make explicit, but which are embodied in its structure, or in its interactive relation with the environment in which it is embedded. There are a number of different kinds of these, distinguished by where and how in the system they occur.

● Those which comprise the virtual machine interface to the subcognitive system, and so are directly implemented as distinct identifiable modules (Behavioural modules) within the subcognitive system, and consequently exist in the form of labelled operations within the cognitive system. The relevant properties of these are encoded procedurally in the cognitive system, not in the previous sense of being algorithmically encoded, but in the sense of governing the structure of the system, such as the form of the general part-fitting schemas, and so emerge from the general structure of the planner.

● Those which comprise parameters of these top level Behavioural modules (i.e. those used by the planner). In some cases these are simple numerical representations of physical quantities, such as degrees of rotation. In other cases they are partial instantiations of such representations, the full instantiation of which is completed only at plan execution time, such as the size of the parts. These parameters are labelled in both the cognitive and subcognitive systems, and are computed at least in part by the cognitive system. In the SOMASS 1 system this instantiation is simple numeric evaluation. The SOMASS 2 system will perform encapsulated symbolic computations on intermediate representations in the subcognitive system. In a number of cases intermediate representations which could have been entirely collapsed by the planner into a single parameter are in fact carried into the subcognitive system and collapsed (finally computed) there for no other reason than improving the comprehensibility of the system to the designer and debugger.

- Those Behavioural modules, and their parameters, which are purely internal to the subcognitive system. It so happens that there are none in this category in the sensorless SOMASS 1 system, but as soon as the use of vision for part location is implemented this category will exist.

- Those behaviours which are not encapsulated within specific Behavioural modules, but emerge from the collaboration of the effects of various Behavioural modules upon the world. These are mostly to do with the control of uncertainty, and will be considered in detail under that heading.

3.4.5. The Control of Uncertainty

Let us consider the various ways in which this system represents and handles uncertainty, recalling that the guiding principles of the implementation [27] were that uncertainty should be handled:

- entirely within the subcognitive system;
- at as low a level as possible;
- the residual uncertainty in the output of a behavioural module should be less than the range coped with on the input;
- so that the planner can work in an ideal (certain) world.

Location uncertainty

The simplest kind of uncertainty is the uncertainty in the initial location of the parts: the system is supplied with nominal part locations, about which a few degrees of rotation and a few millimetres of translation are permitted. The part acquisition Behaviour handles this, by acquiring the part with an uncertainty at least an order of magnitude better than than that permitted about the initial location. The current implementation (SOMASS 1) being sensorless, it does this by simple constrained motions (nudgings), which have to be planned to the simple extent of computing the enclosing rectangle of the shape of the base of the part. Although the purpose of this computation is the control of uncertainty, as far as the planner is concerned this is simply a question of supplying

the Behavioural module with the requisite parameter set. The next implementation (SOMASS 2) will use vision to perform this job, and consequently this uncertainty controlling computation will disappear entirely from the planner. Whichever version is considered, this particular uncertainty (part location) is controlled entirely by the part acquisition Behaviour.

Thus this kind of uncertainty obeys the guidelines, with the qualification that the Behavioural module needs some parameters, which are specifically required for the uncertainty control, to be computed by the planner.

Shape uncertainty

The second kind of uncertainty is uncertainty of form. This either translates directly into the final uncertainty of presentation with which the part is brought into its fitted position in the assembly, or is partly transformed into additional location uncertainty by rotations and regrasping. Where regrasping takes place there are also added uncertainties of location due to the variously caused movements which can occur when a part is released from the gripper. Most of these several uncertainties compound into simple uncertainty of location in the regrasping position. It would have been easy to add the nudgings already used in the initial part acquisition to the regrasp, thus controlling these uncertainities, but this proved unnecessary, since the method adopted to handle uncertainty of form in the fitting of the part into the assembly proved capable of coping with this extra regrasp uncertainty as well.

So in this case uncertainty was permitted to develop unchecked by the regrasp Behaviour, on the grounds that subsequent Behaviours can cope with this. This is hardly local control at the lowest level, though arguably omitted only because unnecessary. Thus it could be seen as an optimisation, a shortened form of the proper principled design for the sake of efficiency.

The "spacing-out" strategy

The control of this regrasp uncertainty is partly accomplished by the *spacing out* computations which ensure that there is a space between all the vertical faces which are intended to be against one another. These spaces permit the parts to be placed into the assembly despite errors of presentation, and previous errors in the assembly itself. The

---

[27] Published before implementation in [41], and recapitulated in more detail in [33].

spaces have been designed to be large enough to accommodate the worst combinations of the these various errors. They end up as computed offsets to the nominal final destinations of the parts in the assembly. These spaces, and the errors they contain, are removed at the end of the assembly, when the final Behaviour nudges the whole assembly as tightly packed together as the shapes of the parts will permit. This postponement of error management contradicts the initial "less uncertainty out than in" guideline.

What is worse (from the point of view of the initial guidelines) is that this *spacing out* uncertainty management technique involves computed offsets by the planner to the part destinations within the assembly, i.e., the "spaces" are intermediate results which disappear into the computed part destinations, and consequently are quite invisible to the subcognitive system. Thus although the subcognitive system could be said to accomplish this strategy in the sense that it is inherent in the final destinations of the parts, this is a rather empty sense of "accomplish" since there is no distinct action or parameter or combination thereof within the subcognitive system which can be associated with this *spacing out* strategy. Clearly this is a case where the bulk of the work of uncertainty management is actually performed by the planner.

Part-fitting uncertainty

There is one more kind of uncertainty control involved in the SOMASS system. We mentioned that the planner insists on fitting the parts with vertically downwards fitting trajectories. Now clearly it is also possible to push parts in from the side. Unfortunately uncertainties of form mean that this will not always succeed, because the hole may be fractionally lower than the part trying to fit into it, and the effect of gravity means that we cannot employ a *spacing out* strategy between horizontal faces. Consequently this assumption that vertical fitting is the thing to do is part of the uncertainty management. So this is a clear case where there is not even the feeblest argument that some of this uncertainty management is done by the subcognitive system, since it is accomplished purely by the failure to employ any other than vertical fitting trajectories. Furthermore, this decision to avoid all but vertical fitting (with a special exception) is not taken by the cognitive system,

but has simply been built into the way it operates by the designer.

The original guidelines in retrospect

In summary, out of these four cases of uncertainty, there is one case where the subcognitive system is largely concerned with the management of uncertainty, one case where it simply left uncontrolled (i.e., handled later), and two cases where the planner arguably does all the work, in one case by explicit computation, and in the other simply by virtue of its design.

Might it be that the expectation that the planner be unconcerned with matters connected with uncertainty was phrased too crudely? After all, it is a feature of the Explicit-World-Model approach that the planning level must be concerned with *explicitly* represented uncertainty, whereas all that has been shown of the SOMASS system is that it is programmed willy nilly to use *strategies* which are concerned with the control of uncertainty. The planner itself has no knowledge of uncertainty *per se*, nor does it know in any way that these strategies are in part concerned with the control of uncertainty. These are things known only to the *designer* of the planner, i.e. which have been built-in *tacitly* to the planner. So it seems that the proper assertion is the more qualified one that Behaviour-based planners should have no concern with *explicit* or *implicit* uncertainty, i.e., *symbolic* uncertainty; and that *tacit* concern with uncertainty is one of the ways of avoiding this.

What about the assertion that Behaviour-based planners work in an *ideal* world with *no* concern with uncertainty?

An ideal world is an abstraction of the real world. Consequently while there is only one real world, there are as many ideal worlds as there are ways of abstracting from it. In the Behaviour-based assembly paradigm, the ideal world in which the planner operates is defined for it by the particular Behavioural modules in terms of which it plans. If each of these modules handles all the uncertainty that concerns its part of the assembly process safely within itself, then the ideal world of the planner will not even contain any *tacit* references to uncertainty. If, on the other hand, these modules deal with the assembly uncertainty *in world-mediated collaboration with one another*, then the ideal world they define for the planner *will* be concerned with some details of assembly strategy which happen to be (but as only the designer knows) concerned with control of uncertainty – in other words, *tacit* uncertainty management.

Thus this experiment (of constructing the SOMASS system) suggests that it is dealing with *explicitly* or *implicitly* (i.e., *symbolically*) represented uncertainty (and which therefore must be thought about) that causes the complexity which mires the Explicit-World-Model paradigm; to be concerned with uncertainty only *tacitly* (and so not reasoning about it at all) is compatible with simplicity and reliability. In other words, *tacit* consideration of uncertainty is compatible with the Behaviour-based approach. The originally stated aim of managing uncertainty entirely within a Behavioural module still applies, but only to what would otherwise have to be reflected into the planner as explicit or implicit consideration of uncertainty; the reflection of tacit considerations of uncertainty into the planner is acceptable. These tacit representations are the representational consequence of emergent behaviours, i.e., behaviours which are not encapsulated in distinct Behavioural modules, but emerge from their world-mediated collaboration.

4. Conclusions

There are some domains, such as assembly, where the logical complexities of subtask interaction require prior planning, i.e., an autonomous assembly system will require an assembly planner. We refer to this part of the system as the *cognitive* part. We argue that the common label of *symbolic* presumes a symbolic implementation; while we do use a symbolic planner, nonsymbolic planners are possible. Likewise, we refer to the real-time plan-execution part of the system as *subcognitive*. The common label of *subsymbolic* presumes a nonsymbolic implementation. While subcognitive information processing is likely to be modular (encapsulated), there is no special reason not to employ symbolic computation where it offers advantage.

Our SOMASS assembly system is a careful marriage of a Behaviour-based subcognitive system, and a symbolic planner. We refer to this kind of careful marriage as a *hybrid* system. The interface between these two components of the system is a virtual machine. The Behaviour-based system,

comprising task-achieving part-motion Behavioural modules, is constructed to be a plan interpreter, with the aim of simplifying the job of the planner as much as possible. The most important aspect of this is that uncertainty is handled entirely by the subcognitive Behaviour-based part of the system, in the sense that the planner has no need to reason about uncertainty or sensing. The planner is only *tacitly* concerned with uncertainty, in the sense that some aspects of uncertainty management are built-in to the design of the whole system. This tacit representation of uncertainty handling strategies occurs when uncertainty is handled by behaviours which are not encapsulated in distinct Behavioural modules, but emerge from their world-mediated collaboration.

Given the uncertainty in the research community about the fundamental principles involved in the construction of intelligent autonomous systems, and the extremely modest scale of successful implementations, we consider it wise to restrict experimental ambitions to relatively simple tasks performed in the *real* world, so that the cycle of hypothesis and experimental test occurs as rapidly as possible, and the assumptions inherent in simulation are avoided.

Reducing the complexity of plans by improving the subcognitive competence of the agent executing the plan has proved to be a powerful method of simplifying overall system complexity in automated assembly systems. It has enabled the implementation of a working model of a fully automated assembly system, the SOMASS soma assembly system, which illustrates this hybrid architecture. This system requires little more information than the shape of the assembly and the shape of the parts from which to devise and execute assembly plans, and does so with pleasing reliability. Further development of this system is part of a long-term research programme into Behaviour-based robot systems at Edinburgh, which we began in 1986.

Acknowledgements

During the development of the SOMASS system Chris Malcolm was supported by the ACME Directorate of the UK Science and Engineering Council, grant GR/D/2400.6. Further research using this system is supported by ACME grant

GR/E 68075 (1989-1991). We have been assisted in the development of these ideas by our colleagues and students of the Behaviour-based Systems Research Group. In particular we wish to thank John Hallam (Edinburgh University) and Wade Troxell (Colorado State University). Rodney Brooks and his team at MIT's Artificial Insect Laboratory have been a great source of inspiration. We thank Patti Maes, Luc Steels, and Walter van de Velde of the Free University of Brussels for the memorable workshop which motivated the development of this paper.

References

[1] Fodor, Jerry Alan, *Modularity of mind : an essay on faculty psychology*, Bradford Books, MIT Press, 1983.

[2] E Yourdon, L L Constantine *Structured Design*, Prentice-Hall, New Jersey, USA, 1979.

[3] Hoare, C.A.R., *Communicating Sequential Processes*, Prentice-Hall International, 1985.

[4] Lyons, D., *Robot Schemas*, Ph.D. thesis, 1985, University of Massachussetts, Amherst, USA.

[5] Albus, J.S., *Brains, Behaviour, and Robotics*, BYTE Books, McGraw-Hill, 1981.

[6] Brooks, R.A., *Achieving Artificial Intelligence Through Building Robots*, AI Memo 899, MIT, AI Lab, May 1986.

[7] Brooks, R.A., *A Robust Layered Control System for a Mobile Robot*, IEEE Journal of Robotics and Automation, RA-2, April, 1986, 14-23.

[8] Brooks, R.A., *Real, Synthetic Autonomous Agents*, in proceedings of Representation and Learning in an Autonomous Agent, Nov 16-88, 1988, Lagos, Portugal; revised in this issue.

[9] G Beni, S Hackwood, L A Hornak, J L Jackel, *Dynamic Sensing for Robots: an analysis and implementation*, Robot Res., 2(2), Summer 1983, 51-60.

[10] Aloimonous, J., Weiss, I., Bandopadhay, A., *Active Vision*, Proc 1st Int. Conf. on Computer Vision, June 1987, 35-54.

[11] Olson, S.J., Potter, R.D., *Real-Time Vergence Control*, Tech Rep 264, CS Dept., University of Rochester, NY, Oct 1988, 17 pages.

[12] Brown, Christopher M, (ed), *The Rochester Robot*, Technical Report, Computer Science Department, University of Rochester, New York, August 1988.

[13] Newell, A., Simon, H.A., *GPS – A Program that Simulates Human Thought* in Computers and Thought eds Feigenbaum and Feldman, McGraw-Hill, 1963, p279-276.

[14] Dennett, D., *Styles of Mental Representation*, Proc Arist Soc., n.s., 83, 213-216.

[15] Polanyi, Michael, *The Tacit Dimension*, Routledge and Kegan Paul, 1967.

[16] Smith, B.C., *Reflection and Semantics in a Procedural Language*, PhD dissertation, Report MIT/LCS/TR-272, MIT, Cambridge, MA, 1982. See also, chapter 3 of Brachman, R.J. and Levesque, R.J., Eds, Readings in Knowledge Representation, Morgan Kaufmann, California, 1985, 31-40.

[17] Pylyshyn, Z.W., *Computation and Cognition: Toward a Foundation for Cognitive Science*, MIT Press, Cambridge Mass., 1984.

[18] Harnad, S., (ed) *Categorical Perception: the Groundwork of Cognition*, Cambridge University Press, 1987.

[19] Harnad, Stevan, *Minds, Machines, and Searle*, Journal of experimental and Theoretical Artificial Intelligence,

[20] Harnad, Stevan, *The Symbol Grounding Problem*, submitted to Physica D, preprints available from author.

[21] Dennett, Daniel C, *Intentional Systems*, The Journal of Philosophy, 68 (1971) 87-106.

[22] Dennett, D., *Intentional Systems in Cognitive Ethology*, BBS 6, p343-390, 1983.

[23] Ryle, Gilbert, *The Concept of Mind*, London New York Hutchinson's University Library, 1949; Penguin 1963.

[24] Rosenschein, S.R., Kaelbling, L.P., *The Synthesis of Digital Machines with Provable Epistemic Properties*, in Theoretical Aspects of Reasoning about Knowledge, ed Halpern, J.Y., proc 1986 conf, pub Morgan Kaufmann, 1986, 83-98.

[25] Steels, L., *Artificial Intelligence and Complex Dynamics*, paper presented at the IFIP workshop on Concepts and Tools for Knowledge-based Systems, Mount Fuji, Japan, November, 1987. Also available as AI Memo no 88-2, VUB AI Lab., Pleinlaan 2, 1050 Brussels, 1988.

[26] Nevins, J.L., and Whitney, D.E., *Computer Controlled Assembly*, Scientific American, February, 1978.

[27] Maturana, H.R., Varela, F.J., *The Tree of Knowledge: The Biological Roots of Human Understanding*, New Science Library, Shambala, Boston Mass., 1988.

[28] Bateson, Gregory, *The Cybernetics of Self*, in *A Theory of Alcoholism*, in Psychiatry, Vol 34, no 1, pp 1-18, 1971; reprinted in *Steps to an Ecology of Mind*, Ballantine Books, NY, 1972.

[29] Stallman, R.M., Sussman, G.J., *Forward Reasoning and Dependency-Directed Backtracking in a System for Computer-Aided Circuit Analysis*, MIT AI Memo 380, September 1976.

[30] Fleming, A., *Analysis of Uncertainties in a Structure of Parts 1*, and *Analysis of Uncertainties in a Structure of Parts 2*, DAI Research Papers No. 271 and 272, Department of Artificial Intelligence, University of Edinburgh, 1985.

[31] Durrant-Whyte, H.F., *Uncertain Geometry in Robotics*, Proc 1987 IEEE Int Conf on Robotics and Automation, 851-857, March 1987.

[32] Taylor, R.H., *Planning and Execution of Straight Line Manipulator Trajectories*, IBM J. Res. Dev., vol. 23, no 4, 424-436, 1979.

[33] Smithers, T., and Malcolm, C.A., *Programming Robotic Assembly in terms of Task Achieving Behavioural Modules*, Journal of Structural Learning, vol 2 no 10, 1989, 15 pages; also Edinburgh University DAI RP 417.

[34] Popplestone, R.J, Ambler, A.P, Bellos, I, *RAPT: A Language for describing assemblies*, Industrial Robot, Sep 1978, 131-137.

[35] Winograd, T., Flores, F., *Understanding Computers and Cognition*, Norwood, N.J. Ablex Publishing 1986.

[36] Chapman, D., Agre P.E., *Abstract Reasoning as Emergent*

from Concrete Activity, in proc workshop Reasoning about Actions and Plans, eds Georgeff and Lansky, pub. Morgan and Kaufmann, 1987.

[37] Malcolm, C.A., and Smithers, T., *Programming Assembly Robots in terms of Task Achieving Behavioural Modules: First Experimental Results*, Proc International Advanced Robotics Programme, Second Workshop on Manipulators, Sensors and Steps towards Mobility, Manchester, UK, Oct 24-26 1988; also Edinburgh University DAI RP 410.

[38] Malcolm, C.A., *Planning and Performing the Robotic Assembly of Soma Cube Constructions*, MSc Dissertation Edinburgh University, September 1987, 87 pages.

[39] Berlekamp, E.R., Conway, J.H., Guy, R.K., *Winning Ways*, vol 2, Academic Press, 1982.

[40] Sloman, Aaron, *Afterthoughts on Analogical Representations*, in Proc Theoretical Issues in Natural Language Processing, Cambridge MA, 1975, p164-168; also Brachman, R.J. and Levesque, R.J., Eds, Readings in Knowledge Representation, Morgan Kaufmann, California, 1985, 431-440.

[41] Smithers, T., and Malcolm, C., *A Behavioural Approach to Robot Task Planning and Off-Line Programming*, Proc International Advanced Robotics Programme, First Workshop on Manipulators, Sensors, and Steps towards Mobility, May 1987 Karlsruhe, KfK 4316, ISSN 0303-4003, ed Dr T Martin, Kernforschungzentrum Karlsruhe, Projecttragerschaft Fertingunstechnik, Postfach 3640, 7500 Karlsruhe 1, Federal Republic of Germany, 313-326, (DAI Research Paper 306).

Animal Behavior as a Paradigm for Developing Robot Autonomy

Tracy L. Anderson and Max Donath

Robotics Laboratory, Dept. of Mechanical Engineering and the Productivity Center, University of Minnesota, Minneapolis, MN 55455, USA

We have been examining naturally occurring examples of autonomous systems in order to identify characteristics that might provide insight into our research on autonomy. In the first part of this paper, we review relevant research which has occurred in the area of animal behavior. Based on certain observations, we have proposed a number of primitive reflexive behaviors which are then used to develop several useful emergent behaviors. These emergent behaviors were demonstrated on a simulated mobile robot and then successfully implemented on Scarecrow, an actual robot. Scarecrow allows us to demonstrate that behavioral control strategies do indeed provide us with a powerful strategy for robust operation in dynamically changing unstructured environments in which one cannot impose unrealistic expectations on the performance of the machine or its sensors. A consequence of this is, that given the unpredictability of human actions, such behavioral control strategies may facilitate the safe interaction of man and machine.

Keywords: Mobile robots; Robot control; Ethology; Emergent reflexive behaviors; Stimulus response characteristics.

1. Introduction

Much of the research in the area of robotics has had as its long term goal the development of a robot which exhibits varying degrees of autonomous behavior. Autonomy is desirable in tasks which involve manipulation and mobility but for which human intervention is difficult. While much effort has been expended in the development of systems to handle specific classes of problems, considerably less effort has been directed towards the issue of autonomy itself.

How does one develop a robot which exhibits autonomy across a broad range of unstructured and dynamically changing environments, in support of many tasks which may have little in common with each other?

We begin with a fundamental assumption: in order for a robot to act autonomously over a wide range of tasks and environments, it must be capable of exhibiting a variety of different behaviors. This is supported by ethological observations on the behavior of animals [27,28] and differs from traditional approaches to robot control which have

Tracy Anderson is currently pursuing a Ph.D. at the University of Minnesota in the area of autonomous mobile robots. His Master's research concentrated on behavioral control strategies applied to a mobile robot. In addition, he is currently employed by 3M Company and is responsible for development of knowledge based applications and architectures to support the research, development and commercialization of advanced composite materials.

Max Donath received his B.Eng. degree from McGill University in 1972 and the S.M., Mech.E., and Ph.D. degrees from M.I.T. He is currently Associate Professor of Mechanical Engineering at the University of Minnesota where he has been since 1978, except for the 1986–87 period when he was a Visiting Associate Professor at Stanford University.

Major interests are in the mechanisms of integrating sensors, intelligence and motor control function in order to provide the flexibility and adaptability associated with human capabilities. His research in the areas of walking and prosthetics, robot hand and arm control, sensor development, and autonomous mobile robots have implications to both industrial and rehabilitation activities.

He has received a number of awards over the years, some of which include the Military Order of the Purple Heart Award for Research for the Handicapped, the NSF Presidential Young Investigator Award and the SME Outstanding Young Manufacturing Engineer Award. He is an Associate Editor of the ASME Journal of Dynamic Systems, Measurement and Control.

North-Holland
Robotics and Autonomous Systems 6 (1990) 145–168

concentrated on the development of a single behavior, often to the exclusion of others.

The issues with which we are concerned are fundamental and are not all addressed here. Can autonomy result from simple reflexive stimulus/response forms of behavior or is reactive behavior required? Is memory an essential requirement for autonomy and if so, what form must this memory assume? How does the concept of "self autonomy" (i.e. behavior which may be characterized as supporting self survival) differ from that of "imposed autonomy" (i.e. behavior which does not benefit the robot but fulfills some desired task which we impose upon the system)?

We will first review the relevant research in animal behavior and then briefly introduce the primitive reflexive behaviors which we have constructed for a mobile robot. These form the basis for a set of emergent behaviors, some of which will be subsequently described. These provide a starting point for our investigations in autonomy.

2. Animal Behavior

Nature has often been used as a source for the design of man made artifacts. In robotic design, nature has provided many examples for emulation, ranging from the various structures which allow different animals to grasp and manipulate objects to the variety of structures used for locomotion. These biological examples have provided us with a basis for the design of robot hands, flexible and rigid manipulators, and various walking machines.

Besides the many different morphological models that nature provides, it also provides us with many examples of different types of behavior which allow both vertebrates and invertebrates to successfully interact with their environment. Successful interaction is essential to their survival. Examples include both the attack and escape behaviors, mating, feeding, and nest building behaviors.

A review of the literature in this area [27,28,35, 18,36] provides valuable insight into how the different behaviors of an animal are interrelated and what types of factors govern the appearance of such behaviors. In this paper we will review several examples, taken from the literature, illustrating important observations on animal behavior which

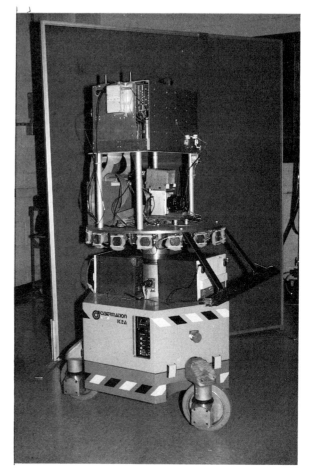

The Scarecrow robot.

have served as motivation for the development of robot behaviors.

2.1. Different Approaches in the Study of Animal Behavior

Two basic approaches have been used in the study of animal behavior. The first approach is based on a topdown strategy which attempts to explain the behavior of the animal without complete knowledge of the underlying physical mechanisms [1]. The second approach taken by physiolo-

---

[1] This is the same strategy that has been taken in the development of the natural sciences. Simon points out "We knew a great deal about the gross physical and chemical behavior of matter before we had any knowledge of molecules, a great deal about molecular chemistry before we had an atomic theory, and a great deal about atoms before we had any theory of elementary particles" [Simon, 1985; p. 20].

gists is based on the analytical decomposition of the organism into its various physical subcomponents.

2.1.1. Top Down Approach

The topdown approach in the study of animal behavior is shared by both ethologists and behavioral psychologists.

Ethologists study the behavior of animals under natural settings with the belief that behavior is largely a result of the animal's innate response to certain environmental stimuli. Their interests are biological in nature; in addition to the cause of the behavior, they are interested in determining what function it provides the animal and its evolutionary consequences. It's their belief that types of behavior are specific to certain species. Related species will exhibit similar behaviors while unrelated species will exhibit dissimilar behaviors. Survival of a given species depends not only upon the physical structure but also upon possessing the necessary behavioral characteristics.

As opposed to the approach of ethologists [2], behavioral psychologists study the behavior of animals in a controlled laboratory environment. They believe that the response exhibited by an animal to certain stimuli is not an innate response but instead is primarily a learned response. They largely ignore the natural habitat in which the animal exists. Their aim is to uncover general principles which describe the behavior of an animal in terms of its ability to learn to respond to certain stimuli. Thus, they desire to formulate general laws of learning.

2.1.2. Bottom Up Approach

The physiologist attempts to explain animal behavior in terms of the interactions between the physical components of the animal. They approach animal behavior from an analytical perspective by decomposing the animal into physiological subcomponents, and then focus upon understanding the underlying mechanisms of each of the subcomponents. They are primarily concerned with the functioning of the animal at the neural level.

However, knowledge of how each component operates individually is not sufficient to allow a complete understanding of the behavior of the organism. We must also have an understanding of how these components are structured and interrelated.

2.1.3. A Lack of Framework

Describing the behavior of an animal presents a serious problem to the observer. Unlike in other physical sciences, where observations can easily be quantified in units such as voltage, current, and force, the description of behavior depends upon the behavior being investigated and as a result, is somewhat subjective [27].

Since it is recognized that accounting for behavior in terms of the physiological interactions of neurons is some time away, ethologists develop explanations of behavior based upon external observations expecting that the underlying physical interactions can be deduced from them [3].

The most fundamental method in which to describe behavioral response would be to describe the precise muscular movements as a function of time. This description is incomplete however, since it conveys no information about the function of the behavior, i.e. its purpose. A more complete method of description is to describe each behavioral pattern in terms of its consequences. This method avoids unnecessary detail and allows analysis at a higher level.

2.2. A Theory of Animal Behavior

The ethological approach to the study of animal behavior began in the late 1930s, mainly through the early work of Konrad Lorenz and Niko Tinbergen. It was Konrad Lorenz who introduced a model to explain the predictable behavior of certain animals when exposed to specific stimuli. Lorenz's model consists of an internal center based in the central nervous system, receiving sensory information from the environment. He refers to this as an *innate releasing mechanism*. The function of the innate releasing mechanism is to cause a specific response from the animal when certain situations in the environment were detected. A

---

[2] These two different approaches to the study of animal behavior resulted from differing views on this question of nature versus nurture although it is now recognized that the answer lies somewhere in between [Baker, 1981].

[3] This is the same approach which has been taken by meteorologists in predicting the weather.

stimulus which evokes the response was called *a releaser* [4] and the pattern of behavior exhibited was called a *fixed action pattern*.

2.3. On Instinct and Learning

How is it that an animal possesses the ability to feed itself, produce and raise offspring, build nests, and avoid predators? The answer is believed to be due to a combination of inherited responses to certain situations and the ability to adapt to situations for which no response is available. As examples of both extremes [5], consider first the female digger wasp:

> "A female digger-wasp emerges from her underground pupa in spring. Her parents died the previous summer. She has to mate with a male wasp and then perform a whole series of complex patterns connected with digging out a nest hole, constructing cells within it, hunting and killing prey such as caterpillars, provisioning the cells with the prey, laying eggs and finally sealing up the cells. All of this must be completed within a few weeks, after which the wasp dies." [27, p. 22]

Lorenz's model explains this complex behavior as the aggregation of a series of sequential behaviors, where the results of one behavior act as the trigger for the next one to begin. In this example, the releaser would be the presence of a male digger wasp which would evoke a mating behavior, the result of which would evoke a nest building behavior, the result of which would evoke a predator behavior, and so on. Note that under this hypothesis, if the female digger wasp was isolated from the male digger wasp, then none of the other behaviors should occur. Experiments with female digger wasps isolated from males verify this.

This is an example of an innate behavior which has been genetically passed on from previous generations. The wasp is not acting to accomplish some specific goal but instead acts as it does because its ancestors acted this way. That is what

allowed them to be ancestors in the first place. Thus, the selective process is not only the result of an individual being physically suited to a particular environment but is also the result of the individual possessing certain behavioral characteristics. This is a central thesis of the ethological approach to the study of animal behavior.

As an example of behaviors explicitly learned, consider the early life of the lion cub;

> "Born quite helpless, it is sheltered and fed by its mother until it can move around. It is gradually introduced to solid food and gains agility in playing with its litter mates. It has constant opportunities to watch and copy its parents and other members of the group as they stalk and capture prey. It may catch its first small live prey when 6 months old, but it is 2 years or more before it has grown sufficiently to feed itself. Its behaviors, and particularly the methods and stratagems it uses in hunting, may change according to circumstances throughout its life." [27, p. 22]

This is an example of an animal which learns to adapt to the environment in which it lives. Adaptation has the obvious benefit of allowing the animal to react to new situations. However, an innate response has the benefit of immediacy, since no time is required in order to develop a learned behavior.

Manning makes some interesting points regarding these two examples; the first is that a clear distinction between behaviors which involve only innate abilities versus those which involve learned behaviors can sometimes be misleading. For example, in experiments on the digger wasp [39], it was shown that the digger wasp learns to identify the location of its nest based upon local landmarks. The experiments consisted of surrounding the nest by a ring of pine cones. When the wasp first emerged from the nest, it exhibited a behavior in which it circled the nest repeatedly before leaving to capture its prey. During this period, the pine cones were moved a distance away from the nest, but the pinecones' arrangement was maintained. Upon its return, the wasp was observed to orient itself towards the pinecones, not the nest. Likewise, the lion cub exhibits certain predatory behavior which is instinctive.

Secondly, the degree to which an organism develops learned behavior may be related to the average life and body size of the organism. Innate behaviors are more important for insects which have an average life on the order of weeks or hours. Learning capacity requires large amounts of brain tissue which may not exist in small

---

[4] This approach has been used in the control of mosquito populations. It is known that male mosquitos are attracted to female mosquitos based upon a high frequency sound the female produces. This sound (a releaser) is reproduced electronically to attract the males into a device which destroys them electronically.

[5] These examples were taken from "An Introduction to Animal Behavior" by Aubrey Manning [Manning, 79] however, many other examples can be found in the literature on animal behavior.

animals and hence, they must rely on their innate ability to interact with their environment.

2.4. Environmental Stimuli

2.4.1. Responses to Environmental Stimuli

When there is a rigid relationship between a stimulus and a response in an animal, the response is referred to as a reflex response. Reflex responses provide the animal with protective behaviors. Such responses have been shown to be present in animals which have been isolated from birth and is thus considered instinctive. Reflex responses are elicited independent of environmental factors.

Most behaviors exhibited by an animal are more complex than the reflexive type of behavior. For example, certain animals such as the male robin will exhibit aggressive behavior towards an approaching animal when within its own territory. When the robin is outside its territory under identical conditions, it will exhibit a nonaggressive behavior such as that of fleeing. A dog may show a strong response to a food stimulus when some time has passed since its last meal but may show a very weak response once it has finished eating. Both examples illustrate that the relationship between stimulus and response is not necessarily rigid but may also depend upon external environmental factors as well as the internal state of the animal.

2.4.2. Sensory Interpretation

The type of stimuli required to activate a reflexive response is typically not very complex. It is well established that the stimuli required to activate a complex behavioral pattern is usually only a very small subset of the total amount of sensory information available to the animal. This subset is referred to as the sign stimuli. For example, Tinbergen showed that the sign stimulus for attack behavior in a male stickleback during its reproductive cycle was the red belly of another male stickleback [27]. By introducing many different models of the male stickleback, he found that the details of surface texture and the shape of the model were unimportant. Male sticklebacks would attack very crude models provided that the bottom portion of the model was red but would completely ignore a very accurate model lacking the red underbelly. In addition, the attack rate was found to increase in relation to the amount of red contained on the model.

Often, a combination of specific stimuli are found to evoke a certain response. What is important is not that all the stimuli are present, but that some weighted sum of the stimuli is greater than some threshold value. Thus, in the absence of one sign stimulus, the same response occurs when the intensity of the other is increased. This summing effect of input stimuli is referred to as 'heterogeneous summation'.

Manning points out that sign-stimuli are usually involved in those types of behavior in which it is absolutely critical to never miss responding to the stimuli, such as that which occurs in predatory responses. To guarantee this response, the animal typically responds to other objects which pose no threat but still possess the sign-stimuli needed to activate the specific responsive behavior. Male sticklebacks attack almost all red objects including red flower petals placed in their aquatic environment. Small birds possess the ability to evade larger birds of prey such as hawks and owls which typically have large, dark circular eyes. The sign stimulus is the appearance of a pair of large, dark circular 'eyes'. It is interesting to note that small birds' prey such as moths and butterflies will spread their wings when touched, exposing patterns which show a remarkable resemblance with the eye patterns of the large predators of the small birds. This provides them with some level of protection from the small bird predators.

As another example of how specific behavioral patterns can be triggered by specific stimuli, consider the predator behavior of the frog:

> "The frog does not seem to see or, at any rate, is not concerned with the detail of stationary parts of the world around him. He will starve to death surrounded by food if it is not moving. His choice of food is determined only by size and movement.
>
> ...He can be fooled easily not only by a bit of dangled meat but by any moving small object." – [What the Frog's Eye Tells the Frog's Brain, 25].

Matters are further complicated by the fact that different aspects of the same object can serve as sign-stimuli for different types of behavior. Consider a particular mode of behavior in which the herring gull will steal the eggs of other herring gulls. For this to occur, the eggs must be normally shaped and undamaged. These two attributes of the egg are the sign stimuli for this behavior. However, during the mode of behavior characterized by the incubation of its own eggs, eggs will often roll from the nest requiring the herring gull to retrieve them. In this case, the shape is unimportant for the task. The gull will retrieve models of eggs shaped like cylinders, cones, or balls providing they are normally speckled and colored. It seems that other attributes of the egg are important to activate the behavior which results in retrieving the eggs. Once the egg has been retrieved however, the shape and size again become important attributes for the incubation behavior. The herring gull will choose the largest of the available eggs to incubate provided the egg has a rounded shape.

2.4.3. Specialized Environmental Detectors

How does an animal, given a diverse set of sensory information about the environment, select which information to respond to and which information to ignore?

The first answer can be found by examining the sense organs themselves. The sensory organs of many animals have developed into a system of specialized detectors allowing the animal to sense certain environmental conditions.

The visual system of the frog is such that it readily detects the movement of small, dark circular objects at close range, while it is unable to detect movement of other objects which are large and at a greater distance. This is well suited to the frog which relies on flies for its primary food source.

The wings of a female mosquito oscillate at a characteristic frequency which is different from that of the male mosquito. The male mosquito has small hairs on its antenna formed such that they have a resonant frequency equivalent to the characteristic frequency of the female's wings. This in effect provides the male mosquito with a female mosquito detector.

Moths have developed a tympanic organ which is highly sensitive to the ultrasonic emissions of bats, their primary predator [35]. The moth is capable of detecting a bat at a distance of up to 100 feet. It is interesting to note that the predator avoidance behavior of the moth depends upon the intensity level of the signal received by its tympanic sense organ. For low levels which correspond to distances of the bat between 15 and 100 feet, the moth makes a directed response away from the source of the signal. Since it is believed that the

bat cannot detect the presence of the moth until it is within 10–15 feet, this provides advance notice to the moth which may then be able to move out of the feeding area of the bat. What is even more interesting however, is that moths which first detect the bat when the bat is within 10 feet, do not exhibit a directional avoidance behavior, but instead exhibit a nondirectional response such as: folding their wings and falling to the ground, erratic flight patterns, or movement from a stationary location [6]. Thus, depending on the distance of the bat, different strategies are used for avoidance behavior.

2.4.4. Complex Sensory Interpretation

Although specialized sense organs are found in many different animals, it does not completely explain the behavior of the herring gull which can detect the attributes of shape, size, color, and patterns of speckles of the herring gull egg. For one type of behavior, shape is the sign-stimulus while for another type of behavior size, color, and pattern of speckles are the sign-stimuli. Thus, we know that the herring gull is capable of detecting all of these attributes, but somehow selects which ones are important depending on the type of task that it is performing. This implies that there is some internal process by which this occurs. This is what led Lorenz to formulate the concept of an innate releasing mechanism: the idea that the brain is actively selecting a subset of the available, sensory information and directing the response of the animal accordingly.

2.5. Factors Influencing Behavior

Simple causal relationships between stimulus and behavior do not always exist. In addition to external stimuli, other factors influence the behavior of an animal. Behaviors which depend upon some internal factor are classified according to their consequences. Using a functional method of classification, certain activities which support one type of behavior can be distinguished from those which support another. One method of classification used in animal behavior is referred to as

---

[6] This behavior has been observed for some time. It has been noted that the behavior of moths usually becomes erratic when exposed to high pitch sound such as the jingle of keys [35].

motivation[7]. This term is used to classify differences in observed behavior in terms of the consequence of the observed behavior, not as an explanation in of itself. Motivation is that class of internal processes responsible for changes in behavior [28]. Thus, for example, certain observed behaviors are classified as being connected with feeding, courtship, hunting, sleeping, etc. and the animal is said to internally possess a motivational potential towards the specific behavior.

It is believed that associated with each possible mode of behavior, there is a motivational potential. The current mode of behavior is that behavior which has the highest motivational potential and the proper combination of external stimuli. The motivational potentials may also be a function of time as occurs in the mating behavior of certain species[8], or may be due to hormonal changes within the animal.

2.6. A Hierarchy of Behaviors

Manning notes that, complex behavioral patterns can often be decomposed into other more simple behavioral patterns and that such decomposition occurs hierarchically with simpler behavioral patterns such as standing, walking, biting and swallowing being subordinated to higher level behaviors such as attacking, fleeing, and feeding [27]. Just as different types of reflex behaviors have to compete for control of the "final pathway" (i.e, control of the muscles which lead to overt response), it is believed that these higher level behaviors must compete for control of the lower level behaviors.

---

[7] One must be careful not to ascribe anthropomorphic characteristics to the behavior of animals since it will lead to erroneous conclusions. Rather, one must view the behavior in terms of what selective advantage it provides the individual. It is interesting to note that humans have no difficulty in describing the behavior of animals in terms of human behavior but resist the idea that their own behavior is animal like in many ways. This is due to the tendency of humans to see themselves as the center of the universe. Any evidence otherwise, is met with great reluctance as evidenced by the work of Copernicus and that of Darwin, both of whom experienced much opposition to their theories of the universe and of natural selection [McFarland; 87].

[8] The mating behavior of certain species are cyclical in nature based upon an "internal clock." This internal clock is referred to as its circadian rhythm.

2.7. Conflicting Behaviors

Not all the behaviors which an animal can exhibit are compatible with each other. For example, an avoidance behavior may conflict with a feeding behavior if the food is offered to the animal by a human, a resting behavior may conflict with a courtship behavior, etc. Conflict "denotes a state of motivation in which tendencies to perform more that one activity are simultaneously expressed" [28]. It is thought that an animal has many tendencies such as the tendency to sleep or eat; however, at any one moment, only one of these tendencies are dominant.

When competition arises between these tendencies, conflict behavior is said to occur. For example, a male stickleback that is guarding its territory against other males, will show conflicting tendencies of aggression and courtship in the presence of female sticklebacks. In fact, the territorial boundary of the male stickleback is determined by the point of equilibrium when the tendencies to flee balance with the tendencies to attack. A duck being fed by a human in a park oscillates between approach and retreat until some point of equilibrium occurs. Often, seemingly unrelated activities occur when a conflict situation arises. Two male sticklebacks, in conflict at their territorial boundary will start displacing sand, a behavior which occurs in nest building. Since the nest is already built, this behavior is irrelevant to either that of defence or that of nest building. Some believe that the two conflicting tendencies cancel each other out thus allowing some other tendency to gain dominance.

2.8. Animal Behavior as a Model for Robot Control

The following points summarize some of the important observations regarding animal behavior that we have used in our research on robot behaviors:

(a) To some degree, all animals possess a set of innate behaviors which allow the animal to respond to different situations.

(b) The type of behavior exhibited at any given time is the result of some internal switching mechanism.

(c) Complex behavior can occur as a result of the sequential application of different sets of primitive behaviors with the consequence of a given behavior acting as a mechanism which triggers the next one.

(d) Simple reflex types of behavior occur independent of environmental factors and provide the animal with a set of protective behaviors.

(e) Activation of more complex types of behavior typically depend upon external and internal constraints.

(f) Animals typically only respond to a small subset of the total amount of sensory information available to them at any given time. Animals have developed specialized types of detectors which allow them to detect specific events.

(g) Behavior is often organized hierarchically with complex behavioral patterns resulting from the integration of simpler behavioral patterns.

(h) Conflicting behavior can occur in animals. These will require either a method of arbitration between such behaviors or the activation of alternate behaviors.

3. Robot Behavior

In this section, we introduce the different forms of robot behavior which we have investigated. We will first discuss several issues associated with autonomy and its relationship to the underlying behavioral control strategies. We will then be describing a set of primitive reflexive behaviors that we have developed and will discuss their relationships to the above observations of animal behavior. We will go on to illustrate some of the emergent behaviors which can be formed from this set using both a simulated robot and an actual machine, named Scarecrow.

3.1. Single Behavior Approaches to Autonomy

The majority of research which has occurred on autonomous mobile robots has concentrated on developing a vehicle which can exhibit a single type of behavior supporting a specific task: that of moving between two positions in its environment while avoiding collision with objects [9].

---

[9] While this statement may seem at first to be an overgeneralization of the research which has been done to date, examination of the literature will reveal otherwise.

Consider a mobile robot capable of autonomous navigation. What degree of autonomy does such a robot exhibit? One might conclude that its behavior appears to be autonomous since the robot is capable of successfully moving to a specified location in the environment without colliding with obstacles. However, if a traditional path planning approach were to be used to affect such behavior, the degree of autonomy would be limited. The robot would be capable of exhibiting autonomous behavior only for a specific type of task: that of moving between two positions in the environment. While such a behavior is of obvious benefit, a robot limited to exhibiting a single type of behavior may not provide the degree of autonomy required in situations where human intervention is undesirable or impossible.

Single behavioral approaches to autonomy (i.e., navigation) [26,30,31,16,40,17,29,32,34,12,24] tend to result in autonomous systems which perform reasonably well for a specific class of applications, but do not degrade gracefully when dynamic and highly unstructured environments are encountered.

These approaches have inherent limitations when one considers the variety of different behaviors which may be required for complete autonomy. If one were interested in other types of behavior, the desired behavior would have to first be decomposed into some assemblage of temporally ordered navigational behaviors. Decomposition of many types of tasks such as "patrol the area", "follow the perimeter", "clean the floor", "mow the lawn", "turn down the corridor", "find the door", "clear the snow off the driveway" or "stay clear of approaching objects" is difficult if one is required to decompose the desired task into navigational subtasks. Clearly, real world autonomous systems (i.e. animals) do not behave in this manner.

Secondly, these approaches to autonomy are such that the ability to avoid collisions with obstacles cannot be separated from the ability to move between two positions in the environment. They are one and the same. The problem of obstacle avoidance is only solved for those cases in which the robot is to move from an initial position to some goal position. Once the robot has reached its goal position, no protection is provided from collision with approaching objects.

3.2. Multi-Behavioral Approaches to Autonomy

While most research has been directed towards supporting single-behavior navigational tasks, there has indeed been work on developing robots capable of exhibiting multiple behaviors in support of a variety of tasks.

Brooks presents a multi-behavioral approach which is aimed at developing a robot capable of exhibiting a wide range of different behaviors, among them "flee," "wall following," and "exploratory" behaviors [11,9,10]. The goal of this work is to incrementally develop a robot with increasing levels of competence with the expectation that such an approach will eventually lead to a complex form of intelligent behavior.

Other multi-behavioral work reported by Arkin [6] incorporates the concept of multiple concurrent behaviors (which he calls schema) such as "avoid-static-object," "move-ahead," "move-to-goal," and "stay-on-path". Similarly, Payton [33] reports on a set of reflexive heuristic behaviors which when combined, form other types of behaviors such as "wander," "seek-heading," and "back-and-turn." However, as with Arkins' approach, such behaviors are intended to support navigational tasks and are implemented as parameterized procedures.

Kadonoff [21] presents a set of local navigation strategies which in effect, leads to a set of different behaviors of the robot such as "avoid," "path-follow," "wall-follow," "aisle-center," and "beacon-track." These strategies are used in support of navigational tasks for the patrol robot which they manufacture. While each strategy results in a different behavior of the robot, no attempt is made to use such strategies for any task other than navigation.

3.3. Mechanistic Autonomy

Our approach to the development of an autonomous mobile robot is a multi-behavioral one in which we define a set of behaviors, each of which causes the robot to respond in a specific manner to detected stimuli [2]. Initially, we have limited ourselves to reflexive forms of behavior in which there exists a rigid relationship between a specific stimulus and the exhibited response of the robot. We consider each of these behaviors as "behavioral entities" and as such, refer to them as "primitive reflexive behaviors" [10].

One of the most interesting aspects which we have observed in our research and other multi-behavioral approaches to autonomy is that when individual behaviors are allowed to operate concurrently, behavioral patterns emerge (i.e., the observed response of the robot) which take on characteristics not previously ascribed to the individual component behaviors. It is this attribute of the multi-behavioral approach that leads to the use of the term "emergent behavior" [11].

An underlying assumption of our approach is that such emergent behavior results in a form of automatism, "the performance of an act without conscious control, as in the operation of the reflexes" [4]. Our view is mechanistic; we believe that it is possible for a mobile robot to perform useful tasks simply as a result of its innate, underlying structure. Our view is that many natural organisms function in this manner. This perspective is not new or unique but has existed for many years in the debate of nature versus nurture.

While we clearly recognize that the ability to learn new behaviors in response to situations not previously encountered or envisioned is a characteristic of higher life forms, we also recognize that many life forms possess innate forms of response which act to protect the organism and to facilitate functionality.

The definition of autonomy is highly domain specific. For example, we could provide a robot with an avoidance behavior which causes it to actively move away from objects in its environment. For example, in *Fig. 1*, Scarecrow moves away from all objects including the walls (for an explanation of the graphical representation, see the introduction for section 3.6). One might conclude that the robot is autonomous since it exhibits a self-governing behavior; it continually avoids collision with objects in its environment. However, the problem lies in that it only exhibits autonomy with respect to one particular behavior, certainly not sufficient for "survival". Although autonomous, it will be incapable of providing for

---

[10] At this point, we make no claims regarding what constitutes a primitive behavior.

[11] Similar to the notion that the whole is greater than the sum of the parts.

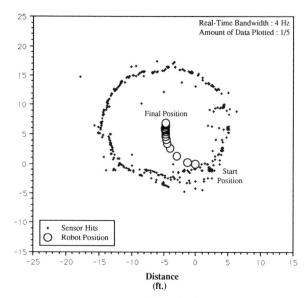

Fig. 1. Object avoidance for Scarecrow.

regeneration of its batteries with only this behavior.

The ethologist views the selective process to result from an individual being physically suited to a particular environment and possessing certain behavioral characteristics; we view autonomy as a direct result of a robot's ability to physically exist in its environment and to exhibit the necessary behavioral responses.

3.4. Specification of Robot Behavior

Traditional approaches to task planning for mobile robots result in a mapping of the desired task into a static, fixed specification of the desired behavior. Such formulations of behavior assume that the world is highly predictable (i.e. the world in which the plan is formulated will be the world in which the plan will be executed) and as a result, the behavior of the robot can be specified in advance of its execution. Arkinson [7] elucidates the problems associated with this approach when applied to autonomous robots:

"A plan to achieve each goal must be created. A plan specifies an ordering of actions whose collective effects logically achieve a desired goal or goals. In a sometimes malevolent and only partially modelled real world, a robot executing the indicated actions may not actually achieve the desired effects of each action while still obeying any constraints imposed by the plan. There are a host of potential problems which may create a divergence at execu-

tion time from the expected effects of actions as described in the plan."

...Industrial robotics has combated the problem by highly constraining the environment and tasks of the robot. However, in less controlled environments where complex behavior is required, the potential for any robot action to produce a variety of outcomes cannot be eliminated. Robust and successful robot actions require that this uncertainty be accommodated in the control of the robot, especially where autonomy is desired."

Thus, under traditional approaches to task planning, specification of what the robot should do in order to successfully complete the task is made in advance of the execution of the task. Assumptions have been made about the ordering in which certain situations will occur as the robot moves through its environment. Such an approach to planning will be inadequate in situations in which events occurs unexpectedly [12] during the execution of the task. To overcome this problem, researchers have concentrated on issues such as task monitoring [7] and error recovery methods [19].

Task monitoring and error recovery allows one to recover from situations which may occur unexpectedly as the robot executes its task and thus avoids the computationally expensive process of replanning. If plan execution differs significantly from that which was expected, replanning may be required. Replanning results in the formulation of a new plan which is then mapped into a representation which again results in a fixed, static description of behavior. If the environment differs significantly from what was expected, such an approach will require frequent replanning, and in the worst case (i.e. one in which the environment is completely different from that which is expected), will be unable to provide a plan for the robot.

Our approach to behavioral specification is to provide the robot with a set of reflexive behaviors, each of which provides the robot with a specific

---

[12] It is important to differentiate between an unexpected situation and a situation which occurs unexpectedly. An unexpected situation is one for which no response has been provided, such as would occur if the robot, while moving through a group of expected objects, suddenly encounters a deep ravine. A situation which occurs unexpectedly would be the presence of a new object placed into the path of the robot where an open space was assumed. The path planner is capable of handling situations which occur unexpectedly if it is aware of them when the plan is created.

response to detected stimuli. It is our intention to develop a robot capable of exhibiting many different types of behaviors which in turn, will support a wide variety of tasks.

We make no assumptions regarding the ordering in which certain situations will occur as the robot moves through its environment. We do not express behavior as a quantitative description of robot state but instead, express it in terms of stimulus/response mechanisms which cause the robot to respond to its environment in a manner similar to that of certain organisms. From a dynamics point of view, our approach results not in the specification of a trajectory constraining robot state, but in the modification of the dynamics of the robot through the addition of different reflexive behaviors. The result is that the robot can exhibit a variety of behavioral patterns in an unstructured dynamically changing environment.

It is our belief that such an approach will lead to a greater degree of autonomy, and as a result, will provide for robustness in the face of uncertainties (due to for example, sensor limitations) and unpredictable situations.

3.5. Primitive Reflexive Behaviors

In what follows, we will describe a set of *primitive reflexive behaviors*, each of which causes the robot to respond to a subset of the total stimuli present in the environment and internal to the robot. We refer to the resulting motion of the robot in its environment as a *behavioral pattern* and the processes which affect it as *behavior* [13].

Each primitive reflexive behavior which we construct is actually an assemblage of computational devices which interprets sensory data, processes the data in some manner, and issues a signal which acts as a reference command to the robot actuators. Thus, each behavior is considered as separate from the robot control system. In effect, we are adding computational devices which couple the robot dynamics with the environment.

These devices are discussed in detail in [1].

In this paper, we limit ourselves to constructing behavior from computational devices which do not contain internal state. This results in the construction of behavior which may be characterized as *reflexive* [14]. Such behavior in effect contains no form of memory. The result is that the output of each primitive behavior at time $t + 1$ (i.e. response) is completely deterministic and is determined by the inputs (i.e. stimuli) to the behavior at time t.

From an ethological perspective, each primitive reflexive behavior 'models' the fixed reflexive response observed in animals when presented with specific stimuli. The resulting behavioral pattern is equivalent to what Lorenz termed as a *fixed action pattern*.

Many of the reflexive behaviors which we have developed model very simple forms of stimulus/ response behavior. The primitive reflexive behaviors are of two distinct types: avoidance and attraction. Avoidance behaviors cause motion away from some stimulus while attraction behaviors cause motion towards some stimulus. Each of the behaviors which we construct maps sensory data into a potential field which is then applied to the robot. In the potential field approach, the robot is viewed as a point mass subject to repulsive "forces" which act to protect obstacles in the environment, and to an attractive "force" which acts to draw the robot towards specific locations in the environment [23,5]. One of the properties of potential fields is that of superposition, which provides a convenient mechanism for combining the output from multiple behaviors which may operate concurrently.

The attraction set of behaviors that we have developed and investigated include (in descending order of complexity): Location Directed Open Space Attraction, Wide Open Space Attraction, Narrow Open Space Attraction, Follow Object CW, Follow Object CCW, Object Attraction, Lo-

---

[13] This definition of behavior is consistent with that presented by [Manning 79] : "Behavior includes all those processes by which an animal senses the external world and the internal state of its body, and responds to changes which it perceives." Thus, behavior is associated with internal processes whereas the behavioral pattern is associated with our observation and interpretation of physical phenomenon.

[14] We refer to a behavior as reflexive if it results in a fixed behavioral pattern in response to a set of external and/or internal stimuli. Our definition is consistent with that presented in [McFarland 87]: "Reflex behavior is the most simple form of reaction to external stimulation. Stimuli such as a sudden change of tension in a muscle, a sudden change in the level of illumination, or a touch on some part of the body, induce an automatic, involuntary, and stereotyped response."

cation Attraction, and Forward Attraction. The avoidance behaviors are Active Avoidance and Passive Avoidance.

The computational architecture which forms the basis of our implementation is characterized by (1) a separation of the devices which affect each primitive reflexive behavior from the overall control of robot behavior (i.e. each of our primitive reflexive behaviors is completely independent and uncoupled and as a result, can exert no control over other behaviors); (2) a lack of internal state within each behavior (i.e. memoryless behavior); (3) separation of the mechanism for combining behavioral output from the devices which affect behavior; and (4) our desire to model each behavior as a nonheuristic "innate" response to external and/or internal stimuli.

Our purpose in this paper is to focus on the emergent behaviors that are possible given a limited set of primitive reflexive behaviors. In the following, we will only briefly describe the functionality of each of these primitive reflexive behaviors. More detail can be found in [1] and in [2].

3.5.1. Avoidance Behaviors

Animals exhibit many different types of avoidance behavior. They avoid collisions with objects as they move through their environment. They avoid various predators and avoid environments which do not offer conditions optimal to their survival. We have defined two primitive reflexive behaviors which together form the basis of a collision avoidance behavior.

Passive Avoidance   The most fundamental method of avoiding a collision with an object is to halt the forward motion of the robot if a potential collision is detected [15]. This is the purpose of the passive avoidance behavior. It is equivalent to the freeze or startle behavior which has been observed

in many different animals. It acts as a reflexive type of behavior which protects the robot in those situations in which a meaningful response cannot be formulated due to limitations in the rate at which sensory data becomes available and the computational time required to generate a response.

Active Avoidance   The purpose of the active avoidance behavior is to provide a directed response in order to avoid a collision with an approaching object. The term active is used since unlike the passive avoidance behavior, this behavior will continually issue commands directed at avoiding a collision with an approaching object. This behavior allows the robot to exist in dynamic environments [16].

3.5.2. Attraction Behaviors

The following sections describe the different types of attractive primitive reflexive behaviors which have been constructed.

Location Attraction   The purpose of this behavior is to provide the robot with location directed motion where the location is specified by a desired position of the robot in a global frame of reference. A robot acting with this behavior will continually generate commands which result in motion in the direction of the desired location. This behavior provides no protection from objects which may block the path of the robot, or any protection from approaching objects once the robot is at its desired location. It simply causes straight line motion from the current robot location to the desired location.

This behavior is similar to the goal oriented behavior observed in many different animals and has been shown to be a component behavior of migratory behaviors [8]. During migratory behavior, when the animal is displaced from its current location, it has been observed to exhibit a directed

---

[15] This immediately poses the following question: if one is interested in determining the necessary characteristics which an autonomous robot must possess, how does one deal with the issue of "self knowledge" (e.g. in order to detect a potential collision with an object in the environment, the robot must have knowledge of its own dimensions, how its sensors are arranged, etc). While we have kinesthetic sensors which, for example, provide internal feedback such that we 'know' where our hands are, it is nevertheless unknown how the gains on this feedback are set. Are they learned, or are we born with them?

[16] There is a limit to the degree to which this behavior can avoid collisions with dynamic objects in the environment. These are due to limitations in the ability to sense such objects, limitations in the rate at which such objects can be detected, and the limited power available to the robot for response. These limitations are not limitations in the approach but in the current state of technology. If such limitations did not exist, one would not need the passive avoidance behavior.

motion which causes it to re-orient itself towards a goal. It is thought that migratory behaviors are a result of the animal's ability to sense its own orientation relative to the magnetic fields produced by the earth [28,8].

Forward Attraction The purpose of this behavior is to provide the robot with forward directed motion. A robot acting with this behavior will continually generate commands which result in motion along the current orientation of the robot. In effect, this behavior results in a robot which sustains forward motion, regardless of detected objects in the environment. As with the location attraction behavior, this behavior provides no protection from objects which may lie in front of the robot.

Object Attraction The object-attraction behavior functions to generate motion in the direction of an object. The object is represented by its surface normal which is calculated from the range data obtained from the sensor. When an object is detected, an attractive force is generated to cause motion towards the object.

A robot acting under this behavior will exhibit no movement (i.e, response) unless an object is detected (i.e, stimulus). When an object is detected, movement will occur in the direction of the object.

Object Following CW In contrast to the object-attraction behavior which generated motion in the direction of the surface normal, these behaviors generate motion in a direction perpendicular to the object such that motion occurs in a clockwise direction around the object.

Object Following CCW This behavior is identical to the object-following-cw behavior except that the attractive potential field associated with this behavior causes motion in a counter clockwise direction around the object.

Open Space Attraction Behaviors The stimulus-response behaviors which we have defined so far have been primarily concerned with the locations and shapes of objects in the environment. A group of primitive reflexive behaviors can be defined based upon the regions of space in which no objects were detected. Such regions are defined when a set of sensory measurements returns no range value (i.e. no object detected). These regions indicate completely open regions of space which provide unobstructed travel. At any given position in the environment, multiple regions of open space may exist (e.g. corresponding to the case when multiple objects are detected) or a single region of open space may exist (e.g. when no objects were detected).

To detect such regions, we have constructed a device which functions as an open space detector. Its purpose is to translate sensory range data into representations of open space. Conceptually, this detector is not unlike the specialized environmental detectors found in animals.

The resulting model of open spaces is a very simple one based on an understanding of the arrangement of the sensors on the vehicle and their maximum range. From these two quantities, one can calculate the angular width of the open spaces, a value which allows one to differentiate between wide open regions of space and narrow open regions of space.

Note that such sensors can be constructed using very crude approximates of distance to objects in the environment (e.g. using a low resolution proximity sensor). The open space detector derives its functionality from the many range sensors (which together provide a high angular resolution) that are arranged in a radial manner around the robot.

Based upon the interpretation of range data, three different primitive reflexive behaviors are defined, each of which causes a different type of open space attraction.

Narrow Open Space Attraction The purpose of this behavior is to provide the robot with a directed motion such that attraction to narrow open spaces occurs. This behavior will generate an attractive force which will result in motion towards the center of the region of open space which possesses the smallest angular width (as perceived from the robot). This behavior provides protection from collision with objects in the sense that the behavior generates an attractive force in the direction of a region of open space which, by its very definition, contains no object.

Wide Open Space Attraction The purpose of this behavior is to provide the robot with directed motion such that attraction to wide open spaces occurs. This behavior will generate an attractive force which will result in motion of the robot towards the center of the region of open space which possesses the largest angular width. This behavior results in a robot which "seeks" regions of wide open space.

Such a behavior may itself prove valuable from the standpoint of sensory interpretation (e.g. landmark recognition) by causing motion which is directed towards regions of open space which provide a maximal view of the surroundings.

Location Directed Open Space Attraction The purpose of this behavior is to provide the robot with a directed response such that motion occurs towards regions of open space which lie in the direction of some specified location in the environment. The location-directed-open-space-attraction behavior results in a robot which constantly moves in the direction of the open regions of space which are most closely aligned with the goal direction.

3.6. Emergent Robot Behavior

In the multi-behavioral approach to autonomy, emergent behavior occurs as a result of the spatial ordering of behavior (i.e. the concurrent activation of a set of primitive reflexive behaviors), also referred to as static arbitration; or through the temporal ordering of behavior (i.e. the sequential activation of different sets of primitive reflexive behaviors), also referred to as dynamic arbitration.

In the subsumption approach of [9,10], each new behavior (i.e. level of competence or control) is built on top of a lower level behavior and operates by spying on and interjecting data into the interconnections of the lower level behavior. Thus, there is an inherent "built-in" coupling between each of the behaviors. It is through this coupling that the spatial and temporal ordering of behavior occurs.

A variant to the subsumption approach is investigated in [13], in which they view goal-achieving behaviors as simple difference engines which act to reduce the difference between the actual state of the world and a desired state of the world. Their primary interest is in developing a more formal mechanism to merge behaviors together. A general arbitration point is suggested for ordering behavior, however in the paper, they limit themselves to ordering based upon the use of predetermined timeouts.

In our approach, each of the primitive reflexive behaviors is completely independent and uncoupled from each other. Our primary motivation in decoupling each of these behaviors is based upon the combinatorial nature of combining behavior spatially. Obviously, the more general case in which temporal ordering is included is even more problematic. This has led us to separate the mechanism which controls when a particular behavior is active from the actual computational elements which form the basis for each of the primitive reflexive behaviors.

To facilitate control of when each of the primitive reflexive behaviors is active, we have added computational elements, which act as binary switching devices, to each of the input wires for each of the behaviors [17]. Since downstream computation leading to a response of the robot is only performed when new values are placed on the input wires, the binary switches function to minimize the total amount of computation which occurs as the robot moves through its environment. Using this feature, we can affect a variety of different emergent behaviors by simply opening and closing the appropriate switches. We are currently investigating the development of a formal methodology for constructing more complex *reactive* forms of robot behavior in which the set of primitive reflexive behaviors active at any given time depends upon the occurrence of specific events in the environment [3].

In the follow section, we illustrate some of the different emergent behavioral patterns which we have observed while experimenting with the primitive reflexive behaviors. Our experimental results were obtained by simulation and by tests on an actual vehicle.

The simulation is of a robot with circular cross-section operating in an unknown environment (constructed of static polygon objects). Each of the larger circles represents a position of the

---

[17] Another approach would be to add a continuously valued weight to the output of each of the behaviors, in effect dictating the degree to which a given behavior participates in the overall behavior of the robot. While such an approach may ultimately allow for some form of learning mechanism by adjusting the values of the weights, its investigation is beyond the scope of this paper.

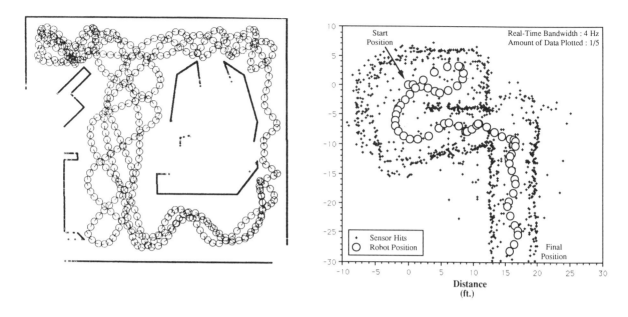

Fig. 2. (a) Generalized wandering behavior for simulated robot. (b) Generalized wandering behavior for Scarecrow.

robot at a given instance of time while the internal radial segment indicates the current orientation and direction of motion of the robot. The diameter of the robot was fixed at 2.2 feet (the diameter of our real robot). The robot detects the location of objects by using sixty point range sensors distributed around the robot at fixed angular intervals. The simulated sensors provide distance measurements to unknown objects within their maximum range of 11.0 feet from the robot's position at that moment in time. Each point on the surface of an unknown object that is detected (i.e. a sensor 'hit') is represented by the smaller dark circles.

The real robot, Scarecrow, is an untethered 400 pound multiprocessor-controlled pseudo-omnidirectional vehicle. Sixteen ultrasonic range sensors are equally spaced around the unit. Each has a range of 30 feet and a field of view which can be approximated by a 20° cone. There are a number of machine limitations, not the least of which is the fact that there are blind spots between adjacent sensors. Artifacts due to the particular properties of ultrasound lead to further aberrations in the perceived range. Nevertheless, the following results based on experiments with

Scarecrow demonstrate the remarkable robustness of the emergent behavioral approach [18]. The data that is plotted represents every fifth set of that collected as Scarecrow moves through the lab and adjacent corridor at approximately 1.5 ft/sec. The control and data acquisition bandwidth is 4 Hz. As with the simulation, the robot is represented as a circular object; the sensory range data as small crosshairs. For more details on Scarecrow, see [38].

Our purpose is not to compare the exact motion of Scarecrow with the simulated results since such comparisons would not be meaningful. Our objective is to compare the resulting patterns to verify whether the behaviors function as expected.

[18] In addition, the environment in which Scarecrow exists is a real world laboratory, cluttered with tables, chairs, and cabinets. Furthermore, besides other sensor limitations, the robot's wheels slip. As a result, the wheel encoders provide inaccurate information as to the robot's global position. (These encoders are only used for the location attraction based behaviors. We have avoided, whenever possible, to use this type of information.) People come and go as they please, and consequently, Scarecrow's operating domain is constantly changing. The walls in the area are not smooth and can be best characterized as backdrops for various steam, water, power and air conduits.

3.6.1. Generalized Wandering

A behavioral pattern characterized as generalized wandering emerges when the forward-attraction behavior is activated concurrently with the passive-avoidance and active-avoidance behaviors. Wandering provides a useful behavior which may support such tasks as mapping or patrolling of an area. Typically, the robot will wander throughout its environment.

The resulting behavioral pattern is shown in *Figs. 2a* and *2b* which illustrate that the robot has moved throughout a large portion of its environment.

One should note that environments may exist in which the robot may be limited to a form of "localized wandering". Such localized wandering occurs due to the weighting (i.e. the relative magnitudes of the potential fields generated) between the active-avoidance behavior and the forward-attraction behavior. Such regions correspond to local minima in the combined potential field. By varying the field strength associated with each of these behaviors, the robot may cover additional territory. This weighting effect has not yet been investigated. Furthermore, note that the exact path is completely deterministic and is a function of the geometric locations of all surfaces sensed by the robot. If the simulation were to be run again with

the same initial location of the robot and the same object positions, the resulting behavioral pattern would be the same. Since we cannot start Scarecrow at the "exact" same position each time and since we cannot ensure that its environment is always the same, its path will vary from run to run.

3.6.2. Simple Navigation

A primitive form of navigational behavior emerges when the passive-avoidance, active-avoidance, and location-attraction behaviors are allowed to operate concurrently.

The term "primitive" is used since this behavior appears to an outside observer to be equivalent to a form of navigation in which the robot moves between two positions in its environment. While the robot appears to navigate between these two positions, such is not the case. Navigation in a more formal sense is "the art and science of determining a ship's or aircraft's position at any time and of conducting a ship or aircraft from one position to another. The problems of navigation are those of position, direction, and distance on the water or in the air" [15]. The practice of navigation involves detailed a priori preparation which includes construction of a proposed route, estimation of environmental disturbances, as well

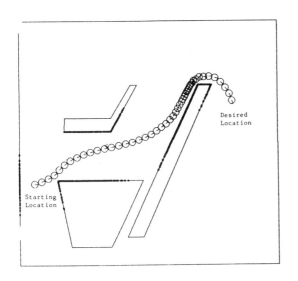
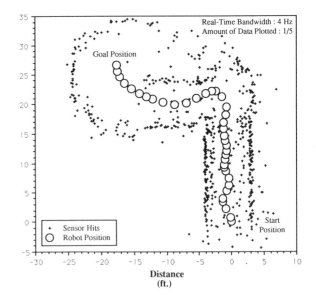

Fig. 3 (a) Simple navigation behavior for simulated robot. (b) Simple navigation behavior for Scarecrow.

as using the appearance of terrestrial landmarks and knowledge of celestial objects to increase one's estimate of position.

Baker [8] provides a clear distinction between navigation and pilotage: "navigation is the method of determining the direction of a familiar goal across *unfamiliar* terrain whereas pilotage is the method of determining the direction of a *familiar* goal across familiar terrain". This definition implies that most previous approaches to autonomous navigation based upon path planning methodologies are not navigation but instead pilotage.

Figs. 3a and *3b* illustrate the resulting behavioral pattern associated with this behavior. The robot exhibits a behavioral pattern which causes it to move to a specified location without colliding with objects in its environment.

While this combination of primitive behaviors often results in successfully moving the robot to a desired location, it is not guaranteed. It is possible that the location-attraction behavior may become incompatible with the the avoidance behaviors such as shown in *Figs. 4a* and *4b*.

At this point in the environment, the potential field associated with the active-avoidance behavior when combined with the potential field associated with the location-attraction behaviors has resulted in a combined field with a local minima which does not correspond with the desired location in the environment. The resulting "artificial forces" which are imposed on the robot from each of the potential fields balance and as a result, each behavior's contribution to the overall behavior of the robot cancels each other. The result is that the robot velocity drops to zero at this position in the environment.

This problem has been observed for some time and is referred to as "stagnation" [5]. A variety of strategies have been suggested for overcoming such situations including imposing an additional potential field upon the robot which models random noise [6], the use of other types of field functions [5] such as generalized potential fields [24], and the use of supervisory systems to recognize such situations [5].

We believe that such situations arise due to the reflexive nature of the robot. It has been given a statically defined set of reflexive behaviors and as a result, the overall behavior of the robot is completely reflexive. The behavior of the robot is completely determined by the stimuli upon which

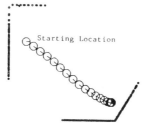

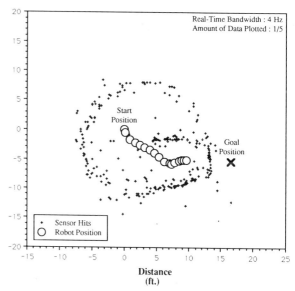

Fig. 4 (a) Stagnation occurs for simulated robot. (b) Stagnation occurs for Scarecrow.

each of its reflexive behaviors depend. Other unrelated events such as having a zero velocity can have no effect upon its behavior. We characterize the overall behavior of the robot as nonreactive (i.e. it cannot affect other types of behavior in response to such situations).

Limiting oneself strictly to the stimulus/response form of reflexive behaviors proposed reveals an important observation: an essential characteristic of autonomy is the ability to change one's behavior in response to the external environment (i.e, the ability to react to different external events).

3.6.3. Perimeter Following

A perimeter following behavior emerges when the primitive reflexive behaviors of passive-avoi-

 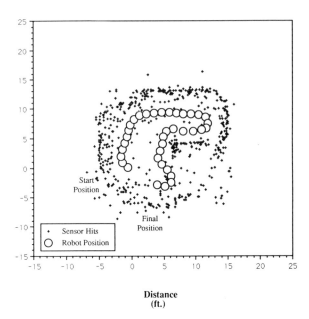

Fig. 5 (a) Perimeter following behavior for simulated robot. (b) Perimeter following behavior for Scarecrow in a room with an interior wall.

dance, active-avoidance, object-attraction, and either of the follow-object behaviors operate concurrently.

The follow-object behaviors provide the motion parallel to the perimeter while the object-attraction behavior and active-avoidance behaviors act to keep the robot close to the objects. *Figs. 5a* and *5b* illustrate the resulting behavioral pattern for clockwise perimeter following.

Note that in order for the robot to follow the perimeter of the environment, the robot must first be able to detect it. If the robot, acting under this set of primitive reflexive behaviors is initially placed at a location in which no objects are detected, the robot will remain idle. Thus, the robot responds to the detection of an object(s) by exhibiting a behavioral pattern in which it follows the perimeter of the object. If these stimuli are not present, it does not exhibit any form of directed response.

Different approaches are possible to cause the robot to exhibit motion for those cases in which it does not detect any objects. One approach would be to simply modify the object-attraction and object-following reflexive behaviors in order to elicit motion in the absence of objects. However,

the resulting behavior would then not adhere to the proposed reflexive stimulus/response paradigm: it would contain "heuristics" or special fixes.

The approach which we advocate would be the specification of a more general purpose behavior in which the robot reacts to such situations by exhibiting a different form of behavioral pattern such as generalized wandering.

This simple example further reinforces the notion that to achieve greater degrees of autonomy

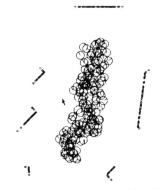

Fig. 6. Behavioral pattern associated with wide open space wandering for simulated robot.

requires reactive forms of behavior. In [3], we show that it is indeed possible to construct reactive robot behavior strictly in terms of a set of reflexive behaviors and without resorting to heuristics.

3.6.4. Constrained Forms of Wandering

To illustrate how other types of behavioral patterns emerge when primitive reflexive behaviors are allowed to operate concurrently, we have experimented with different forms of the wandering behavior.

Wide Open Space Wandering We can construct a robot which wanders in open regions of space by allowing the wide-open-space-attraction behavior to operate concurrently with the active-avoidance, passive-avoidance, and forward-attraction behaviors. Notice that constructing such a behavior involves simply activating an additional primitive behavior in addition to those which constitute the generalized wandering behavior discussed earlier. *Fig. 6* illustrates the resulting behavioral pattern.

This behavioral pattern exhibits characteristics of the generalized wandering behavior and the wide-open-space-wandering behavior. The result is a behavioral pattern which constrains the robot to wander in locally large open regions of space.

Narrow Open Space Wandering As with the wide-open-space wandering behavior, we can create another type of wandering behavior by allowing concurrent operation of the narrow-open-space-attraction behavior with the active-avoidance, passive-avoidance, and forward attraction behaviors.

Fig. 7 illustrates the resulting behavioral pattern. Examination of this figure reveals a behavioral pattern which is very similar to the generalized wandering behavior presented previously except for portions of the environment in which multiple, distinct regions of space can be detected.

In these regions of the environment, the effect of the narrow-open-space-attraction behavior constrains the overall behavior of the robot such that wandering remains localized. The result is a behavioral pattern which may be characterized as narrow-open-space-wandering.

Location Directed Open space Wandering A useful type of wandering behavior results when the

Fig. 7. Behavioral pattern associated with narrow open space wandering for simulated robot.

location-directed-open-space-attraction behavior operates concurrently with the active-avoidance, passive-avoidance, and forward attraction behaviors. As in both of the previous wandering behaviors, a new type of wandering behavior occurs by simply allowing an additional primitive behavior to be active concurrently with those which constitute the generalized wandering behavior. *Figs. 8a, 8b* and *8c* illustrate the resulting behavioral patterns.

The robot exhibits a behavioral pattern which shares characteristics associated with the generalized wandering behavior when a single object is detected and characteristics associated with a location directed behavior when the robot is in completely open space or when multiple regions of open space exist.

To illustrate how cyclical behavior is possible when the robot is limited to a set of statically activated primitive reflexive behaviors, examine *Fig. 8a*. Very few other goal locations could be found within this environment to cause such severe cyclical behavior. In the majority of cases, the robot successfully reached the target location without exhibiting any form of cyclical behavior (see *Fig. 8b*).

In *Fig. 8c*, the robot encounters a large barrier in the direction of the desired location and exhibits a characteristic associated with the generalized wandering behavior. This generalized wandering behavior causes the robot to move back into an open region of space in which no objects are detected. At this point, the location-directed-open-space-attraction behavior causes the robot to move in the direction of the desired location and the process repeats until eventually, the robot wanders within view of the passage way which leads to the desired location. In effect, it does not "remember" where it has been or what it has "seen".

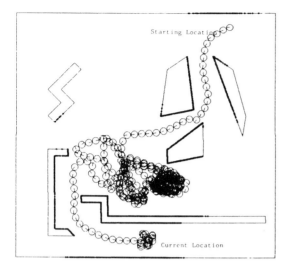

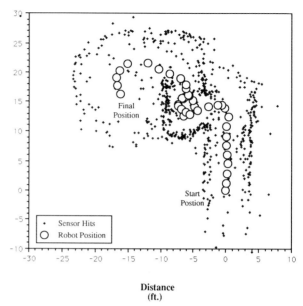

Fig. 9. Location directed open space wandering for Scarecrow.

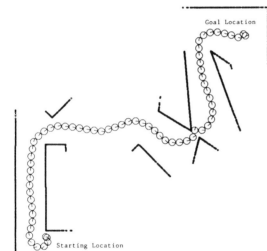

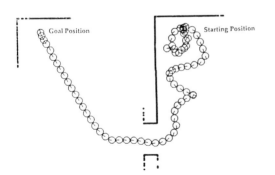

Fig. 8 (a) An example of a cyclical behavioral pattern for location directed open space wandering (simulated robot). (b) Location directed open space wandering for simulated robot (no cyclical behavior) (c) Location directed open space wandering for simulated robot.

Fig. 9 illustrates the corresponding behavioral pattern for Scarecrow. The robot is shown with a starting location in the hallway and a desired location in the lab. As shown, large barrier partitions have been placed inside the laboratory in order to block access to Scarecrow's destination. Under the simple navigation behavior, the robot would have stagnated before it could have reached its goal. In this case, however, the robot successfully moves to the desired location. Some cyclical behavior is clearly visible.

This cyclic behavior is due to: (a) limitations in the robot's ability to adequately sense its environment, (b) the inability of the robot to respond to events which happen over several time periods, (c) the deterministic nature of the robot's response, and (d) the reflexive nature of the robot. This problem was observed by Culbertson [14]

> "These memoryless robots will exhibit certain behavioral maladjustments, since, having no memory, they cannot react to events occurring over an interval of time. What reaction is suitable to a given input may depend on previous inputs, and such distinctions are a closed book to the memoryless robot.
>
> ...Also, these robots might easily get hung up or trapped even in a completely inanimate environment."

In fact, such cyclical behavior may indicate that an essential characteristic of a truly autonomous robot is that of memory (i.e, the ability to react to events which occur over a number of intervals of time and the ability to alter behavior depending upon previous behavior). Cyclical behavior has also been observed in the wandering and wall following behaviors of Brooks and Connell [11].

3.7. Combinatorial Expansion of Behaviors

We have illustrated seven different behavioral patterns which emerge when various primitive reflexive behaviors are allowed to operate concurrently. What other forms of behavioral patterns are possible from the currently defined primitive behaviors?

This presents an interesting prospect since it is usually not easy to predict the resulting behavioral response from a combination of concurrent processes. The prospect of additional types of useful behavior, not envisioned previously, is extremely powerful since it may provide one with new types of behaviors to support given tasks and provide additional insight into the process of building robot behavior.

The location-directed-open-space-wandering behavior was a result of a bottom-up composition in which we originally intended to experiment with the location-directed-open-space-attraction behavior, in which the robot was attracted towards open spaces in the direction of some location in the environment. We quickly found that, often, due to obstacles in the goal direction, the only open space for the robot to move towards was that which it had just come from. What was really needed was some type of behavior which acted concurrently to cause the robot to move to other regions so that some open space in the goal direction might be found. To achieve this characteristic in the behavioral pattern, we allowed the primitive reflexive behaviors which made up the generalized wandering behavior to also be active. The result was that the behavioral pattern exhibited characteristics of both a location directed response and a generalized wandering response.

We have found, however, that arbitrarily adding additional primitive reflexive behaviors to the robot eventually results in an overall behavior of the robot which serves no meaningful purpose. The total number of unique behaviors possible from n different primitive reflexive behaviors, combined spatially and assuming binary methods of combination, can be computed. By considering the i possible combinations of n items taken k at

a time:

$$i = \sum_{k=0}^{n} \frac{n!}{k!(n-k)!}$$

we get 1024 behaviors for 10 primitive behaviors. Thus, we see that a combinatorial explosion in the number of possible behaviors can occur when constructing spatially ordered behavior. In actuality, this number is *much* larger if one allows for temporal ordering of behavior, or if the more general problem is addressed, in which behaviors are each weighted by a continuously varied value. As behaviors are continuously added to form emergent behaviors, this issue of scaleability becomes a significant challenge which must be addressed in a multi-behavioral approach to autonomy. This represents an area for future research.

3.8. Relationship to Other Work

Our approach to defining robot behaviors is built upon previous research in the area of autonomous mobile robots [9,10] and is strongly influenced by ethological observations [27,28,35]. It also shares similarities with the works of [21,33,6,22]. Each of these approaches is based upon a vertical decomposition. A thorough conceptual review of our approach as compared to others is presented in [1] and in [2].

First, in our approach, the elements which affect behavior are separated from the mechanism which controls when a particular behavior is active. Thus, we do not allow for temporal ordering of behavior (e.g. ordering based upon the use of timeouts) nor do we allow for the prioritization of behavior within the definitions of each of the primitive reflexive behaviors. This allows us to decouple the control of behavior (i.e. spatial and temporal ordering) from the actual implementation of each of the reflexive behaviors.

Secondly, each of the primitive reflexive behaviors which we have constructed models a simple stimulus/response mechanism which does not incorporate heuristics or localized path planning algorithms. Each behavior models a directional response to a specific stimulus.

Thirdly, each of our primitive reflexive behaviors map their response into a potential field [23,20,5]. This combination mechanism occurs *ex-*

ternal to each of the primitive reflexive behaviors. Thus, we can easily add additional primitive reflexive behaviors, provided that their response is expressed in the form of a potential field.

Finally, each of our primitive reflexive behaviors does not contain any form of memory. Our motivation has been to explicitly investigate the role of memory in autonomy (i.e. is memory required and if so, what form should such memory take). As such, we wished to first experiment with behaviors which are completely reflexive.

Some of the emergent behaviors which we achieve through different combinations of primitive behaviors are functionally equivalent to those proposed by other researchers, while others produce much different results.

Our passive-avoidance and active-avoidance behaviors are derived from the zeroth level of control used by Brooks [9,10]. These two behaviors also serve to model the observed predator-prey behavior between moths and bats [35]. The active-avoidance behavior is also equivalent to a portion of the "vector sum" local navigation strategy reported in [21] and other approaches to obstacle avoidance based upon the use of potential fields [5,23,6].

The simple navigation behavior which we use is functionally equivalent to the approach taken by [5,23,21,10].

Our generalized wandering behavior is different than that reported in [11] in that Brooks builds a wandering behavior by constructing a new level of control (i.e, the first level of control), on top of his avoidance behavior. This avoidance behavior generates a random heading periodically and uses "a simple heuristic to plan ahead to avoid possible collisions which would otherwise need to be handled by the zeroth level". This results in a robot which periodically moves in the direction of a random location. To complete the wandering behavior, an additional level of control (i.e, the second level of control) is added to the existing levels of control. This level of control generates headings which cause the robot to move towards regions of space such as corridors. To insure that both the first and second level of control do not issue control commands at the same time, level two is allowed to inhibit the first level of control, resulting in temporal ordering between behaviors. If the robot has not reached the position specified by the second level within 2 minutes (a timeout

value), control is passed back to the first level which then generates a random heading. Under our generalized wandering behavior, no use of heuristics or path planning is made. Furthermore, our wandering occurs as a result of a spatially ordered set of primitive reflexive behaviors: no temporal ordering or timeouts are used.

Kadonoff [21] reports on a local navigation strategy referred to as "avoider" which causes a wandering behavior; however, no details or results are reported. Payton [33] also proposes a wandering activity composed of "slow for obstacle" and "turn for obstacle" behaviors but no results are given on its performance.

Our perimeter following behaviors are conceptually derived from the wall following behavior of Brooks [11] except that in their implementation, additional modules are added which cause the robot to move through doorways. As in their implementation of the wandering behavior, this behavior is affected by the built-in control structure which temporally orders the wall following from that which causes the robot to move through doorways. A timeout mechanism is included which causes the robot to revert to wall following if the robot has not successfully passed through the door in a set amount of time. Kadonoff et al. report on a local navigation strategy which follow walls without providing details on its implementation or performance [21].

The location-directed-wandering behavior appears to be similar to the "seek-heading" activity proposed in [33] but again, no results on its performance are given.

4. Closure

4.1. Summary

The central thesis which we have put forth is that autonomy in robot behavior can be developed from simple forms of primitive reflexive behavior. While we clearly recognize that the ability to learn new behaviors in response to situations not previously encountered or envisioned is a characteristic of higher life forms, we also recognize that many life forms possess innate forms of response which act to protect the organism and which allow it to function.

In the area of mobile robots, our research builds upon and is most closely related to that of [9,10] in that new types of behavioral patterns emerge from the combination of more primitive forms of behavior. We view our results as complementary to that of Brooks. Our approaches differ primarily in the details of our architectures and in our desire to begin by investigating the limitations which may arise due to the strict use of reflexive, memoryless forms of behavior.

Our approach is based upon a fundamental assumption that a significant degree of autonomy for a wide range of differing tasks will require a variety of different types of behavior. We classify our approach as a multi-behavioral approach to autonomous mobile robot control. As a guide to our research in autonomy, we have relied upon ethological observations of animal behavior and have summarized some of the relevant points regarding such observations.

We illustrated how new forms of behavioral patterns emerge when different primitive reflexive behaviors are allowed to operate concurrently. An important observation is that the new behavioral patterns which emerge take on characteristics not previously ascribed to the component behaviors. Furthermore, such emergent behavior still represents reflexive behavior in that the set of primitive reflexive behaviors active at any given time is fixed in advance. We also showed that it is possible to achieve these behaviors without taking advantage of memory, heuristics or path planning.

Finally, we presented experimental results for Scarecrow, an actual mobile robot operating continuously under real-time motion control, in a completely unknown, unstructured and dynamic environment. The forms of the behavioral patterns which emerged were functionally equivalent to those predicted by simulation. These experiments showed that the emergent behaviors are robust, in that they achieve their functionality despite sensor and vehicle limitations. Experience to date, has also shown that Scarecrow functions reasonably well despite the presence of the most unpredictable obstacles, humans themselves.

4.2. Conclusions

In the course of our research in autonomy, we have arrived at a number of conclusions:

1. A limited degree of autonomy can result from behaviors which are strictly reflexive in nature.
2. Reflexive behavior is possible without the use of memory.
3. Autonomy requires some form of self knowledge such as the arrangement of sensors on the robot or the dimensions of the robot.
4. New behavioral patterns emerge when differing primitive behaviors are allowed to operate concurrently. Such emergent behavior takes on characteristics not previously ascribed to each of the component behaviors.
5. Greater degrees of autonomy require reactive forms of behavior in which the robot is not limited to a fixed set of primitive reflexive behaviors which can be active.
6. Cyclical behavioral patterns can occur when a robot is limited to reflexive, memoryless behavior.
7. It is possible to exhibit useful behavioral patterns without the explicit use of robot state information.
8. Due to the combinatorial nature of constructing emergent robot behavior, it is necessary to maintain the independence of each of the primitive reflexive behaviors and separate the mechanism which allows for control of robot behavior from the actual devices which affect each reflexive behavior.

Acknowledgements

This research has been supported with funds provided in part by the University of Minnesota Productivity Center, the CIM Consortium, the CyberOptics Corp., and the Office of Naval Research under Contract N0004-85-C-0847. We also appreciate the loan of equipment by MTS Systems Corp. and CyberOptics Corp. We would like to thank Jay Talbott for his efforts in designing large portions of Scarecrow and for orchestrating the experiments.

References

[1] T.L. Anderson, A Reflexive Behavioral Approach to the Control of a Mobile Robot. M.S. Thesis. Dept. of Mechanical Engineering; University of Minnesota (1989).

[2] T.L. Anderson and M. Donath, Synthesis of reflexive behavior for a mobile robot based upon a stimulus-response paradigm, in *Mobile Robots III, Proc. of the SPIE*, Vol. 1007 (Cambridge, MA, November, 1988).

[3] T.L. Anderson and M. Donath, A computational structure for enforcing reactive behavior in a mobile robot, in *Mobile Robots III, Proc. of the SPIE*, Vol. 1007 (Cambridge, MA, November, 1988).

[4] *The American Heritage Dictionary of the English Language.,* *New College ed.* (Boston, Houghton Mifflin Company, 1980, c1969) (W. Morris) ISBN 0-395-20360-0.

[5] J.R. Andrews, Impedance Control as a Framework for Implementing Obstacle Avoidance in a Manipulator, S.M Thesis, Dept. of Mechanical Engineering (Massachusetts Institute of Technology, 1983).

[6] R.C. Arkin, Motor schema based navigation for a mobile robot: an approach to programming by behavior, *IEEE Int. Conf. on Robotics and Automation* (March, 1987, Raleigh, NC).

[7] D. Atkinson et al., Autonomous task level control of a robot, in: *Proceedings of Robotics and Expert Systems: 2nd Workshop* (June, 1986, Instrumentation Society of America).

[8] R.R. Baker, *Human Navigation and the Sixth Sense* (Simon and Schuster, New York 1981; ISBN 0-671-44129-9).

[9] R.A. Brooks, Achieving artificial intelligence through building robots, A.I. Memo 899 (May, 1986).

[10] R.A. Brooks, A robust layered control system for a mobile robot, *IEEE J. of Robotics Automat.* (March 1986).

[11] R.A. Brooks and J.H. Connell, Asynchronous distributed control system for a mobile robot, *In: SPIE's Cambridge Symposium on Optical and Optoelectronic Engineering* (October, 1986, Cambridge, Massachusetts).

[12] J.L. Crowley, Dynamic world modelling for an intelligent mobile robot using a rotating ultrasonic ranging device, *1985 IEEE Int. Conf. Robotics and Automation* (March, 1985, St. Louis, MO).

[13] P.W. Cudhea and R.A. Brooks, Coordinating multiple goals for a mobile robot, source unknown (1986).

[14] J. Culbertson, *The Minds of Robots: Sense Data, Memory Images, and Behavior in Conscious Automata* (University of Illinois Press, Illinois 1963).

[15] D. Dutton, *Navigation and Nautical Astronomy* (George Banta Publ. Co., Menasha, Wisconsin 1948).

[16] A. Elfes, A sonar-based mapping and navigation system, *Proc. 1986 IEEE Int. Conf. Robotics and Automation* (1986).

[17] A.M. Flynn, Redundant sensors for mobile robot navigation (Cambridge, MA, Massachusetts Institute of Technology, 1985; AI-TR-859; 70 pp document, Artificial Intelligence Laboratory, Cambridge, MA 02139).

[18] G. Fraenkel and D. Gunn, *The Orientation of Animals*, 2nd ed. (Dover Publ., New York 1961).

[19] M. Gini, Symbolic and qualitative reasoning for error recovery in robot programs, in: *Proc. NATO ASI on Languages for Sensor Based Control in Robotics* (1986).

[20] N. Hogan, Programmable impedance control of industrial manipulators, In: *Conf. CAD/CAM Technology in Mechanical Engineering* (March, 1982, Cambridge, MA).

[21] M. B.Kadonoff et al., Arbitration of multiple control strategies for mobile robots, *SPIE Mobile Robots* (1986) 727.

[22] L.P. Kaelbling, Goals as parallel program specifications, in: *Seventh Nat. Conf. Artificial Intelligence* (August, 1988, St. Paul, MN).

[23] O. Khatib, Real-time obstacle avoidance for manipulators and mobile robots, *1985 IEEE Int. Conf. Robotics and Automation.*

[24] B.H. Krogh and C.E. Thorpe, Integrated path planning and dynamic steering control for autonomous vehicles, *1986 IEEE Int. Conf. Robotics and Automation.*

[25] J.Y. Lettvin et al., What the frog's eye tells the frog's brain. in: W. McCullock, *Embodiments of Mind* (MIT Press, Massachusetts 1970; c1965) 230; 25p.

[26] T. Lozano-Perez and M. Wesley, An algorithm for planning collision-free paths among polyhedral obstacles, Comm. ACM (October 1979, 22(10)) 560-570.

[27] A. Manning, *An introduction to Animal Behavior*, 3rd ed. (Addison-Wesley Publ. Co., Reading, Massachusetts 1979; c1967. (Barrington, F. R. S. Contemporary Biology) ISBN 0-201-04446-3.

[28] D. McFarland, (Ed), *The Oxford Companion to Animal Behavior* (Oxford University Press, 1987; c1987) ISBN 0-19-281990-9.

[29] A. Meystel and D.Gaw, Minimum-time navigation of an unmanned mobile robot in a 2–1/2d world with obstacles, *1986 IEEE Int. Conf. Robotics and Automation.*

[30] D.A. Miller, A spatial representation system for mobile robots, *1985 IEEE Int. Conf. Robotics and Automation.*

[31] H.P. Moravec, *Robot Rover Visual Navigation* (UMI Research Press, Ann Arbor, Michigan, 1981) ISBN 0-8357-1200-1.

[32] A.M. Parodi et al., An intelligent system for an autonomous vehicle, *1986 IEEE Int. Conf. Robotics and Automation.*

[33] D.W. Payton, An architecture for reflexive autonomous vehicle control, *1986 IEEE Int. Conf. Robotics and Automation.*

[34] S.V. Rao et al., Concurrent algorithms for autonomous robot navigation in an unexplored terrain, *Proc. IEEE Int. Conf. Robotics and Automation* (April, 1986).

[35] K.D. Roeder, *Nerve Cells and Insect Behavior* 2nd ed. (Harvard University Press, Cambridge, Massachusetts 1969; c1963. (Griffin et al., Harvard books in biology, No. 4) ISBN 674-60800-3.

[36] H. Schone, *Spatial Orientation: The Spatial Control of Behavior in Animals and Man.* (Princeton University Press; Princeton, NJ 1984) ISBN 0-691-08364-9.

[37] H. Simon, *The Sciences of the Artificial* (Massachusetts Institute of Technology, 1985) ISBN 0-262-69073-X.

[38] J. Talbott, T.L. Anderson and M. Donath, SCARECROW: An implementation of behavioral control on a mobile robot, in *Mobile Robots IV, Proc. SPIE*, Vol. 1195 (Philadelphia, PA, November, 1989).

[39] N. Tinbergen, *The Study of Instincts* (Oxford University Press, London, England 1951).

[40] R. Wallace et al., Progress in robot road-following, *1986 IEEE Int. Conf. on Robotics and Automation* (April, 1986, San Francisco, CA).

A Biological Perspective on Autonomous Agent Design

Randall D. Beer [1,2], Hillel J. Chiel [2], and Leon S. Sterling [1]

Departments of [1] Computer Engineering and Science, and [2] Biology and the Center for Automation and Intelligent Systems Research, Case Western Reserve University, Cleveland, OH 44106, USA

The inability of current "classical" AI systems to handle unconstrained interaction with the real world has recently lead to a search for new control architectures for autonomous agents. We argue that simpler natural animals already exhibit most of the properties required by an autonomous agent, and suggest that designers of autonomous agents should draw directly upon the neural basis of behavior in these animals. The relevant behavioral and neurobiological literature is briefly reviewed. An artificial nervous system for controlling the behavior of a simulated insect is then developed. The design of this artificial insect is based in part upon specific behaviors and neural circuits from several natural animals. The insect exhibits a number of characteristics which are remarkably reminiscent of natural animal behavior.

Keywords: Autonomous behavior; Artificial insect; Artificial nervous system; Heterogeneous neural networks; Computational neuroethology; Behavioral hierarchy; Motivated behavior; Insect locomotion; Artificial intelligence; Situated action.

1. Introduction

The real world is complex, unpredictable, and dynamic. It is simply not possible for a designer to foresee all of the circumstances that might be faced by an agent in continuous, long-term interaction with such an environment. Any truly intelligent agent must therefore possess a considerable degree of autonomy. It must be capable of flexibly adapting its behavioral repertoire to the moment to moment contingencies which arise without explicitly being told what to do in each situation. How should the control architecture of such an autonomous agent be organized?

The classical AI answer to this question is largely drawn from introspection on conscious

Dr. Hillel Chiel graduated from Yale University in 1974 with a B.A. in English, and received a Ph.D. from M.I.T. in 1980 in Neural and Endocrine Regulation. As a postdoctoral fellow at the Center for Neurobiology and Behavior at Columbia University's College of Physicians and Surgeons, he studied the cellular basis of feeding behavior in the marine mollusc *Aplysia.* He then became a Consultant in Neurobiology in the Department of Molecular Biophysics Research at AT &T Bell Laboratories. He is currently an Assistant Professor in the Departments of Biology and Neuroscience at Case Western Reserve University. He is interested in experimental and modeling studies of behavior in simpler organisms.

Leon Sterling is Associate Professor in the Department of Computer Engineering and Science at Case Western Reserve University (CWRU), and co-Director of the Center for Automation and Intelligent Systems Research there. He received his B.Sc.(hons.) from the University of Melbourne in 1976 and his Ph.D. in Pure Mathematics from Australian National University in 1981. He spent three years in the Artificial Intelligence Department at the University of Edinburgh, and one year at the Weizmann Institute before joining CWRU in 1985. His interests include logic programming, expert systems and new foundations for artificial intelligence.

Randall Beer received a B.S. in Computer Engineering (1985), and an M.S. (1985) and Ph.D. (1989) in Computer Science from Case Western Reserve University. He is currently an Assistant Professor in the Departments of Computer Engineering and Science, and Biology at Case Western Reserve University. He is interested in computational neuroscience, artificial intelligence, and symbolic programming languages.

human reasoning. Essentially the same process by which we deliberately reason through, say, an anagram is hypothesized to underlie all intelligent behavior. Abstractly, this technique can be formulated as the appropriate manipulation of symbolic representations of the situation. The problem of crossing a room, for example, can be formulated as a search over symbolic descriptions of the possible paths through all of the intervening obstacles in much the same way that solving an anagram can. The actual manipulations involved in the former problem may be very much more complex than for an anagram, and the structure of the symbolic representations may be very intricate, but the idea is essentially the same. This notion finds its strongest and most explicit expression in the Physical Symbol System Hypothesis, which states that formal symbol manipulation is both a necessary and sufficient mechanism for general intelligent behavior [27].

In many ways, this methodology has served AI well. Though various issues were more difficult than originally anticipated, numerous fragments of intelligent behavior have now been generated in this manner. From the point of view of research on autonomous agents, however, all of these systems currently suffer from several rather glaring deficiencies: (1) they are incapable of flexibly coping with contingencies not explicitly foreseen by their designers, (2) their performance is extremely sensitive to the representational choices made by their designers, and brittle in the face of inevitable small deviations of the real world from these abstractions, and (3) their time complexity scales very poorly with problem size, becoming intractable for even simple real world tasks.

Of course, current shortcomings of the classical AI methodology do not necessarily compromise its fundamental soundness. The exploration of techniques for addressing these limitations is currently an active area of AI research. However, in light of the continuing difficulties encountered by these efforts, we must at least face the possibility that much of our intelligent behavior, particularly that which involves taking action in the real world, is really not at all like conscious reasoning. For this reason, a number of researchers have begun to explore alternative architectures for the control of autonomous agents (e.g. [8,25,1,17]).

Historically, AI has almost exclusively attempted to emulate *human* behavior. Our own approach to designing architectures for autonomous agents is grounded in the recognition that human beings are not the only natural agents which exhibit interesting autonomous behavior. Given our current level of understanding, people may not even be the best examples to study at this time. When even the most mundane contingency arises in our everyday interactions with the real world, we may draw upon an incredibly diverse collection of cognitive skills and a lifetime's worth of accumulated knowledge to cope with it. But human beings are simply too complex to model whole, and very little is known about the mechanisms underlying human cognition.

Therefore, our work has focused on the behavior of simpler natural animals, such as insects. While such animals cannot play chess or prove theorems, they are capable of autonomously adapting their limited behavioral repertoires to the moment to moment contingencies of the real world in ways that no current AI system can match. In order to tap this very rich source of potential insights for autonomous agent control structures, we have undertaken a careful study and simulation of the biological mechanisms underlying the autonomous behavior of simpler natural animals [4]. We call this endeavor *Computational Neuroethology*, since Ethology is the study of the behavior of animals in their natural environments [24], and Neuroethology is the study of the neural mechanisms underlying this behavior [9].

This paper is organized as follows. The next section describes some important principles of animal behavior. A brief introduction to some of the neural mechanisms which are known or hypothesized to underlie this behavior is then provided in Section 3. With this background, Section 4 describes an initial exploration into biologically-inspired control architectures for autonomous agents which we call the Artificial Insect Project. By drawing upon specific behavioral principles and their underlying neural circuits from several natural animals, we have designed an artificial nervous system for controlling the behavior of a simulated insect. Finally, Section 5 discusses the advantages and disadvantages of this approach to designing autonomous agent control architectures, and suggests some directions for future research.

2. Concepts in Animal Behavior

Before embarking upon a detailed consideration of the underlying biological mechanisms, it is instructive to briefly consider the problem of natural autonomous behavior from an ethological perspective. Unlike most artificial systems, natural animals obviously thrive very well in the real world. What are the common behavioral principles exhibited by animals engaged in the everyday business of their existence? Which of these principles might be useful in artificial autonomous agents?

Perhaps the most important principle, readily apparent to even a casual observer, is that all animal behavior is *adaptive* in the following sense: as an animal confronts its environment, its behavior is continuously adjusted to meet the everchanging internal and external conditions of the interaction. For example, a feeding insect will suddenly turn and run if it is attacked by a predator [31]. In addition, a running insect will continuously alter its gait to compensate for changes in terrain and load, and can even adjust for amputations of one or more legs [15].

Broadly speaking, animal behavior can be divided into a number of major classes. Perhaps the simplest form of animal behavior is a *reflex*, in which some fast, stereotyped response is triggered by a particular class of environmental stimuli. The defining characteristic of a reflex is that the intensity and duration of the response is entirely governed by the intensity and duration of the stimulus [10]. Reflexes allow an animal to quickly adjust its behavior to sudden environmental changes. Reflexes are commonly employed for such things as postural control, withdrawal from painful stimuli, and the adaptation of gait to uneven terrain.

Taxes or orientation responses are another simple class of behavior [9]. These behaviors involve the orientation of an animal toward or away from some environmental agent, such as light, gravity, or chemical signals. For example, female crickets exhibit positive phonotaxis during courtship, that is they orient to the calling song of a male [26].

Fixed-action patterns are a somewhat more complex form of behavior [24]. A fixed-action pattern is an extended, largely stereotyped response to a sensory stimulus. The triggering stimulus for a fixed-action pattern is generally more complex and specific than for reflexes. The response usually involves a complex temporal sequence of component acts. While such a pattern may be triggered by the occurrence of a specific sensory stimulus, its intensity and duration is not particularly stimulus-governed. In fact, once a fixed-action pattern has been triggered, it will usually run to completion even if the triggering stimulus is removed. An example of a fixed-action pattern is an escape response, in which some distinguishing characteristic of an imminent predator attack triggers a sequence of evasive maneuvers on the part of the prey (e.g. cockroaches escaping from toads; [31]). The fixed-action patterns of individual animals can also be interrelated in intricate ways, as is demonstrated by the elaborate courtship rituals between the male and female members of many animal species (e.g. guppies; [3]).

Despite the ubiquity of such responses as reflexes, taxes and fixed-action patterns, animal behavior is by no means solely reactive. Factors internal to an animal can also play an important role in the initiation, maintenance, or modulation of a given behavior. The sign or intensity of reflexes, for example, can change depending upon internal factors. The threshold for triggering most fixed-action patterns similarly varies with internal state.

Behaviors which show no simple or rigid dependence on external stimuli, but are instead governed primarily by the internal state of the animal, are known as *motivated behaviors*. In these behaviors, an animal's propensity to exhibit a given behavior such as feeding depends not only upon the presence of the appropriate environmental stimuli (i.e. food), but also upon internal *motivational* variables (i.e. hunger). Motivated behaviors are typically characterized by (1) grouping and sequencing of component behavior in time, (2) goal-directedness: the sequence of component behaviors generated can only be understood by reference to some goal, (3) spontaneity: the behavior can occur in the complete absence of any eliciting stimuli, (4) changes in responsiveness: the modulatory effect of the motivational state varies depending upon its level of arousal or satiation, (5) persistence: the behavior can greatly outlast any initiating stimulus, and (6) associative learning [21].

Any individual animal consists of a large collection of reflexes, taxes, and fixed-action patterns, many aspects of which are under at least some motivational control. As an animal confronts its environment with this diverse behavioral repertoire, it must properly coordinate its many possible actions into coherent behavior directed toward its long-term survival. Toward this end, the behavioral repertoire of a natural animal typically exhibits a certain organization. Some behaviors normally take precedence over others. Some behaviors are mutually exclusionary (i.e. any behaviors which utilize the same motor apparatus for incompatible actions). Switches between different behaviors depend both upon environmental conditions and internal state. These relationships are often described as rigid and strictly hierarchical, with cleanly delineated behaviors and simple all or nothing switching between them. In reality, the relationships may be nonhierarchical, the organization can change depending upon the behavioral context, and behaviors can partially overlap so that discrete switches between them are sometimes difficult to identify.

Though the number and variety of behavior clearly varies from species to species, all of the principles described above are exhibited in one form or another by all natural animals. This basic organization of behavior supports the ability of natural animals to flexibly cope with real world environments. In addition to this propensity for adaptive behavior, however, natural animals also exhibit various forms of *plasticity*. Aspects of their future behavior can be modified as a result of their past history of interactions with the environment. The time scale of these modifications may range from seconds to years.

Several simple forms of plasticity have been identified in natural animals [18]. In *habituation*, the magnitude of response to a given stimulus decreases with repeated exposure to the stimulus. For example, while a loud clap may initially produce a startle response in an animal, subsequent claps will produce a progressively weaker response. In some cases, the startle response may disappear altogether. *Dishabituation* is the sudden restoration of an habituated response following a particularly strong or noxious stimulus to the habituated sensory apparatus. An extremely loud clap, for example, might restore the habituated startle response. *Sensitization* involves an enhancement of a response to a wide variety of

stimuli following the presentation of another strong stimulus. For example, a strong pinch might increase the sensitivity of the startle response to sound. These simple forms of plasticity allow an animal to adjust its responsiveness to its environment.

None of the above forms of plasticity depend upon a pairing of the strong stimulus with the weaker one. In *associative learning*, on the other hand, pairing between two stimuli is crucial. In one form of associative learning, called *classical conditioning*, repeated pairing of an initially neutral stimulus with one which normally elicits some response will eventually lead to a situation in which the neutral stimulus alone triggers the response. A common example of classical conditioning is when dogs salivate at the sound of a bell if the bell has been paired with the appearance of food in the past. In another form of associative learning, called *instrumental conditioning*, an animal's behavior is reinforced by events in its environment. For example, a rat will learn to avoid a particular food if prior ingestion of that food was followed by sickness [13]. These associational forms of plasticity allow an animal to take into account the causal relationships within its particular environment. However, it is important to realize that most animals cannot make arbitrary associations, but only those that are biologically relevant. For example, though a rat can easily learn to associate illness with a particular odor or taste, it by and large cannot learn to associate illness with auditory or visual stimuli.

Though there are several other forms of behavioral plasticity, we will mention only one more here. *Latent learning* is plasticity which does not involve particularly strong stimuli or obvious reward or punishment, as when an animal learns about its environment through exploration. For example, even ants can learn to run a maze simply by repeatedly being placed within it [33]. By these and many other forms of behavioral plasticity, animals fine-tune the behavioral repertoire with which they are genetically endowed to the exigencies of the particular environment in which they find themselves.

In this section, we have focused primarily on characterizing the behavior of simpler animals. This emphasis should not be misunderstood. Human beings are obviously not insects, and there are many aspects of human behavior of interest to

AI which clearly cannot be directly addressed through a study of simpler animals. We maintain, however, that there are many more which can. In particular, we strongly believe that the behavior of simpler animals has all of the ingredients which artificial autonomous agents require in order to flexibly cope with the real world: it is goal-oriented, adaptive, opportunistic, plastic, and robust. While the specifics of any given animal behavior are unlikely to be of direct use to an engineered agent, the general principles most certainly are.

Furthermore, it is important to stress that simpler animals are not simple. Even C. elegans, a millimeter long worm with only 302 nerve cells (it has less than 1000 cells in its entire body!) has been shown to be capable of associative learning [20]. In addition, several species of insects are known to possess elaborate social structures and to employ complex forms of communication [42]. Finally, and perhaps most importantly from our perspective, the neurobiological mechanisms underlying many of the abovementioned behavioral principles are beginning to be worked out in simpler animals. It is to these neural mechanisms which we now turn.

3. Neurobiological Basis of Animal Behavior

Consider the following problem: You must design the control system for a device which can autonomously accomplish some open-ended task (such as "stay out of trouble" or "keep this area clean") in a complex, dynamic, unpredictable, and, in many ways, openly hostile environment. You have considerable general information about the structure of this environment, but cannot assume that this information is complete in any sense. Your system must therefore be capable of flexibly applying whatever behavioral repertoire you choose to give it to the actual situations it encounters. At the same time, it must be capable of modifying aspects of that repertoire to better fit the particular environment in which it finds itself. This task is far easier than the one that evolution faces, because evolution cannot benefit from the knowledge of any conscious designer. The only information that it has about the environment is whether or not a given design succeeds in reproducing itself. On the other hand, because it has so little information to go on, its designs make the

fewest possible assumptions, resulting in the most robust control systems in existence. Evolution's answer to this challenge is nervous systems.

One of the most important facts about nervous systems is that they are extremely heterogeneous. Individual nerve cells possess complex intrinsic dynamics which endow them with often unique response properties. The activity of a nerve cell at any point in time is a function not only of the activity of other nerve cells which synapse upon it, but also of its shape, the characteristics and distribution of its current channels, its chemical environment, and its internal biochemical state. Far from being unimportant biological details, most of these properties appear to be functional: nervous systems actually take advantage of them for controlling the behavior of animals [34,23].

Nervous systems are not only heterogeneous in their elements, but also in the interconnections between those elements. Nervous systems consist of a great many specific circuits which are organized into highly structured architectures. These architectures are constructed during the development of an animal, and have been designed over the course of evolution. They are responsible for the basic complement of behavior with which an animal is endowed [36].

How are nervous systems organized to support the behavioral principles discussed in the previous section? By a careful analysis of both the behavior and the underlying neural circuitry, this question is beginning to be answered in simpler animals. Underlying reflexes in all animals, for example, are essentially direct connections between the sensory neurons which recognize the sensory stimulus and the motor neurons responsible for the response. Because these reflex circuits typically consist of short, fast pathways involving no more than one or two synapses, they are capable of only rudimentary sensory analysis and stereotyped motor responses. However, these reflex circuits may be affected by other circuits which interact with the neurons involved in the reflex [38]. Similarly, taxes and other orientation responses appear to be controlled by circuits which compare information from sensory receptors on each side of an animal's body [32].

All behaviors more complex than reflexes and taxes require the generation of temporally extended patterns of motor activity (e.g. fixed-action patterns). What is the neural basis of such patterns of behavior? How are the sequencing and timing of the individual components controlled? These questions have been most fully addressed in the context of rhythmic patterns of behavior, such as swimming or walking. The neural circuits underlying rhythmic behaviors are called *central pattern generators* [12]. They can be divided into two general categories: those employing pacemaker cells and those employing network oscillators. Pacemaker cells are neurons which are capable of producing rhythmic bursts solely by virtue of their own intrinsic dynamics. Network oscillators, on the other hand, are networks of neurons which generate rhythmic patterns due to the synaptic interactions between their component neurons, none of which are capable of rhythmic activity in isolation. Often, central pattern generators involve networks of neurons with intrinsic bursting properties, so that the final pattern depends both upon the intrinsic dynamics of each cell as well as the interconnections between them (e.g. [34]). In addition, the details and phasing of the basic pattern produced by a central pattern generator can be greatly affected by sensory feedback, sometimes making it difficult to distinguish between a *central* pattern generator and a *peripheral* one [29].

What are the neural mechanisms by which the internal state of an animal affects its behavior? There is no simple answer to this question. Many internal processes exist which can effect the function of particular neural circuits over time: (1) as already described, individual nerve cells have intrinsic cellular dynamics which influence their operation; (2) reverberating pathways exist in which any activity in a circuit leads to increased activity within that same circuit via positive feedback loops; (3) the activity of one nerve cell can dynamically alter the interactions between several others because neurons form connections on different parts of other neurons; and (4) the activity of a given neural circuit can be greatly influenced by a variety of chemical means, such as hormones [35].

Many situations require that a decision be made whether or not to generate a specific behavior (e.g. some fixed-action pattern) in a given context. An early notion regarding the neural basis of such decisions was that of a *command neuron* [22]. In this view, sensory information converges on a single neuron which initiates the response by activating the appropriate pattern generation cir-

cuitry only when the proper sensory stimulus is present. A few examples of putative command neurons have been found. However, though neurons whose activation can elicit specific motor patterns certainly exist, the notion of a single neuron being uniquely responsible for a given behavior has proven to be an oversimplification. Even for simpler animals, it now appears that behavioral choice is a much more distributed process. In general, decisions regarding which behaviors to generate in a given environmental context appear to be achieved by consensus involving interactions between the circuits responsible for each behavioral pattern [2].

The cellular basis of several forms of behavioral plasticity have been extensively studied in some invertebrates. For example, in the marine mollusc *Aplysia*, studies of habituation have shown that the decrement in the animal's response to a repetitive stimulus is associated with synaptic depression: due to the nature of the biochemical processes responsible for synaptic transmission, the efficacy of a specific synapse between the sensory neuron and the motor neuron involved in the response decreases with repeated use. Similarly, sensitization is caused by an enhancement of synaptic transmission within the affected pathway. This enhancement is triggered by another neuron associated with the sensitizing stimulus which forms a synapse near the affected synapse and releases chemicals which increase its efficacy. Finally, associative conditioning has similarities to sensitization in that the efficacy of a neural pathway is enhanced. In *Aplysia*, it appears that the prior activity of the neuron that receives reinforcement allows the affected synapse to be further enhanced by the mechanisms previously described for sensitization [19].

As a solution to the problem posed at the beginning of this section, nervous systems have many advantages. The flexibility and complexity of the individual neurons allow them to be configured in a large variety of ways. Because of their complexity, individual nerve cells can be utilized to process large amounts of information in parallel. The architectures that are typical of nervous systems are also highly distributed, with different parts performing overlapping, but not identical functions. Finally, the intrinsic properties of neurons, and their complex interactions, endow them with a rich dynamics that may be capable of responding much more effectively to the rapidly changing exigencies of the real world than more discrete, centralized systems.

4. The Artificial Insect Project

In the preceding sections, we have argued that artificial autonomous agents should aspire to the behavioral capabilities of simpler natural animals. Given the current state of the art, a robot with "only" the behavioral repertoire of an insect would, we believe, be quite an impressive achievement. We have further argued that the control architectures we design for our autonomous agents could benefit from a knowledge of the neural mechanisms underlying natural animal behavior. To test these ideas, we have undertaken the construction of a simulated insect whose behavior is controlled by an artificial nervous system. The overall design of this insect is inspired by the principles of natural animal behavior described in the previous two sections, and its nervous system is based in part on specific neural circuits in several natural animals. At present, the simulated insect is capable of locomotion, wandering, edge-following, and feeding, as well as properly managing the interactions between these behaviors in order to survive within its environment for an extended period of time. In this section, we provide an overview of this *Artificial Insect Project*, which represents a first cut at designing a complete, biologically-inspired artificial agent. Full details can be found in [4].

4.1. Physical Models

As for a natural animal, the physical characteristics of an autonomous agent's body and environment have a significant impact on the design of its controller. The body model we have chosen for the artificial insect is shown in *Fig. 1*. Though this design is loosely based on the American Cockroach [7], it resembles the basic body plan of many insects. The antennae contain tactile and chemical sensors. The mouth can open and close, and also contains tactile and chemical sensors. The insect has an internal store of energy, as well as a simple metabolism in which energy is consumed at a fixed rate. If its energy level ever reaches zero, the insect is removed from its environment. When the

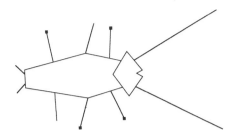

Fig. 1. Body model.

insect's mouth closes over a patch of food, a fixed amount of energy is transferred from the food patch to the insect's internal energy store.

The artificial insect has six legs, each with a foot that may be either up or down. When its foot is up, a leg assumes a fixed length and any forces it applies cause it to swing. When its foot is down (denoted by a black square), a leg stretches between its foot and the body, and any forces it generates may result in movement of the body. Despite the fact that the insect is only two-dimensional, it can fall down. The insect becomes statically unstable whenever its center of mass lies outside of the polygon formed by the feet which are down. If this condition persists for longer than 40 msec, the insect is considered to have fallen down and the legs are no longer allowed to move the body.

The environment in which the artificial insect exists contains unmovable obstacles and food patches. When an insect encounters an obstacle, it bounces back along its direction of motion a small, fixed amount. Food patches are circular areas of the environment which contain energy. These patches emit an odor whose strength is proportional to the number of food units in the patch, which is in turn proportional to its area. As odors diffuse through the environment, their intensity falls off as the inverse square of the distance from the center of the food patch.

4.2. Neural Model

In order to utilize neurobiological principles for controlling the behavior of an artificial agent, we must choose a neural model which strikes the proper balance between biological reality and computational and conceptual tractability. We cannot possibly model an entire nervous system at the detailed biophysical level. On the other hand,

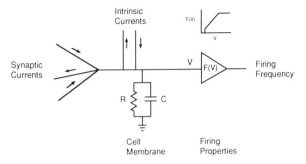

Fig. 2. Neural model.

as discussed in Section 3, certain biological characteristics appear to be fundamental to the way nervous systems control behavior. Our neural model is therefore intermediate in complexity between biological nerve cells and the formal neurons typically employed in artificial neural networks. The model is shown schematically in *Fig. 2.*

The output of a model neuron corresponds to the firing frequency of a nerve cell. In the model, this frequency is a nonlinear function of the neuron's potential. We have employed saturating linear threshold functions with an initial jump discontinuity to represent this relationship (see inset). Three parameters characterize this function: the threshold voltage at which the neuron begins to fire, the minimum firing frequency, and the gain. An RC circuit is used to capture the ability of nerve cells to temporally sum their inputs. Model neurons are interconnected by weighted synapses through which they can inject current into one another. These aspects of the model are similar, though not identical, to several neural models that have been previously explored in the field of artificial neural networks (e.g. [16]).

One of the most striking differences between real nerve cells and the formal neurons that are typically employed in artificial neural network research is their rich internal dynamics. Nerve cells are not simple functions, but dynamical systems which are capable of spontaneous activity and whose input/output characteristics change over time. Without modeling the detailed biophysical mechanisms responsible for these characteristics, we have nevertheless captured their net effect through the addition of intrinsic currents to our model. These currents may be both time and voltage dependent. For example, we have used a

pair of intrinsic currents to design a model pacemaker neuron which is employed in several circuits within the artificial insect's nervous system.

Finally, our neural model supports compound synapses, in which the output of one neuron effects the connection between two others. Compound synapses come in two varieties. *Gating* synapses allow the activity of one neuron to enable or disable connections between two others. *Modulatory* synapses, on the other hand, allow a neuron to modify the strength of a connection between two others in a multiplicative fashion.

4.3. Locomotion

All of the other behaviors require some means for the artificial insect to traverse its environment. Therefore, the first behavior we sought to implement was locomotion [6]. In locomotion, each leg must swing rhythmically. However, because the insect can fall down, the controller must also properly coordinate the movements of the six individual legs in order to achieve successful locomotion.

The design of the neural circuit which controls locomotion in the artificial insect is largely based on the work of Pearson and his colleagues on the neural basis of locomotion in the American cockroach [28]. While a complete circuit has not yet been worked out, several principles of its operation have been identified [30]. (1) each leg is probably controlled by a separate central pattern generator, (2) reflexes involving leg position and load play an important role in shaping the output of the central pattern generators, and (3) the central pattern generators controlling different pairs of legs are probably coupled by some form of inhibition.

During walking, each leg rhythmically alternates between a swing phase and a stance phase. During the *swing phase*, the foot is up and the leg is swinging forward. During the *stance phase*, the foot is down and the leg is swinging back, propelling the body forward. These basic movements are produced by the pattern generator circuit shown in *Fig. 3.* There are six copies of this circuit, one for each leg, except that a single command neuron LC makes the same two connections on all six leg controllers. The design of this circuit is based upon Pearson's Flexor Burst-Generator Model [28].

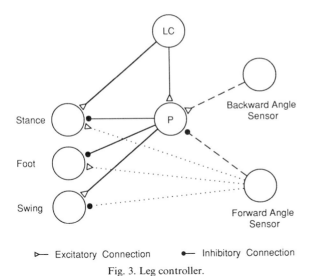

Fig. 3. Leg controller.

⊳— Excitatory Connection   ●— Inhibitory Connection

The alternating swing and stance movements of each leg are primarily produced by the central pattern generator shown in sold lines in *Fig. 3*. Each leg is controlled by three motor neurons. The *swing* and *stance* motor neurons determine the force with which the leg is swung forward or backward, respectively, while the *foot* motor neuron controls whether the foot is up or down. A stance phase is produced when the foot is down and the stance motor neuron is active. Periodically, a swing phase is initiated by a burst of activity produced by the pacemaker neuron P. This activity lifts the foot and swings the leg forward by inhibiting the foot and stance motor neurons and exciting the swing motor neuron. Another stance phase begins when the pacemaker burst terminates. The alternating swing/stance cycle required for walking can thus be produced by rhythmic bursting in P. Note that both the force applied by the leg during each stance phase and the time between bursts in P depend upon the steady level of excitation supplied by the locomotion command neuron LC.

Most central pattern generators require some sensory feedback to fine-tune the basic pattern. In our controller, this information is supplied by two sensors which signal when a leg has reached an extreme forward or backward angle (shown with dashed lines in *Fig. 3*). When a leg is all the way back, the *backward angle sensor* encourages it to swing by exciting the pacemaker. The *forward angle sensor*, on the other hand, encourages the leg

to terminate the current swing by inhibiting the pacemaker. In addition, the direct connections from the forward angle sensor to the motor neurons (shown with dotted lines in *Fig. 3*), comprise a stance reflex which smooths the transition from swing to stance.

In order to generate statically stable gaits, the movements of each individual leg must be properly coordinated or the insect will fall down. This coordination is achieved by appropriate coupling of the central pattern generators controlling each leg. One useful rule of thumb is that adjacent legs should not swing at the same time. This constraint is implemented by mutual inhibitory connections between the pacemakers of adjacent legs, as shown in *Fig. 4*. For example, when the middle right leg is swinging, the front and back right legs and the middle left leg are discouraged from also swinging, but the other legs are unaffected.

While these constraints generate statically stable gaits at high speeds of walking, at lower speeds they are not sufficient to guarantee statically stable gaits. The slower gaits of many animals exhibit a stepping sequence known as the *metachronal wave*, in which a wave of swings progresses from the rear of the animal to the front. In insects, for example, the back leg swings, then the middle leg, then the front leg on each side of the body. This appears to be a particularly stable pattern of stepping. Metachronal waves were implemented in our model by increasing the leg angles of the two rear legs, which lowers the natural frequency of their pattern generators due to the sensory feedback [14]. Because of the inhibitory coupling between the pacemakers of adjacent legs, this results in entrainment between the pacemakers on each side of the body. In the stable phase relationship

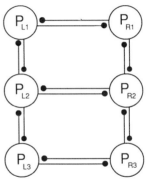

Fig. 4. Central coupling between pacemakers.

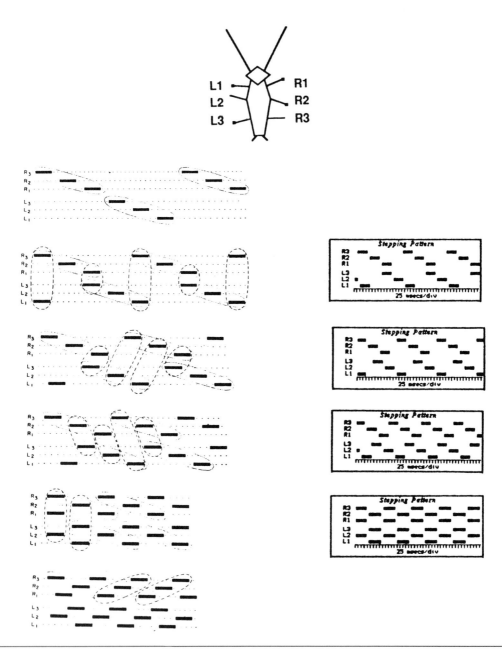

Fig. 5. A comparison of the gaits generated by the artificial insect (right) and natural insects (left; [41]). Leg labeling conventions are shown at top.

results from this entrainment, the swing of any given leg immediately follows the one behind it.

Using this locomotion controller, the insect exhibits a continuum of statically stable gaits as the firing frequency of the locomotion command neuron LC is varied. Gaits can be conveniently de-

scribed by their *footfall patterns*. In this representation, a black bar is displayed during the swing phase of each leg. The space between bars represents the stance phase. Selected gaits exhibited by the artificial insect are shown at the right in *Fig. 5* as the firing frequency of LC is varied from lowest

(Top) to highest (Bottom). At low levels of LC activity, the metachronal waves on each side of the body are very apparent. However, they increasingly overlap as LC activity increases until the *tripod gait* appears at the fastest walking speed. In this gait, the front and back legs on each side of the insect swing and stance together with the middle leg on the opposite side. This sequence of gaits bears a striking resemblance to those that have been described by Wilson [41] for natural insects (*Fig. 5; Left*).

This sequence of gaits emerges from the interaction between the dynamics of the neural circuitry responsible for locomotion and the body and environment in which it is embedded. In order to better understand the operation of this neural network, we undertook a series of lesion studies, in which the response of the controller to the removal of various elements was examined [11]. We briefly summarize some of our results here.

In general, we found the locomotion controller to be remarkably robust to removal of any single element or connection. The lesion of one component often led to compensatory effects in other components, although the overall robustness of the controller to further perturbations always decreased with any lesion. Indeed, we found the interaction between the central and peripheral components of the controller to be quite unexpectedly subtle. For example, lesioning connections from the backward angle sensors to the pacemakers in the rear legs completely abolished the metachronal wave in slower speed gaits, but left the tripod gait virtually unaffected. In contrast, higher speed gaits were more sensitive to lesions of the central inhibitory connections between pacemakers than were lower speed gaits. This suggests that the higher speed gaits are primarily generated centrally, while lower speed gaits are more dependent upon sensory information.

While the command neuron would appear to be important to the generation of all gaits, it is not, in fact, essential. For example, the full range of normal gaits were exhibited even after complete removal of LC if the insect was pushed along by an external force. In addition, removing all of the connections from LC to the six pacemakers had no effect whatsoever on a walking insect. When these same six connections were removed before an insect was allowed to establish a normal

gait, the reason for these remarkable results became clear. A normal insect usually establishes a stable gait within a single step. However, an insect with this lesion required well over a dozen steps to achieve the proper coordination. On the other hand, once a normal gait was established, the lesioned insect was indistinguishable from a normal one. It appears that LC normally acts to set the burst frequency of the pacemakers close to the final value required for a given speed of walking, and then the sensory information simply fine-tunes them. However, in the complete absence of this central information, the sensory feedback alone is still sufficient to establish normal gaits, though this process is cruder and takes longer than normal.

4.4. Wandering

Once an insect is capable of locomotion, it can begin to wander through its environment if it also has an ability to turn. In straight-line locomotion, the legs apply forces which translate the insect's body. Turning was implemented by also allowing the legs to apply lateral forces to the body, thereby rotating it. Since the neural circuitry responsible for wandering behavior in insects has not yet been worked out, we designed a simple neural network which is capable of generating the necessary motor patterns [4]. In this controller, two pacemaker-like neurons whose burst and interburst characteristics vary randomly are used to excite the motor neurons controlling the lateral extension of the front legs at random intervals and for random periods of time.

4.5. Edge-Following

An animal must have some means for coping with any obstacles it encounters as it wanders through its environment. One strategy that is commonly employed by insects is edge-following ([7], p. 373). During edge-following, an insect maintains a nearly parallel orientation between its body and the edge of the obstacle it is following. If the angle between the insect and the edge is too small, the insect must turn toward the edge so as to increase this angle. If this angle is too large, the insect must decrease it by turning away from the edge. In addition, a momentary loss of contact with the edge should not terminate the behavior.

Of course, if the insect is unable to reestablish contact within a certain period of time, then its attempts to do so should cease. Thus, edge-following exhibits behavioral hysteresis: once triggered, it persists for a short period of time even after the sensory stimulus which initially triggered it has been removed. Unfortunately, the neural circuitry controlling edge-following behavior in insects is currently unknown. We therefore designed a neural network which is capable of generating edge-following behavior with the characteristics described above [4]. There are two copies of this controller, one for each antenna.

4.6. Feeding

As previously discussed, motivated behaviors are among the most interesting and complex behaviors exhibited by simpler animals. Feeding is a prototypical motivated behavior in which attainment of the goal object (food) is clearly crucial to an animal's survival. In this case, the relevant motivational state is hunger. When an animal is hungry, it will exhibit a sequence of *appetitive* behaviors which serve to identify and properly orient the animal to food. Once food is found, *consummatory* behaviors are generated to ingest it. On the other hand, a satiated animal may ignore, or even avoid, sensory stimuli which suggest the presence of food [21].

An animal's interest in feeding (its *feeding arousal*) may be a function of more than just its energy requirements. Other factors, such as the exposure of an animal to the taste, odor, or tactile sensations of food, can significantly increase its feeding arousal. This relationship between feeding and arousal, in which the very act of feeding further enhances an animal's interest in feeding, leads to a form of behavioral hysteresis. Once food is encountered, an animal may feed well beyond the internal energy requirements which initiated the behavior. In many animals, this hysteresis is thought to play a role in the patterning of feeding behavior into discrete meals rather than continuous grazing [37]. At some point, of course, the ingested food must be capable of overriding the arousing effects of consummation, or the animal would feed indefinitely.

Because the artificial insect possesses a simple metabolism and a limited energy store, it too requires some form of feeding behavior in order to

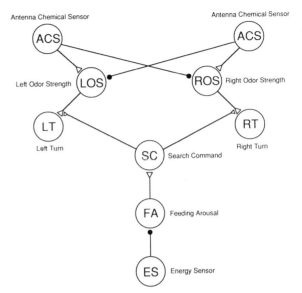

Fig. 6. Appetitive controller.

survive for any extended period of time. Based in part upon neuroethological data on the feeding behavior of the marine mollusc *Aplysia*, we have designed neural controllers for feeding in this insect. An appetitive controller is responsible for finding food when the insect is in need of energy by following the odor which diffuses from a food patch. Once a food patch has been found, a separate consummatory controller is responsible for the actual ingestion. This controller also implements the arousal and satiation characteristics described above.

The appetitive component of feeding behavior in the artificial insect is an example of a taxis. The appetitive controller is shown in *Fig. 6*. Its design follows the general outlines of several proposed neural circuits controlling taxes in various animals, but it is not directly based upon any specific circuit. This controller consists of two components. The first is responsible for orienting the insect to a food patch by following its odor. These odor signals detected by the chemical sensors in each antenna (ACS) are compared (by LOS and ROS) and the difference between them is used to generate a turn toward the stronger side by exciting the corresponding turn interneuron (LT or RT) by an amount proportional to the strength of the odor gradient. These turn interneurons connect to motor neurons controlling the lateral extension of the front legs.

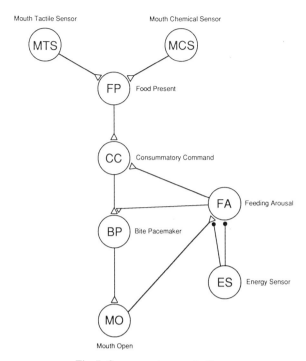

Fig. 7. Consummatory controller.

patches and to prevent consummation from beginning before the food is actually reached (due to the diffusion of odors). Once CC fires, it triggers the bite pacemaker neuron (BP) to generate the rhythmic bursts necessary for driving the motor neuron (MO) which opens the mouth. Because the threshold of the consummatory command neuron (CC) is lower than that of the search command neuron (SC), an insect which is not sufficiently aroused to actively search for food may nevertheless consume food that is presented directly to its mouth.

The motor neuron controlling the mouth also makes an excitatory connection onto the feeding arousal neuron, which in turn makes an excitatory modulatory connection onto the connection between the command neuron and the bite pacemaker. The net effect of these excitatory connections is a positive feedback loop: biting movements excite FA, which causes BP to burst more frequently, thereby generating more frequent biting movements which further excite FA until its firing frequency saturates. This positive feedback loop is inspired by work on the neural basis of feeding arousal maintenance in *Aplysia* [39].

As the insect consumes food, its energy level begins to rise. This increasing activity both inhibits FA directly, and decreases the gain of the positive feedback loop via an inhibitory modulatory synapse onto the connection between MO and FA. At some point, this effect will overcome the positive feedback and activity in FA will cease, causing the insect to stop feeding. This neural mechanism is based upon a similar one hypothesized to underlie the satiation of feeding in *Aplysia* [40]. Thus, complex interactions between the energy sensor (ES) and the feeding arousal neuron (FA) implement the motivational state governing feeding behavior in this insect.

With these two neural controllers in place, the feeding behavior of the artificial insect exhibits four of the six characteristics of motivated behavior defined by Kupfermann (1974) and presented in Section 2:

Grouping and sequencing of behavior in time. A "hungry" artificial insect generates appetitive and consummatory behaviors with the proper sequence, timing, and intensity in order to obtain food.

Goal-Directedness. Regardless of its environmental situation, a hungry insect will generate

The second component of the appetitive controller is responsible for controlling when the insect orients to food. Though the odor gradient is continuously being sensed, the connections from the odor strength neurons (LOS and ROS) to the turn neurons (LT and RT) are normally disabled, preventing this information from actually turning the insect. As the insect's energy level falls, however, so does the activity of its energy sensor (ES). This gradually releases the spontaneously active feeding arousal neuron (FA) from inhibition. When the insect becomes sufficiently aroused to fire the search command neuron (SC), the connections between the odor strength neurons and the turn neurons are enabled by gating synapses from SC, and the insect begins to orient to food.

The consummatory component of feeding behavior is a fixed-action pattern which is triggered by the presence of food. The consummatory controller is shown in *Fig. 7*. When chemical (MTS) and tactile (MCS) sensors in the mouth signal that food is present and the insect is sufficiently aroused to feeding, the consummatory command neuron CC fires. Both tactile and chemical signals are required to prevent attempts to ingest nonfood movements which serve to obtain food. Thus, at certain times, the behavior of the artificial insect can be understood only by reference to an internal goal.

Changes in responsiveness due to a change in internal state. While a hungry insect will attempt to orient to and consume any nearby food, a satiated one will ignore it. In addition, once a hungry insect has consumed sufficient food, it will walk right over the food patch which initially attracted it.

Persistence. If the artificial insect is removed from food before it has fed to satiation, its feeding arousal will persist for some time.

One technique that has been applied to the study of arousal and satiation in natural animals is to examine the time interval between successive bites as an animal feeds under various conditions. In *Aplysia*, for example, the interbite interval progressively decreases as an animal begins to feed (showing a buildup of arousal) and increases as the animal satiates. In addition, the rate of rise and fall of arousal depends upon the initial degree of satiation [37].

It is interesting to compare these results to those obtained from similar experiments on the artificial insect. Food was directly presented to artificial insects with differing degrees of satiation, and the time interval between successive bites was recorded for the entire resulting consummatory response. Above approximately 80% satiation, insects could not be induced to bite. Below this level, however, insects began to consume the food. As these insects fed, the interbite interval decreased until some minimum was reached as feeding arousal built up (*Fig. 8*). The rate of arousal build-up was slowest for insects with the highest initial level of satiation. In fact, an insect which was already 75% satiated never achieved full arousal.

As the feeding insects neared satiation, the interbite interval again increased as arousal waned. It is interesting to note that, regardless of the initial level of satiation, all insects in which biting was triggered fed until their energy stores were approximately 99% full. The appropriate number of bites to accomplish this were generated in all cases. Feeding behavior in the artificial insect thus exhibits a number of very interesting characteristics which are quite reminiscent of natural animals. These issues are further explored in [5].

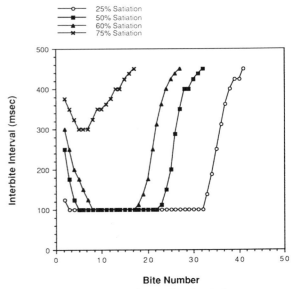

Fig. 8. Build-up of arousal and satiation.

4.7. Behavioral Choice

As described above, the artificial insect is capable of locomotion, wandering, edge-following, and feeding (which in turn consists of appetitive and consummatory component behaviors). Many of these behaviors are potentially incompatible because they share the same motor apparatus. For example, the wandering, edge-following, and appetitive controllers all utilize the lateral extensors of the front legs to turn the insect, often in opposite directions. In addition, while locomotion is crucial to these three behaviors, locomotion during the consummatory behavior would be disastrous. The artificial insect must therefore constantly decide what to do next given its current internal and external situation. How should its nervous system be organized so that the many individual neural controllers always generate globally coherent behavior?

Generally speaking, feeding should take precedence over edge-following, which in turn should take precedence over wandering. The artificial insect's behavioral repertoire can therefore be organized as shown in *Fig. 9*. Each major behavior is represented by an ellipse. Locomotion is not explicitly represented as a separate behavior, since it is implicitly utilized by most of the other behaviors. In addition, certain other important interactions, such as that between the edge-following

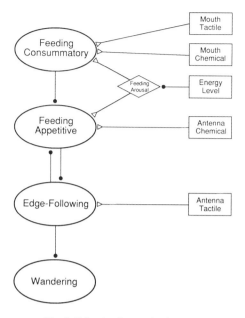

Fig. 9. Behavioral organization.

controllers on each side of the body (crucial in corners), are not explicitly represented in this diagram. Sensory stimuli which play a role in triggering a given behavior are shown as rectangular boxes, while the motivational state governing feeding is represented by a diamond. The interactions between these various components are illustrated by excitatory and inhibitory connections. This diagram roughly corresponds to that which an Ethologist might construct to describe the interrelationships between the various behaviors of a natural animal.

In general, whenever a higher order behavior is triggered, it suppresses lower order behaviors. Note, however, that the diagram in *Fig. 9* is not strictly hierarchical. While feeding normally takes precedence over edge-following, this precedence reverses if an obstacle blocks the insect's path to food. In this case, the insect follows the edge of the obstacle in the hopes of getting around it. The relationship between these two behaviors is therefore dependent upon the environmental context.

The excitatory and inhibitory connections in *Fig. 9* are meant only to illustrate the interactions between the artificial insect's various behaviors. How can the interactions in this diagram be implemented neurally? In some cases, the required interactions between two behaviors can be directly implemented by explicit connections between the

corresponding command neurons. For example, edge-following behavior can suppress wandering via direct inhibitory connections from a key neuron in each of the edge-following controllers to a key neuron in the wandering controller.

The neural implementation of other interactions is more complex. The edge-following and appetitive controllers are particularly interesting in this regard. Neither of these controllers can simply suppress the other because situations exist in which either one should dominate. The neural implementation of this relationship therefore requires additional circuitry which modifies the interaction between these two controllers depending upon the environmental context. Thus, behavioral choice in the artificial insect is implemented in a distributed fashion: decisions are made by consensus among the various neural controllers rather than by a centralized decision module. A complete discussion of the neural circuitry which mediates these behavioral interactions can be found in [4].

The artificial insect's complete nervous system, which implements the behavioral repertoire illustrated in *Fig. 9*, contains a total of 78 model neurons and 156 model synapses. The capabilities of this nervous system are illustrated in *Fig. 10*, which shows the path followed by an artificial insect as it solves a simple but important problem in its environment. At (1), the insect is low on energy and immediately begins to locomote toward the food patch at the upper left (note that obstacles do not block the diffusion of odor). At (2), however, it collides with the intervening wall

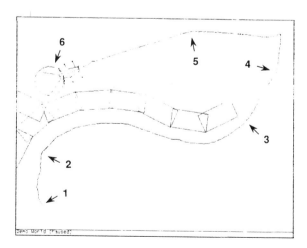

Fig. 10. An illustration of the artificial insect's behavioral repertoire.

and begins to follow its edge. When the insect loses contact with the wall at (3), it briefly tries to reestablish contact by turning back toward it. When no further contact is forthcoming, the insect begins to wander. Note that, due to the inverse square decay of odor intensity with distance, the insect's chemosensors can no longer detect the food patch at this point. After a short period of wandering, it collides with the right wall at (4) and begins to follow it, negotiating a corner in the process. As it continues to follow this edge, the insect once again comes within range of the odor at (5). It immediately leaves the wall it was following and heads toward the food patch, finally feeding successfully at (6).

5. Discussion

While it would certainly never be mistaken for a natural insect, the artificial insect described above nevertheless exhibits a number of characteristics which are strikingly reminiscent of the autonomous behavior of simpler natural animals. It is capable of locomotion, wandering, edge-following, and feeding. Its locomotion controller, which is directly based upon the neurobiological data for cockroach walking, can generate a continuum of statically stable gaits simply by varying the activity of a single neuron. These gaits are quite similar to those that have been described for natural insects. Lesion studies of this controller have demonstrated a remarkable robustness and subtlety of operation. The feeding behavior of the artificial insect similarly displays many of the characteristics associated with motivated behavior in natural animals, including a build-up of arousal and satiation as feeding progresses. Finally, the artificial insect is capable of flexibly organizing its behavioral repertoire in a variety of ways in order to survive within its simulated environment. We believe that this richness is a direct consequence of the biological details which we have incorporated into our model.

The artificial insect currently suffers from a number of limitations in its present form. While portions of its nervous system are based directly upon neurobiological data (e.g. locomotion and feeding), other portions are rather *ad hoc*. Even the biologically-inspired controllers had to be fine-tuned by trial and error (there are over 500

parameters in the insect's nervous system). We would have preferred a more principled approach to these issues, but the required neurobiological data was simply not available. Because we were interested in designing a complete autonomous agent rather than modeling only isolated pieces of behavior, we were forced to fill in many missing details. Only further study of natural nervous systems and considerably more design experience with artificial ones will increase the sophistication of our neural controller designs and deepen the principles upon which they are based.

The behavioral repertoire of the artificial insect is also currently rather limited. While it does exhibit, in one form or another, most of the behavioral characteristics described in Section 2, its repertoire is still quite impoverished compared to that of any natural animal. In addition to locomotion, wandering, edge-following, and feeding, insect behavior typically includes fleeing, fighting, nest building, foraging, grooming, mating, and communication. Some of these behaviors would certainly be useful to an artificial agent, and they are all interesting objects of study in their own right. Unfortunately, although there is a rich body of literature on the ethology of these behaviors, neural circuitry for many of them is not currently available.

Also conspicuously absent from the artificial insect is any form of plasticity. Plasticity is clearly crucial to an autonomous agent, and several neural mechanisms for it were mentioned in Section 3. However, we chose to focus first on nervous system design. Plasticity is a means by which evolutionarily good designs are fine-tuned to the particular environment of an individual animal. It is not a process for producing good designs in the first place from unstructured controllers. Now that we have designed a nervous system which is capable of endowing the artificial insect with the basic behavior essential to its survival, we can begin to explore the behavioral implications of introducing plasticity into specific portions of this nervous system.

In conclusion, we believe that the behavior of even simpler natural animals already exhibits most of the characteristics which we seek to instill in artificial autonomous agents. Animal behavior is goal-oriented, adaptive, opportunistic, plastic, and robust. All of these qualities are crucial for continuous, long-term interaction with the real world.

Furthermore, we feel that the current level of understanding of the neural basis of behavior in simpler animals is sufficiently mature that fruitful interactions between Neuroethology and AI are possible. The artificial insect that we have described represents only one example of such interaction. A great many others are possible.

Acknowledgements

We would like to thank Roy Ritzmann for his comments on an earlier draft of this paper. We are also grateful to Yoh-Han Pao and the Center for Automation and Intelligent Systems Research. RDB was supported in part by a grant from the Cleveland Advanced Manufacturing Program. HJC was supported by NSF grant BNS 88-10757.

References

[1] P. Agre and D. Chapman, Pengi: An implementation of a theory of activity. *Proceedings of the Sixth National Conference on AI* (AAAI 87) (Morgan Kaufmann Publishers, 1987) 268–272.

[2] J.S. Altman and J. Kien, New models for motor control, *Neural Computation* 1 (1989) 173–183.

[3] G.P. Baerends, R. Brouwer and H.T.J. Waterbolk, Ethological studies on *Lebistes reticulatus* (Peters), I. Analysis of the male courtship pattern, *Behaviour* 8 (1955) 249–334.

[4] R.D. Beer, *Intelligence as Adaptive Behavior: An Experiment in Computational Neuroethology*, Ph.D. Dissertation, Dept. of Computer Engineering and Science, Case Western Reserve University (1989). Also available as Technical Report TR 89-118, Center for Automation and Intelligent Systems Research.

[5] R.D. Beer, and H.J. Chiel, (forthcoming), Neural implementation of motivated behavior: Feeding in an artificial insect, to appear in D.S. Touretzky (Ed.), *Advances in Neural Information Processing Systems 2* (Morgan Kaufmann Publishers).

[6] R.D. Beer, H.J. Chiel and L.S. Sterling, Heterogeneous neural networks for adaptive behavior in dynamic environments, in D.S. Touretzky (Ed.), *Advances in Neural Information Processing Systems 1* (Morgan Kaufmann Publishers, San Mateo, 1989) 577–585.

[7] W.J. Bell and K.G. Adiyodi, (Eds.) *The American Cockroach*. (Chapman and Hall, New York, 1981).

[8] R.A. Brooks, A robust layered control system for a mobile robot, *IEEE Journal of Robotics and Automation* RA-2(1) (1986) 14–23.

[9] J.M. Camhi, *Neuroethology* (Sinauer Associates, Sunderland, MA, 1984).

[10] T.J. Carew, The control of reflex action. In E.R. Kandel and J.H. Schwartz (Eds.) *Principles of Neural Science* (Elsevier, New York, 1985) 457–468.

[11] H.J. Chiel and R.D. Beer, A lesion study of a heterogeneous neural network for hexapod locomotion, *Proceedings of the First International Joint Conference on Neural Networks* (IJCNN 89) (1989) 407–414.

[12] F. Delcomyn, Neural basis of rhythmic behavior in animals, *Science* 210 (1980) 492–498.

[13] J. Garcia, W.G. Hankins, K.W. and Rusiniak, Behavioral regulation of the milieu interne in man and rat, *Science* 185 (1974) 824–831.

[14] D. Graham, Simulation of a model for the coordination of leg movement in free walking insects, *Biological Cybernetics* 26 (1977) 187–198.

[15] D. Graham, Pattern and control of walking in insects, *Advances in Insect Physiology* 18 (1985) 31–140.

[16] J.J. Hopfield, Neurons with graded responses have collective computational properties like those of two-state neurons, *Proc. Natl. Acad. Sci.* 81 (1984) 3088–3092.

[17] L. Kaelbling, An architecture for intelligent reactive systems, *Proceedings of the 1986 Workshop on Reasoning about Actions and Plans*, (Morgan Kaufmann Publishers, 1987) 395–410.

[18] E.R. Kandel, *Cellular Basis of Behavior*. (W.H. Freeman, San Francisco, 1976).

[19] E.R. Kandel, Cellular mechanisms of learning and the biological basis of individuality, In E.R. Kandel and J.H. Schwartz (Eds.), *Principles of Neural Science* (Elsevier, New York, 1985) 816–833.

[20] N. Kumar, M. Williams, J. Culotti and D. van der Kooy, Evidence for associative learning in the nematode *C. elegans*, *Society for Neuroscience Abstracts* 15 (1989) 1141.

[21] I.J. Kupfermann, Feeding behavior in *Aplysia*: A simple system for the study of motivation, *Behavioral Biology* 10 (1974) 1–26.

[22] I.J. Kupfermann and K.R. Weiss, The command neuron concept, *Behavioral and Brain Sciences* 1 (1978) 3–39.

[23] R.R. Llinás, The intrinsic electrophysiological properties of mammalian neurons: Insights into central nervous system function, *Science* 242 (1988) 1654–1664.

[24] K.Z. Lorenz, *The Foundations of Ethology*. (Simon and Schuster, New York, 1981).

[25] P. Maes, The dynamics of action selection, *Proceedings of the Eleventh International Joint Conference on AI* (IJCAI 89) (Morgan Kaufmann Publishers, 1989) 991–997.

[26] R.K. Murphey and M.D. Zaretsky, Orientation to calling song by female crickets, *Scapsipedus marginatus(Gryllidae)*, *J. Exp. Biol.* 56 (1972) 335–352.

[27] A. Newell and H.A. Simon, Computer science as empirical inquiry: Symbols and search, *Comm. of the ACM* 19(3) (1976) 113–126.

[28] K.G. Pearson, The control of walking. *Scientific American* 235 (1976) 72–86.

[29] K.G. Pearson, Are there central pattern generators for walking and flight in insects? in W.J.P. Barnes and M.H. Gladden (Eds.), *Feedback and Motor Control in Invertebrates and Vertebrates* (Croom Helm, London, 1985) 307–315.

[30] K.G. Pearson, C.R. Fourtner and R.K. Wong, Nervous control of walking in the cockroach, in R.B. Stein, K.G. Pearson, R.S. Smith and J.B. Redford (Eds.), *Control of Posture and Locomotion* (Plenum Press, 1973) 495–514.

[31] R.E. Ritzmann, The cockroach escape response. in R.C. Eaton (Ed.), *Neural Mechanisms of Startle Behavior* (Plenum Press, New York, 1984) 93–131.

[32] C.H.F. Rowell, H. Reichert and J.P. Bacon, (1985). How Locusts fly straight, In W.J.P. Barnes and M.H. Gladden (Eds.), *Feedback and Motor Control in Invertebrates and Vertebrates* (Croom Helm, London 1985) 337–354.

[33] T.C. Schneirla, Basic problems in the nature of insect behavior, in K.D. Roeder (Ed.), *Insect Physiology* (Wiley, New York, 1953) 656–684.

[34] A.I. Selverston, A consideration of invertebrate central pattern generators as computational data bases, *Neural Networks* 1(2) (1988) 109–117.

[35] G.M. Shepherd, *Neurobiology.* (Oxford University Press, New York, 1988).

[36] N.C. Spitzer, (Ed.) *Neuronal Development* (Plenum Press, 1982).

[37] A.J. Susswein, K.R. Weiss and I. Kupfermann, The effects of food arousal on the latency of biting in *Aplysia, J. Comp. Physiol.* 123 (1978) 31–41.

[38] A.H.D. Watson and M. Burrows, The synaptic basis for integration of local reflexes in the Locust. In W.J.P. Barnes and M.H. Gladden (Eds.), *Feedback and Motor Control in Invertebrates and Vertebrates* (Croom Helm, London, 1985) 231–250.

[39] K.R. Weiss, H.J. Chiel, U. Koch and I. Kupfermann, Activity of an identified histaminergic neuron, and its possible role in arousal of feeding behavior in semi-intact *Aplysia, J. Neuroscience* 6(8) (1986) 2403–2415.

[40] K.R. Weiss, H.J. Chiel and I. Kupfermann, Sensory function and gating of histaminergic neuron C2 in *Aplysia, J. Neuroscience* 6(8) (1986) 2416–2426.

[41] D.M. Wilson, Insect walking, *Annual Review of Entomology* 11 (1966) 103–122.

[42] E.O. Wilson, *Insect Societies* (Harvard University Press, 1971).

Index

Note: Italicized page numbers indicate illustrations.

A priori knowledge, 118–120
A* search algorithm, 94–96
Abstraction
    in behavioral module, 133
    as unnecessary, 102
Abstraction barriers
    and hierarchical planning, 100–101
    and linguistic plans, 92
Action(s)
    data as resource for, 101
    leading to goal, 39
    plans as resource for, 89, 101
    as strategies, 39–40
    theories of, 49
Action networks, 49
Action selection, 49
    characteristics of, 52
    and deliberative thinking paradigm, 49
    on different abstraction levels, 69
    dynamic, 52–57
    as emergent property, 53
    as open, 59–60
    parameters to, 69
    problem of, 50–52
Action-perception cycle, 107
Activation, of competence modules, 53–57
Active avoidance, 156, 166
Active vision, 125n3
    movement toward, 4
Activity
    dynamics of, 21
    and interaction, 32
    nature of, 25–26
    in plan-as-program view, 20
    theory of, 21
Actors, defined, 76
Actuators, and sensors, 10
Adaptation, benefits of, 148
Adaptivity, 59–62
Add list, 53, 56–57
ADEPT, 137
Adequacy, as criterion, 31
Affordances, 110–111
Agent(s)
    behavior of, 76
    defined, 76
    embedded, 35–48
    goal, 83
    moving-object, 83

    obstacle, 83
    pull-field, 83
    qualities of, 87
    state of, 76
    world-object, 80
Agent design
    approaches to, 36–37
    software tools for, 38
Agre, Philip E., 23, 90, 106, 132
AI. *See* Artificial intelligence
Algorithm
    complexity of, 67–69
    control structure of, 68–69
    for dynamic action selection, 53–57
    limits to, 69
    planning capabilities of, 57–59
    results of, 57–67
Allen (robot), 7, 8
ALV experiment, 90–91
Amarel, S., 107
AML, 129
Amord, 23
Analogical representations, 1–2, 72
    advantages of, 85
    vs. categorical representations, 72–74
    computational architecture for, 76–79
    exploiting, 71–87
    in key role, 82–83
    mixed, 73
    operations of, 74–76
    types of, 77–78
Animal behavior, 146–152
    concepts in, 171–173
    as model for robot control, 151–152
    neurobiological basis of, 173–175
    organization of, 172
    and robot autonomy, 145–167
Anytime algorithm, 46
Aplysia, 180–182
Appetitive behaviors, 180
Appetitive controller, *180*
Arbib, M., 107
Arbitration, 106
    network of, 9, 32
Architecture
    agent-based, 76
    of artificial creatures, 128–134
    for autonomous agents, 49

behavior-based, 49
    hybrid, 123–143
    layered, 101
    schema-based, 130
    subsumption, 3, 6–7, 49
Arkin, R.C., 98, 153
Arkinson, D., 154
Artificial forces, 161
Artificial insects, 169, 175–184
    vs. *Aplysia*, 182
    behavioral organization of, *183*
    behavioral repertoire of, *183*, 184
    characteristics of, 184–185
    feeding behavior of, 184
    limitations of, 183
    neural model of, 175–*176*
    physical models of, *175*
Artificial intelligence (AI), 105, 169
    methodology of, 169–170
    and nouvelle AI, 3–4, 13–14
Artificial nervous system, 169, 183–184
Assembly, defined, 134
Assembly planner, 137–138
Assembly planning, 123
Assembly robots, 123
    grounding in, 131
    uncertainty in, 128–129
Associative conditioning, 174
Associative learning, 172
Attraction behaviors, 155, 156–158
Augmented finite state machine (AFSM), 6–7
AuRA. *See* Autonomous Robot Architecture
Automatism, 153
Autonomous agent
    biological perspective on design of, 169–185
    contribution to research in, 87
    organization of, 1, 169–170
Autonomous assembly system, symbol grounding in, 123–143
Autonomous behavior, 169
Autonomous mobile system, 134
Autonomous Robot Architecture (AuRA), 105, 111–117
    and cognitive psychology, 106–107
    flexibility and, 118
    reactive control in, 106
    subsystems of, 111, 112, *112*, *113*, 114, *114*
Autonomous vehicles, 89
Autonomy
    and ability to change, 161
    conclusions regarding, 167
    defined, 153
    as domain specific, 153
    imposed, 146
    mechanistic, 153–154
    multi-behavioral approaches to, 153
    self, 146
    single behavior approaches to, 152
Avoidance, 155, 156
Avoider, 166

Backward angle sensor, *177*
Bateson, Gregory, 126

Behavior(s)
    appetitive, 180, 182
    combinatorial expansion of, 165, 166
    control of, 165
    coupling of, 82
    defined, 155, 155n13
    emergent, 153
    global, 14
    goal-directed, 49
    hierarchical organization of, 152
    independent, 8
    interaction of with environment, 146
    migratory, 156–157
    motivated, 169
    primitive reflexive, 155–158
    prioritization of, 165
    reflex types of, 152
    as reflexive, 155n14
    reflexive heuristic, 153
    set of, 155–156
    spatial ordering of, 158
    and stimulus/response mechanisms, 155, 165
    temporal ordering of, 165
    vision-based, 11–12
    See also Animal behavior; Robot behavior
Behavioral choice, 182–184
Behavioral hierarchy, 169
Behavioral hysteresis, 180
Behavioral knowledge, in reactive navigation, 105–121
Behavioral model, vs. Explicit-World-Model, 133
Behavioral modules, 29, 30, 123
    as abstraction devices, 136–137
    and encapsulation, 132
Behavioral pattern, 155
Behavioral psychologists, 147
Behavior-based architectures, 49
Behavior-based paradigm, 123
    and ideal world, 141–142
Behavior-based robot control systems, 130
Beni, G., 125n3
Bias, to ongoing plans, 62–63
Binding environment (Gapp), 42
Borrowed semantics, 128
Bottom up approach, 68–69, 147
Brooks, Rodney A., 19–20, 30, 36, 90, 92, 101, 106, 124, 126, 130, 134, 153, 166
Bureaucratic modules, 53

Case-based planning, 24
Categorical representations, 72–74
Category, defined, 72
Central pattern generators, 174
    coupling of, *177*
    and peripheral generator, 179
    reflexes and, 176
Chapman, D., 27–29, 90, 106, 132
Church-Turing thesis, 124n2
Circuit, generating, 42–43
Circulation, 99–100
Classical conditioning, 172
Cognitive penetrability, 134

Cognitive psychology, 106–107
Cognitive/subcognitive interface, 131–133
Cognitive systems, 127, 132–133
Combinational explosion problem, 67
Command neuron, 174, 179
Communicated plans, 91–92
Competence module, 53, 134
    activation in, 54–56
    types of links in, 53–54
Compilation, vs. interpretation, 136–137
Complex behavior, 151–152
Complexity theory, 18
Computation, 76, 124
Computational neuroethology, 169, 170
Conditional program, evaluation of, 42
Conditioning
    in *Aplysia*, 174
    forms of, 172
Conflict behavior, 151
Conflicter links. *See* Competence module
Conjunctions, prioritized, 44
Conjunctive goal expressions, 43
Connectionist representations, 72n1
Constantine, L.L., 124n2
Consummatory behaviors, 180
Consummatory controller, *181*
Contingencies, 19
Contour markers, 73
Control
    reactivity, and loci of, 32
    theme of, 30
    zeroth level of, 166
Control structure, 68–69
Copernicus, 151n7
Co-rountines, 124
Cudhea, P.W., 101
Culbertson, J., 164
Current situation
    activation by, 54
    and relevant modules, 59
Cyclical behavior, 164, 165

DAP, 76
DARPA Autonomous Land Vehicle (ALV), 90
Darwin, C., 151n7
Data, as action resource, 101
Data structure, semantices of, 36–38
Deductive closure axiom, 38
Deictic representation, 21–22
    and variables, 67
Delete list, 53, 56–57
Deliberative thinking paradigm, 1, 49
Dennett, D., 125n4, 126, 127
Description, 126, 127
Detectors, animals', 152
Development strategy, 37
Diffusion operations, 77–78
Dijkstra search algorithm, 94–95
Discrete states, 93
Dishabituation, 172
Docking, 108, 155, *119*

Domain program, 40, 44
Drunken sailor behavior, 115
Durrant-Whyte, H.F., 128n8
Dynamic goals, 37
Dynamic vision, 125, 125n5

Edge-following, 179–180
Effective capability, 133
Effector control hierarchy, 129
Effectors, and sensors, 71
Embedded agents, 35–48
Emergent behavior, 145, 153
Emergent functionality, 1, 50, 68–69
Emergent properties, 5
Encapsulation, 132
Environment
    embeddedness in, 126
    and functionality, 50
    and patterns of activation, 55–56
    and situated automata model, 35–36
Environmental detectors, specialized, 150
Environmental stimuli, 149–152
Error recovery, 154
Ethologists, 147
Ethology, 145, 170
Evolution, and physical grounding, 5–6
Executable, module as, 53, 59
Execution
    in plan-as-program view, 17, 18
    process of, 19
    reliability of, 136
    use of term, 20
Expert system, 125, 130–131
Explicit, use of term, 125n4
Explicit goals, 51–52
Explicit representations, 138–139
Explicit-World-Model paradigm, 126, 133

Fault tolerance, 62
Feeding, 180–*182*
Feeding arousal, 180, *182*
Firby, R.J., 106
Fixed action pattern, 148, 155, 171, 173–174, 181
Floating point arithmetic processors, 125
Flores, F., 132
Footfall patterns, *178*
Force sensors, 9
Forgetting
    and commitment, 38
    functional mapping as, 37
Forward angle sensor, 177
Forward attraction, 157
Frame problem, 1, 5, 49
Framework, lack of, 147
Free space, 85
Friction, 128n8
Functionality, 1, 50, 68–69

Gaits, *178*–179
Gapps, 35, 38–44
    compiler, 40, 45

extending, 44–48
  and run-time planning system, 46
Gating synapses, 176
Generalized wandering, *159*, 160
Generativity, Pengi's, 23
Genghis (robot), 7, 9–10
George (robot), 114, *115*
Gibson, J.J., 110
Gladwin, Thomas, 21
Global behavior, 14
Global clock, 76
Global functionality, 82
Global goals, 59
Global parameters, 53n3, 56
Gnat robots, 12
Goal(s)
  activation by, 54
  classes of, 37
  explicit, 51–52
  global, 59
  and information, duality of, 37
  orientation, 59, 61
  protected, 54
  types of, 39
Goal-achieving behaviors, 158
Goal agents, 83
Goal conflicts, avoiding, 63–65
Goal-directedness, 49, 181–182
Goal lists, prioritized, 43–44
Goal reduction rules, 39, 40
Goals, types of, 39, 42
Gradient field
  and lightsource, 75
  pull-field as, 82–83
Gradient representation, 93–95

Habituation mechanism, 69, 172
Hackwood, S., 125n3
Hand-coding, 50–51
Hand-eye coordination, 83–87
Harnad, S., 132, 134
HARV, 115
Herbert (robot), 7, 8–9
Heterogeneous neural networks, 169, 173
Heterogeneous summation, 149
Heuristic planning, 29
  meanings of, 30–31
Heuristics, in traditional AI, 14
Hierarchical planner, 112
Hierarchical planning, 100–101
Hit, sensor, 159
Hoare, C.A.R., 124
Horizontal bias, 62
Hutchins, Edwin, 21
Hybrid, 123
Hybrid architecture, 133–134
  symbol grounding via, 123–143
Hypotheses, for dynamic action selection, 52–53
Hysteresis, behavioral, 180

Ideal world, defined, 141
If case, 47

Implementation, 126
Implicit, use of term, 125n4
Implicit representations, 139
Imposed autonomy, defined, 146
Improvisation, 17
  and interleaved planning, 30
  vs. planning as programming, 21
  and redecision, 18
Inclinometer, 9, 115–116
Incremental development, modularity in, 124, 124n1
Incremental planning. *See* Interleaved
  planning
Indexical-functional aspect, 67–68
Indexical-functional representation, 21–22
Indexicality, 28
Inherent semantics, 128
Inhibition
  in central pattern generators, 176–179
  of conflicters, 55
  among modules, 53n3
  by protected goals, 54
  rules of, 63–64
Innate behavior, 147, 148–149
Input, 124
Insect locomotion, 169
Insect metaphor, 137
Instinct, 148–149
Instrumental conditioning, 172
Intelligence
  AI view of, 125
  foundation of, 13
Intelligent agents, 35
Interactional systems, 49
Interbite interval, *182*
Interleaved planning, 29–30
Internal clock, 151
Internal representations, 71, 72
Internal sensors
  as agents, 77
  vs. external sensors, 72, 74
Internal switching mechanism, 15
Internalized plans
  defined, 89, 92, 102
  as representation for action resources, 89–102
  vs. situated automata, 93
Interpretation
  vs. compilation, 136–137
  vs. evaluation procedure, 47
IRDATA DIN, 129
it evaluation functions, 5
it fundamentalist AI, 3
it physical grounding hypothesis, 3
it polynomials, 5
it situated activity, 3

Joint-interpolated motion, 129

Kadonoff, M.B., 106, 153, 166
Kaelbling, L.P., 106, 126
Knowledge
  perceptual, 105–121

representational, 107
tacit, 137
world, 93, 105–121
Knowledge-based paradigm, 125
Knowledge-based system, 105
Explicit-World-Model as, 126
Knowledge representation hypothesis, 123–125

Landmark knowledge, 99
Language
internal vs. external, 27
operator-description, 45
See also Natural language
Latent learning, 172
Layered architecture, 101
Leg controller, *177*
Lesion studies, on locomotion controller, 179
Lightsource markers, 74–75
Linguistic plans, 91–92
Linguistic routines, 29
Links, types of, 53
Localized wandering, 160
Location agent, 80
Location attraction, 156–157
Location-directed open space attraction and wandering, 158, 163, *164*, 165
Location uncertainty, 140
Logical advice taking, vs. situated instruction use, 27
Locomotion, artificial insect's, 176–179
Locomotion controller, *177*, 184
Long-term memory (LTM), 111
Lorenz, Konrad, 147, 150, 155
Lozano-Pérez, Tómas, 19–20
Lyons, D., 124, 130

Malcolm, Chris, 30
Manning, A., 151
Map, acquiring, 79–83
Map-based plans, 89
Map building (behavior), 80–81
Markers, 73
MAS, 87
Mataric, Maja J., 11
Maturana, H.R., 126
McFarland, D., 151n7
Mechanistic autonomy, 153–154
Memory, in autonomous robot, 164, 166
Mentality, as functionally modular, 123
Metachronal wave, 117–179
Migratory behavior, 156–157
Mission constraint, 101
Mobile robots, 3, 105, 145
experiments with, 115
subsumption-based, 124
Models, 71
Modularity
functional, 124
in incremental development, 124, 124n1
Modulatory synapses, 176
Monostables, 7
Morphology, transform-centered, 124n2

Motivated behavior, 169
characterization of, 171, 181–182
Motivation, as classification, 150–151
Motor schemas, 107–108, *109*
Multi-agent automata, 76–77
Multi-agent system (MAS), 76
Multi-behavioral approaches in robots, 153

Natural language, 27
Navigation, *160*, 160–161
Negation, handling of, 41–42
Neisser, U., 107
Nerve cells, artificial insect's, 176
Nervous system
artificial, 169, 183–184
heterogeneous, 173
Network oscillators, 174
Neural networks, heterogeneous, 169, 173. *See also* Nervous system
Neuroethology, 169, 170
Non-monotonic reading, 1, 49
Nonsymbolic operators, 72
Nonsymbolic systems, 125, 126
Norman, D., 107
Nouvelle AI, 3–4

Object attraction, 157
Obstacle agent, 83
Obstacle avoidance behaviors, 92
and artificial potential field method, 97–98
Odometry, 8
Operations, analogical, 77–79
Operator(s), 45
nonsymbolic, 72
Operator-description language, 45
Opportunities, 19
Orientation response, 171
Output
data, 124
motor, 124
symbolic, 124

Pacemaker cells, 174
Parallelism, 69
Part-fitting uncertainty, 141
Participation, in activity, 20–24
Passive avoidance, 156, 166
Path planning, 46
Path tree concept, 95
Payton, D.W., 106, 153
Pearson, K.G., 176
Pearson's Flexor Burst-Generator Model, 176
Pengi, 21–24
circuitry of, 23
reactive control in, 106
Perception
action-oriented, 108
as AuRA subsystem, 111–112
Perception-based split, 36–37
Perceptual knowledge, in reactive navigation, 105–121
Perceptual schemas, 108–111
Perimeter following, 161, *162*, 163

Peripheral pattern generator, 174
Persistance, 182
Persistent knowledge, 111
Physical grounding hypothesis, 5–7
    defined, 5
    evolution and, 5–6
    strategy for, 13
Physical Symbol System Hypothesis, 170
Physically grounded systems, 7–12
Pilotage, 161
Plan(s)
    action selection vs. AI, 57–58
    communicated, 91–92
    different meanings of in AI, 31–32
    internalized, 89–102
    in linguistic form, 91
    map-based, 89
    relevance of, 20
    representation of, 90–91
    as resources for actions, 89
    role of, 21
    and shared understandings, 26, 27
    subplan hierarchy view of, 19–20
    using, 20–21
Plan as communication .
    factors of, 29
    variations in, 25
    view, 17, 24–27
Plan as constraint, 29, 32
Plans-as-programs, 18–24
    difficulties with, 18–20
Planner, 19, 23
Planning, 3
    as AuRA subsystem, 112, 113–114
    case-based, 24
    deliberative thinking approach to, 49
    heuristic, 30–31
    interleaved, 29–30
    reactive, 31–32
    universal, 45–46
Plan construction
    forms of, 18
    vs. plan execution, 30
Plan execution. See Plans-as-programs
Plan execution agent
    vs. plan, 131
    as subcognitive system, 127
Plan execution subsystem, AuRA's, 112
Plan spaces, 31
Plan use
    nature of, 24
    views of, 17
Plasticity, 172
Position controlled robot, 129
Potential field methods
    vs. gradient field methods, 97–98
    viability of, 121
Precondition list, 53, 56–57
Predecessor link. See Competence module
Predecessors, activation by, 55
Primitive reflexive behaviors, 153, 155–158, 155n14
    additional 165–166

and potential fields, 165–166
    types of, 155
Probabilistic correctness, 31
Program(s)
    conjoining, 41
    defined, 39
    disjoining, 41
Program structuring methods, 124
Projection, 28
Protected goals, 54
Pull-field, 82
Pull-field agent, 83
Puzzlitis, 12–13
Pylyshyn, Z.W., 134
Pyroelectric sensors, 9

Randomness, 69
RAPT (assembly programming language), 132
Raw map data, 98–99
RDL, 87
Reaction-diffusion, 77–79
Reaction operations, 78–79
Reactive action packages (RAPs), 106
Reactive architecture, 106
Reactive navigation, 106–107
    advantages of, 105
    characterization of, 117–118
    over contoured terrain, 115–117
    examples of, 115–117
    integrating knowledge in, 105–121
Reactive control, 105
Reactive planning, 29, 31–32, 89
Reactive systems, 35, 49
    appraisal of, 71–72
Reactivity, 32
Recursive goal evaluation, 40–42
Re-evaluation, 60
Reflex responses, 149
Reflexive behavior(s), 106
    memoryless, 167
    as simplest form, 171
Reflexive heuristic behaviors, 153
Reflexivity, 28
Regression function, 45
Releaser, 148
Remote centre compliance, 126, 126n7
Replanning, 154
    dynamic, 97
Representations
    analogical, 71–87
    deictic, 21–22
    explicit, 138–139
    implicit, 139
    indexical-functional, 21–22
    internal, 71
    mixed, 73
    nature of, 24–25
    participatory theory of, 21–22
    within SOMASS system, 137
    tacit, 139–140
Representational knowledge, 107
Resource usage constraints, 98

Responsiveness, changes in, 182
Rex, 38
Robot(s)
    assembly, 128–129
    autonomy in, 145–146
    gnat, 12
    mobile, 3, 105, 145
    position-controlled, 129
    reflexive nature of, 161
    virtual, 129
Robot autonomy, and animal behavior, 145–167
Robot behavior, 152–166
    emergent, 158–166
    reactive forms of, 158
    specification of, 154–155
    See also Behavior(s)
Robot control program, 128, 145
Robot manipulation task, 19–20
Robot navigation, and representational knowledge, 107
Robotics, Asimov's laws of, 44
Rosenschein, S.R., 126
Route planning, 89
    and gradient field information, 94–97
Route plans, internalized, 93–98
Routines, 49
    Pengi's, 22–23
Rule set, fixed/recursive, 47
Running argument system, 23–24
Run-time arbitration, 50–52
Run-time environment, 77
Run-time expression, 39
Run-time goals, 46–48

Scalar function, 94, 98
Scaleability, 165
Scarecrow (robot), *159*, 159n18, *160*, *161*, *162*, *164*, 167
Schema(s), 105, 153
    goal-reduction, 45–46
Schema-based architecture, 130
Schema-theory, 108–111
    motivation for, 107
Scher, Bob, 21
Schopper, Marcel J., 45
Scribner, Sylvia, 21
Search approach, 85
Search-food agents, 82
Search tree, 58
Self-autonomy, 146
Self-knowledge, 156n15
Semantic loan, 128
Sensitization, 172, 174
Sensor(s)
    coupled to actuators, 10
    external, 72, 74
    force, 9
    internal, and effector, 72,74
    kinds of, 129
    mapping of, 71
    programming use of, 128–129
    pyroelectric, 9

Sensor-processing hierarchy, 129
Sensory interpretation, 149
    complex, 150
    and wide open space attraction behavior, 157–158
Seymour (robot), *7*, 11–12
Shallice, T., 107
Shape-dependent part-fitting, 134
Shape uncertainty, 140
Shared understandings
    plans and, 26, 27
    and communications, 29
Short-term memory (STM), 111
Sign stimuli, 149
Simon, H., 146n1
Simulation, three-dimensional, 115
Situated action, 169
Situated activity, 3, 17, 49
    limitations on, 50
    natural language in, 27
    role of plans-as-communications in, 26
    theory of, 25
Situated agents, and action selection, 50–69
Situated automata theory, 35–38, 49
    model for, 35–36
Situated instruction use, 27
Skinner, B.F., 106
Smith, Brian, 125, 126
Smithers, Tim, 30
SOMA, 123
SOMASS robotic assembly system, 123
SOMASS Soma assembly system, 134–142
    as cognitive system, 127
    experimental approach to, 134–136
    as hybrid system, 142
    as plan executor, 127
    reliability of, 136
    robustness of, 136
Sonja, 27–29
Spacing out, 138
    as strategy, 140–141
Speed, of action selection, 66–67
Squirt (robot), *7*, 10
Stagnation, *161*
Stance phase, 176, 177
State(s), proximity of, 120
Static arbitration, 158
Static goals, 37
Steels, L., 72, 126
Sticklebacks, 149
Stiction, 128n8
Stimulus/response characteristics of autonomy, 146
Structural coupling, 126
Subcognitive component
    influence on cognitive component, 132
    and signal/symbol transformation, 127
Subgoals
    defined, 59
    protection of, 64
    purpose of, 91
Subplans, hierarchy of, 19

Subsumption, 123
    in emergent robot behavior, 158
    new, 6
    new language of, 7
    old language of, 6–7
Subsumption architecture, 3, 6–7, 49, 89
    debugging, 13
    defined, 6
    layers of control in, 8, 9
Subsymbolic system, 125–127
Successor(s), activation by, 54–55
Successor link. *See* Comptence module
Suchman, Lucy, 21
Superposition, 98, 155
Swing phase, 176
Symbol(s), 4–6
Symbol grounding, in autonomous assembly
    system, 123–143
Symbolic computation, 124
Symbolic functional approach, 126
Symbolic/signal transformation, 125–126
Symbolic system, 123, 125–127
    and emergent properties, 5
    grounding of, 130–133
Symbolic system hypothesis, 4–5
    as flawed, 3
Synapses, varieties of, 176
Syntax, theory of, 29
Systems
    cognitive, 127
    nonsymbolic, 125, 126
    subcognitive, 127
    subsymbolic, 125–127
    symbolic, 125–127

Tacit, use of term, 125n4
Tacit knowledge, 137
Tacit representations, 139–140
Target location, 85
Task level decomposition, 1
Task monitoring, 154
Task planning, 154
Taxis (es)
    appetitive controller as, 180
    defined, 171
Thoughtfulness, 65–66
3-block blocks-world problem, 45–46, 64–65
Three-dimensional simulation, 115
Tick period, 7
Tinberger, Niko, 147, 149
Tom and Jerry (robots), 7, 8
Top down approach, 147
Toto (robot), 7, 10–11
Trace, construction of, 85
Trail agent, 77
Trail-value, 77
Transformation, intelligent, 124
Transitory knowledge, 111
Tripod gait, 179

Ullmann, S., 87
Uncertainty, 123
    and assembly agent, 132
    in assembly robots, 128–129
    control of, 140–142
    location, 140
    part-fitting, 141
    shape, 140
    tacit contern with, 141–142
Unexpected situation, 154n12
Universal planning, 45–66
Universal plans, 49
    defined, 45
    as program for action, 100

VAL2, 129, 136
Variables
    issue of, 67–68
    motivational, 171
Vector sum navigation strategy, 166
Vertical bias, 62–63
Vestibular-ocular system, 12
Viritual machine interface
    and decoupling, 133n17
    intermediate interpreted, 132
    as rational reconstruction, 134
Virtual robot, 129–130
Virtual sensors, 1
Vision
    active, 4
    dynamic, 125
Visual operations, 1–2
Visualization, Pengi's use of, 22
Voronoi diagram, 96
Voronoi edge, 96
    and zero circulation, 99
VLSI techniques, 130
Vygotsky, Lev S., 21, 27

Wandering (behavior), 80
    artificial insect, 179
    constrained forms of, *162*, 163–165
    generalized, 160
    localized, 160
Waves, as communication tool, 81–82
Wertsch, James W., 21
Whiskers, function of, 9
Wilson, D.M., 179
Winograd, T., 132
World knowledge
    in reactive navigation, 105–121
    in terms of discrete states, 93
    types of, 111
World-mediated collaboration, 141–142
World models
    in AuRA, 118, 120
    development of, 128–129
World-object agents, 80

Yourdon, E., 124n2